Alternatives to Imprisonment

CRIME & SOCIETY

Series Editor
John Hagan, University of Toronto

Alternatives to Imprisonment: Intentions and Reality,
Ulla V. Bondeson

Inequality, Crime, and Social Control, *edited by*
George S. Bridges and Martha A. Myers

FORTHCOMING

Great Pretenders: A Study of Property Offenders,
Neal Shover

Poverty, Ethnicity, and Violent Crime,
James F. Short

Criminological Controversies, *John Hagan,*
A. R. Gillis, and David Brownfield

Crime, Justice, and Public Opinion,
Julian Roberts and Loretta Stalens

Crime, Justice, and Revolution
in Eastern Europe, *Joachim J. Savelsberg*

Alternatives to Imprisonment

Intentions and Reality

Ulla V. Bondeson

Westview Press
BOULDER • SAN FRANCISCO • OXFORD

Crime & Society

Published in 1994 in the United States of America by Westview Press, Inc., 5500 Central Avenue, Boulder, Colorado 80301–2877, and in the United Kingdom by Westview Press, 36 Lonsdale Road, Summertown, Oxford OX2 7EW

Library of Congress Cataloging-in-Publication Data
Bondeson, Ulla, 1937–
Alternatives to imprisonment : intentions and reality / Ulla V. Bondeson.
p. cm.—(Crime & society)
Includes bibliographical references.
ISBN 0-8133-2011-9
1. Alternatives to imprisonment. 2. Sentences (Criminal procedure) I. Title. II. Series: Crime & society (Boulder, Colo.)
HV9276.5.B66 1994
364.6—dc20 94-2285
CIP

Printed and bound in the United States of America

The paper used in this publication meets the requirements of the American National Standard for Permanence of Paper for Printed Library Materials Z39.48-1984.

10 9 8 7 6 5 4 3 2 1

Contents

Foreword

This study of community corrections in Sweden provides policy guidance, based on highly original research and profound thought, that should interest and benefit all who are concerned with alternatives to imprisonment everywhere.

Professor Bondeson's findings utilize recidivism rates, their correlates and predictors, for those receiving three kinds of community penalty: conditional sentence, probation with regular supervision and probation that begins with one month of confinement before release to supervision. She then presents a very distinctive study of the supervisors of these cases, detailing how they perceive the types of assistance and control that they provide as well as the perception of this supervision by their clients.

All of this occurs in a recent type of community correction in Sweden in which most of the supervisors are volunteers with case-loads of one to five cases who also have full-time jobs of diverse types, most often as social workers, policemen or teachers. Four institutions, each with a capacity of only forty inmates, were built specially for probationers for whom initial confinement was prescribed. Professor Bondeson's research includes systematic interviews with inmates and staff in these facilities that probe their relationships to each other, the issues that concern them and the effects of these places on the criminality of their residents.

But this is not simply a research report. It also provides a historical perspective, reviews other pertinent research in many nations, considers the relevant theory and sociology of the law, raises issues of values and ideologies and closes with imaginative ideas for the reform and improvement of corrections. This is not only a study of alternatives to prisons; it is itself a valuable alternative to the less thorough and thoughtful studies of community corrections that have preceded it.

Daniel Glaser
University of Southern California

Preface

Although during the last two decades several Nordic official committees have recommended a reduction in the use of imprisonment and an increased use of community sanctions, incarceration rates have been going up in Sweden, Denmark and Norway. Only Finland, which historically has had much higher incarceration rates than the other Scandinavian countries, is an exception to this pattern. A comparison of the number of persons found guilty of offenses against the Penal Code shows that in 1991 Finland had a conviction rate that was almost double that of Denmark and Sweden while the Norwegian conviction rate was less than half that of the latter two countries. The number of offenses registered by the police in Finland is, however, far less than the number registered in Sweden and Denmark, and, according to a victimology study, Finland is down to the level of Norway (van Dijk et al. 1990; Bondeson 1991).

With the exception of Norway, fines are the most commonly used sanction; this is particularly true of Finland. Sweden makes the most use of other community sanctions (defined in the *Yearbook of Nordic Statistics* as "conditional sentence, waiving of prosecution, etc."), followed by Denmark and, at a much lower level, Norway and Finland. These rates have been fairly stable in all four countries.

Comparisons between the Scandinavian countries are complicated by reason of differences in legislation and ways of compiling statistics. The Nordic Committee on Penal Law has described in detail the various community sanctions available in Scandinavia and, after scrutinizing the statistics, has also concluded that there is a greater tendency to use probation and waiving of prosecution in Sweden than in the other Nordic countries (NUA 1980:13; see also Bondeson 1980a; Sveri 1986).

A distinct intention of the new Swedish Penal Code, which came into force in 1965, was that the use of probation would be increased and enhanced by giving supervision a true treatment content. However, during the ensuing ten-year period the use of probation increased only modestly while the use of the conditional sentence (a penal warning without supervision) more than doubled in frequency.

As long ago as 1970, Sparks, in a survey conducted for the Council of Europe, urged research that would compare the effectiveness of conditional sentences without supervision—as used in many European countries—and probation. The present study does exactly that, but it has to be said that not much similar research has been carried out.

There are certain advantages to conducting evaluative research on alternative sanctions in Sweden. Apart from the fact that these sanctions are used extensively, an important feature has been that of requiring a thorough pre-sentence social inquiry to enable the court to decide between imposing a conditional sentence or probation. This has been so because the law emphasizes the importance of individual prevention. The court has therefore had to have access to personal and social information about the offender in order to decide whether supervision appeared necessary or could be dispensed with. In Denmark, by contrast, such pre-sentence inquiries are not obligatory and are not usually undertaken when a conditional sentence appears to be the most likely sanction. The choice of probation tends more to be governed by proportionality considerations, i.e., to be imposed for repeated offenses or those of greater gravity. Furthermore, Denmark possesses neither a correctional organization exclusively equipped to deal with probationers nor such a developed practice of using lay supervisors as is the case in Sweden.

The detrimental effects of imprisonment have been well documented (see Bondeson 1989) and have been generally acknowledged in most western countries. As a consequence, we have witnessed an intensive search for alternatives. For a recent analysis of non-custodial alternatives in Europe, see the report by Bishop (1988), and for a presentation of the sanction systems of member States of the Council of Europe, see van Kalmthout and Tak (1988; 1992).

Probation today seems to be going through a transitional and stressful period, one that offers many challenges (see, for example, Mathieson 1992). As early as the 1960s American research demonstrated that manipulating case-load size made little difference to the success or failure of probation. A similar conclusion emerged from the English experiment with intensive and matched treatment in the mid-1970s (Folkard et al. 1976). More recently, studies by Petersilia et al. (1992) have indicated that intensive probation supervision reduces neither recidivism nor drug misuse and naturally costs more than routine supervision.

Although probation costs much less than imprisonment and apparently does not produce worse results, a conditional sentence without supervision costs even less and seems, at least in many cases, to be equally effective (Bondeson 1975).

Despite current interest in the expansion of alternatives to imprisonment, we still have limited precise knowledge about their relative effectiveness. In order to study their functioning and impact, I have conducted research into three forms of alternative sanctions, namely, conditional sentence, ordinary probation and probation with initial institutional treatment.

In the present research I wanted to study to what extent the legislator's aims with conditional sentence and probation were realized (Bondeson 1977 in Swedish; 1979a in Russian). Detailed attention has been given to the legislator's individual preventive intention with probation and the attempt to give the sanction an enhanced treatment content.

An unusual combination of a socio-legal and criminological approach has been used in this study. I have scrutinized the legislator's intentions and their subsequent implementation by the courts, professional probation officers, lay supervisors and institutional staff. The recidivism rates of random samples of offenders given a conditional sentence, ordinary probation and probation with institutional treatment have been ascertained and compared using a prediction instrument to permit valid comparisons. The perceptions of probationers and their supervisors of the treatment provided have been compared totally and pairwise. An in-depth study of a probation institution has been conducted using participant observation and interviews with staff and inmates. Finally, the reasons for the partial failure of the probation treatment have been analyzed and reform proposals presented.

Subsequently, changes have been introduced into criminal policy in accordance with some of the suggestions presented. Thus, probation with institutional treatment has been abolished with reference made to research demonstrating its inefficacy. Supervision times have been shortened. A division of labor between professional probation staff and lay supervisors has occurred with the former providing formal control and practical assistance to a greater extent and the latter undertaking more of a personal support function. Treatment planning now takes place and should be followed up continuously. Offenders with a better prognosis are conditionally sentenced to an even greater extent. (For an account of developments see Appendix II by Bishop). It is my belief that most of these observations and their implications for reform are also relevant for other countries.

The comprehensive research project described in this book has only been possible with the help of many devoted persons. The major portion of the empirical data was collected under my guidance by graduate students of Lund University. Recidivism, the sentencing process, supervision and a probation institution were studied by Thomas Hansson, Pawel Chylicki, Monika Hultén, Irene Ek and Zolt Tajthy respectively. Their results have been further analyzed in Chapters 4–7.

Translating, adapting and updating the Swedish text to make it suitable for publication in English has been a long and tortuous process. The translation was made by Aina Bonner. Peter Garde gave amicable assistance in checking part of the manuscript, and Gitte Høyer incorporated a great number of amendments. Later, Norman Bishop, drawing on his wide experience and knowledge, skillfully revised and assisted in condensing the text. Finally, the word-processed manuscript was adapted by Siv Sandberg to meet the publisher's requirements. Although invaluable help has been given by very competent persons, to all of whom I wish to express my gratitude, I am naturally solely responsible for the final product.

Grants for translation and revision of the book have generously been provided by the Danish and Swedish Social Science Research Councils and by the Torsten and Ragnar Söderberg Foundation.

Ulla V. Bondeson
University of Copenhagen

1

Problems and Theories

This research has four principal aims:

1. to describe and analyze non-institutional treatment,
2. to evaluate the sanctions of conditional sentence and probation,
3. to analyze and explain the effects of the law,
4. to propose reforms based on the findings of points 1–3 with the purpose of rendering non-institutional treatment more effective.

This study may be described as falling within the discipline of sociology of law insofar as it provides a sociological description of legal institutions and the effects of law. Since the laws which have been subjected to analysis are governed by penal law, the study may also be described as criminological.

The design of the research is somewhat complicated because its aims vary and are, at the same time, interwoven. The individual studies which make up the entire project are distinguished by different problems, theories and methods, but together they should provide answers to the four principal aims set forth above. The problem areas with their related theories will be presented in this chapter while more specific problems and theories related to the individual empirical studies will be discussed in the later chapters.

Description of Non-Institutional Treatment

Despite the fact that non-institutional treatment has long been more common than imprisonment in Scandinavia and now is used with several times as many offenders, we still know very little about how it functions. Research on imprisonment has clearly been more comprehensive, particularly internationally, than research on non-custodial sanctions. Factors which contribute to this concentration on imprisonment probably include its more dramatic character and the fact that it can be studied under more controlled social conditions; probation seems in many ways to be more obscure and elusive. Hauge (1970), one of the few Scandinavian criminologists who has studied probation in relative depth, writes: "Despite the fact that articles, books and other publications which discuss probation would fill a medium-sized public library, only a fraction of these are based on empirical investigation. While there are large volumes describing the way the supervision of offenders should be carried out, there are very few descriptions of how supervision is conducted in reality." (p. 4)

Before the beginning of the 1960s very little research had been conducted on probation. The research efforts of the following twenty years have mainly consisted of inquiries ordered by correctional administrations, justice departments and the like. These include the Swedish Sundsvall experiment with reinforced resources, the English Home Office project IMPACT and some of the American studies conducted by the California Youth Authority and the Department of Corrections. These projects have resulted in a number of publications, often of a preliminary or a technical nature. Thus, there is still a deficiency of comprehensive research monographs published on non-institutional correction.

Evaluation of Conditional Sentence and Probation

If descriptive studies of non-institutional correction are few it is obvious that strictly evaluative studies are even scarcer. Sparks (1970) compiled a report for the Council of Europe on the use and effectiveness of *probation, parole and measures of after-care*. Almost all the research described had been conducted in England or the United States. He gives two reasons for this: "The first is that, at least until very recently, those two countries have accounted for almost all of the empirical research in all areas of criminology and penology, and in particular have had, between them, a virtual monopoly on research on the effectiveness of treatment. The second is that they have—again, until very recently made by far the most extensive use of probation, parole and the kinds of after-care considered in this report." (p. 249)

Sparks was certainly right in his claim that studies of the effectiveness of punishment and treatment had been neglected outside Anglo-Saxon countries but he is hardly correct in claiming that probation and parole are less common in all other countries. Probation seems to be used in Sweden to a greater extent than in many other countries and to about the same extent as in the Anglo-Saxon countries.

It is therefore important to supplement international reviews with the findings from other countries such as Sweden. Since the latter country's sanction system is constructed differently from that of many other countries it provides a basis for a different approach to evaluation than those hitherto used. This applies, among other things, to the comparison made here between conditional sentence and probation.

Wilkins (1969) has pointed out that the relatively few studies made of correctional treatment mostly concern its outcome and not what goes on inside institutions. Clarke and Sinclair (1973) criticized correctional outcome studies for being founded on a medical myth and institution studies for not being sufficiently evaluative: "Thus two general tendencies have been found in treatment research; an evaluative trend, which aimed at comparing the effects of treatment which had not been described, and a sociological, which devoted itself to describing treatment which had not been compared." (p. 5)

Comparative studies of different correctional institutions, such as those conducted by Glaser (1964), Street, Vinter and Perrow (1966), and Bondeson (1974; 1989), are still relatively rare.

As the two methods for measuring the effects of treatment answer different questions and at the same time supplement each other, it would be natural to *combine* them. Hood and Sparks (1973) also think this should be made the primary task of treatment studies and they also urge research which would pay heed to offender experience inside and outside the prison.

Since studies of the effects of treatment and impact studies of institutions require their own special measurement techniques, each of which can be sufficiently complicated, criminologists have seldom combined the methods. However, I attempted this in an earlier project (Bondeson 1968) and was able to demonstrate that the indoctrination of youths into criminal values and norms at a reform school affected their subsequent adjustment.

The present project has an unusual design in that it combines a description of treatment with an evaluation of the effects of penal measures, thus meeting the requirement of Hood and Sparks cited above. Since the research also compares different sanctions it meets Clarke and Sinclair's demand for comparative studies (pp. 25–26).

Only studies of both treatment content and outcome permit comprehensive interpretation of research data. When information is obtained on the content and outcomes of *different* forms of treatment, then the likelihood of interpreting the results with certainty is increased.

Unfortunately the ideal research situation with controlled experiments is seldom available to the treatment evaluator and almost never in Scandinavia. Considerations of justice and equality before the law usually prevent the random assignment of offenders to an experimental group which is studied before and after a sanction is imposed, and a control group which is also studied on both occasions but which has not received treatment. The design of the present research attempts to approach the ideal as closely as possible. By choosing the two sanctions, probation and conditional sentence, of which only one involves supervision, a *quasi-experimental* situation is obtained in which, with the aid of prediction techniques, the attempt can be made to attempt to study the effect of treatment. Furthermore, the probation sanction exists in two different forms: ordinary probation which involves only supervision in the community and probation with institutional treatment in which an initial short period of institutional treatment precedes supervision in the community. This makes it possible to compare two different treatment measures with no treatment at all. Moreover, we have access to data from different periods of time for the three sanction groups. The project's design is shown, somewhat simplified, in Figure 1.1.

If a quasi-experiment is to replace a true experiment, the sanction groups, which may be presumed to differ on background variables, must be rendered comparable. Fortunately, prediction techniques are relatively well developed and in using them I have tried to avoid a number of the possible sources of error pointed out by earlier Nordic critics (Börjeson 1966; Andenaes' and

	Before Sentence: Childhood, Personal and Social Conditions	After Sentence: Adjustment during Probation Supervision	During or after Probationary Period: Social Adjustment, Recidivism
Conditional sentence	X		X
Probation without institutional treatment	X	X	X
Probation with institutional treatment	X	X	X

FIGURE 1.1 Information on the Three Sanction Groups from Different Periods

Quensel's criticism 1966; Börjeson's response 1967). A more detailed analysis of this type of sources of error will be found in Chapter 5.

A Socio-Legal Analysis of the Effects of Legislation

Definitions of the subject area of the sociology of law vary. It has been asserted that the sociology of law attempts by sociological analysis to describe how legal institutions function in our society and how laws affect people's attitudes and behavior (Aubert 1972). In general, it can be said that the sociology of law studies the mutual interaction between law and society, i.e., how legislation affects a variety of societal conditions and how these effects in their turn contribute to the formation of new laws. The legal system is not a closed system but is influenced by different subsystems in the surrounding society and the prevailing culture, and it itself exerts an influence on these social systems (see Friedman and Macauley 1969, 197). An essential task for the sociology of law is to study how the structure of society influences, and is influenced by, the formation of different legal and other norm systems.

In the present research I shall to some extent deal with the way in which different social and legal systems have influenced the origin of the legislative provisions governing the sanctions studied. But the main questions on which I concentrate concern how the intentions of the legislator are translated into practice both at the sentencing and implementation levels and how these intentions are realized in terms of the aim of regulating behavior.

Traditional treatment research, often limited to the study of the effect of a given treatment modality within a particular sanction, has lacked this wider perspective. Thus, for example, studies have been conducted on the effect of group therapy with prisoners, vocational training at a youth reform institution and the case-loads of probation officers. It might be wise to abstain from talking about treatment research when, as in the present research, the total effects of a sanction and especially a comparison of the effects of different sanctions, are studied. The term treatment research is euphemistic and falsely associated with treatment as therapy. Nor is it usually expected to lead to a broader socio-legal analysis. I use the term despite these objections because the methods developed in the field of treatment research are superior to those available in the sociology of law. My approach may be summarized by saying that the methods used here have been borrowed from treatment research but the theoretical analyses belong to the sociology of law.

Some Earlier Scandinavian Studies of the Effects of Law

Space does not permit a complete description of earlier Scandinavian studies dealing with the effects of law to be given but it will be useful to indicate the direction such research has taken. And the first thing to be said is that although the subject is of crucial importance only a limited number of empirical studies are available.

For the legal scholar, the problem of discovering how legislation achieves the effects which are intended is relevant both in studies *de lege lata* (i.e., how the law is constituted) and *de lege ferenda* (i.e., how the law ought to be constituted). But, in fact, most effort has been devoted to reflections on purpose and not to working out suitable scientific methods for this type of analysis. Aubert (1972) writes as follows on this matter: "But these reflections on purpose have often been based on inadequate experience and have the character of wishful thinking rather than critical scientific analysis. Investigations using proven scientific methods of how laws actually function seem to be born out of well-known juridical problems but jurisprudence has not been able to find methodologically satisfying solutions. It is too early to say with certainty whether the sociology of law can supply a satisfactory solution." (p. 51)

Socio-legal scholars can scarcely be said to have presented any general conclusions based on the empirical investigations which have hitherto been conducted (see Aubert 1972, 50–58 and Dalberg-Larsen 1991, 229–268 for a review of these studies). A summary by Aubert (1976) has a final heading "Conclusions?" in which he writes: "That which has been summarized here should be seen as an illustration of problems rather than answers to general questions about whether, and under what conditions, laws are obeyed or function as intended." (p. 164)

Yet this research tradition of the sociology of law is not completely new; it has been developed contemporaneously with treatment research. Some of the most well-known studies of the effects of laws have been conducted, at least in Scandinavia, as early as four decades ago by juridically trained research workers using more or less developed sociological methods; see, for example, Schmidt et al. (1946), Aubert, Eckhoff and Sveri (1952) and Stjernquist (1973).

When the Scandinavian studies on the effects of law are classified, there would seem to be a clear predominance of civil legislation. When penal law has been studied, the emphasis has been placed almost exclusively on *general prevention*, i.e. the deterrent effect of laws or their contribution to the establishment of general moral values in society. The *individual preventive* effects of penal law (by which is meant how the law, through treatment, deterrence or incapacitation, keeps the offender from committing further offenses) seems to have been relatively neglected by the sociology of law. Treatment research has with few exceptions only studied different forms of treatment within a given sanction—not the entire sanction system.

Yet an important function of the sociology of law ought to be the comparison of laws with different characteristics and the study of their different modes of operation. The knowledge that some laws have certain advantages by comparison with others is of importance when law reforms are under consideration. Thus, for instance, Christie has argued that conflicts should be handled through civil law and that all involved parties should have the right to participate (1975, 164ff. and 1976).

Another limitation of many socio-legal studies on the effects of law, at least in Scandinavia, is that they have focused on individual effects and less often on courts and administrative agencies. Earlier studies of courts, such as Geijer and Schmidt's study of the Swedish Labor Court (1958) and Goldschmidt's study of judges in Greenland (1957), do exist however. But emphasis has usually been placed on the law's influence in regulating behavior, i.e. how defined groups of citizens conform in their behavior to special legislative provisions.

Aubert's Model of the Communication of the Content of Law

The way that law achieves its effects can be conceptualized as a question of general communication. Communication presumes a sender, a receiver and a message which is conveyed from the sender to the receiver. If the content of legislation is to be spread from the parliament to the people, then we can speak of mass communication. Aubert (1972) drew up a model for the communication of legislative content in order to illustrate this process. The primary purpose of the model is to show the different channels through which the legislative message can pass and the various factors that need to be taken into consideration when making assessments of the effects of law. As examples of particularly important components of the model, mention can be made of the legislator's official orders and notifications, the courts, advocates, administrative bodies, the press and personal influence.

Later, Aubert (1976, 135–140) discussed *feedback* on legislation in more detail where he, like Wiener, envisaged legal rules operating as a closed loop of norms in society. Nowadays, particularly in the United States, demands can be made on legislatures to evaluate the effects of the laws they draft. Usually the relevant ministries receive complaints concerning their subordinate administrations, requests and appeals from individuals, pressure groups and various administrative bodies together with research findings and mass-media reports. Reactions to legislation or proposals for reforms come through parliamentary debates and questions. Even if, under the constitution, it is parliament that is responsible for creating new laws, government has increasingly taken the initiative. Similarly, it has become increasingly customary for administrations to initiate work on law concerning administrative matters.

Since we know that it is often difficult to change social realities through legislation, I have tried to illumine and account for the differences between *the law in books* and *the law in practice.* In addition, I have tried to follow the legislator's intentions down through the sentencing and enforcement levels to see if deviations from the legal norms can be found. By trying also to see the interaction of legal rules with other formal and informal rules, it is possible to throw light on various legal and social institutions.

The Law on Probation—A Combination of Coercion and Support

Aubert distinguishes between *coercive laws,* which belong to traditional penal law, and *resource laws,* which are more common in administrative law. The former generally state a norm to be observed backed up by the use of negative sanctions. The latter often communicate values and goals which are to be realized with the help of positive sanctions.

Legal rules have usually been defined as rules behind which there is a coercive threat. For example, Austin, the founder of analytic legal positivism, and the Uppsala philosophers Lundstedt, Ekelöf, and, in particular, Olivecrona, believed that coercive power lay behind all laws.

The English legal philosopher, Hart (1961), distinguishes between rules imposing obligations, rules backed by coercive power and rules conferring powers and competence. He points out that the definition of laws also has implications for a theory of how laws function in society.

When Aubert (1976, 43) introduced the resource aspect of legal rules in addition to the coercive aspect, his intention was to lay the foundation for a more realistic theory of the functions of law in the modern welfare state. The powerful expansion of administrative law with the ensuing increase in the number of resource laws, seems to justify such a perspective.

Aubert's distinction between coercive laws and resource laws seems especially fruitful for an analysis of the law on probation since this law also has some characteristics of administrative law owing to the significant role accorded to such administrative authorities as supervision boards and the probation service.

The law governing probation has the interesting characteristic of *simultaneously constituting both a coercive law and a resource law.* Many laws have elements of coercion and support but the law of probation combines these to such an extent that it is difficult to say if one element predominates. Historically, the Commission responsible for reviewing the sanctions in the Penal Code sought to eradicate the traditional notion of punishment as far as possible and replace it with a philosophy that the offender through treatment would be assisted to adjust in society.

The law of probation is a coercive law since it provides for supervision to be imposed on the offender. It can be regarded as a resource law since the provision of a supervisor is considered to be an offer of assistance. Hence, supervision consists of both *control* and *assistance*. If an offender evades control various sanctions can be imposed. These sanctions are considered to be positive measures but since they may involve limiting the offender's freedom of movement and can also involve a degree of deprivation of liberty, the offenders upon whom they are imposed would probably describe them as negative measures. Like the obligation to engage in treatment, which may also be imposed, their existence and use is justified by reference to the offender's need of support or the necessity of investigating his situation in order to select a suitable treatment alternative.

The probation sanction, which is justified by considerations of individual prevention, offers treatment or support since the law states that the sanction may only be applied if the offender in question *needs* supervision. The latter requirement applies even if probation is accompanied by an initial period of institutional treatment. Special conditions and certain sanctions for breach of conditions are also justified by reference to the offender's need of such measures.

The concept "need" is usually associated with the desire of a person to receive a treatment which is, therefore, experienced positively. However, the concept as used in the law on probation has a wider meaning and includes the authorities' assessment of the offender's supposed need of support or control. Insofar as the offender does not expect to gain anything in the short or long term from correctional treatment, we may suspect that other needs are being met, namely those of society. On this the law is silent. The ambiguity can be expected to have consequences for the various stages of the implementation of the law.

Probation may constitute a resource for the offender if he considers himself to be in need of a contact person and can find the desired support in this person. Even if the offender does not regard supervision as constituting a positive resource, but rather sees it as a serious encroachment on his freedom, he may nevertheless consider it an "offer" in so far as a greater evil, in the form of imprisonment, can thereby be avoided. Probation, then, can be seen as a resource—*but in a negative sense*. Similarly, probation with institutional treatment, despite the deprivation of liberty involved for about one month, can be regarded as a negative resource when the alternative is a significantly longer loss of freedom.

So, too, the sanction *conditional sentence* (penal warning) can also be seen as a resource in the negative sense. It is seen as a proof of confidence in the offender when the court makes the sentence conditional upon future crime-free behavior instead of imposing imprisonment or probation. In this sense, a conditional sentence is probably regarded as a resource by those upon whom it is imposed.

The majority of resource laws have a built-in coercive element. The Act on Compulsory School Attendance, for example, involves an offer of free education but at the same time school attendance is made obligatory for nine years. The possibility which exists within the school system of granting exemption corresponds to the possibility of shortening supervisory periods. Both positive and negative sanctions seem to exist in the school system. Theoretically however, there are better possibilities to make use of more support instead of more control when a pupil finds it difficult to make use of the instruction offered by the school. But, for the probationer who has difficulties in making use of supervision, control can be introduced *de facto* instead of better support.

But there is probably a certain combination of coercion and support in most human activities. This can be observed within work and family life and in the sphere of leisure.

A Model for Studying the Effects of the Law on Probation

As with other coercive legislation, the law on probation formulates a *norm* that must be followed since a general condition stipulates that the offender must lead a law-abiding life. But as with legislation providing resources, we can also discern a *value* to be upheld or a *goal* to be attained with the sanction—the offender is to be given the opportunity to adjust in society.

But it might be said that whilst the norm is directed at the offender, the formulated goals are intended for the authorities and other persons whose task it is to implement the sanction. It might be said that the norm is to be seen as a *primary rule* or, to be more precise, as the implementation instructions which are intended to realize the goals whilst the purpose of the law—or, more precisely, the implementation instructions which are intended to achieve that purpose—is to be considered a *secondary rule* (Hart 1961).

There is a given relation between the norm and the purpose in the form of implementation instructions: both deal with the offender's resocialization. And of this it might be said that whilst the research worker interested only in treatment effects focuses on the study of how clients comply with the norm of living in obedience to the law, the sociologist of law studies how the goals of law are realized. By combining both these research foci it becomes possible to ascertain whether any deficiency in following the norm can be better explained by deficiencies in the formulation of the goal or in the methods of implementation.

The norm requiring the offender's general obedience to the law and the goal of adjustment in society are the same for the sanction of *conditional sentence* as for probation. The value to the offender of making the sentence conditional is not, however, that of offering him positive resources but can instead be formulated negatively, i.e. the offender need not be deprived of his liberty. The sanction is justified by reference to individual prevention in that the conditionally sentenced offender is spared the destructive effects of a prison sentence.

My starting point then for this research is that the sanctions studied have as purpose the adjustment of the offender in society and I seek to determine how this purpose was realized in reality. In other words, I have studied *how the individual preventive value was formulated, converted into action and subsequently realized.*

Although the Swedish Penal Law of 1864 bore the marks of the classical school of penal law, the 1965 Penal Code gave a more individual preventive emphasis to the system of sanctions. The Protective Law Commission, which drafted the preparatory legislation on conditional sentence and probation, had a largely individual preventive perspective. However, some conflict can be discerned between the individual and general preventive emphases in both the preparatory work and the law itself. This conflict of emphases can be presumed to have implications for the implementation of the law since both those concerned with implementing the law and those subject to its provisions can be expected to experience certain inconsistencies or contradictions when these opposing considerations have to be taken into account.

The model used to study the effects of the law is complex. Account must be taken of the preparatory legislative work and the law itself, the courts' interpretation of the law when choosing the sanction, the supervision boards' activities in heading and overseeing the implementation of probation, the probation service which is responsible for the practical work of the non-institutional services under the leadership of the Swedish Prison and Probation Administration, the staff of the correctional institutions and, finally, the laymen who undertake the greater part of supervision. The sentencing and enforcement bodies can, however, interpret the law and its enabling orders and directives differently. Those whose task it is to enforce the law bring other formal and informal norms to the carrying-out of that task and may define their duties in different ways. Offenders too may react to the various ways in which the law is interpreted and applied. In short, complex interactions take place between the bearers of a number of different roles with varying expectations.

The research has therefore involved a study of the preparatory legislative work and the ensuing law, an analysis of the courts' sentencing documentation, statistical analysis and direct observation of supervision board behavior, personal interviews with probation staff, participant observation of, and standardized interviews with the staff and inmates of a probation institution and the use of standardized questionnaires with supervisors and their offender clients (see Appendix I for the methods and samples used).

Whether the individual preventive intention can be carried through in reality depends to a great extent on how the offenders in question interpret the support and control measures taken. But non-legal factors can also play a significant part in the success or failure of a client's readjustment. The individual offender's personal and social circumstances, as well as his reference and membership groups, are also important. However, the legislator's intentions included the idea that even these social circumstances should be influenced by the various support and treatment measures. On the other hand, the law governing probation has scarcely any possibility of influencing factors on a macro-level and we would expect a variety of societal conditions to have some bearing on rehabilitation efforts. Various social and economic circumstances in all probability are factors which increase the difficulties.

In general, there is a close interplay at both macro- and micro-levels between legal and non-legal factors. The division of society into social classes is probably caused to a great extent by other than purely legal factors, but the latter may consolidate and even strengthen it (see for instance Aubert 1976; Friedman 1976). The notion of prognosis, which dictates the choice of sanction as between conditional sentence and probation, can function, for instance, as just such a reinforcement mechanism. The sentence may trigger off a labelling process, which is strengthened by the attitudes of the public and becomes a part of the offender's identity. An act is defined as a crime and the public then defines the offender as a criminal on the basis of his having been sentenced (Becker 1963). This influences the offender's self-concept, which in turn influences his choice of reference and membership groups, which further confirms the public's judgment, and so on ... Because such *stigmatization processes* are auto-reinforcing and often irreversible they can be presumed to play an important role and to no small extent render the offender's adjustment in the community much more difficult.

Figure 1.2 shows the different legal and non-legal factors which can be thought to have some bearing on the realization of the individual preventive goal although it cannot do justice to the totality of possible factors. Among the legal institutions that are responsible for realizing the individual preventive intention we may note the law itself, the courts, the supervision board, the National Prison and Probation Administration, the probation organization, the lay supervisors and the correctional institutions. The probation organization must also work together with the social welfare agencies, the medical services, the employment services and other bodies. The legislature's intentions are conveyed through the law, governmental orders and administrative instructions and they are spread via opinion-forming activities. The various legal actors may also be influenced by other formal and informal rules, by their social roles and expectations and by a variety of societal circumstances. The client's social role and expectations can also be expected to have repercussions on the legal actor's attitudes and behavior.

In addition to the legal factors the offender, in his turn, is also influenced by various personal, social and societal conditions. Such personal and social factors as poor education, alcohol abuse and lack of work make the offender's rehabilitation more difficult. On the other hand, the discovery of new personally important values (e.g. a partner for life, or a religious or political conviction), may facilitate adjustment. Such problems as social rejection resulting from class prejudices, unemployment and public prejudice against deviants may all be expected to render the offender's readjustment in society more difficult. The interaction between the various legal and non-legal factors can also result in the client being stigmatized and this can be expected to impede his readjustment very considerably.

These opposing social forces may be so strong that *negative* individual prevention is achieved instead of the legislator' goal of positive individual prevention, i.e. the effect may be the opposite of what was intended (cf. Bondeson 1974; 1989).

It should be emphasized that the model, like that of Aubert, cannot tell us

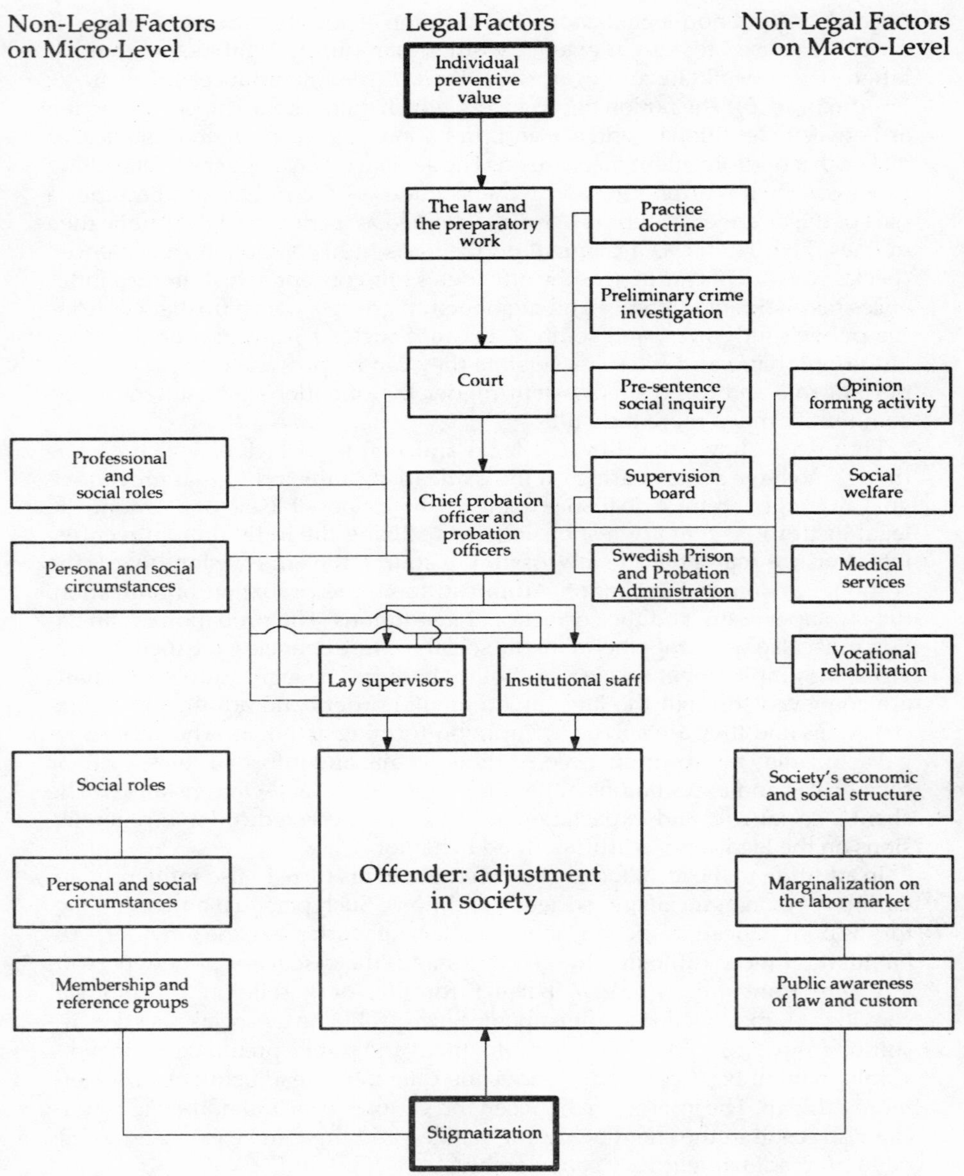

FIGURE 1.2 Legal and Non-Legal Factors of Relevance for the Realization of the Individual Preventive Aim of Probation

under what conditions a law has one or the other effect. Still less can it give guidance when we want to quantify the different factors' reciprocal significance for the realization of the goal. What, however, we can do is to obtain a measure of the extent to which the goal is realized, i.e. the extent to which the offenders are or are not rehabilitated.

The built-in quasi-experimental design enables us to gain some insight into the extent to which successful or unsuccessful adjustment can be accounted for by the legal factors. It is, of course, a debatable point whether this level of ambition justifies calling the diagram a model (see Kaplan 1964, for a discussion of various types of models). But contemporary theories within the sociology of law are not yet sufficiently developed to allow the construction of a model with any greater degree of precision. It does not seem reasonable to try to present a model of the effects of law which is intended to enable general predictions to be made.

Explanations of Deficient Legislative Effects

The model described above can also facilitate an interpretation of deficient legislative effects. Knowledge of the recidivism rates makes us suspect that the legislator's intentions concerning individual prevention are not realized. Some possible explanations as to why a treatment program envisaged by the legislator is not implemented or why the goal of individual prevention is not attained, will be given below. I list them at this point to help the reader who wants to find alternative interpretations of the text that follows (a systematic examination of alternative explanations is undertaken in Chapter 8).

1. The manifest purpose of individual prevention is not necessarily that which is really intended. The theory of individual prevention may in fact be a treatment ideology which has other, legitimating, aims.
2. The theory of individual prevention is not expressed with sufficient lucidity and lack of ambiguity to allow for reliable application. This can be due to such things as contradictions in the law itself, caused in their turn by compromises made during the preparation of the legislation.
3. The legislator's theory of individual prevention is not put into practice by the implementing bodies. Deficiencies in implementation can be caused by:

   - Vagueness in the law and the preparatory work as well as in subsequent orders and implementation instructions creates uncertainty among both sentencing and implementing authorities.
   - The theory of individual prevention or the treatment ideology need not necessarily be embraced by the legal actors responsible for implementing the law. This can lead to open or concealed conflicts.
   - The organizational structure and decision-making functions can hinder the communication of the treatment theory with paralysis of action as a result.

- Administrative expansion can create a bureaucracy in which means are transformed into ends.
- It may be difficult for both professional and lay supervisors to apply the treatment theory by themselves.

4. Offenders do not perceive the treatment in accordance with the legislator's intentions. Apart from the reasons already given, this may also be due to suspiciousness felt by offenders as a consequence of the threat of sanctions implicit in the treatment.
5. There are faults in the treatment theory itself.
   - It is difficult for offenders to make use of treatment which is a combination of control and support.
   - The offender does not need treatment.
   - The offender is in need of welfare instead of treatment.
6. The treatment fails because of the offender's personal and social circumstances. A selection hypothesis could mean that "the offenders are so bad that it makes no difference what is done".
7. The treatment fails because of other societal conditions which result in the rejection of handicapped or deviant groups.
8. The treatment fails because the offender is stigmatized as a result of the combined effects of legal and non-legal factors.

The above explanations are not mutually exclusive; on the contrary, they can be expected to supplement each other. The legislation may be somewhat ambiguously formulated and this can create uncertainty among those who must implement it. The offender who comes from a socially impoverished environment may find it difficult to accept treatment from the representatives of the correctional system. At the same time, he needs various material resources which, because of his legal situation, are not easily obtained from the social services. The sentence he received labels him in the eyes of the people in his surroundings which in turn affects his assessment of himself. He meets difficulties on the labor and housing market, which further strengthen his view of himself as a social reject.

Reform Proposals

If, in the end, it appears that the legislator's intentions concerning individual prevention are not realized, it is necessary to try to explain how this discrepancy between the law in books and the law in practice arises and to find out how a better agreement might be reached. The socio-legal analysis made should then, as far as possible, be the basis both for a diagnosis of the difficulties as well as any proposals for change either of the law or the reality in which it is implemented (see Chapter 9).

If the conclusion is that the probation legislation was intended to achieve individual prevention but the treatment ideas were not formulated sufficiently clearly and those sentenced to this sanction have therefore unmet treatment needs, then the recommendation must be that the treatment theory needs to be expressed more explicitly and concretely.

If the conclusion is that the legislator's aim was the rehabilitation of offenders but that he proceeded from an invalid treatment theory and that offenders do need some kind of assistance, then we should try to specify the offenders' needs and say how they could be satisfied so as to facilitate social adjustment.

If, on the other hand, it becomes apparent that differences between the law's manifest and latent functions depend on the fact that the legislator had no real individual preventive intention but wished to conceal traditional penal notions behind a more progressive-sounding treatment ideology, then a discrepancy between the law in books and in reality is only to be expected.

At this point the question becomes, at least in part, a political one: what do we want to achieve with our criminal policy and what policies are politically feasible?

2

The History of Non-Institutional Correction

This chapter deals with the national and international development of non-institutional correction and also provides a historical description of the probation organization in Sweden. The differences between the *common law* and the *codified law* systems (see Fuller 1921, 120) have played a decisive role for successive reforms.

The Social Background of Modern Criminal Policy

The origin and development of different penal and treatment measures can be seen both in relation to the legal system as a whole and against the background of cultural, social, technical and economic forces in society (see Rusche and Kirchheimer 1939). The primary goal of criminal policy is the reduction of crime. However, the methods used to reach this goal vary with national traditions, the level of available knowledge and the nature of social, economic and other conditions. The development of such penal measures as conditional sentence and probation must be seen as a part of the general movement in modern societies away from a traditional repressive system. Imprisonment seems in many ways to be not well suited for many, more or less distinct, categories of offenders. The earlier aim of retaliation and general prevention is being replaced in principle by more humanitarian and directly utilitarian considerations. The most important goal of criminal policy has been stated to be the rehabilitation of offenders and attempts are made by rational means to reach this goal. This development in criminal policy parallels improvements in social conditions and social services in order, among other things, to prevent crime.

Development of Probation in the Anglo-Saxon Countries

Legal Background in Common Law

Opinions differ as to whether England or the United States should be credited with having introduced the methods which became the models for later

Swedish laws on conditional sentence and probation (see Tappan 1969). The English *common law* system probably provided, however, the necessary conditions for the introduction of probation as it allows for the flexible adaptation of law to new, emerging demands by society.

The *judicial reprieve* was clearly a precursor of the conditional sentence. It involved a deferment of the imposition or the enforcement of punishment with the aim of giving the defendant an opportunity to seek a pardon.

The recognizance, dating from the fourteenth century and also called *binding over to be of good behavior*, was a promise made by an offender who had not yet been sentenced that in future he would live a law-abiding life. The offender promised to pay a *bond* or *bail*, with or without a guarantee, and was returned to the court if he violated any of the specified conditions. The use of this method for first and minor offenders was not authorized until 1861 and not until 1879 for offenders sentenced for felonies.

This form of obligation was introduced early into the colonies. As early as 1836, Massachusetts gave legislative support to the practice in the lower courts of allowing minor offenders, at any stage in the proceedings, to be released against a guarantee of good behavior—a practice which was a true forerunner of probation. The use of the recognizance increased during the nineteenth century, the aim being to reduce the suffering caused by rigorous penal laws but there was also a growing awareness of its rehabilitative possibilities.

The *provisional release on bail* was frequently used both in England and the United States and is also considered to have had historical significance for the development of probation.

The *provisional filing or deferment of cases* seems to have been specific to Massachusetts. After a defendant was declared guilty, the court might defer sentence unless the general demands of justice required that an immediate sentence be imposed. The case was "filed away" until further notice and could be taken up again if circumstances demanded it.

With the increased use of different forms of deferment of sentence or enforcement, the courts' right to make sentences conditional for an indefinite period was called into question. The higher courts in different American jurisdictions adopted different positions on this issue. Finally, the Supreme Court decided, in a case that attracted a great deal of attention (*Killits Case*, 1916), that the courts did not have such a right in the absence of statutory provisions. It was held that judicial discretion must not involve a permanent refusal to enforce the law. This doctrine that the courts should have the inherent power to postpone sentence indefinitely was quashed, however, at a time when probation was already a well-established correctional method and when the public was already accustomed to this new way of treating offenders. For this reason, the Supreme Court's decision had the effect of stimulating the enactment of statutes that clearly authorized the use of a conditional sentence, with or without supervision.

From the socio-legal perspective this is an interesting example of how a legal practice can be established without the support of legislation. Paradoxically, the courts' extra-legal practice only became legal after it had first been declared illegal by the Supreme Court and this had led to the enactment of statutes authorizing the *status quo.*

The First Amateur Efforts with Supervision

Some American criminologists claim that true probation, i.e. with supervision, originated in Massachusetts in the 1840s. Supervision was, however, also employed in England by certain courts and, as early as 1820, was used with young offenders. In the early stages, families or policemen were used as supervisors but later the services of volunteers or charity organizations were employed.

A meritorious pioneer effort was that of John Augustus, a Boston shoemaker who in 1841 became a guarantor for a drunk and disorderly offender and persuaded the court to impose a nominal fine of one cent and court costs instead of the usual imprisonment in the *House of Correction.* He continued to act as guarantor for other inebriates and even for other kinds of offenders. During the eighteen years that elapsed until his death he helped about 2,000 persons. He undertook a simple prior investigation of the case, made sure that his wards received education or were given employment, often found them a place to live and, on request, sent in a report to the courts.

After Augustus' death, his work was continued by a prison chaplain, Rufus Cook, and other less known volunteers. In principle, they undertook the various tasks of which probation later came to be composed, namely presentence social inquiries, regular reports and home visits. The supervisory period was generally short, often only a few weeks. Their work was not based on any scientific principles of human behavior or rehabilitation methods but was pervaded by a spirit of simple humanitarian endeavor to spare lesser offenders the destructive effects of a prison sentence. It seems that they had many successful cases.

In 1869 a law was passed allowing Massachusetts to have a representative attached to the *Board of State Charities.* This representative took part in court proceedings against children and was authorized to place them under supervision in a suitable home. Probation for all categories of offenders was regulated first in legislation in 1878 and made possible the appointment of a paid *probation officer* in Boston. This first probation law made an explicit distinction between supervision and punishment since its provisions applied to defendants who could reasonably be expected to readjust without being punished. It is of interest that this law was not limited to certain types of offenders or offenses. The only criterion was the likelihood that the defendant could be rehabilitated without being punished.

In 1891 a law was passed in Massachusetts authorizing the obligatory appointment of probation officers throughout the state. However, the law provided that these should not be working policemen. The probationary period extended from three weeks to one year and supervision generally lasted six to twelve weeks.

Even at that time importance was attached to the lower costs involved in non-institutional supervision as compared with institutional treatment and to the general success that was achieved in rehabilitating offenders. These considerations probably contributed to the first probation law in the world being adopted without any real public debate or conflict. It should be added that the new law did not replace but supplemented the earlier practice of deferring sentence which grew out of common law. This new law dealt mainly with the appointment, salaries and duties of probation officers and the control of these duties—and allowed the courts to use probation more freely and effectively.

Federal probation was not established until 1925. Mississippi did not introduce legislation on probation until 1956. Great differences still exist between the American states in the way their laws are formed and implemented.

Professionalization of Supervision

As early as 1880 the voluntary laymen began to be replaced by salaried probation officers. Like their predecessors, they had no special training and to a large extent their methods—helping, guiding and moralizing—were similar. Not until the beginning of the twentieth century was there a training movement within social work when, in 1904, the *New York School of Philanthropy* was founded. Human wickedness was seen as a consequence of harmful social and economic forces and welfare work—consisting primarily of material assistance intermingled with humanitarian and moral values—became the most important work method. During the First World War, the philosophy and techniques of *casework* were introduced and Mary Richmond's "Social Diagnosis" (1917) had much influence. It was partly sociological in its perspective and it emphasized the importance of a social inquiry into the client's situation and personality so that treatment of the family could take place in the natural social environment.

During and after the First World War a marked change took place in the ideology of social work as a result of the growth of *psychiatry and, especially, psychoanalytic theory.* The theories of Freud, Adler and Jung were imbibed uncritically by the American schools of social work. This new interest in the individual and his emotional dynamics displaced the earlier interest social workers had taken in the influence exerted by the offender's environment. The search for professional status resulted in casework derived from a relatively orthodox psychiatry, setting its stamp on social work for several decades. That these psychiatric methods had been developed for voluntary neurotic patients in private clinics was disregarded and probation was seen quite simply as casework conducted under special conditions.

Sociologically speaking, once a social institution has been created it is often difficult to re-assess it critically and modifications are usually carried through with a view to completing an accepted pattern of ideas. Both prison and probation experience clearly demonstrate *the normative influence of the prevailing situation.* The predominant definition of what constitutes probation has been a significant obstacle to attempts to give it renewed content.

From the standpoint of *organizational theory* it can be asserted that once a form of treatment in freedom has been established, it tends to develop in the direction of formalism and ritualism. From the original voluntary humanitarian work has grown a *profession* and a *bureaucracy* with its own specific problems. Of these, by far the most serious is probably the ease with which means are transformed into ends (Merton 1957).

Although the development of non-institutional treatment in Sweden started later similar problems arise today in connection with professionalization and a service organization's bureaucratic growing pains (see Chapter 8).

The Development of Conditional Sentence and Probation in Sweden

While the Anglo-Saxon countries were introducing new kinds of sanctions divorced from classical punishment theories and based only on what seemed practical—and therefore subject to modification in the light of experience—the European continent preferred to devote itself to speculating about the basic principles of penal law. In order to understand the discussions which took place—and still do take place—in Sweden about the new sanctions of conditional sentence and probation a short historical description of the principles of penal law is necessary.

General Penal Law Background

The provincial laws of the Middle Ages introduced fines for the majority of crimes with the aim of limiting revenge and providing satisfaction for the injured person. As late as 1734 Swedish law provided for the use of fines for a number of serious crimes. Allowing the injured party to receive them as redress was only abandoned with the advent of the 1864 Penal Code. After the Reformation, penal law was made more stringent because of the belief that its provisions should be based on the Mosaic principle of retribution. During the eighteenth century, the French philosophers of the Enlightenment reacted against the powers of the courts which enabled them to impose cruel and arbitrary punishments. They demanded that punishment be imposed in reasonable proportion to the crime (see Anners, 1965). The German idealists Kant and Hegel, starting from a retributive perspective, arrived at the same conclusion. The English philosopher Bentham argued though that crime prevention should be the goal of the administration of justice and that the offender should not be made to suffer more than was necessary to reach this goal.

The *Swedish Penal Code of 1864* adopted the principles of *classical penal theory,* i.e. that every crime should be followed by punishment, that both crimes and punishments should be precisely stated in the law and that punishment should be in proportion to the seriousness of the offense. This view accorded well with a liberal view of society, i.e. that the individual should be allowed freedom to act within a legal framework which specified his rights and duties. This system satisfied both the advocates of retribution and crime prevention (Strahl 1967).

The desire to make punishment proportionate to the crime led to a penal system which chiefly provided for fines for the less serious offenses, deprivation of liberty for the more serious and the death penalty for the most serious. The idea of proportionality, still strongly rooted in penal law, comes to clear expression in the Penal Code of 1965, at least with respect to the traditional punishments of fines and imprisonment.

The weakness of the classical penal system lies in the fact that it constitutes a schematic construction built on certain philosophical and juridical principles instead of being based on observation of the criminal and the influence which punishment may have on him. Criminologists started to call attention to these shortcomings towards the end of the nineteenth century. The most radical opposition came from the *Italian positive school of criminology* represented by Lombroso, Ferri and Garofalo.

Ferri proposed that the penal law's sole purpose was the prevention of crime and rejected every thought of retribution and punishment, replacing these concepts with the notion of reaction. The criterion of guilt was replaced by that of danger which, in turn, led to notions of the protection of society and the treatment of the offender.

Within the *International Association of Criminalists,* which was founded in 1889 by the German professor of penal law, von Liszt, the notion was put forward that occasional offenders should be spared harmful prison sentences and have their sentences suspended.

The factors discussed here—the growth of criminology, the establishment of other schools of penal law than the classical school and the example from the Anglo-Saxon countries—prompted European criminal policy to supplement the classical penal system with various sanctions which were intended to restrain the offender from committing further offenses.

Legislative Reforms in the Twentieth Century

The Conditional Sentence Act of 1906. Conditional sentence was introduced in several European countries toward the end of the nineteenth century and somewhat later in Sweden.

In accordance with the classical principle that crime should be followed by punishment, it was thought that a punishment should always be pronounced and that offenders should only be spared its immediate enforcement, which in its turn was made conditional upon law-abiding behavior during a probationary period. If the conditionally sentenced offender committed another offense during the probationary period the conditional sentence could be revoked and another sanction imposed.

Compared with the American provisions, the Swedish conditional sentence was limited by exacting conditions. It applied only to occasional criminals who could be corrected without being punished and could be imposed for an offense which would otherwise lead to at most forced labor for three months or prison for six months. It could also be imposed with a sentence to fines if it was feared that the fines might not be paid and their conversion to imprisonment might prove necessary. The enforcement of such an imprisonment could be conditionally deferred for a probationary period of three years. The aim of conditional sentence was thus to save occasional offenders from short prison sentences. Even at that time there was an awareness of the serious harm caused by imprisonment. The offender was torn away from his work and family and placed among asocial individuals who could influence him negatively.

Conditional release from prison was introduced in the same year as a means of shortening prison sentences for the offender who was so well-behaved that it seemed unnecessary for him to serve the entire time in order to deter him from committing further crimes. Other reasons for this reform were to facilitate the transition from institutional life to life in freedom and to encourage prisoners to conduct themselves well during confinement.

The 1918 Conditional Sentence Act. Under the 1918 Conditional Sentence Act the conditions for imposing a conditional sentence were widened so as to allow it to be used for offenses punishable with forced labor for up to six months and imprisonment for up to one year. At the same time the courts were empowered to require the offender to be under *supervision* during the probationary period of a conditional sentence and could, as well, order a *social inquiry* to be made on the defendant and his personal circumstances. This was intended to facilitate the court's assessment of whether an offender's sentence should be made conditional. An offender who was under 21 years of age, could be required to obey his supervisor in either particular or general matters. Behavior that could be regarded as reprehensible, even if it did not involve relapse into new crime, could result in revocation. The courts were required to appoint a suitable person to supervise the sentenced person's conduct.

The 1939 Conditional Sentence Act. In 1939 a law, which did not take effect until 1944, was passed which transformed the conditional sentence into sanction comparable with American probation. The upper limit for its use was raised to one year's forced labor or two year's imprisonment and the courts were given power to impose *special conditions* concerning such matters as employment, residence, abstinence from intoxicating liquor and the payment of damages. As before, the courts could still pronounce a sentence of deprivation of liberty in the conditional sentence but grant a conditional deferment of enforcement. But a new possibility was that the conditional sentence could be imposed without a pronouncement of such punishment if special conditions were also imposed.

In connection with the 1939 Act, a *probation organization* was brought into being. The probation officers were to be responsible for the supervision of offenders whose sentences had been made conditional, prisoners who had been conditionally released and, in addition, those released from the institutions set up for the newly-created sanctions of youth imprisonment, preventive detention and internment. The courts of first instance were to act as *supervision courts* for the conditionally sentenced offenders placed under supervision. A special supervision board could also be appointed by a court of first instance to deal with certain matters in the competence of the supervision court.

Thus, the conditional sentence developed into a fairly diversified form of reaction to crime. It could be limited to a conditional waiving of sanction intended for defendants with good prognoses for whom a warning would suffice. For other offenders it could be combined with supervision and special conditions which could significantly restrict the sentenced person's freedom. The conditional sentence could also be used to deal with an offender in accordance with certain social welfare laws. This meant that even those who were well advanced in a criminal career and with poor prognoses could be conditionally sentenced.

Further reforms were introduced up until 1965 when a new Penal Code came into force. In 1959 the courts were given the power to combine a conditional sentence with *day-fines,* originally introduced in Sweden in 1931. The number of days in the day-fine is determined by the seriousness of the offense and the amount to be paid per day is determined by the defendant's income. The number of days multiplied by the amount per day gives the total amount of the fine.

The 1965 Penal Code. Those involved in preparing the new Penal Code considered it unsuitable that so many widely differing measures had been brought together under the heading of conditional sentence. In consequence, the conditional sentence was split into two penal measures with two different names. The conditional sentence was reserved for cases where the offender was not placed under supervision while the term probation was introduced where offenders were placed under supervision and, possibly, made subject to special conditions. Furthermore, surrendering an offender to child welfare, temperance care and psychiatric care were re-classified as independent sanctions and thereby released from the conditions applicable to a conditional sentence.

The conditional sentence is a sanction which means that *a conditional waiving of certain other sanctions* is granted. The probationary period is two years. The offender is subject neither to supervision nor any special conditions. He is, however, under an obligation to be of good conduct and to pay any damages owing. The court may specify the time and manner of the payment of damages. The court also has the power to impose *day-fines*—not more than 120—in conjunction with the conditional sentence even if fines are not stipulated for the offense. A conditional sentence is intended for offenders whose favorable prognosis makes any other measure unnecessary for their correction.

Probation is the name given to *non-institutional treatment in the community* as opposed to institutional treatment. It is not a conditional waiving of sanction but an independent penal sanction. Probation lasts for three years. The sentenced person is placed under the supervision of a supervisor appointed by the court for at least the first part of the probationary period. The court may impose special obligations concerning such matters as place of residence, use of leisure, disposal of wages, training, employment and the consumption of alcoholic beverages. These special conditions may also require the offender to undertake treatment for alcohol misuse or some other behavioral difficulty. The special conditions apply for a specified period or until further notice. If the offender is under an obligation to pay damages, special conditions may be imposed for their payment. Probation can also be combined with, at most, 120 *day-fines* even if a fine is not stipulated for the offense.

A new provision in the 1965 Penal Code made it possible for probation to be combined with *institutional treatment*. If the defendant was over 18 years of age and it was deemed necessary for his subsequent adjustment, the court could order treatment in an institution for at least one and not more than two months—the exact period to be determined during the institutional treatment—as part of the probation.

With misconduct, the supervision board could intervene by giving a warning or ordering that the offender be taken into provisional custody. If the offender appeared to be unable to manage in the community, the supervision board could apply to a prosecutor for the probation to be revoked. If the court agreed to this it could decide on another sanction for the original offense.

The 1973 Correctional Reform. The 1973 correctional reform (Government Bill 1973:131), which came into force in 1974, involved certain small changes in the provisions of the Penal Code concerning conditional sentences and probation (SFS 1973:918).

An earlier provision permitting an extension of the probationary period to three years for offenders with *conditional sentences* who misbehaved was annulled (Penal Code, Chapter 27, Section 6:3) and the general conduct requirement was reformulated (Penal Code, Chapter 27, Section 4).

Another earlier provision permitting the extension of the probationary period to five years with *probation* was also annulled as was the possibility of requiring compliance with a special condition on pain of a financial penalty (Penal Code, Chapter 28, Section 7). Some of the special conditions were abolished and it was recommended that those that remained should be used cautiously. An addition to the Code provided that the offender must have "seriously ignored his obligations" for action to be taken to revoke probation or institutional treatment (Penal Code, Chapter 28, Section 8). A further provision required that supervision be terminated when two years of the probationary period had passed (Penal Code, Chapter 28, Section 5) and an obligatory review of the need for supervision after one year was recommended. The aim of these reviews was to shorten unnecessarily long periods of supervision.

So far as changes in the Penal Code were concerned, the 1973 correctional reform meant mainly that certain sanction possibilities disappeared. What the reorganization meant for augmented resources within the non-institutional sector will be taken up later (see Chapter 8 and Appendix II).

Organization of the Non-Institutional Service

Historical Review

In 1910 a Discharged Prisoners' Aid Society was formed in Stockholm. Branches were soon established in the larger towns and in 1925 the Swedish Association of Discharged Prisoners' Aid Societies was formed. Their financial resources were, however, limited and inadequate. A state probation organization was provided for in legislation in 1939.

Although the police were often given the task of supervision initially, the county councils had the power to appoint "another suitable person" as supervisor. After 1918 the courts appointed supervisors for conditionally sentenced offenders while the county councils appointed a supervisor for parolees. Thus, the first supervisors were public servants even if they could scarcely be considered to be professional supervisors. They seem mostly to have undertaken control activities, the support function being mainly provided by laymen from the voluntary help organizations.

In 1944 the state probation service was set up and took over the functions of the Discharged Prisoners' Aid Societies and the supervisory duties of the county councils and the police.

The Probation Service

General Organization. There are 46 probation districts distributed throughout the country's various correctional regions. The chief probation officer is in charge of the activities in his district and is accountable to the regional director. Formally, he is subordinate to one or several local supervision boards as well as the national supervision board (which decides on parole for long term prisoners).

Administratively, the probation service comes under the Swedish Prison and Probation Administration and the supervision boards. However, the national and the local supervision boards are directly accountable to the Ministry of Justice.

Local Supervision Boards. The local boards are responsible for over-seeing all non-institutional treatment under the Penal Code and the probation offices are their service agencies. They direct the work of the probation officers, provide them with advice and instructions and appoint supervisors. They decide when supervision should be terminated and what measures should to be taken with misconduct.

The chairman of the board, who must be a jurist, is appointed by the government and must have served as a judge. The other four members of the supervision board are appointed by the county council and must have had experience of youth service work, labor exchange work or some other suitable employment qualifying them for the position. Another jurist acts as secretary of the board and the chief probation officer or an ordinary probation officer informs the board about the clients being supervised. In urgent cases the chairman can make independent decisions (Elwin, Heckscher and Nelson 1975, 181).

Probation Work. The probation service has not been the subject of the detailed central regulation which is characteristic for the prison service. In consequence, it is not easy to describe its activities as a clear definition of objectives it is to some extent lacking, the duties are varied and the routines relatively few.

The chief probation officer and his probation officer assistants are social workers and are assisted by an administrative personnel. As already mentioned, it is their duty to inform the supervision boards about the offenders in their charge in order that decisions can be made about the termination of supervision, special conditions and disciplinary measures. They also conduct social inquiries, train other persons as social inquiry investigators and prepare reports about clients who are appearing again before the courts. Probation staff are also responsible for recruiting, assisting, guiding and training lay supervisors and for making sure that the latter compile and send in supervision reports. The probation officers work chiefly with the cases that are assessed as difficult. Their work involves arranging accommodation, employment, training, medical treatment, etc. for their clients. The probation organization has been given only limited resources for the direct support of its clients. The probation officers are required to collaborate with such social services as employment offices, youth services, temperance services and the health care services. They are also expected to disseminate information in the community which will facilitate understanding, and thereby the implementation, of non-institutional sanctions.

Lay Supervisors. The lay supervisors are appointed by the courts, the supervision boards or the chief probation officers. Supervisors are subordinate to the chief probation officer and are under an obligation to report to him.

On average, the lay supervisors handle two cases at a time, but some supervisors work with many more. Even if the majority of supervisors are assigned only one case, this does not mean that supervisors work with only one person since some supervisors take on cases referred from other social services. This fact—significantly lacking in the official statistics—throws light on the conditions of supervision from the perspective of those controlled rather than that of the authorities responsible for controlling.

Non-institutional care is based largely on the participation of lay supervisors. About 90% of the offenders under supervision are supervised by laymen. The true proportion is even greater among those sentenced to probation since the professional probation officers tend to supervise the difficult cases, i.e. those conditionally released from prison. For about 20,000 supervised offenders in total there were more than 10,000 lay supervisors and less than 200 probation officers at the time of the study.

Supervisors are required to support and control their clients. The fact of being laymen and not officials is held to be advantageous for their work with offenders as it is thought that this makes it easier for the clients to establish contact with them. At the same time, the fact that lay supervisors must generally do their supervising in their leisure time makes it more difficult for them to collaborate with the different authorities responsible for arranging work, housing, social welfare benefits or medical assistance (see more about the supervisors, Chapter 6).

The *Swedish Association of Lay Supervisors,* formed in 1968, represents lay supervisors working within any social service—not just those engaged in probation and parole work. It arranges study courses and stimulates the recruitment and training of supervisors as well as representing their interests. It emphasizes the molding of favorable opinion throughout the country.

3

The Legislator's Intentions

Problems in the Interpretation of Law

The interpretation of law is part of the process of applying law and is normally not a theoretical, scientific activity but rather the solving of problems using value judgments and considerations of what would be appropriate (Strömholm 1973). Sociologists of law therefore encounter problems of interpretation when they attempt to determine the legislator's intentions.

First, it is often *difficult to distinguish between theory and ideology*. Thus, when the legislator maintains that a certain treatment should promote the offender's adjustment in society, he may or may not be basing this view on a theory that a certain form of treatment leads to a certain result. However, it is almost impossible to determine whether the legislator considers or does not consider some theory of individual prevention to be scientifically valid or whether he believes or does not believe in the theory. Treatment arguments such as individual prevention may also be used because these seem rational although the legislator's view may be based on quite other values. Thus, a treatment theory could be used to justify milder sanctions which in reality might be based on humanitarian values. And, theoretically, it could also legitimate an apparently individual preventive but extremely long treatment which in reality was based on a general preventive ideology.

Second, even if the legislator bases his views on a treatment theory, he usually does not support his arguments with empirical data. The theory which is depicted as a treatment theory may in fact be only wishful thinking—the legislator thinks that the treatment *ought* to have certain effects.

Third, the legislator describes the system's *manifest functions* and almost entirely neglects its latent functions. This neglect of the unintentional and often dysfunctional effects of law enforcement results from the absence of an empirical basis.

Fourth, the legislator proceeds almost exclusively from his *own value system* and fails to appraise the measures from the perspective of the person who will be subjected to treatment. When treatment measures are described as positive, the statement is generally based on the legislator's value judgement of the intended effects. The treatment measures may not, however, be experienced in the same way by the offender who may well regard them as negative.

Fifth, the legislator rarely undertakes a proper *ends-means analysis.* Crime reduction is set up as a goal and penal methods are seen as the instruments to reach it. By neglecting to analyze the effects of other social measures, an exaggerated picture is painted of the effects of pure penal measures.

Sixth, *legal language* gives rise to certain problems. Although legal terminology allows for considerable precision in distinguishing between details, it is seldom that clear definitions of basic concepts are given. Thus, in the preparatory work for the law on probation it is often difficult to determine whether "treatment" means some form of therapy or is merely a jurist's term for some legal measure. Linguistic ambiguity adds to the problem of distinguishing between theory and ideology.

Finally, it is sometimes difficult to say *who is the legislator* and what weight should be given to legislative preparatory work, to doctrine and to practice. Jurists are chiefly interested in knowing to which legal sources normative significance should be attributed whereas the social scientist is as, or more, interested in the people and institutions who exercised influence on emerging legislation and their value judgments.

Sources of the Law

The Swedish Penal Code contains the fundamental provisions on non-institutional sanctions. The main sources for the preparation of these provisions were the Protective Law Commission's final report "Protective Law" (SOU 1956:55), the 1956 After-care report "Non-institutional Treatment" (SOU 1961:16) and the Government Bill and Proposals 1962:10. Implementation instructions for probation were given in Government Ordinances SFS 1964:632, SFS 1973:920 and SFS 1974:514. The Swedish Prison and Probation Administration issues circular instructions to professional staff and publishes advice for lay supervisors from time to time. The courts and supervision boards can issue special directives about how supervision shall be implemented.

The Genesis of the Penal Code

As early as 1909 work was begun on formulating the principles for, and drawing up a draft of, new penal legislation. Continued preparatory work on reforms was entrusted to legislative committees. The *Penal Law Committee* was set up in 1937 to deal with offenses and the *Protective Law Commission*—a literal translation of its Swedish title—was set up in 1938 to deal with sanctions. The members of both committees were all officials—who thereby had a marked influence on the subsequent proposals for legislation (discussed by Elwin et al. 1975, 52–53).

Both committees made recommendations for successive reforms concerning, for instance conditional sentence, open prisons, prison work, conditional release, etc. The Protective Law Commission's work was based on the notion of social defense and its proposals were called protective law recommendations (SOU 1956:55).

There were objections to the abolition of the notion of punishment and the term protection, proposed by the Commission, was considered empty of content and misleading. When the recommendations were finally brought together in a new Penal Code (in Swedish *Brottsbalk,* literally translated means a Crime Code), it was decided to retain the term punishments to denote fines and imprisonment. However, the Swedish term used for probation (skyddstillsyn) means, in literal translation, "protective supervision". The proposed legislation, which was presented to the parliament in 1962, was adopted with only minor amendments (Nelson 1967). The Penal Code took effect on 1 January 1965.

General Goals of Criminal Policy

The movement for social defense maintained that the primary task for the administration of justice was to prevent crime; no room was allowed for retribution. The Protective Law Commission asserted that the purpose of society's criminal policy was to protect the community and its members against criminal activity by *preventing* crime (SOU 1956:55, 28).

However, the Commission pointed out that criminal policy has only limited possibilities of preventing crime. It called attention to the problem of the causation of crime and referred to research showing that the majority of inmates in the correctional institutions had been brought up in environments characterized by antisocial behavior, criminality or mental abnormality. The importance of the early years of childhood and a good upbringing was stressed.

As a result the Commission considered that there was a great need for different kinds of treatment measures to "remove physical or mental weaknesses, ensure that the offender gets a job and see that he does it properly, place him in a suitable environment and in general bring order to his living conditions" (SOU 1956:55, 32).

The Protective Law Commission clearly adhered to a treatment theory but it also cautiously stated: "There is no doubt that many offenders can be made more capable of leading a law-abiding life even if it is not certain that they will in fact do so" (SOU 1956:55, 32).

It also expressed the idea that in the interest of prevention it might be best to do as little as possible (SOU 1956:55, 32). In support of this idea, the Commission referred to studies which showed that young first offenders who were granted waiver of prosecution, recidivated less than those conditionally sentenced. These, in turn, recidivated to a considerably lesser extent than offenders who were deprived of their liberty. The Commission also noted that the recidivism rate is very high for offenders sentenced to sanctions depriving them of their liberty and particularly high when these are of long duration (SOU 1656:55, 34).

But penal intervention cannot, the Commission held, be limited to those cases where intervention is justified from the point of view of providing treatment, nor is it possible to allow the type of intervention to be based completely on such a view. Since the use of sanctions has some, albeit uncertain, general preventive effect the Commission considered that crime should be followed by a criminal law sanction and that exceptions could only be made if the circumstances warranted.

It seems clear that the Commission was chiefly interested in resocializing the offender and avoiding the detrimental effects of punishment but by clinging to certain principles of classical penal law—the principle that crime shall be followed by punishment and by referring to of general prevention—the treatment ideas are not followed through consistently. The Commission's discussion tells us little about how the *contradictory goals* of punishment and treatment are to be attained.

Guiding Principles for Choosing a Sanction

Chapter 1, Section 7 of the Penal Code states: "In the choice of sanctions, the court, with an eye to what is required to maintain general obedience to the law, shall keep particularly in mind that the sanction shall serve to foster the sentenced person's adaption in society".

Here the contradiction is embodied in a single formula intended to guide sentencing practice. The preparatory work, however shows that when the contradictions became all too evident, a smoke-screen was created to hide them. Statements of the type "the problem will right itself when the law is applied" and "the demands for consistency must not be too stringent" serve to camouflage very real contradictions and problems.

It was pointed out in the Penal Code Commentary I that, in fact, the general provision concerning the choice of sanctions had been supplemented in nearly every chapter dealing with particular sanctions by a list of prerequisites for their use. These prerequisites set limits to the court's possibilities to freely follow the principles of the general provision but give advice on the appropriate indications for the use of the sanctions.

The Commentaries also stress that since the range of punishment permitted by the various scales is often very broad it must be very difficult to judge with any certainty how much punishment is required to deter the defendant and others from criminality. It would be disquieting from the point of view of legal guarantees of fairness if every court in each case had the duty, or was authorized, to determine the punishment within the appropriate scale according to its own assessment of what is necessary or suitable. This argues for determining punishment chiefly with regard to the seriousness of the offense, including the intention and in general the offender's volition and emotional state at the time of the offense. Considerable weight was also attached to whether he had committed an offense previously. "Exactly what circumstances shall be taken into account when determining punishment and the weight that shall be assigned to them has in all essentials been laid down through a tradition in the determination of punishment which has in the main long been followed (1965, p. 55)."

The Commentaries take us quite a long way from the Protective Law Commission's discussion of goals. The legislator's intentions have been successively watered down. It would be strange if such a vaguely formulated section of the law, interpreted as it is in different ways by different authorities, did not engender uncertainty among the judges who had to apply it.

Conditional Sentence

In accordance with the proposals of the Protective Law Commission, the provisions of the Penal Code divide the earlier conditional sentence into two different sanctions—conditional sentence and probation.

General Pre-Conditions for the Use of Conditional Sentence. The new conditional sentence was intended for occasional offenders with a good prognosis.

Special Pre-Conditions. Chapter 27, Section 1 of the Penal Code provided for four pre-conditions for the use of the conditional sentence:

1. that the offense is punishable by imprisonment;
2. that it is not necessary to place the defendant under supervision;
3. that no more far-reaching measure is necessary to restrain him from further criminality;
4. that no other sanction should be used by reason of the seriousness of the offense or with regard to general obedience to the law.

The courts must arrive at a prognosis as to whether the defendant can be expected to live a law-abiding life in the future. This prognosis is primarily based on the social inquiry report which ordinarily is required before the imposition of a conditional sentence.

So far as the seriousness of the offense is concerned, the provisions set a lower limit by stating that it must be punishable by imprisonment. No upper limit is set.

Combining a Conditional Sentence with a Fine. In order to extend the field of application of the conditional sentence, the Protective Law Commission proposed on both general and individual grounds that the courts, in addition to a conditional sentence, should be empowered to sentence to day-fines for the same offense. However, the end result was that Chapter 27, Section 2 of the Penal Code provides as follows: "If it is necessary for the reformation of the offender or with regard to general obedience to the law, up to a maximum of one hundred and twenty day-fines may be imposed together with a conditional sentence whether fines are provided for the offense or not".

This provision on fines weakens the individual preventive pre-condition proposed by the Protective Law Commission, i.e. to widen the field of application of the conditional sentence by making it possible to combine it with fines.

Combining a Conditional Sentence with an Obligation to Pay Damages. Chapter 27, Section 5 of the Penal Codes provides, as previously, that the court may require the sentenced person to make good any damage arising as a result of the offense and to do what lies in his power to discharge that responsibility.

The Protective Law Commission held that it was of the greatest importance that anyone causing damage through crime should be required as far as possible to make good that damage. This was called for not merely out of sympathy for the plaintiff, but also on grounds of individual and general prevention. At the same time, however, the court must see to it that the offender is not so burdened by the payments for damages that his adjustment in the community is hindered. Nor should payment of damages be ordered in order to make the sanction more severe. Payment of damages could well obviate the necessity to impose fines.

Probationary Period, Good Conduct Provisions and Measures to Be Taken with Misconduct. The Protective Law Commission's recommendation that the earlier three-year probationary period should be reduced to two years was introduced into the Penal Code at Chapter 27, Section 3. The Commission's recommendations also contained a limitation of the offender's obligations insofar as nothing was proposed that corresponded to the earlier provision on good conduct. The only requirement put forward by the Protective Law Commission was that the offender should abstain from further crime.

The Penal Code provision in Chapter 27, Section 4 reads: "The sentenced person shall lead an orderly and law-abiding life during the probationary period, avoid bad company and seek to the best of his ability to support himself". If the sentenced person fails to comply with the conditions laid down as a consequence of the conditional sentence, the court, if the prosecutor institutes proceedings before the end of the probationary period, may

1. decide that the sentenced person shall be warned;
2. impose a condition in accordance with Section 5 or alter a condition previously imposed;
3. prolong the probationary period to three years;
4. revoke the conditional sentence and decide on another sanction for the offense.

Concurrence of Crimes. If a fresh offense is committed before the end of the probationary period, the conditional sentence may be vacated or certain other measures taken. Thus, if a person who has been sentenced to imprisonment, conditional sentence, probation, youth imprisonment or internment is found to have committed another crime prior to the sentence, or if he commits a new crime subsequent to the sentence but before the sanction has been fully implemented or otherwise terminated, the court may

1. order that the sanction imposed earlier shall also apply to the second offense;
2. impose a separate sanction for that offense or, if the earlier sentence has acquired legal force,
3. revoke the sanction imposed and impose a different kind of sanction for the offense (Chapter 34, Section 1).

Probation

As has already been mentioned the former conditional sentence was split into two sanctions when the Penal Code came into existence. Probation was the name reserved for that sanction which was to be used where supervision, with or without special conditions, was considered necessary.

General Pre-Conditions for the Use of Probation. The Protective Law Commission urged that when it came to reforming offenders so that they lived law-abiding lives, treatment in the community had undoubted advantages over imprisonment. By splitting up the former conditional sentence into two sanctions and providing an organizational reinforcement for treatment in the community, the Protective Law Commission sought to widen the field of application of probation. The Commission emphasized that probation was to be seen as an independent sanction, one which, unlike the earlier conditional sentence, was not a suspension of the imposition of a sanction or of the enforcement of a stated punishment: "It is intended for offenders who stand in need of positive measures in the form of support and help together with control if their adjustment in the community is to be promoted" (p. 132).

The importance of securing the sentenced person's co-operation in order that treatment in the community can be carried out successfully was emphasized although it was also pointed out that the probationer could be subjected to a certain degree of coercion.

Special Pre-Conditions. Chapter 28, Section 1 of the Penal Code sets forth five pre-conditions for the choice of probation as a sanction for a criminal offense:

1. that the offense can give rise to imprisonment;
2. that it is necessary that the defendant be placed under supervision;
3. that no more far-reaching sanction is called for;
4. that the minimum punishment for the offense is ordinarily not more than one year's imprisonment;
5. that ordinarily the defendant shall be more than eighteen years old.

The pre-condition that "no more far-reaching sanction is called for" was clearly meant by the Protective Law Commission to mean "from an individual preventive standpoint" but as interpreted by the Minister of Justice it refers also to a general preventive standpoint.

The fourth pre-condition is not to be found in the Protective Law Commission's proposal. A number of bodies were, however, in favor of limiting the field of application of probation.

Probation Combined with a Fine. Chapter 28, Section 2 provided for fines in connection with probation and has the same wording as for conditional sentence. The Commission held, however, that even if the purpose of probation was of individual preventive character, this did not prevent the sanction from having a more general preventive effect. This was so because treatment in the community could be made more intervenient by special conditions or institutional treatment. It was therefore neither necessary nor desirable to augment the penal value of the sanction by making it possible to sentence to fines in combination with probation. It was also pointed out that when the defendant was required to make good any damage occasioned by the offense, fines could not be adjudged if they placed the aggrieved person's possibilities of securing recompense in danger.

This reasoning is not to be found in the explanations to the Bill. Against this background it is perhaps not surprising that the Commentary to the Penal Code III simply says that probation may not be imposed merely because being under supervision makes the reaction to the offense more severe. For that purpose another sanction must be chosen instead—a conditional sentence combined with a fine or a fine or imprisonment. But this conclusion—that probation with a fine should not be used to make the sanction more severe—finds no support in the reasoning of the Protective Law Commission.

Probation with Institutional Treatment. An important innovation was the Commission's proposal that probation might be combined with an initial short period of institutional treatment. The provision took the following form in Chapter 28, Section 3 of the Penal Code: "If the defendant is eighteen years of age or older, the court may, if it is deemed necessary for his correction or for some other reason, order that the probation shall include treatment in an institution. Such treatment shall continue for at least one and at most two months depending on decisions made as it progresses ... If the defendant has not attained twenty three years of age, the court may decide that the order shall take effect even though the sentence to probation has not acquired legal force."

The Protective Law Commission's view was that for these young persons there was a need for some intermediate measure lying between the more lengthy youth imprisonment and ordinary probation in the community. The Commission argued that short institutional treatment could be utilized for both individual and general preventive reasons but only if deprivation of liberty is proven individually necessary. It emphasized that the kind of cases envisaged are essentially those which fall outside the field of application of the conditional sentence. The aim of the proposal was primarily to widen the scope for use of probation and permit this sanction in certain cases to be a substitute for sanctions which would entail deprivation of liberty for a relatively long period.

There is a built-in conflict in this argument. Probation with institutional treatment is justified by reference to individual prevention but at the same time is also be a substitute for another and longer form of deprivation of liberty—which thereby raises the issue of general prevention. This contradiction created a number of difficulties which became apparent in the discussion on the nature of the treatment in general.

The Protective Law Commission had recommended that the period for the institutional treatment be two months. The Commission had abstained from suggesting a scale of from one to three months at the court's discretion since this could easily result in setting the sanction level in accordance with the other normal criteria, i.e. mainly in relation to the seriousness of the offense.

Various arguments were advanced against this view and a compromise solution emerged as the provision in the Penal Code quoted at the beginning of the present section. But what appears, however, to be a compromise became in my view an entirely new form of contradiction since a partially determinate period prevents both the imposition of the sanction in strict accordance with the seriousness of the offense and, at the same time, makes it impossible to vary the treatment by reference to the offender's treatment needs.

The Protective Law Commission considered that the *probationary period* should, as a general rule, be counted from the day of sentence. It was considered important with youthful offenders that treatment should be started promptly. The professional association of advocates objected to this, *inter alia* on the ground that the proposal meant that a deprivation of liberty would be enforced immediately regardless of whether an appeal was being made against the sentence.

The result—as with many other matters—was a compromise solution. In fact it is far from clear whether immediate enforcement is to be justified by reference to treatment, deterrence or containment.

So far as the *nature of the institutional treatment* was concerned, the Commission preferred only to emphasize that the intention was not to introduce the "short sharp shock" of the English detention centres but rather "a psychological and pedagogic influencing of the offender so that he arrives at an insight on the importance of abstaining from crime in future" (p. 145).

In this connection the Commission proposed that a new type of institution, called probation institutions, should be set up, so that the probationers, who were presumed to be first offenders, should not be mixed with recidivist offenders. The probation institutions should be provided with a " well-qualified staff able to make use of the short period of treatment in the most suitable fashion".

Probationary Period. The Penal Code provision on the probationary period followed the recommendation of the Protective Law Commission: "The probationer shall remain under supervision during the term of probation. When supervision is deemed to be no longer necessary it shall be ordered terminated. As long as the probation lasts, the probationer may be placed under supervision anew if there are reasons for such a course of action. A decision on this matter is rendered by a supervision board (Chapter 28, Section 5)."

The Protective Law Commission emphasized that the probationary period comprises the maximum time for supervision. Just as probation should be not used unless there was a real need of supervision, so should supervision cease as soon as it no longer fulfilled any function. The Commission also pointed out that it could well serve treatment ends to taper off supervision before the end of the probationary period so that there was no sudden change from supervision to unlimited freedom.

General and Special Conditions. Chapter 28, Section 6 of the Penal Code provides that what is stated about imprisonment in Chapter 26, section 12–17 shall also apply to probation. Chapter 26, Section 13 provides that a person conditionally released from prison shall keep the supervisor informed of his place of residence and occupational status, shall visit the supervisor as required and in general follow any instructions given and maintain contact with the supervisor. Section 14 provides that the conditionally released person shall live an orderly and law-abiding life, avoid bad company, maintain himself to the best of his ability and in general seek to live in accordance with what is required of him in under instructions or advice conveyed with the support of the Code.

Section 15 provides that special conditions may be laid down that appear suitable for the promotion of his adjustment in the community. The special conditions may obtain for a given period or until further notice.

The Protective Law Commission considered on grounds of individual prevention that the supervision board and not the court should lay down the conditions with the exception of the question of damages.

The Minister of Justice and a number of other bodies, however, did not accept this view. In particular, the professional association of chief judges emphasized that it was the courts which had responsibility for seeing that sanctions were chosen with due regard to the need for general prevention and the general preventive effect of probation was largely a matter of the conditions imposed. Moreover, the Protective Law Commission's proposal that conditions and instructions should be part of a treatment plan was not taken up in the proposed legislation. Once again, we see that measures proposed by the Commission for reasons of individual prevention were accepted but that the guarantees which the Commission built in to prevent their use for reasons of general prevention were ignored.

Conditions would seem therefore to be mainly for use as mechanisms of augmentation—which means that they risk to lean towards punishment instead of treatment. If the offender does not observe the general conditions, special conditions can be made. If these, in their turn, are not observed the sentenced person can be the subject of further measures decided on by a supervision board. The conditions can in this way have more the character of threats and impositions through which an element of repression enters into the probation sanction. Despite the fact that, formally speaking, the conditions are there for individual preventive reasons the circumstances described here can mean that there is a risk that the sentenced person's resettlement in the community is not promoted and may even be counteracted.

Measures with Misconduct. Chapter 28 and Sections 7–11 of the Penal Code deal with the various measures which can be taken in the event of misconduct. If the probationer does not comply with what is required of him as a consequence of the sentence to probation, a supervision board may:

1. decide that the probationer be given a warning;
2. extend the term on probation to at most five years;
3. order him, under threat of a monetary penalty, to comply with a special condition imposed (Section 28, Section 7).

Furthermore, if the probationer has ignored his obligations and it can be presumed that he will not let himself be corrected by a measure which the supervision board is empowered to take, the board shall request the prosecutor to raise the question of revoking the probation or the treatment referred to in Section 3 with the court (Chapter 28, Section 8).

If the probation is revoked, the court shall decide on another sanction for the offense. In so doing, fair consideration shall be given to what the probationer has undergone as a consequence of the probation as well as to any fines imposed with the probation in accordance with the provisions of Section 2. The court may impose imprisonment for a shorter period than that provided for the offense (Chapter 28, Section 9).

If a question arises concerning the revocation of probation or concerning treatment in accordance with the provisions of Section 3 or a measure referred to in Section 7, the supervision board or the court before which a proceeding has been instituted under Section 8 may, if the circumstances require it, order that the probationer be appropriately detained while awaiting a further decision for up to a week or, under special circumstances, for a further week.

The possibility of a temporary detention was also an innovation in the Protective Law Commission's proposal. What the Protective Law Commission wanted to do was to introduce a possibility to intervene if there were an acute danger for a relapse into crime or some other misconduct on the part of a probationer. However, it seems astonishing that the Commission, knowing that the police must give assistance in this situation with detention in inadequate police cells as a frequent consequence, could imagine that such a detention was a means as it desired "to influence the probationer" and "restore his mental balance".

All of the measures with misconduct—the issuing special directives, taking up supervision anew, warning, prolongation of the probationary period, obedience to directives under threat of monetary penalty, institutional treatment and revocation of probation—could all be considered to be repressive components in what was intended to be a positive treatment modality. Formally speaking, it only required misconduct—and with temporary detention not even that—for far-reaching interventions to be brought into use.

If the probationer ignored his responsibilities, the court had the possibility of ordering institutional treatment as a sanction—which thereby gives the probation institution the character of a punishment. And the court was also empowered to revoke the probation and sentence the offender to another sanction for the offense which originally gave rise to the probation. "The new decision can be one of imprisonment but also some other sanction prescribed for the offense" (Commentary to the Penal Code III). This means that what was intended to be a treatment in freedom could be exchanged for a traditional imprisonment without any new offense being committed.

The Content of Positive Treatment. Although there are a number of specific provisions concerning various negative sanctions which can be used in the event of misconduct, there is only one kind of positive incentive, namely that supervision can be terminated. But there are no legislative provisions about the form of the so-called positive treatment.

Here the provisions of the Penal Code differ radically from the Protective

Law Commission's proposals. The Commission attempted to define the content of the proposed treatment in the following terms.

1. ***Professionally Trained Workers for Social Inquiry Reports.*** The Commission urged that the social inquiry report which should precede a sentence to probation should not only take up the offender's personal circumstances and situation but also provide a basis for a treatment plan. The Commission proposed that in order to avoid poor treatment planning these inquiries should be carried out more often by specialists, such as probation officers.

2. ***Independent Superintendence Boards.*** The reasoning on positive measures also emphasized the need for professional supervisors and independent superintendence boards. "In order to ensure the effectiveness of probation as a treatment modality it is a necessary condition that the treatment should be guided by an expert body with appropriate authority which, during the probationary period, can follow the treatment and flexibly adjust it to changed circumstances" (p. 138–139). The Commission proposed local superintendence boards as such a body.

The proposal to set up superintendence boards was followed, although with the retention of a title from the 1939 Act—supervision boards. But a recommendation that they should have an independent position vis-à-vis the courts was not completely accepted since the Penal Code provided that special conditions could also be imposed by the courts.

3. ***Professionally Trained Supervisors and Contact Persons.*** The Commission proposed that the supervisor for a person sentenced to probation should always be a professionally trained person and, as a rule, the chief or other probation officer. The Commission nevertheless held that in addition to the public servant there was value in having a private individual offer time and interest as helper and friend on behalf of the probationer. For this reason voluntary workers, designated by the superintendence board, should continue to be used in probation work.

However, the Minister of Justice considered that even with a marked increase in the number of chief probation officers and probation officer assistants, it would probably still be necessary to give more cases to laymen for supervision than the Commission had supposed. He proposed that chief probation officers and probation officers should more often than hitherto be used as supervisors of difficult cases.

4. ***Treatment Planning.*** The Commission had urged that careful treatment planning was a *sine qua non* for successful probation and stated that more detailed provisions on the form for a treatment plan should be worked out administratively. But no such administrative provisions had come into existence at the time when the Penal Code entered into force.

5. ***Increased Resources.*** Finally, the Protective Law Commission emphasized that an essential condition for bringing a law on social defense into operation was that adequate resources should be available for the treatment of sentenced persons. In particular, a considerable increase in the number of professionally trained chief probation officers and probation officers was necessary having regard to the widened responsibilities which they would have

to assume. The relatively limited extra expense to the State's budget would be more than recouped through the savings effected by reduced institutional costs.

Other Legal Provisions

The legal provisions regulating the activities of the various bodies concerned with probation are now described in more detail.

Legal Provisions Concerning Supervision Boards. The activities of the boards are regulated in Chapter 37 of the Penal Code. However, the Protective Law Commission's intention to create a relationship of confidence between the probationer and the board can scarcely be said to be presented positively or with clarity in the Penal Code provision: "In a matter dealt with by a supervision board and relating to some question other than the termination of supervision or a special condition imposed, the offender shall be given an opportunity to express himself if this can conveniently be arranged and hearing him would not be unprofitable. If the offender requests that he be heard orally in a matter before the board, he shall be given the opportunity." (Chapter 37, Section 6)

As has been shown earlier, the means available to the supervision boards to achieve the aim of getting the supervised person to lead a law-abiding life consisted mainly of sanctions with misconduct.

Legal Provisions Concerning the Probation Service. The probation service is considered to be the service agency for the supervision boards. The duties of the chief probation officer include acting as a go-between for the supervision boards on the one side and the supervisors on the other. He is also to keep himself informed on how supervisors and clients fulfil their various responsibilities. The chief probation officer's responsibilities vis-à-vis the supervisor and the client, are not, on the other hand, regulated by any specific provisions.

Legal Provisions Concerning the Supervisor. The supervisor's responsibilities to the chief probation officer are clearly defined in a 1964 Ordinance on treatment in freedom (SFS 1964:632). The reporting responsibility of the supervisor is defined in Section 31 and requires him within one month of the start of the supervision and thereafter at quarterly intervals to report to the chief probation officer on the probationer's conduct, housing and occupational status, the supervisor's visits to the probationer and what has been observed on these occasions together with any other circumstances of importance for the supervision.

Section 26 requires the supervisor to report on non-observance of imposed conditions or on any proposed modification of conditions or supervision.

The provisions dealing with the supervisor's control function are more clearly stated than those dealing with the support function. The main section in the Ordinance, Section 17, requires the supervisor to hold himself informed on the probationer's conduct and see to it that the latter does what is required of him in accordance with the Penal Code or a special condition imposed or instruction given on the basis thereof as well as provide him with help and support to lead an orderly and law-abiding life. "The supervisor should perform his task with firmness. He should seek to win the probationer's confidence by showing goodwill and consideration".

It is significant that the word "shall", which is used in all provisions concerning the supervisor's duties vis-à-vis the chief probation officer and his control function vis-à-vis the probationer, is replaced by the word "should" whenever reference is made to the helping function. More precise instructions about how lofty supervision objectives are to be attained are not to be found in the Ordinance.

The Swedish Prison and Probation Administration issues a circular instruction, Instructions for Supervisors. Whilst the instructions published in 1964 emphasize control more than support, it is support which is brought out more in the 1972 version and, in the 1974 version, the attempt is made to secure a balance between them. Although the instructions give a more concrete description of the content of supervision, or at least the forms of supervision, the norms are still vaguely formulated. The support function is still optional by comparison with the obligatory control function. The idea of a treatment plan on the lines desired by the Protective Law Commission is never mentioned.

Legal Provisions Concerning the Social Inquiry Report. The purpose of a social inquiry report as defined in Section 1 of the Act on Social Inquiry Reports in Criminal Cases (1964 and as amended 1973) is to obtain information on the personal circumstances of the accused and the measures which might be considered suitable to promote his adjustment in the community and improve his possibilities for personal development. The wording indicates a clear individual preventive purpose.

Although the Protective Law Commission laid emphasis on the importance of using well-trained investigators, it made no recommendations about the special qualifications of an investigator. It is still true today that it is a matter of using anyone who is suitable and willing. We shall later return to the question of the quality of social inquiry reports and the importance attaching to the social inquiry investigator's recommendation on the sanction.

Legal Provisions Concerning the Client. The sentenced person is not given any collected information to enable him to ascertain his rights about, for instance, a proposal on choice of supervisor, attendance at the supervision board, an appeal against its decisions, etc. Nor are the client's rights vis-à-vis the chief probation officer and the supervisor defined in any legal provisions.

At least until as late as 1973 the client only received the following information after sentence had been passed: "The purpose of supervision is to help you to live a useful and law-abiding life. If you misbehave the supervision board can give you a warning and prolong the probationary period up to five years".

Probation with supervision is considered officially to be an offer of treatment, but at the same time more supervision is threatened if the probationer misbehaves. The question can well be asked: Is this really the best way of promoting contact and creating a relationship built on confidence?

4

The Judge's Choice of Sanction

Problem, Theory and Method

The aim of this chapter is to examine the extent to which individual prevention was taken into account with choice of sanction. A first step in this inquiry is to present a systematic analysis of the offenders' personal and social circumstances. In order to ascertain whether the judges also gave consideration to general prevention aspects when choosing the sanction, factors concerning current offense and previous criminality are analyzed as well.

The Judge's Decision-Making Model

Philosophers of law have described the sentencing process in a variety of ways. Blackstone maintained, for example, that the passing of a sentence is simply a mechanical application of a set of legal rules to the facts of special cases. Other legal theorists, particularly those known as legal realists, have put forward a partially opposing thesis, namely that a judicial decision is the product of the judge's background and attitudes and not of rational deduction. However, when a judge must decide if a rule can be applied to a special set of facts, his task does not necessarily constitute either a mechanical process of deduction or an arbitrary personal decision. As Hart has pointed out, theoretically, judicial decisions can be both rational and consistent, even if the judge's decision is not always one or the other.

Different *theories of the interpretation of law* are often described as *subjective* (the "will of the legislator" is sought primarily in the text of the law and the preparatory work), *objective* (the meaning of the law is sought in the text and its meaning in common language as well as from observations of its consequences) or *teleological* (which to an even greater extent emphasizes the aim of the law as the only or the most important principle of interpretation). However, it is not always clear whether the interpretation theories of some philosophers of law refer to what is objectively the *correct* method of interpreting law or are merely a recommendation for the interpreter concerning how he *ought* to proceed or are statements about how the interpreter *usually* proceeds (Eckhoff 1975, pp. 112–116).

It is usually asserted that judicial decisions are not exclusively determined by the judge's model of what is legally correct but that even *non-legal factors* influence the outcome of a case. Scholars have most often emphasized motives which cannot be understood by examining the law itself (see e.g. Aubert 1972, p. 188).

A number of studies have shown that variations exist in sentencing practices among individual judges and among different types of judges. In almost every case, researchers have attributed these variations to non-legal factors, such as the judge's personality, or what might be called arbitrariness.

However, with few exceptions, no definitions are given of "the personal factor" or other undefinable elements, nor are the individual differences related to the different attributes of the judges (Hood and Sparks 1973, p. 122). And in no case, it seems, has research been undertaken to determine whether the variations can be accounted for by *legal factors* other than those connected with the offense, its seriousness and similar circumstances.

As a rule, researchers have started from a *decision-making model based on traditional ways of assessing punishment;* judges, on the other hand, may have worked with a model that takes individual prevention into account. It is not surprising that researchers find inexplicable variations under such circumstances. I know of no study which takes a *model of individual prevention* as its point of departure and attempts to establish the extent to which judges make use of it. Such an approach makes for a markedly more difficult research task since it is not so easy to ascertain what might be the judicially relevant factors.

In this study I take as my starting point just such a more complex model. As we saw in Chapter 3, Swedish judges are required primarily to take individual prevention into consideration when choosing the sanctions of conditional sentence and probation. However, it is left to a large extent to the judge to decide which personal and social factors should be considered. Considerations of general prevention—usually related to the type and seriousness of the offense—also come into the picture. But, in principle, general prevention should not be considered when a choice is made between the sanctions of conditional sentence and probation. The judge should choose probation rather than conditional sentence if the offender is seen to need supervision for his readjustment. He can also choose probation with institutional treatment if the defendant is found to need supervision and an initial period of treatment in an institution. In choosing between probation with or without institutional treatment, consideration may, however, at the same time be given to other aspects, among them those of general prevention.

To the extent that the judges act in accordance with the legislator's intentions by giving primary consideration to individual prevention when they choose conditional sentence or probation, we would not expect to see a traditional assessment of punishment based on the seriousness of the offense. But if there should be covariance between the social factors (which the judge must pay attention to when making his prognosis) and the crime factors (which are linked to the offense) there is a risk of getting a result on the crime variable which parallels the result on the social factors. We must therefore keep the different types of factors separate by using appropriate statistical methods.

The purpose of the present study is not to try to find variations in judicial decisions and thereafter find the explanation for these in the judges' attributes. Unlike most other studies I have here proceeded from a model of individual prevention in which *personal and social circumstances become the legally relevant factors* and—to express it somewhat provocatively—the crime can almost be regarded as a non-legal factor.

In other words, I am trying to establish what is the *decision-making model of judges.* The reader is referred to Hood and Sparks (1973, pp. 128–129) for a *model representing the structure of the sentencing process* within the common-law system. That model tries to incorporate all the various factors which could influence the judges in the choice of a sanction and assessment of the level of punishment. The present study thus illustrates the differences between the law in books and the law in action. Whether a defendant has a better prognosis if he is sentenced conditionally than if he is sentenced to probation, or whether a defendant who is placed under supervision has as good a prognosis as the offender who is sent to prison, seems to me to be ordinarily more a sociological or social-psychological problem than a legal one. But it becomes legally relevant in the present case to make an assessment of the defendant's chances of adjusting to society, based on the knowledge of an individual's personal and social circumstances and on what is known of the individual preventive effects of imprisonment and probation. If a judge wants guidance in handling this problem, he may refer to the research available on treatment effects. As, however, no certain interactional effects have been found between the individual and treatment, the judge could reduce his problem to one of mainly choosing a sanction on the basis of its general individual preventive effects. But this means that he can well have more use of sociological and evaluative research into the effectiveness of punishment and treatment than of legal theory or methods.

Various Methods of Studying the Sentencing Process

According to Hood and Sparks, three methods have been used in studies of the *various ways sentences are arrived at.* With the first method, simple comparisons are made between different courts, and the proportion of offenders who receive a certain sentence is established. Thus, Grünhut (1956) found great variations among different English juvenile courts in their use of conditional sentence: the proportion of offenders who received this sanction varied from 12% to 79% in two neighbouring towns. With a second, more refined method, a large number of cases are reviewed and the assumption is made that the various types of crime are randomly distributed among the judges. Using just such a method, Gaudet (1949) analyzed over 7,000 sentences imposed by six judges in a New Jersey county court, where the prosecutor distributed the cases among the judges in rotational order. Gaudet found that the "more lenient" judges sent one-third of the offenders to prison, while the other judges imprisoned half or more. In the most sophisticated of the three methods, attempts are made to control for the different types of offender through the use of comparison or prediction methods. Green (1961) examined about 1,500 cases handled in the Philadelphia court of quarter sessions and found that the legal factors surrounding the offense and previous criminality were more important than such non-legal factors as sex, age, race and place of birth. In Sweden considerable variation has been found between both courts of first instance and courts of appeal (Bondeson 1983). The factors which *judges take into consideration* during the judicial process can be studied by the following methods: participant observation, interviews with judges, analysis of the reasoning undertaken by the court in support of the judgment or, by studying the files, investigation of the factors that show covariance with the judgments passed.

The method of *participant observation* appears not to have been used in any published study. However, the observant participant can make available information not easily obtainable by other means. Blumberg, with long experience as a defense counsel, could thus make a study of the public defender (1967) which demonstrated the lack of agreement between legal ideals and the fact that, in practice, the defense counsel plays the part of a court functionary.

A useful method for the scientific observer is conducting *interviews with judges* to ascertain how judges reason when they impose sentences. An early study of this kind was made by the Danish legal scholar, von Eyben (1951). Similar studies have been carried out by Mäkelä (1966) in Finland, Lauridsen (1972) in Denmark and Bondeson and Bodin (1977) in Sweden.

Content analysis of the court's reasons for the sentences imposed presents certain difficulties. When preparing the present study it was found that the reasoning about the judgments passed was often vaguely formulated and incomplete in content.

Using *investigation of the factors which show covariance* with the judicial decision is not subject to the same disadvantages as the other methods mentioned above because it eliminates the judge's subjective evaluation of his actions. Aubert (1964, p. 124) pointed out if we wish to exclude reliance on the judge's own account of the different factors influencing his decision-making we should examine the factors that are statistically related to the decision.

In the present study, we have used various statistical methods to investigate the factors that are correlated with judicial decisions and, in addition, a content analysis of the courts' written reasons for the sentences imposed.

Description of the Sanction Groups

The following description of the client group provides a background to the judges' choice of sanction and also forms the basis of the prediction study (Chapter 5). By comparing the sanction groups with each other and with a normal group, we can gain insight into the probable causes of their registered criminality.

A relatively large number of variables relating to the offender's childhood, his personal and social circumstances and previous and current criminality, will be presented. Such a comprehensive review of these background variables is justified because the legislator has not mentioned what variables the judges should take into consideration when they decide on a sanction. Had a smaller number of variables been used it could have been objected that we had missed just those factors which the judge uses for his assessment of whether the sentenced person needed supervision or institutional treatment.

The sample consists of 413 convicted males who are relatively evenly distributed between the three sanction groups. They were randomly selected from among the sentences passed in 1967 by thirteen different courts within the probation districts of Malmö, Lund and Helsingborg. The data are the same for both the sentencing and the prediction study. After pre-testing a measuring instrument using eighty variables was constructed. There were no missing external data. Internal missing data, sampling, data collection and data analysis are described in Appendix I.

General Background Information

The *age distribution* was as follows. Those sentenced to probation with institutional treatment (PI) had a median age of 20.5 years, whilst ordinary probationers (P) and conditionally sentenced offenders (CS) had median ages of 24.5 and 25.5 respectively. The mean ages (21, 29 and 31 respectively) show somewhat greater variation.

Although probation with institutional treatment was intended primarily for young offenders, one-fifth of those so sentenced were between 24 and 50 years of age and none were under 18. Two of the P-group and six of the CS-group were under 18. An offender must be 18 or more before he can be sentenced to institutional treatment and offenders under 18 may not be sentenced to probation unless this sanction is considered more suitable than treatment under the provisions of the Child Welfare Act.

Birthplace and place of upbringing showed more PI-offenders to have been born in towns and more CS-offenders to have been born in the country. Almost half the offenders from all groups resided in a large town at the time of sentence and about twice as many resided in a large town when they came before the court as were actually born and brought up in a town. Thus, there was considerable geographic mobility in all the sanction groups.

There are distinct differences of *nationality* between the groups. Twenty-six percent of the CS-offenders were born in a foreign country and had foreign citizenship. This was true for 9% of the P-group. Of the PI-group, 11% were born in a foreign country and 9% had foreign citizenship. One-third of the foreign citizens in the CS-group and almost all the foreign citizens in the probation groups, resided in Sweden. The courts appear to make considerable use of conditional sentence combined with expulsion from Sweden when offenses are committed by foreign citizens.

The majority of the offenders in all three groups were not married. Nevertheless, the groups clearly differ in the proportions of persons who were married—33% of CS-offenders, 17% of P-offenders and 5% of PI-offenders. This difference in *civil status* can only partly be explained by the differences in age.

The majority of offenders did not have any *children*. One-third of the total number had children under the age of 16 and among these the CS-group generally had two and the P-group one.

Home and Childhood Conditions

Almost twice as many in the P-group and the PI-group as in the CS-group were *born out of wedlock,* (12%, 13% and 7% respectively). Almost every fifth CS-offender and P-offender, and somewhat more than every fourth PI-offender had parents who were *divorced* at the time of our study. Variables related to *stability of environment showed* 68% of the CS-offenders, 54% of the P-offenders and 50% of the PI-offenders to have lived with their parents during childhood. Five or more environments were registered for 1% of CS-offenders, 6% for P-offenders and 8% for PI-offenders.

Fifty-one percent of the CS-group had *fathers or foster fathers* who belonged to social group III (lower class) as opposed to 66% for the probationers' fathers. The number of unskilled laborers is greater among the fathers of probationers than among those of CS-offenders (41% and 30% respectively). Both probation groups deviate from the normal population in respect to social class. Almost every third probationer and one CS-offender in ten were brought up under poor *economic conditions,* i.e. their families were receiving some kind of financial assistance. Two-thirds of the *mothers or foster mothers* were housewives. Among those working, 72% had work which did not require any form of vocational training and 82% had typical lower social class jobs. Thirteen percent of the CS-offenders and 35% of the probationers lived under conditions of *overcrowding,* defined as two or more people to one room. Extreme overcrowding was registered for 14% of probationers. These figures may be under-estimations as information was not available for just over one-third of the sample. In all sanction groups there were on average five people *living together in one household.* Three-quarters of all the offenders had two to three *siblings.* In addition, a small number of half-siblings lived in the same household.

Using definitions developed by Blomberg, the methods of *upbringing* can be described as good for 66% of the CS-offenders, 49% of the P-offenders and 41% of the PI-offenders. No differences were detected between the groups concerning parental strictness. However, there were differences concerning lax methods (CS-group 6%, P-group 22%, PI-group 31%) or inconsistent methods (2%, 8%, 13% respectively). This variable has proved to have predictive value in other studies.

The relationship of the offender's father to the rest of the family was unsatisfactory for 36% of PI-offenders, 25% of P-offenders and 7% of CS- offenders. The relationship between father and son was distinctly negative for 20% of PI-offenders, 14% of P-offenders and 4% of CS-offenders. The *mother's relationship* to all or some members of the family was also less than satisfactory for 23% of PI-offenders, 12% of P-offenders and 7% of CS-offenders.

The highest frequency for *mental disorders* was found among the relatives of the PI-offenders and the lowest among the relatives of the CS-offenders. Mental disturbances were registered for 18% of the PI-offenders' fathers, 23% of their mothers and 8% of their siblings.

Some form of *alcohol misuse* was found among 19% of all the registered fathers, 3% of the mothers and 8% of the siblings. More than six times as many cases of alcohol misuse were registered among the fathers of PI-offenders as among those of CS-offenders (33% and 5% respectively). More than three-quarters of the registered accounts of alcohol misuse by mothers were found in the PI-group.

Intervention by the police or an alcohol misuse agency *as a result of alcohol misuse* was more frequent among probationers' families than among CS-offenders' families—33% of the CS-offenders' fathers, 55% of the P-offenders' fathers and 78% of the PI-offenders' fathers. Similar interventions were found among one-third of the CS-offenders' siblings and more than one-half of probationers' siblings. All interventions arising from the mother's misuse of alcohol occurred in the group of probationers who had been sentenced to institutional treatment.

Known criminal activity within the offenders' families occurred most commonly among siblings (20% of the PI-offenders' siblings and 8% and 2% in the P-group and CS-group respectively). Three times as many of the PI-offenders' fathers had been involved in some kind of criminal activity as fathers of CS-offenders. Criminal activity on the part of mothers was limited to a few isolated cases.

In order to describe the combined effect of the offenders' environment during childhood and adolescence, the twenty most important of the thirty original variables were categorized and summed to form a simple *index* of minus scores (see Chylicki, p. 29 for a description of the individual variables and distribution of minus scores). Sixty-six percent of the CS-offenders, 33% of the P-offenders and 20% of the PI-offenders had a zero score or a score of minus one. Three percent of the CS-offenders, 16% of the P-offenders and 28% of the PI-offenders had more than five minus points. The highest number of minus points in the CS-group was eight and in the probation groups, thirteen. The median number for the three groups are 0.78, 2.56 and 3.78 respectively. The difference is significant ($p < .01$) between the PI-group and the P-group and highly significant ($p < .001$) between the CS-group and the P-group.

More Detailed Information on the Offenders

Personal Attributes and Scholastic Achievements. So far as *intellectual capacity* is concerned, there is a clear over-representation of the less well-endowed in the two probation groups both in comparison with the CS-group and a normal population. Thirty percent of the PI-offenders and 22% of the P-offenders were far below average as compared with 9% among the CS-offenders. As many as 10% of the PI-group were clearly educationally backward.

Nineteen percent of the CS-offenders, 33% of the P-offenders and 39% of the PI-offenders suffered from mild *mental disorders*. One percent of the CS-offenders and 6% of all probationers had mental problems of intermediate severity for which psychiatric consultation had been necessary. Twelve percent of the two probation groups but none of the CS-offenders suffered from severe disorders which had necessitated institutional care. It should be noted that the probation sanction was not intended for use with mentally handicapped offenders.

Almost three-quarters of the sample, but four-fifths of the PI-group, had had no more than *elementary schooling.* Twenty percent of the CS-offenders, 17% of the P-offenders and 14% of the PI-offenders had had some kind of practical vocational training. Of the total sample, 6% were educated in primary school or school for adult education and only 3% in grammar school or college.

The proportions of the groups placed in remedial classes or classes for the mentally retarded were 9% (PI-group), 7% (P-group) and 2% (CS-group). *Poor social adjustment in the school* situation occurred to a greater extent in the probation groups and especially so in the PI-group. The proportions for school maladjustment were 13% (PI-group), 6% (P-group) and 3% (CS-group). For truancy the proportions were 6%, 4% and 1% respectively and for a combination of problems 17%, 7% and 2% respectively.

Prior Offenses—Measures by Child Welfare Authorities. Less than one-fifth of the CS-offenders were registered as delinquents before they were 15 years old while the proportion among the probationers was four-fifths. Previous antisocial behavior (partly criminality and partly behavior resulting in child welfare interventions) was noted among 20% of the CS-offenders, 53% of the P-offenders and 72% of the PI-offenders. The statistical differences between the CS-group and the P-groups are highly significant and are significant between the P-group and the PI-group.

Less than one-third of the offenders from the CS-group who were registered for antisocial behavior were only brought to the child welfare authorities' attention. But in 70% of the cases involving P-offenders and 86% of the cases involving PI-offenders active interventions were instituted. Three percent of the CS-offenders, 29% of the P-offenders and 51% of the PI-offenders had been placed under supervision or had been turned over to some social agency for care. Furthermore, the child welfare authorities had taken such steps as placement in a foster home, observation centre or youth reform school in the case of 1% of the CS-offenders, 18% of the P-offenders and 28% of the PI- offenders.

Current Social Adjustment I: Alcohol and Drug Misuse. *Alcohol misuse* occurred with highly significant differences between the CS-group (22%) and the probation groups (P 59% and PI 54%). Of the alcohol misusers, *intervenient measures* were taken with 44% of the CS-offenders, 70% of the P-offenders and 60% of the PI-offenders.

Only 5% of the total sample misused narcotics or pharmaceutical drugs. The proportions are 1% for the CS-offenders, 5% for the P-offenders and 8% for the PI-offenders. Almost half the cases were classified as misusing pharmaceutical drugs. Misuse might well have occurred to a greater extent without becoming known to the authorities.

Current Social Adjustment II: Employment and Residence. The percentage of the sample belonging to the *lower social groups*—especially unskilled laborers—is higher than that in the general population. Seventy-three percent of the CS-group, 83% of the P-group and 95% of the PI-group belong to social group III; of these 42%, 56% and 65% respectively were unskilled laborers.

When these figures are compared with those for the offenders' fathers there is a downward shift in the social class scale. It is uncertain whether this *downward mobility* results from social inheritance in consequence of which the offenders lived under the same or worse conditions as their fathers (see Jonsson 1967) or whether it resulted from early intervention by the authorities. It could also be said that social heritage and the interventions of society are included in an offender's social inheritance.

The proportions who were *unemployed* at the time sentence was passed varies greatly—13% of CS-offenders, 26% of the P-offenders and 58% of the PI-offenders. The difference between the CS-group and the P-group is statistically significant and the difference between the two probation groups is highly significant.

Stability of employment was measured by noting the number of times a change of employment occurred. Although the CS-offenders were, on average, older, they changed jobs less frequently. Twenty-one percent of the CS-offenders, 37% of the P-offenders and 31% of the PI-offenders changed jobs nine times or more. So far as the longest period of employment is concerned, 70% of the P-offenders and 77% of CS-offenders had been employed for at least one year as compared to 43% of the PI-offenders.

With respect to *financial circumstances*, we found that the average annual income of the sample ranged from 10,000 to 15,000 Swedish crowns (approximately 1,400–2,300 US$). The PI-offenders had the lowest annual income and the CS-offenders the highest. Of the total sample, 67% had an income below 15,000 Swedish crowns but this was true of only 53% of national wage-earners in 1966 (Statistisk årsbok 1968). Since women and part-time workers are included in the latter figure, the difference is, in fact, even greater.

The offenders' *housing conditions* were poorly described in the social inquiry reports but the majority of them had some form of ordered living accommodation. Six percent of the CS-offenders, 6% of the P-offenders and 11% of the PI-offenders did not have somewhere to live at the time sentence was passed. But it should be remembered that most of the CS-offenders were short-stay foreigners with no permanent residence in Sweden.

Nevertheless, the majority of the sample solved their accommodation problems in makeshift fashion. Eighteen percent of all the offenders lived with their wives with the majority of these being CS-offenders. Eight percent lived together with someone else and 12% lived alone in their own apartment. Forty percent lived with their parents; the majority of these were from the PI-group. Lastly, 14% boarded with someone else.

Twenty-eight percent of all offenders had below-standard housing and a further 20% lived in semi-modern conditions (missing data on 29% is not included). Although the difference in the housing standard of these offenders is not great between the sanction groups, the difference between the total sample and the national population is great.

Prior Convictions. The *number of previous convictions*, reveals highly significant differences among the three sanction groups. Twenty-eight percent of the CS-offenders, 57% of the P-offenders and 77% of the PI-offenders had at least one previous conviction. Only 4% of the CS-offenders had three or more previous convictions as compared with 18% of the probationers.

On *type of previous sanction,* 5% of the CS-group, 21% of the P-group and 13% of the PI-group had been deprived of their liberty. The CS-offenders had generally been imprisoned for short periods for drunken driving. Forty-four percent of the PI-group had been previously been given ordinary probation.

Current Offense. In all the sanction groups, offenses of theft and fraud were the dominant *types of principal offense.* The proportion of CS-offenders who had committed violent offenses was similar to that of P-offenders (10%) but for the PI-offenders it was only 3%. The CS-group contains a larger number of civil servants and owners of small business enterprises. Not surprisingly, book-keeping offenses had been committed almost exclusively by offenders in the CS-group. Only insignificant differences were found between the sanction groups concerning other types of offenses. By and large, there were only small differences among the sanction groups concerning the nature of the offense for which the offenders received their current sentence.

In order to measure the of *degree of seriousness of the principal offense,* serious offenses (i.e. offenses designated as serious in the Penal Code and usually carrying a minimum penalty) were distinguished from other offenses. Thirteen percent of CS-offenders, 38% of P-offenders and 56% of PI-offenders had committed serious offenses.

An index was constructed of the *severity of combined criminality* by calculating the average number of months actually in prison per offense and adding them together. Although the method has weaknesses the criminality of the various individuals ought to be relatively comparable with this reckoning system. The median values for the index were 18 for CS-offenders, 28 for P-offenders and 48 for PI-offenders.

Both methods of measurement reveal highly significant statistical differences between the CS-group and the P-group and significant differences between the P-group and the PI-group.

Searching for Factors Behind the Sentence

Individual and General Prevention

Clearly judges have taken the offenders' upbringing, previous offenses, alcohol misuse and employment circumstances into consideration when choosing the sanction. The judges have followed the legislator's intentions inasmuch as the CS-offenders have better social prognoses and probationers poorer ones in terms of social and personal circumstances. The judges appear to have taken account of *individual prevention* aspects when sentencing.

However, the number of previous convictions and the degree of severity of the current offense also differentiate the groups, indicating that the judges also took *general prevention* into account when sentencing. Since the degree of severity of the offense differentiates the groups, it appears that the judges gave some thought to *proportionality.* Proportionality notions do not spring from any theory of prevention. They are determined by the conventions of legal thinking. In theory, general prevention and proportionality have little in common but, in practice, they seem to coincide to a great extent. In what follows I shall speak only of a general preventive viewpoint, even if that includes notions of proportionality, since they both stand in opposition to individual prevention.

In theory, the judge who takes the factors connected with the offense into consideration may be motivated by a desire to deter the offender from committing further crimes i.e., his decision is based on an individual preventive deterrence model. However, since according to the law and its preparatory work, the individual's adjustment in society is to be facilitated, it is treatment which is intended and not deterrence. In practice, it is probably impossible, in the majority of cases, to tell the difference between deterrence which is based on individual prevention and that which is based on general prevention. The term "deterrence" as used in Anglo-Saxon countries usually includes both forms.

Since the social and criminal factors are so closely linked and differentiate the sanction groups in a similar way a *methodological problem* arises in separating out the different types of factors. An estimate of the effects of the social factors must be made independently of those of the criminal factors in order to determine whether the judges based their decisions primarily on considerations of individual or general prevention. Various analyses have been used in an attempt to overcome this difficulty.

Controlling for the Nature and Seriousness of the Offense

To ascertain the extent to which judges take account of factors other than the offense when sentencing means controlling for the effects of the nature and seriousness of the offense. A first step was therefore to select cases that were as representative as possible of all the sanction groups in relation to the nature and seriousness of the offense. *Theft* was chosen so far as the nature of the offense was concerned whilst the *seriousness* of all offenses in the current sentence was assessed using Penal Code definitions. Since nationality was considered to have a distorting effect only *Swedes* were included in the analysis. Since the age variable also differentiated between the groups it too was held constant and only offenders in the age group 20 to 23 (the majority) were included in the selection. A total of *twenty-four individuals* met all the above requirements. The next step was to ask how the social and criminal background factors of these individuals were distributed within each sanction group.

To a great extent, the trends are almost exactly the same as those already described. Although all groups were represented in this analysis, it is difficult to draw conclusions about variations in the sanction groups because of the small size of the representative group. When we hold the current offense variable constant, we find that the sanction groups differ with respect to previous antisocial behavior and convictions on the one hand, and alcohol misuse and circumstances of employment on the other. The judges seem to have given weight to both criminal and social background factors. We have not therefore been able in this analysis to determine whether the judges gave greater weight to considerations of individual or general prevention.

Analysis of Negative Cases

So far we have seen that the offender's degree of social handicap is to a great extent proportional to his degree of criminality. For this reason it is difficult to isolate the kind of factors to which the courts assign the greatest importance when choosing a sanction. The judges' impose conditional sentence, probation and probation with institutional treatment in direct relation to the defendants' increasing degree of social handicap and criminality.

By picking out individual cases which differ from these main trends, we can attempt to find out if these deviant or so-called negative cases can be explained by uncovering new factors or discovering new combinations of factors of importance for the choice of the sanction or whether the deviant cases confirm the trends seen earlier (see Lazarsfeld and Rosenberg 1962, pp. 67–174, for *deviant case analysis*).

An analysis of the negative cases was therefore undertaken to try to provide answers to such questions as whether an individual who bears a heavy social handicap, or has committed serious offenses, can be given a conditional sentence and, if so, the reason for this. Alternatively, are there offenders living under orderly social conditions who were sentenced to probation with institutional treatment? If so, why? The negative cases will be studied in relation to each sanction.

Conditional Sentence. As we have already seen, CS-offenders were in the main individuals who had no previous criminal record or only a minor one and they had well-ordered conditions of employment and residence. Conditional sentence was used chiefly with property offenses which were petty or of medium seriousness.

On an index of previous criminality, 80% of the CS-offenders have no more than two minus points. The remaining 20% is made up of thirty individuals registered for antisocial behavior or previous offenses, or those against whom measures had been taken because of their early antisocial behavior and/or because of alcohol abuse. Six offenders from this group had been sentenced for offenses which are, under the Penal Code's provisions, to be classified as serious. Five of these deviant cases were unemployed and two had no place to live at the time sentence was passed. Why were these individuals given conditional sentences despite their dubious prognoses?

An analysis of these thirty individuals reveals that eight are *foreign nationals* resident outside Sweden, a circumstance which seems to be of some importance for the choice of sanction. Three of the eight foreigners were expelled and in two cases the court made reference to a current treatment under the aegis of foreign authorities which would be resumed when the offender returned to his home country.

The court's reasoning varies in the remaining negative cases. Sometimes the courts justify their decisions by referring to the offender's *age*. The following extract from the courts written reasons for the sentence concerning a 73-year-old, sentenced for drunken driving and with two previous convictions for the same type of offense provides an example of this: "Considering N's age and poor state of health, the court does not believe that general obedience to the law necessarily requires that he be sent to prison. There are special reasons in this case, which justify a lesser sanction. On these grounds and also because having regard to N's age and circumstances in general supervision is not deemed necessary, the sanction must be one of conditional sentence."

It was also clear that conditional sentence was used primarily for reasons of individual prevention. The majority of the twenty-two Swedes led *relatively orderly lives at the time of sentence.* It was probably for this reason that they were thought to have good prognoses.

It is more difficult to discover from the written sentencing reasons why conditional sentence was imposed on the unemployed Swedes. All of them showed poor work stability and relatively poor work adjustment. They had previously been fined for traffic offenses. In one case, the reason may have to do with the long time that elapsed between the offense and the trial.

A final assessment of the negative cases seems to show that nationality was the primary reason for the sentence but that age too was accorded importance. In the sample, there were twenty-six foreign nationals who resided in countries other than Sweden, of whom twenty-five were given conditional sentences and one was placed on probation. Fifteen of the twenty-one offenders over 50 were given conditional sentences and only six were placed on probation.

Finally, it would seem that the offender's living conditions at the time of court appearance was also a factor of importance. When conditional sentence is chosen it would seem that *individual prevention* takes precedence over general prevention. Emphasis on general obedience to the law can be satisfied by imposing fines together with the conditional sentence. Fifteen of the thirty analyzed cases were fined at the same time as they were given conditional sentences. If the defendant is a foreign national residing outside Sweden, general obedience to the law can be emphasized by imposing an expulsion order. This is justified on grounds of general prevention but may also be an attempt to secure at least a temporary incapacitation.

Probation. In the majority of cases, the offenders who were placed on probation were those who had committed many previous offenses, had adjusted badly to the work situation and who in other respects did not lead orderly lives. The degree of seriousness of the offense for which probation was imposed varies between minor offenses (e.g. shoplifting) and serious offenses (e.g. gross larceny or gross fraud).

However, nineteen (14%) of the probationers did not obtain a score on the index for previous record. Possible reasons for this group being placed on probation rather than being given a conditional sentence are that they committed more serious offenses than the CS-offenders, that their employment situation at the time was unsatisfactory or that other, hitherto unknown, factors were present.

When analyzing the seriousness of the current offense, we find that nine offenders in this group of nineteen deviant cases were convicted of serious crimes. Four of these were found guilty of gross fraud or gross embezzlement at their place of work. They had, however, all received good references from their previous employers.

Four of the five remaining individuals who were found guilty of serious offenses committed them in connection with financial difficulties or disordered conditions of living.

Among those who were sentenced for having committed serious offenses, there was one man who had been found guilty of attempted manslaughter, gross fraud and gross embezzlement. A physician and the Swedish Board of Health and Welfare were consulted in this case. The report submitted by the Board was quoted by the court: "N's mental abnormality may be seen as constituting a special reason for imposing a milder punishment for the offense. A suitable sanction would be probation combined with open psychiatric treatment". The court noted that the Penal Code does not provide for this suggested combination of sanctions. The offender was therefore sentenced to probation on condition that "during the probationary period N undergoes psychiatric treatment in accordance with the Supervision Board's more detailed decision."

Probation in the majority of these cases did not appear to be justified by reference to individual prevention or, at least, not on the basis of any documented need of supervision. Four of the nine offenders who had committed serious offenses had no previous record and had received good references from previous employers. The remaining four had committed serious offenses when they were in financial difficulties and had been placed under supervision without any reason for the supervision being given. In the last-quoted case in which the offender was placed on probation and required to submit to open psychiatric treatment, there is no mention of supervision being considered necessary from the point of view of individual prevention. An analysis of the ten deviant cases where the offense was not gross shows that the court usually held that supervision was necessary, but even in these cases it does not seem to me to be always clear in what way this was actually indicated. In some cases, the intention of the court was to stop gang activity. In two other cases it was a question of financial distress or actual poverty.

The court placed the offenders on probation despite the fact that it considered the offenses to be isolated incidents. This seems to contrary to the intentions of the legislator.

In some cases the court has justified placing an offender on probation by referring to his poor work stability and general life circumstances. The extent to which supervision is considered necessary to render assistance in these cases depends, among other things, on the expectations entertained about what a supervisor can accomplish. It is my view that the majority of supervisors find it very difficult to manage problems of the kind referred to here, i.e. financial, linguistic, health or work problems.

In some cases the court seems to say that supervision is needed when the person in question lives in ordered circumstances if, for example, he had been brought up in a broken home and is believed to need a father-figure, or if he is depressed and suffers from a gastric ulcer.

Probation with Institutional Treatment. The offenders who were sentenced to probation with institutional treatment were chiefly those with a criminal record, those who had adjusted poorly to the work situation, and those whose living conditions were less than satisfactory. The offenses for which probation with institutional treatment was ordered were, in the majority of cases, of a serious nature.

Twelve individuals (9%) had no previous record or at the most only an insignificant one (0–1 points on the index). Ten of these were unemployed, one was registered as a student and one had lost his job in connection with the offense for which he was charged. Seven of this group were convicted for serious offenses and five for offenses of a somewhat less serious nature. Since none of them had committed any prior offenses it is natural to ask why they were sentenced to probation with institutional treatment.

If we first look at the seven offenders who were convicted of serious offenses, the following example concerning a 19-year-old convicted of gross theft and attempted gross theft, unlawful appropriation of a vehicle on repeated occasions, etc will serve as an illustration: "The court considers it important that N be placed under supervision. In view of N's repeated criminality and other circumstances, the court believes that probation should be combined with institutional treatment. As N does not lead an ordered life the sentence should take effect immediately."

In this and similar cases it is apparent that the sentences are justified by general preventive considerations arising from repeated criminality. But at the same time reference is also made to individual prevention in connection with life circumstances.

One case of an offender who lived under relatively stable conditions concerns a 23-year-old with previous antisocial behavior who had been sentenced to probation on a previous occasion and whose current conviction was one of gross theft. An extract from the court's reasons for sentencing him to probation with institutional treatment reads: "Although N was sentenced to probation a relatively short time ago, the court considers that in view of his personal circumstances he should continue to receive non-institutional treatment. But for N's correction it is considered necessary to combine probation with institutional treatment."

When it is stated in this and other examples that it is necessary for N's correction or readjustment to combine institutional treatment and probation, it seems doubtful if this can be considered justified by a concern for individual prevention based on some special treatment need. Although it is not clearly stated it does seem as though institutional treatment is instead justified by considerations of general prevention. Theoretically, making the sanction more severe can be justified for reasons of individual prevention.

There are, however, examples of the use of institutional treatment for reasons of pure general prevention. In one case, the defendant led a stable existence as an employee of the Post Office Administration. At his trial it was revealed that he stole goods and money which were supposed to be forwarded to addressees. His wife, who had helped him in this, was sentenced to probation in the same case. The man was convicted of repeated gross theft. "Based on what is stated in the social inquiry report and the defendant's circumstances, the court considers the most suitable sanction to be probation. Out of consideration for general obedience to the law, it is necessary, as far as N is concerned, to include institutional treatment in the sanction."

However, there can be no doubt that the court should not give consideration to pure general prevention when choosing probation with institutional treatment.

Of the five people who were sentenced to institutional treatment for minor offenses, three were foreigners residing in Sweden who had certain difficulties in adjusting.

The PI-group (127 individuals) can be divided into two categories: the unemployed (58%) and those with more or less stable conditions of work and residence (42%). Forty (75%) of the second group of fifty-three individuals were registered for antisocial behavior and thirty-three (62%) had been previously placed on probation. Sixty-eight percent of the offenders in this group were convicted of serious offenses.

I would like to add that in view of the fact that a number of cases involved offenders with either no record or only an insignificant record and living in ordered social circumstances, it seems probable that the sanction, in these cases, was chosen more for reasons of general prevention based on the seriousness of the offense, than for reasons of individual prevention based on a need for treatment. The fact that several of the PI-offenders had previously been sentenced to probation makes it likely that the court chose the new sanction in an effort to render the earlier sanction more severe when new offenses were committed. In theory though this sentencing practice need not be justified by either individual or general prevention.

Content Analysis of the Court's Reasons for Sentence

The courts' written reasons for the sentence chosen have been subjected to a content analysis. In what follows a study is made of references in these reasons to the social inquiry report and to medical reports. The extent to which the proposed and chosen disposition coincided is also studied. Finally, references to previous criminality are studied together with direct references to considerations of general obedience to the law. *References to social inquiries and medical examinations.* As the social inquiry investigator and the physician are required to recommend measures considered suitable for promoting the offender's adjustment in society it could well be assumed that any references made to the social inquiry reports and medical examinations would indicate that the courts were giving consideration to individual prevention.

Social inquiry reports had been carried out in almost all the cases studied here. The report prepared by a probation supervisor or a supplement to a previous social inquiry report has been used as source material in certain cases.

Medical reports are provided only if the court finds it necessary under Section 7 of the Act on Social Inquiry Reports in Criminal Cases. These so-called minor forensic psychiatric examinations were undertaken in fifty-three of the 413 cases. None of the CS-offenders, 12% of the P-offenders and 29% of the PI-offenders were subjected to such an examination. This higher proportion in the institutional treatment group should be seen in relation to the fact that mental disorders are more widespread in this group.

So far as the total sample of 413 cases is concerned, the court referred to the social inquiry report in 70% of the cases. The court also referred to the medical report in 70% of the fifty-three cases in which the offender was given a medical examination. References to both the social inquiry report and the medical examination were made in 18% of the cases from the PI-group. However, in 27% of the cases from this group reference was made to neither the social inquiry report nor the medical examination.

Sanctions Recommended and Sentences Imposed. Social inquiry investigators made no recommendations in forty-one cases (10%). A little more than half of these were sentenced to probation with institutional treatment.

In 93% of the cases for which the social inquiry investigator suggested a sanction there is concordance between the recommendation and the sanction subsequently imposed. In only 7% of the cases (26 of 372) did the court impose a sentence which differed from the one recommended by the social inquiry investigator and in some of these cases the difference concerned only the imposition of fines. If the analysis is restricted to the principal sanction, the agreement between the suggested and the imposed sanction becomes even greater.

We find that in fourteen cases social inquiry investigators recommended a less severe sanction than the one imposed by the court. On the other hand, investigators proposed more severe measures, including imprisonment, in twelve cases.

The fact that the courts' reasons for sentence to such a great extent, refer to the social inquiry report, and, in particular, that the courts, in the vast majority of cases, seemed to follow the social inquiry investigators suggestions may be interpreted to mean that the sanctions in question were imposed in an effort to provide treatment. There are, however, objections to such a conclusion. As previous examples have shown, the social inquiry investigators may have based their recommendations on subjective judgements which were not necessarily intended to facilitate the offender's adjustment in society. Furthermore, the investigators were not always especially qualified or sufficiently trained for their work. The sentence actually chosen is not therefore necessarily well-founded from the point of view of individual prevention just because the court follows the investigator's recommendation.

Moreover, there is an obvious risk that in reality it is not the court that follows the investigator's recommendation but rather that the investigator adjusts his recommendations to his perception of the court's sentencing norms. The investigator may make a suggestion which he believes will meet with the approval of the court, *inter alia,* in order to avoid rejection of his recommendation.

In 15% of the fifty-three cases where a *medical examination* was undertaken, the medical report did not contain a recommendation on the sanction. Of the forty-five cases where a suggestion was made, the court followed it in 88% of cases.

In five cases the recommendation set out in the medical report was not followed by the court. In one of these, the report had recommended probation without institutional treatment but the court imposed institutional treatment. In the remaining four cases the sanction suggested in the report was more severe than the one subsequently imposed by the court. In two cases youth imprisonment was suggested and in two cases imprisonment.

Thus, the situation concerning medical reports is similar to the one described above concerning the recommendations made by social inquiry investigators. Where there was a lack of agreement between the suggested and the imposed sanction it would seem from the nature of the discrepancies that the person submitting the recommendation did not always give consideration solely to the individual preventive aspects—although this should have been the case if the legislator's intentions had been followed.

References to Previous Criminality. In order to examine the extent to which the courts take general prevention into consideration when passing sentence, we now study the extent to which references are made to previous criminality and general obedience to the law.

Both in the earlier description of the sanction groups as well as that of the homogeneous groups it has emerged that previous criminality, measured in terms of prior sentences, is of importance for the choice of sanction.

A systematic content analysis was carried out on all the courts' written reasons for the sentences imposed in order to determine to what extent the courts give weight to this factor when choosing the sanction.

Reference was made to the presence or absence of previous criminality in 45% of cases. This figure confirms our assumption that previous convictions are a factor of great importance in the choice of sanction.

If we look at the distribution of such references within the three sanction groups, we find that they occur twice as often in connection with a sentence to probation with institutional treatment as to the other sanctions (69% PI, 36% P and 35% CS). The fact that the previous criminality of the PI-offenders was mentioned to such a great extent can be seen as a result both of their more extensive criminality as well as of the courts' desire to draw attention to the offenders' previous convictions and at the same time take them into account when deciding on the sentence. Where probation had been imposed previously (44% of the PI-group), it was referred to in each case.

We find therefore that the court made reference to previous criminality in many cases where prior convictions were known, and that this variable plays a decisive role in the sentencing process. Although previous convictions may be said to constitute a prognostic factor, its consideration is probably here more a sign of adherence to general preventive demands. However, in theory, making a sanction more stringent can be justified by considerations of individual prevention. Nevertheless, it seems more likely that such an escalation of punishment is an integral part of conventional proportionality thinking.

References to General Obedience to the Law. Probation as such, with or without institutional treatment, should be used first and foremost for reasons of individual prevention. To the extent that direct references to general obedience to the law were made in the courts' reasons for sentence, consideration has been given by them to general preventive aspects.

From a study of the courts' reasoning for all the *probationers sentenced to institutional treatment* (n=127) we found that in 9% of cases the court did not justify its decision by any form of preventive argumentation. References were made to general obedience to the law in 29% of the remaining cases. In the majority of these cases probation was justified by considerations of individual prevention, while institutional treatment was justified by considerations of general prevention. It was extremely unusual for the courts to present only a general preventive argumentation when they imposed probation, with or without institutional treatment. In the majority of cases (71%) only individual prevention was referred to in the court's justification of the chosen sanction.

No explanatory statements were provided by the court in 8% of the cases where it imposed *probation without institutional treatment.* Of the remainder, an individual preventive formulation was given in 76% of cases. References to general obedience to the law were made in 24% of these cases, of which almost all concerned a combination of probation and fines. Probation was justified by reference to individual prevention and the fines by reference to general prevention.

Thus, in more than one-quarter of all cases the courts seem to have imposed institutional treatment for reasons of general prevention. This can clearly been seen in the references that were made to general obedience to the law in 29% of the cases. Obviously, the courts may have taken account of general prevention in an even greater number of cases without it being explicitly stated in their reasons for sentence. Bearing in mind that probation should only be imposed for reasons of individual prevention and that institutional treatment, which is a part of probation, should be imposed at least mainly for reasons of individual prevention (see Chapter 3), it is worthy of note that the courts refer to general obedience to the law to such an extent. The sanction's primary aim is, after all, to promote the offender's adjustment in society.

Bearing in mind the severity of the personal and social problems of the offenders sentenced to probation with institutional treatment it would be surprising if the court had not taken account of treatment needs when sentencing such offenders to probation. On the other hand, it could be said that just because of the acute deficiencies of this group, the court could perhaps to a greater extent have given consideration to individual preventive aspects. The fact that the judges so often referred to general prevention when they sentenced an offender to probation with institutional treatment may be a consequence of the ambiguity of the law and the preparatory work in relation to Chapter 28, Section 3 of the Penal Code. On the one hand the imposition of institutional treatment might have been justified by reference to individual prevention and, on the other, it might have replaced longer periods of confinement, such as youth imprisonment or imprisonment. In a sanction system which, with the exception of the sanctions studied here, is based on traditional ways of assessing punishment, it is understandable if the judges are to some extent inclined to give consideration to the predominating general preventive aspects even when imposing these sanctions.

The Continued Search for Factors Behind the Sentences

We have seen that with the methods used up to now it has proved difficult to decide whether judges give greater weight to individual or general preventive aspects when choosing the sanction.

I have continued the search for factors underlying the sentences by using multivariate analysis and multiple regression analysis.

Multivariate Analysis

Using multivariate analysis I have tried to better separate out the social factors from the offense factors. A new index of social handicap was constructed which—unlike the earlier one used—only includes pure social factors and excludes any measures taken by society in response to antisocial behavior or criminality. This index consists of four sub-indexes of home and childhood conditions, personal attributes and scholastic achievement, social adjustment in respect of work and residence and, finally, alcohol abuse. The full index consists of some thirty factors. A fifth sub-index concerning antisocial behavior and child welfare measures was by definition excluded but was nevertheless investigated.

The association between the different offense factors and the choice of sanction whilst holding the social handicap factors constant was then studied. All the offense factors—estimates of the seriousness of the offense, type of previous sentence and number of previous convictions—were included and tested.

As can be seen from Tables 4.1–3, the associations are statistically significant between all the offense factors and the choice of sanction for both the low and high social handicap groups (the low handicap groups comprise individuals who obtained 0–5 points on the indexes described above and the high handicap groups are comprised of individuals who obtained 6 points or more). The associations are highly significant in five of the six tables (p. <001) and significant in the seventh (p. <01).

Throughout, the association between the offense factors and choice of sanction is stronger in the low social handicap groups than in the high handicap groups. This is probably related to the fact that there is less scope in the high handicap groups for variation of the offense factors as they to some extent show covariance with the social factors.

The observed patterns are very stable and are scarcely affected by whether current criminality or previous recorded criminality is used as the offense factor. The associations are not appreciably affected by including in the index of social handicap any action taken by child welfare authorities in response to early antisocial behavior; the pattern remains exactly the same.

One might easily conclude from the multivariate analyses that judges are influenced in their choice of sanction by the extent of current and previous criminality, independent of the degree of social handicap. But so as not to jump to hasty conclusions concerning the strength or causal nature of these

TABLE 4.1 Choice of Sanction Related to Seriousness of Offense (percentage proportions of minor, medium and grave offenses by sanction groups) with Social Handicap Held Constant (chi-square, gamma, degrees of freedom, probability)

	Minor Social Handicap Seriousness of Offense					Major Social Handicap Seriousness of Offense				
	Min	Med	Gr	Total	N	Min	Med	Gr	Total	N
CS	67	30	3	100	129	53	42	5	100	19
P	42	32	27	100	60	37	30	33	100	78
PI	16	31	53	100	<u>32</u>	17	38	45	100	<u>95</u>
Totals					221					192
	$\chi^2=58$; df=4 p.000 γ.63					$\chi^2=19$; df=4 p.001 γ.40				

TABLE 4.2 Choice of Sanction Related to Previous Sanctions (percentage proportions sentenced to no previous sanction, only day-fines or at least conditional sentence) by Sanction Groups with Social Handicap Held Constant

	Minor Social Handicap Previous Sanction					Major Social Handicap Previous Sanction				
	None	At Most Day-Fines	At Least Cond. Sent.	Total	N	None	At Most Day-Fines	At Least Cond. Sent.	Total	N
CS	74	9	16	100	129	53	21	26	100	19
P	43	23	33	100	60	31	18	51	100	78
PI	22	13	66	100	<u>32</u>	13	17	71	100	<u>95</u>
Totals					221					192
	$\chi^2=44$; df=4; p.000 γ.60					$\chi^2=20$; df=4; p.001; γ.46				

relationships, I also studied the association between social handicap and the sanction chosen, this time holding the different offense factors constant. It then appeared that these six tables also showed significant associations. We thus find statistically significant associations between social handicap and sanction which are independent of the extent of criminality. This finding illustrates once again the strong link that exists between social and criminal factors and how difficult it is to separate them, even with the aid of multivariate analysis. However, logically, the latter variant of the analyses carried out has less weight than the one preceding it. It seems more natural to hold the social handicap factors constant, since in the majority of cases they precede the crim-

TABLE 4.3 Choice of Sanction Related to Number of Previous Convictions (percentage proportions with 0, 1, 2 or more previous convictions) by Sanction Groups with Social Handicap Held Constant

	Minor Social Handicap Previous Convictions					Major Social Handicap Previous Convictions				
	0	1	2 or more	Total	N	0	1	2 or more	Total	N
CS	75	15	10	100	129	53	32	16	100	19
P	50	28	22	100	60	36	22	42	100	78
PI	22	31	47	100	32	20	38	42	100	95
Totals					221					192
	χ^2=38 df=4; p.000 γ.57					χ^2=14 df=4; p.007 γ.25				

inal activity, and then use the offense factors as the independent variables and the sanction factor as the dependent variable.

Multiple Regression Analysis

Since multivariate analysis failed to give an unambiguous result a further attempt was made using multiple regression analysis. By using this method I wanted to grade the effect which the independent variables had on the dependent variable and examine how great a part of the variation in sanction choice could be explained statistically when studying the social and offense factors separately and together.

It should be said that the statistical requirements for the use of this method are not fully met by my data. The requirements are usually said to be that the variables should form an interval scale for both the independent and the dependent variables and there should be no interaction between the independent variables. Opinions differ, however, as to the importance attaching to these conditions and sociologists have used the method even when conscious of the fact that their material does not meet the requirements. Since the statistical requirements are not met, the data should be interpreted with a certain amount of caution.

Table 4.4 shows the relationship between the independent factors and the choice of sanction in the form of simple product-moment correlations and in the form of the multiple correlations of a stepwise regression analysis.

The simple product-moment correlations show a stronger relationship between the offense factors and the sanction choice than between the social or personal factors and the choice of sanction. The three variables concerning previous and current criminality and interventions to which it gave rise provide the three highest correlations: previous antisocial behavior and intervention by child welfare authorities (.50), type of previous sanction (.48) and the

TABLE 4.4 Stepwise Regression Analysis (product-moment correlation, multiple correlation, squared multiple correlation) of Factors Associated with the Choice of Sanction

Step	Variable	r	MR	MRSQ	Increase in MRSQ
1	Previous Antisocial Behavior and Child Welfare Intervention	.50	.50	.25	.25
2	Degree of Seriousness of Current Offense	.45	.61	.38	.13
3	Type of Previous Sanction	.48	.67	.45	.07
4	Present Social Adjustment	.39	.70	.49	.04
5	Home and Childhood Situation	.42	.72	.51	.02
6	Age	-.31	.73	.53	.02
7	Present Social Adjustment I: Misuse of Alcohol and Drugs	.30	.74	.54	.01
8	Personal Attributes and Scholastic Achievement	.35	.74	.55	.01

degree of seriousness of the current offenses (.45). Only thereafter follow home and childhood factors, employment, and residence. Personal attributes and scholastic achievement, and age come next. Misuse of alcohol and drugs shows, perhaps somewhat surprisingly, the weakest relationship of all the indexes but nevertheless comes up to .30.

Thus, once again we find that the three offense factors are the most important. The multiple correlations for previous antisocial behaviour, the seriousness of the current offenses and the type of previous sanction are .50, .51 and .67 respectively. These three offense factors account for 45% of the total variation in the choice of sanction. When the variables of home and childhood situation, and work and residence are included, the multiple correlations increase to .70 and .72 respectively. But, this only increases the explained variation (mcsq) by 4% and 2% respectively. Including the age variable adds a further 2% to the explained variation whilst including the variables on alcohol and drug abuse and personal attributes and scholastic achievement only increases it by a further 1% each. The total explained variation is thus 55%.

It follows that 45% of the variation in the choice of sanction is unexplained. The unexplained variance can be ascribed to factors other than those included in the analysis. But even random variations, resulting from errors of measurement, may be partly responsible. Thus, we have only been able to account for a little more than half of the variation in sentencing. Compared with other sociological studies, however, this is a very satisfactory result. An explained variance of about 10% is a more usual figure and 20% is normally considered to be a good result (see Carlsson, SOU 1972:76).

The regression analysis has demonstrated that both the simple and multiple correlations show a greater association between the offense factors and choice of sanction than between the social factors and choice of sanction. The judges seem therefore to give greater weight to the nature and extent of previous and current criminality than to the defendant's social conditions or personal attributes. However, if sentencing were to be based on an individual preventive treatment model, personal and social conditions should have been given the greatest weight. As has been shown, the legislator's intention was that primary importance should be attached to considerations of individual prevention so far as the sanctions studied here were concerned. But the statistical analysis shows individual prevention is considered only secondarily. The strong relationship between offense factors and choice of sanction suggests that general prevention was accorded primary importance. However, the importance attached to offense factors can, theoretically, also reflect a desire to deter based on the idea of escalating penal reactions or conventional proportionality thinking.

Fines and Damages Combined with Conditional Sentence and Probation

The following analysis seeks to determine whether the courts further emphasized general prevention when they imposed fines together with conditional sentence or probation. According to the Penal Code Commission, fines combined with the above-mentioned sanctions are to be considered first and foremost as an instrument of general prevention. However, as the provisions of the Penal Code are formulated, they can also be used for reasons of individual prevention. The Protective Law Commission stressed the fact that the courts should take the offender's financial situation into consideration so that the aim of helping the offender adjust in society should not be counteracted. Hence, out of consideration for the defendant's possibilities of paying, fines and damages should therefore not be imposed simultaneously. In order to study to what extent fines and damages were justified by individual or general prevention, their imposition is investigated for each sanction separately and the offender's income is held constant.

Use of Fines

Day-fines were imposed on 57% of the CS-offenders, 41% of the P-offenders and 1% of the PI-offenders. Excluding the PI-group, the proportion of fines imposed in combination with a sanction is relatively large.

Why are fines not imposed on the PI-offenders? A hypothetical answer is that if the judges used institutional treatment for reasons of general prevention—and we have already seen several signs which suggest that this is so—then they would not want to make the sanction yet more severe by combining it with fines. Both institutional treatment and fines have been used to make probation more severe and if the court uses one method it obviously does not resort to the other. This interpretation leads rather to the conclusion that both fines and institutional treatment are imposed for reasons of general prevention. If both were considered as treatment, the one would hardly exclude the other as these "instruments of treatment" have little in common. If, on the other hand, both are regarded as instruments of general prevention, then they can be used as alternatives.

A completely different explanation of the fact that the court did not combine fines and institutional treatment might be that the court did not want to further burden this group which often lives under poor social and economic conditions. A large proportion of the PI-offenders were, for example, unemployed (PI 58%, P 26% and CS 13%). However, this can hardly suffice as an explanation when 42% had some form of employment and only one person was fined. The slight difference in income among the sanction groups cannot explain the discrepancy either.

The risk scores assigned to the offenders sentenced to pay fines (34% of the sample) are substantially lower than that assigned to the other offenders in the sanction groups (5.4 and 8.9 respectively). It thus seems as though those with good social prognoses were fined while those whose prognoses were poor were sentenced to institutional treatment. When the total criminality of those who were fined is studied, we find that they have a lower offense score than those who were not fined (median 20 and 33 respectively). This somewhat unexpected result may be connected with the fact that those who were sentenced to institutional treatment committed the most serious offenses, but it may also reflect the traditional view that pecuniary penalties are most suitable for minor offenses.

We can thus assert that the court often imposes fines combined with conditional sentence and probation. The fact that fines are imposed most frequently on CS-offenders and very rarely on PI-offenders suggests that the court sees fines from the standpoint of general prevention. They can be used to tighten up a sanction such as conditional sentence which otherwise would not be considered sufficiently severe. But they are not imposed where some other augmenting reaction is included in the sanction, as is the case with probation with institutional treatment.

Damages

Damages were ordered for 27% of the CS-offenders, 43% of the P-offenders and 53% of the PI-offenders. The distribution of damages among the sanction groups is thus the opposite of that found for fines.

It might be thought from this inverse distribution of fines and damages that the court imposed fines or ordered damages in accordance with the intentions of the Protective Law Commission, namely that the convicted person's readjustment should not be unnecessarily hindered by burdening his economy. However, a cross-tabulation reveals that the court imposed *both fines and damages* in combination with the sanctions under study in every tenth case (42 of 413). The only person who was sentenced to probation with institutional treatment in combination with fines was sentenced at the same time to pay damages. Fourteen percent of the CS-offenders and 16% of the P-offenders were fined and ordered to pay damages. In view of the fact that it is clearly stated in the preparatory work to the law that such a practice should be avoided, these proportions must be considered to be remarkably high.

When the imposition of fines and/or damages is related to the convicted person's income no clear-cut relationship emerges. A greater number of fines were imposed on persons in the high income groups while the proportion of damages imposed on these offenders was somewhat lower. Among the CS-offenders, damages were considerably more prevalent in the low income groups while fines were somewhat more common in the high income groups. Among the P-offenders, both fines and damages were more prevalent in the high income groups. Among the PI-offenders, damages were somewhat more prevalent in the low income groups. If we relate the combination of fines and damages to income, no relationship is found, i.e. the court imposed a tripartite combination just as often on individuals in the low income groups as on individuals in the higher income groups.

Summary and Discussion of the Judge's Choice of Sanction

Basic Difficulties in Interpreting the Data

As we have seen, it is no easy task to determine to what extent judges follow the legislator's intentions. This is due partly to the wording of the law in which the provisions regarding conditional sentence and probation contain few detailed instructions and leave a great deal of scope for interpretation. The most important decisions about the suitability of the sanctions in the particular case are left largely to the court's discretion. Such vague formulations in the text of the law may be defended by contending that the legislator cannot foresee all the possible situations which can arise in real life. The lack of clearly defined guidelines for choosing sanctions renders the evaluation of sentencing practice of necessity more difficult.

The research worker's interpretation difficulties are further complicated by the fact that the offenders who are guilty of the more serious offenses also have the worst social backgrounds. The factual situation makes the analysis more difficult when it comes to distinguishing the factors underlying the sentence and to determining whether the court gives primary consideration to individual or general prevention.

Conclusions and Reflections

In some respects, the use of conditional sentence and probation follows the guidelines given in the law and the preliminary work preceding that law. But in some respects it does not and in yet others it is unclear to what extent it does so because of the interpretation difficulties which were described earlier. The courts seem to have followed the legislator's intentions in the sense that they have imposed a conditional sentences on persons who have not been unduly socially handicapped and who have a markedly better prognosis. The differentiation made between the different sanction groups appears to have been astonishingly effective.

We also found an increasing weight of criminality as we progressed from C-offenders through P-offenders to PI-offenders. The legislator had not foreseen such a parallel between the severity of the offense and the type of intervention. The rising "punishment scale" we have discovered among the three sanction groups may be said to conflict with the law and the preparatory work to the law.

One explanation for the above finding may be found in the strong relationship between social handicap and criminal record. People with lesser social handicaps have committed less serious offenses. However, this is not full explanation. We have found that some CS-offenders can have considerable social handicaps and some CS-offenders have committed serious offenses. Similarly, there are probationers in the material with only minor social handicaps or none at all and some who have only committed minor offenses.

Using the most sophisticated analyses that could be carried out to distinguish between the social and offense factors, it became apparent that the offense factors showed covariance with the choice of sanction, and contributed to explaining it, to a greater extent than was the case with the social factors. This result of the multiple regression analysis suggests that the courts did not give primary consideration to the individual preventive aspects allied as these are to social factors, but rather gave primary consideration to assessing the level of punishment on the basis of the offense factors. This is tantamount to thinking in general prevention terms. It may also reflect conventional thinking in terms of proportionality.

The findings so far as the individual and general preventive aspects are concerned can be said in some respects to be contradictory. In the majority of cases, the court made references to the social inquiry report and followed the suggestions made there about sanction in almost all cases. This could be interpreted to mean that the individual preventive requirements were, on the whole, given a high degree of consideration. However, the agreement between the social inquiry investigator's choice of sanction and the judge's choice of sanction was so great that we have reason to suspect that the social inquiry investigator adjusts his suggestions to the prevailing sentencing norms of the court. We also know that the social inquiry investigator's qualifications and training for the task leave a great deal to be desired.

The fact that the court made references in its reasons for sentence to previous criminality and general obedience to the law further suggests that the judges consciously took account of the extent of criminality and general prevention.

Without further material it is impossible to decide whether the courts made rightful judicial decisions in the sense that those conditionally sentenced are "occasional criminals with such good prognoses that supervision is *not essential* for their correction", and in particular that those sentenced to probation are those for whom "it is deemed *essential* to place the defendant under supervision". The answers depend on the expectations we have of what the supervisor can accomplish. If we take as our point of departure the legislator's theory that supervision is generally an effective treatment method for the problems found in these groups, the court's choice of sanction would be, on the whole, correct. On the other hand, if we proceed from the opposite view, namely that supervision can be harmful, for example, by stigmatizing convicted persons, we could say that the CS-offenders have a good prognosis because they are *not* placed under supervision. The judges' choice of sanction could then be regarded as a "self-fulfilling prophecy" (Merton 1957, pp. 421–436).

The question whether supervision is required is thus an empirical one which can scarcely be answered solely by analyzing the type of documents and records on which this part of the study is based. In order to better answer that question it is necessary to know what supervision means to the person being supervised, how he experiences supervision and is influenced by it. Normally, of course, the judge does not have access to such information, neither generally nor in the individual case. When a judge sentences a person to probation who lives in impoverished social conditions, his decision can only be justified by reference to individual prevention if the treatment theory, which claims that supervision provides useful support and assistance, is correct.

As we have already seen, the law affords little guidance when it comes to specifying under what conditions supervision is required or what supervision is expected to achieve. Unfortunately, judges too do not state on what grounds they believe supervision necessary in the individual case nor do they say what it is expected to achieve. Even if the law cannot foresee all conceivable situations, the judge has the possibility to make his reasoning known in each individual case. Here one could wish that the court's reasoning was more detailed and precise than has been the case up to now. Only when the expectations regarding the treatment modalities are stated is it subsequently possible to learn if they are fulfilled.

It seems that practice concerning the use of probation with institutional treatment in many respects does not follow the legislator's intentions. It is used for people who are heavily socially handicapped and who have long criminal records. This conflicts with the instructions concerning which state that "the combination is unsuitable for young people who have strong criminal and antisocial tendencies". Moreover, institutional treatment was not intended for persons with mental difficulties and problems with alcohol but it has come to include such groups.

We have also seen an almost automatic escalation of the sanctions illustrated, *inter alia*, by the fact that virtually half the offenders sentenced to institutional treatment had previously been sentenced to probation.

We shall now investigate what consequences the various treatment measures have had for the individual's social adjustment.

5

The Effects of Sanctions—Recidivism and Prediction

The present chapter describes recidivism rates and the factors associated with them for the three sanction groups under study. It also describes the construction of a prediction instrument to determine whether the three sanctions result in different recidivism rates among groups of individuals who are similar so far as risk of recidivism is concerned. A follow-up study describes individual social adjustment after sentence and provides information to explain observed differences in the effects of the sanctions.

Recidivism Study

The traditional method for determining the effects of criminal sanctions is to ascertain what proportion of a given population recidivates after a certain sanction has been imposed. However, these recidivism rates only measure the sanction's ineffectiveness, not its effectiveness. Such information cannot tell us whether the offenders who did not recidivate succeeded because a given measure was used since we do not know what would have happened if other sanctions been imposed instead or if no action had been taken at all. To evaluate effectiveness the recidivism rates must be compared for different sanctions. Moreover, if an experimental approach is not feasible, the different sanction groups must be rendered comparable by means of a prognostic instrument (Glaser 1988).

Determining Recidivism Criteria

Which kinds of offenses are to be defined as recidivism? Over what period shall the commission of such offenses be reckoned as recidivism?

Variation in the definitions of recidivism makes comparisons between different studies difficult (see also Christiansen 1983). In American studies of probation and parole a breach of the supervision conditions imposed is often counted as recidivism. A breach of supervision conditions does not necessarily mean that the offender has committed any criminal act. In Scandinavia recidivism is commonly defined as officially registered new offenses. The usual method in Sweden is to count as recidivism only those relatively serious offenses which are recorded in the *Central Criminal Register*—offenses which, in principle, are those resulting in more severe penalties than day-fines.

Information on *offenses which have not led to this form of registration* have been taken from the case records of those placed under supervision. This information was not always complete since, in the absence of formal arrangements for an exchange of information between the courts and the chief probation officers, probation staff are not able to guarantee the completeness of their information. The definition of recidivism must therefore be based mainly on what is recorded in the Central Criminal Register.

The end of the follow-up period was set at the date for the commencement of our data collection, i.e. at the turn of the year 1969–1970. This means that offenders who were sentenced at the end of 1967 could be *followed for a maximum period of two years.* Ideally, a comparison recidivism study should study all subjects for the same period. As the maximum follow-up time is two years,this limit has been set for all subjects. This two-year follow-up period is reckoned from the time the sentence gained legal force (CS and P groups) or from the date of release from a probation institution (PI group).

Experience suggests that a two-year follow-up period is sufficient for the construction of prediction tables. Precision is not greatly improved when they are based on a longer period (see Mannheim and Wilkins 1955, p. 151 and Börjeson 1968, p. 148). Earlier studies have also shown that approximately three-quarters of the total recidivism occurs within the first two years of a five-year period (Inghe and Lindberg, SOU 1956:55,87f).

Similar results were found in the present research. Thus, for those sentenced conditionally and followed for three years, no case of recidivism was recorded after the first twenty months. The probation cases were followed for approximately the same period. Only one person recidivated after the twenty-four month limit. For the group sentenced to probation with institutional treatment the follow-up period was at least two-and-a-half years and at most four years. Only one case of recidivism was recorded after two years. A two year follow-up period seems therefore to be quite adequate for our purposes.

Findings Concerning Recidivism Rates

Relapse into Offenses Recorded in the Central Criminal Register. The two-year follow-up reveals appreciable differences in recidivism between the sanctions. Thus, 12% of the conditionally sentenced, 30% of those placed on probation without institutional treatment and 61% of those placed on probation with institutional treatment, recidivated *at least once.*

There are also differences between the sanction groups in respect of multi-recidivism (assuming that the original sanction was not revoked after first recidivism offense). *Multi-recidivism* was most common among probationers. Among those sentenced to probation with institutional treatment, one-fifth recidivated more than once. Differences were also found between sanction groups for the *point in time for the first relapse.* For all groups recidivism was greatest during the first three months. This was especially true of the PI-group. During this period, 39% of this group, 26% of the P-group and 28% of the CS-group committed further offenses. Thereafter, there is a steady decline in recidivism with the exception of the conditionally sentenced as can be seen in Table 5.1.

Larceny was the *type of recidivist* offense which was responsible for three-quarters of all relapses in all three groups. Among probationers the next most frequent offense was fraud, whilst among conditionally sentenced offenders the next most frequent type of offense was driving whilst under the influence of alcohol.

The *most common sanction* for conditionally sentenced offenders who recidivated was imprisonment (56%) and thereafter probation (39%) with one person being sentenced to probation with institutional treatment (6%).Among ordinary probationers, imprisonment was also the most common sanction with recidivism (43%), followed by probation (38%), probation with institutional treatment (12%), youth imprisonment (5%) and psychiatric care (2%). Imprisonment was also the most common sanction for recidivists among those sentenced to probations with institutional treatment (57%), followed by youth imprisonment (18%), ordinary probation (14%) and probation with institutional treatment (5%). Conditional sentence, temperance care, psychiatric care and child welfare measures were each imposed in one case following relapse into new offenses (1%).

Revocation of the original sanction on first relapse was ordered for 44% of the conditionally sentenced, 33% of ordinary probationers and 44% of those sentenced to probation with institutional treatment. The new sanction for the majority of the relapsed conditionally sentenced offenders was ordinary probation whilst that for relapsed probationers was imprisonment or youth imprisonment.

Since *multi-recidivism* is defined as relapses which occur within the framework of the original sanction no further relapses were noted among those who had their sentences revoked on first recidivism. This means that the extent of multi-recidivism is underestimated.

There was only one case of multi-recidivism among the conditionally sentenced offenders and for this the original sanction was revoked. Eight of the ordinary probationers recidivated twice whereupon half were sentenced to probation with institutional treatment. In no case was the original sanction revoked. Of those sentenced to probation with institutional treatment, nine recidivated twice, five recidivated three times and two recidivated four times within the framework of the original sanction. Imprisonment was the most common sanction imposed in these cases. Four of the nine offenders who recidivated twice had their original sentence revoked as did one offender who recidivated three times and two who recidivated four times.

Thus, the courts generally augmented the sanction after recidivism. Probation can be used as an augmentation for relapsed conditionally sentenced offenders and probation with institutional treatment for relapsed ordinary probationers.

Relapse into Offenses Not Recorded in the Central Criminal Register. Data on offenses not recorded in the Central Criminal Register exist for the probation groups only. The follow-up period was two years. Fourteen (10%) of

TABLE 5.1 Percentage Proportions of the Sanction Groups Recidivating (first time only) into Central Criminal Register Offenses during Different Periods (months)

Sanction or Release Group	N	Number of Months after Sentence 0-3	4-6	7-9	10-12	13-15	16-18	19-21	22-24	Total
CS	18	28	22	6	11	11	6	17	0	100
P	42	26	24	12	17	7	5	5	5	100
PI	77	39	18	14	9	5	7	4	4	100

those sentenced to ordinary probation committed new offenses, the majority of which were larceny, violent offenses and traffic offenses (mainly driving without a license). Day-fines were imposed in all these cases. Among the those sentenced to probation with institutional treatment, twelve persons (10%) recidivated. Here, the offenses consisted mainly of traffic and violent offenses. The number of day-fines imposed was approximately the same as that for the ordinary probationers.

During a two-year period *the total rate of recidivism* (i.e. all offenses resulting in findings of guilt regardless of sanction) reached at least 41% for those sentenced to ordinary probation and at least 70% for those sentenced to probation with institutional treatment. There is no exact information concerning the total recidivism rate for offenders with conditional sentences but it is estimated to be about 20%.

Prediction Study

General Introduction to Prediction Research

Prognostic research in criminology can have two different objectives. One is to provide general predictions of future criminal behavior from prior available information whilst the other attempts to predict the behavior of groups of individuals who have been sentenced to a specific sanction or undergone a particular kind of treatment. This latter type of evaluation can serve both scientific and practical purposes.

Criminological prediction research has been intensively developed over the last fifty years and a rich flora of literature is now available on the subject (see Gottfredson 1970). Prediction research which aims at evaluating different forms of treatment is, on the other hand, less abundant despite the fact that this method was introduced almost forty years ago by Mannheim and Wilkins (1955). Prediction tables have been used in some North American States to predict the behavior of prisoners released on *parole,* when indeterminate imprisonment should cease and the intensity of supervision needed in individual cases (Gottfredson 1970, 762). Prediction tables have, however, been used less frequently in connection with probation (Sparks 1970, 262).

Main Principles for the Construction of Predictive Instruments

In the present study we have conducted an *ex post facto* experiment where the aim was to determine the effect of the different treatment forms imposed by extra-experimental decision-making bodies, that is, the courts. Thus, the task consisted of optimally seeking to cover and scientifically record all the information these decision-making bodies had at their disposal when sanctions were imposed. This was accomplished by systematically going through the social enquiry reports and medical examination reports. From this information variables have been selected which were used to build up an information matrix.A comprehensive prediction study should be based on the following five points:

1. Outcome criterion categories must be established.
2. The attributes upon which prediction is to be based must be chosen and defined; these so-called predictors are expected to have a significant statistical association with the outcome criteria.
3. The association between the predictors and the outcome criterion must be ascertained from a representative sample of the population for which inferences will be drawn.
4. The association based on the original sample should be validated by testing the predictive instrument on a new sample of the population.
5. Prediction methods can only be applied to the situations for which they were developed.

Validation or cross-validation is usually by-passed because of the extra work and costs involved. If the predictive instrument is to be given practical application in new situations, this constitutes a serious weakness.

What attributes should be chosen for prediction and how should the different predictors should be combined in an instrument? In prediction research there are differing views about whether the predictive factors used are the same as those which *cause* the criminal behavior. Eleanor and Sheldon Glueck held that researchers should use as predictors only those aspects of the individual's living conditions that might give rise to criminal behavior. But Wilkins asserts that any factors which increase the effectiveness of prediction should be used regardless of their possible causal relation to future criminal behavior.

There are different views about the number of *factors* which should be used and their weighting. The Burgess method uses an unweighted procedure or assigns all factors an equal weight. The Gluecks attempted to improve on Burgess's simple system by introducing a weighting method: each attribute was given a weight corresponding to the proportion of offenders who possessed each attribute. But Grygier (1970) asserts that there are no logical grounds for believing that this proportion represents the contribution of the attribute to a predictive instrument. A theoretically improved model, using multiple regression, was introduced into criminology by Mannheim and Wilkins (1955). Other statistical variations of the linear method—for instance discriminant analysis—have also been tested. Later, even non-linear models—for example predictive attribute analysis (Mac Naughton-Smith 1963) and configural analysis (Glaser 1964)—have been put forward.

Simple, unweighted predictive instruments do not take intercorrelations between the different predictors into account. They may therefore be less effective, though if a large number of predictors are used this would probably have little practical significance. Linear multiple regression and discriminant analyses have the advantage of taking into consideration both intercorrelations of predictor variables and the correlation between the predictors and the criterion. The method has, however, been criticized for making certain assumptions about linearity and the assumption that the weights obtaining for the whole sample also apply within the various sub-groups of the sample. Both of these assumptions may be false (Gottfredson, p. 754 and Grygier, pp. 820–830). Later forms of configural or association analysis, which are not based on assumptions of linearity, have been criticized because by successively dividing the sample into sub-groups they are vulnerable to random errors. From the few comparisons made, however, of different methods it appears that the results are relatively similar (Simon 1971). Thus, it would seem that Ohlin's (1962) conclusion remains valid: in reality, a simple combination of completely different favorable and unfavorable factors produces a more useful result than can be obtained with complicated weighting systems (p. 288).

The factors selected for the present predictive instrument are those which in other studies, notably those of Ohlin and Mannheim and Wilkins, have shown high correlations with the criterion as well as those which seem theoretically most meaningful. We carefully studied the predictors used in Börjeson's study (1966) since these had been tested on a population of young Swedish lawbreakers not unlike our sample. For the reasons given we used the calculation methods recommended by Burgess and Ohlin. All the factors have been given the same weight. Almost all the variables in the information matrix have been dichotomized and a score of 0 or 1 assigned to them. Risk points for each individual were summed and a total risk score obtained.

The use of unweighted predictors, dichotomized variables, *a priori,* use of unchecked predictor weights and correlations may limit the instrument's ability to differentiate. We shall discuss this later.

The next step in the analysis is to examine the strength of the association between risk group classification and the criterion. It is only if the prognostic instrument has adequate precision that it can be used to evaluate the effectiveness of the different sanctions by enabling comparisons to be made between the recidivism of individuals belonging to the same risk category but different sanction groups.

The predictive instrument was checked for validity using internal cross-validation.

Construction of the Predictive Instrument

The instrument consists of thirty-six predictors built up around six indexes which deal with different aspects of the individual's background, personal attributes, social problems and previous criminality (see Chapter 4 for a description of these variables). All the variables are dichotomized, with the exception of the criminality variable which is divided into three.

The total sample drawn, with no missing persons, consists of 413 individuals. Representativity can therefore be considered satisfactory. On the other hand, certain variables have had to be excluded because data were missing on too many individuals.

Theoretically, some of the predictors might constitute contributing causes to registered criminality, especially those in indexes 1 and 2, while others, such as those in indexes 3 and 4, describe social maladjustment and measures taken because of it. The predictors in index 5 may be seen both as contributing causes to social maladjustment and as a description of social problems, while index 6 is based on sentences for previous criminality.

Index 1. Information on home and conditions of upbringing

Mobility during childhood
Stability of the environment during upbringing
Financial circumstances
Overcrowded living conditions
Father's abuse of alcohol
Social interventions on account of father's alcohol abuse
Father's criminality
Father's relations with the family
Father's mental status
Father's physical status
Mother's abuse of alcohol
Social interventions on account of mother's alcohol abuse
Mother's criminality
Mother's relations with the family
Mother's mental status
Mother's physical status
Upbringing of child(ren)
Abuse of alcohol among siblings
Social interventions on account of siblings' alcohol abuse
Criminality among siblings

Index 2. The individual's personal attributes and scholastic achievement

Intellectual status
Mental status
Physical status
Education
Social adjustment at school
Scholastic achievement

Index 3. Previous maladjusted behavior and action taken by Child Welfare Board

Previous maladjusted behavior
Measures taken by Child Welfare Board
Improvement of social environment through Child Welfare Board

Index 4. Current social adjustment I: Abuse of alcohol and drugs

Misuse of alcohol and drugs
Misuse of alcohol
Social intervention because of alcohol misuse
Misuse of narcotic and pharmaceutical drugs

Index 5. Current social adjustment II: Occupational status, housing and accommodation.

Occupational circumstances
Work stability
Housing conditions

Index 6. Sentences for earlier criminality

This index consists of one variable which is divided into three parts. Cases of no previous criminality were assigned a risk score of 0, previous offenses resulting in at most day-fines were given a risk score of 1 whilst offenses resulting in registration in the Central Criminal Register were assigned a risk score of 2. The number of previous sentences was not included in the predictive instrument as it showed extensive covariance with earlier type of sentence.

The Predictive Instrument's Discriminatory Power, Totally and for the Different Indexes

A test of the predictive instrument's discriminatory power was based on each one of the above-mentioned indexes. The group of non-recidivists is designated as the "C-group" (*clean*) and the group of *recidivists* as the "R-group" (*recidivist*). The risk scores for the C-group are expected to be at the lower end of the scale and those for the R-group to be at the higher end. Analysis of the distribution of the risk scores in the various indexes demonstrated differences between the two groups which were statistically significant at the 1 percent level.

In the final predictive instrument all the indexes are combined. The total risk scores for each of the two groups clearly differ. The mean value is 10.3 for the R-group and 6.3 for the C-group. The predictive instrument seems therefore to have relatively high discriminatory power.

When placing individuals into different risk groups the raw scores were transformed into stanine scores. This transformation to a *stanine distribution* produces nine different risk groups, the scores of which are normally distributed.

Precision of the Predictive Instrument

It remains to check prognostic precision by testing the association between the various risk categories and the criterion, i.e. relapse into a criminality recorded in the Central Criminal Register during a two-year period.

The two curves of Figure 5.1 show how recidivism clearly increases with the stanine risk groups. The curve for recidivism—offenses recorded in the Central Criminal Register—shows that only 12.5% of the offenders in the first risk group recidivated. This figure rises to 70% for those in the ninth risk group. The total recidivism curve, i.e. the rate based on all known offenses, rises more sharply and shows 90% recidivism in the highest risk group.

Using raw scores and only the offenses recorded in the Central Criminal Register during a two-year period as the criterion for evaluating the instrument's forecasting power, produces a biserial correlation of r = .47. Using total recidivist criminality as the criterion increases the biserial correlation to .54. Using stanine scores as the basis for similar calculations, the coefficients are nearly the same, r = .45 and .52 respectively.

The instrument's true predictive power corresponds to a linear relationship of at least r = .45. This result must be regarded as satisfactory. Using far more complicated statistical calculations both Glueck and Glueck (1930) and Mannheim and Wilkins (1955) also arrived at contingency coefficients of .45. But just how good is the predictive power? One measure for evaluating predictive power is the coefficient of determination, i.e. the square of the correlation coefficient which measures the proportion of variance in the criterion accounted for by the variance in the predictors. Our lowest biserial correlation coefficient of .45 gives an explained variance of 20%.

The highest biserial correlation coefficient of .54, gives an explained variance of 29%. Thus, the predictive instrument explains only a small part of the variation in recidivism rates. What seems an unimpressive result needs, however, to be set in relation to the results obtained in other criminological studies. Persson (1975, 42) states that when using traditional sociological and social-psychological variables, an explained variance higher than 10% is rarely reached for a single background variable and that this proportion almost never exceeds 20% even when a large number of such variables is used (see also Carlsson, SOU 1972:76, 45f).

The Predictive Instrument's Ability to Differentiate Within and Between the Different Sanction Groups

Since the recidivism rates for the three sanction groups differ sharply we would expect risk category adherence for the various groups to differ also. There are in fact statistically significant differences at the 1% level between the mean values on the stanine scale for the various sanction groups (CS = 3.3; P = 5.5; PI = 6.3).

The conditionally sentenced offenders are mainly concentrated at the lower stanine values. This means that the predictive instrument has reduced discriminatory power for this sanction group. Thus, whilst a statistically significant difference was found between the C-group and the R-group for those sentenced to ordinary probation and for those sentenced to probation with institutional treatment, this was not true for the conditionally sentenced offenders. For this reason, the conditionally sentenced offenders are not always included in the analyses which follow.

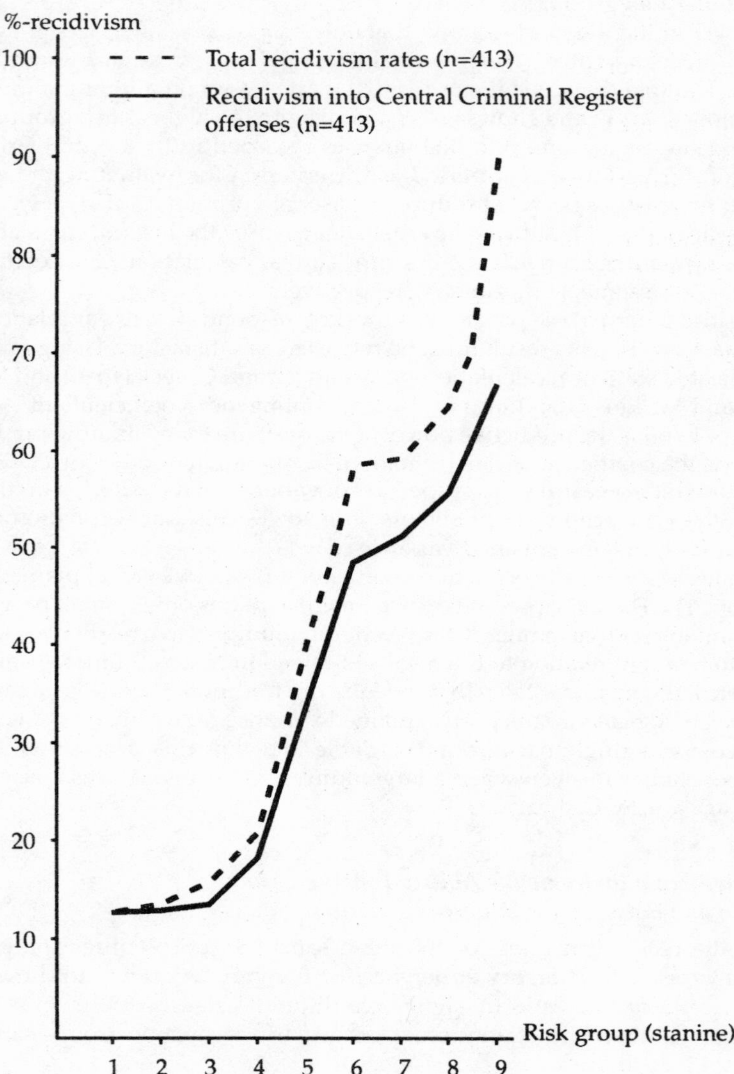

FIGURE 5.1 Recidivism for the Conditionally Sentenced and Probationers by Risk Category (curves for all offenses and for those recorded in the Central Criminal Register)

The Distribution of Recidivism in the Sanction Groups with Risk Categories Held Constant

Figure 5.2 shows the *recidivism curves of the different sanction groups in relation to risk categories.* For all risk categories, the recidivism curve for the PI-group is higher than that for the P-group. Similarly, the curve for the P-group is higher than that for the CS-group in the different risk categories with the exception of the first risk category, in which the P-group only contains two individuals (see Table 5.3). Thus it seems that, for offenders with the same prognosis, the offenders sentenced to probation with institutional treatment recidivate to a greater extent than those sentenced to ordinary probation, and that these, in turn, recidivate to a greater extent than conditionally sentenced offenders.

The fact that the recidivism curves of the PI-group and the P-group are approximately parallel (i.e. recidivism increases largely in proportion to rising risk scores for both sanction groups), shows that institutional treatment, for the majority of individuals in all risk groups, is a less suitable alternative as far as individual prevention is concerned.

In the present diagram, two sanction groups have recidivism curves which climb with higher risk categorization while the third is parallel with the X-axis. For this group, the conditionally sentenced offenders, there comes a point where a higher risk score entails scarcely any increased recidivism. In the first five risk groups, where there is a good representation of individuals, either no relationship can be seen or possibly only a weak curvilinear relationship. The finding suggests that all the individuals studied showed less recidivism when their sentences were conditional and that the recidivism rate for this sanction scarcely increases for the higher risk categories. This finding is particularly noteworthy since the intention of the legislator was that the conditional sentence should only be used for offenders whose prognosis was good. However, in terms of individual prevention, this sanction seems equally effective for those whose prognosis is not so favorable.

Possible Sources of Error in the Recidivism Rates of the Different Sanction Groups

Before the observed differences are accepted as real, however, they must be checked to see if there is any reason to regard them as illusory or as being caused by background factors which were not controlled for. A detailed analysis is justified since these results are central to the investigation.

Could the observed differences in recidivism rates between the sanction groups when the risk categories are held constant have arisen by chance? Other conceivable flaws in the predictive instrument are random errors due to lack of validation, errors of measurement due to, for instance, the dichotomizing of variables, bias connected with the transformation of raw scores into stanine scores and differences in the predictive power of the different indexes. Then, too, the instrument may fail to take certain factors, such as age, nationality and the seriousness of the qualifying criminality into consideration. These and conceivable errors in the criterion variable are discussed. In

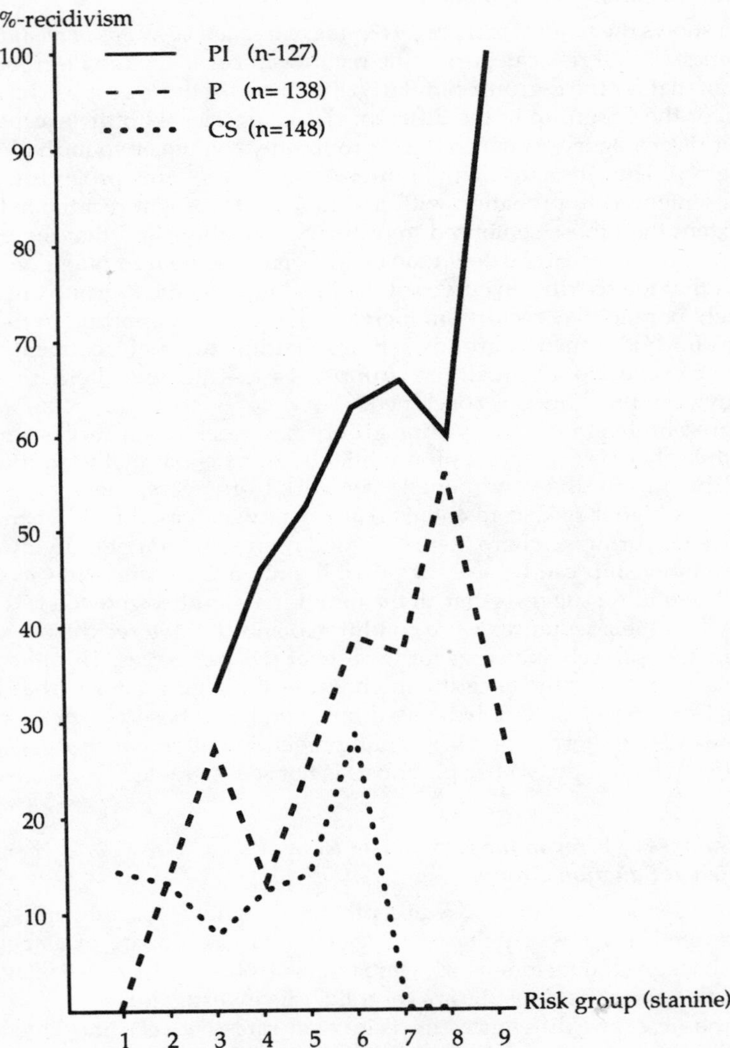

FIGURE 5.2 Recidivism for the Three Sanction Groups by Risk Category (offenses recorded in the Central Criminal Register for the conditionally sentenced, probationers without and with institutionalization)

addition, the fact that conditional sentence and probation may be combined with fines or damages is also examined. Some further possible explanations of the observed results are also touched upon.

1. The Observed Differences in Recidivism May Arise by Chance. As can be seen from Table 5.2, a statistical test of recidivism differences between the P and PI groups shows that the different risk levels have a highly significant total chi-squared value (p = <.001; a McNemar test gives a p-value of .008). Even within the different risk levels we find that four of five testable recidivism differences are almost significant (p = <.04) with only the last one having a somewhat higher probability (p = <.09). We can therefore assert that the differences in recidivism rates between sanction groups are significant despite the small number of individuals in each risk group. The average magnitude of the differences in recidivism is 23% for five risk categories with a relatively even and large distribution, and 28% for all seven categories (unweighted means).

It is more difficult to subject the observed differences in recidivism rates between the P-group and the CS-group to statistical tests because dispersion is poor within the three highest risk categories of the CS-group as is the dispersion within the two lowest categories of the P-group. In consequence, there are therefore fewer comparable categories. A total chi-squared value based on two categories of equal size is as Table 5.3 shows, almost significant (p= <.05). Other non-parametric tests which take account of the fact that the differences within almost all the risk groups point in the same direction, also produce almost significant results (Wilcoxon test p = <.05 and a binomial test p = .06).

The percentage differences in recidivism rates are 11% for four categories with large, even distributions and 18% with all seven categories—somewhat lower than in the foregoing comparison. The observed differences would, however, obviously have been significant if there had been more individuals in each class. If we combine both probation groups to obtain a larger number, we find that the probability value drops still further (Wilcoxon test p = .025). Naturally, even the percentage differences between the sanction groups are increased in this comparison.

The total picture from the two tables is that for nearly every risk group, the more intrusive the nature of the sanction, the greater the recidivism. This indicates that the differences between sanctions are not due to chance.

2. The Predictive Instrument Is Impaired by Random Errors Because of Inadequate Validation. It can be argued that the predictive instrument should be subjected to a test of validity before definite conclusions can be drawn. This can be done either by validating the instrument on other individuals than those who were a part of the original analysis or by performing an internal cross validation.

This criticism, which in itself is of central importance has, however, less relevance for the procedure used in the construction of this predictive instrument. Usually a researcher improves the precision of the instrument by correlating the individual predictors with the criterion in advance, subsequently choosing only those variables which give the highest intercorrelations. More-

TABLE 5.2 Differences in Recidivism between Those Sentenced to Probation with and without Institutional Treatment by Risk Group

	Sanction Group				Recidivism %				Recidivism Difference							
Stanine	PI	(combined)	P	(combined)	PI	(combined)	P	(combined)	P1-P (%)	(combined)	χ^2	(combined)	df	(combined)	p	(combined)
1	0		2		-		0		-		-		-		-	
2	0	14	0	40	-	43	-	18	-	25	-		-		-	
3	3		15		33		27		6		untestable*	3,65	-	1	-	<.04
4	11		23		46		13		33		3,35		1		<.04	
5	25		32		52		28		24		3,38		1		<.04	
6	27		26		63		39		24		3,18		1		<.04	
7	35		27		66		37		29		5,04		1		<.02	
8	20		9		60		56		4		0,05		1		<.45	
9	6	26	4	13	100	69	25	46	75	23	untestable*	1,95	-	1	-	<.09
											17,20		5		<.001	

* Does not satisfy the requirement that all theoretical values shall be >1 and at least three-quarters >5 (cf. Siegel 1956).

TABLE 5.3 Differences in Recidivism between Those Sentenced Conditionally and Sentenced to Ordinary Probation by Risk Group

Stanine	Sanction Group P	(grouped)	Sanction Group CS	(grouped)	Recidivism % P	(grouped)	Recidivism % CS	(grouped)	Recidivism Difference P-CS (%)	(grouped)	χ^2	(grouped)	df	(grouped)	p	(grouped)
1	2		14		0		14		-14		untestable*		-		-	
2	0		31		-		13		-		-		-		-	
3	15	40	40	117	27	18	8	11	19	7	3,61		1		.04	
4	23		32		13		12		1		untestable*	1,10	-	1	-	<.15
5	32		21		28		14		14		1,37		1		.13	
6	26		7		39		29		10		untestable*		-		-	
7	27		2		37	36	0	16	37	20	untestable*		-		-	
8	9	98	1	31	56		0		56		untestable*	4,22	-		-	
9	4		0		25		-		-		-		-	1	-	<.02
											5,32		2		<.05	

* Does not satisfy the requirement that all theoretical values shall be >1 and at least three-quarters >5 (cf. Siegel 1956)

over, the variables are often weighted in accordance with their varying explanatory value. Such a procedure, usually based on a multiple correlation and regression analysis, normally means that random effects get used in a less than satisfactory manner. Börjeson, who used a similar method but proceeded from a so-called iterative variant (with a built-in random correction worked out by Horst) still found a chance component which resulted in an overestimation of prognostic precision. When a cross-validation was performed, the regression coefficient decreased significantly from .78 to .66 (pp. 121–125). However, our procedure has been to choose variables which seem meaningful on logical grounds and which have been shown in previous studies, notably Börjeson's work, to have good predictive power. Indeed, it could be said that we have validated the instrument used by Börjeson. We have *not* under any circumstances utilized random effects by statistically selecting and weighting the predictors in accordance with their relationship to the criterion. Because of this, it becomes much less important to validate the instrument in the way suggested.

A cross-validation was nevertheless performed. This was done by dividing the sample into two groups. After the individuals had been categorized by sanction and age, they were randomly assigned to one or other of these groups. The biserial correlations between risk category and criterion was r = .38 for one group and r = .58 for the other. These correlations should be compared with that discussed earlier, namely r = .47, based on the raw scores of the entire material. The stanine scores of the corresponding correlations in the new sample are .35 and .54 respectively which can be compared with the correlation calculated for the entire material, r = .45.

The correlations are thus somewhat higher in one sample and somewhat lower in the other when comparisons are made with the original population. Where random effects have crept in because of optimizing the relationship between the predictors and the criterion, the correlation obtained with validation using a new sample usually drops substantially. What we have are variations which indicate that the new correlations may be both higher and lower. This shows that we have not capitalized on random variations. The logical objection to the necessity of validating the instrument in the conventional way has thus been given statistical support.

3. The Predictive Instrument Is Impaired by Measurement Errors Primarily Because the Variables Were Dichotomized. One source of error, pointed out by Quensel (1966) in criticism of Börjeson, is the type of measurement error which can be caused by dichotomizing the variables. Different errors in the background variable, among them where the observed values for the background variable deviate from the true values, lead to a reduction in the regression coefficient and less slope in the regression lines. In experimental investigations, where the distribution of the different treatment forms is random and where the background variable is determined later, the difference is insignificant and depends on chance only. With non-experimental investigations where there are two data sets with disparate distributions for the background variable which may then be determined with a not insignificant error, the situation, it is said, may well be different.

If there are several background variables, where each background variable is dichotomized, the situation becomes more difficult to interpret and the effect of dichotomizing cannot easily be assessed (pp. 452–453).

Quensel thinks that if the two treatment forms provide the same effect but the distribution by the background variable is not the same, it is possible for the two adapted straight regression lines not to coincide. Instead an illusory difference may show up. If dichotomizing does not succeed in holding the entire variation of the background variable constant, the true risk scores for the group with a sanction involving deprivation of liberty can be higher, just as the risk scores for the group with sanctions not depriving them of their liberty might be lower. Both errors in background variables and in their dichotomization are said to possibly lead to the regression lines having a diminished slope and to the differences between their heights being increased.

We cannot exclude the possibility of measurement errors in this study as measurement is always marred by some errors. But if these are not systematic in character, they probably do not play a decisive role. The only systematic error I can imagine is a possible underestimation of the conditionally sentenced offenders' characteristics. If this is so, more of these offenders should have been assigned to a higher risk category, which in turn would mean that the differences in recidivism between those sentenced to a conditional sentence and probation would, if anything, become larger. We have tried to keep the random errors as low as possible by using various data checks. It is nevertheless difficult to estimate the size of the remaining measurement errors and it is impossible to say with certainty what effect they have. Since, however, we measure the background variable later, errors in this variable are probably of minor importance.

Quensel thinks it is more difficult to assess the significance of dichotomizing variables. However, he has not stated that such a division of the variables can reduce as well as increase measurement errors. Since most variables are not dichotomized in the raw data, it would not be impossible to recalculate the predictive instrument based on graded variables. However, I assume that this would not essentially alter the result. The information lost because of the dichotomizing procedure is counterbalanced partly by the large number of predictors used and partly by the liberal use of double and triple variables. Such a variable pattern means that one variable measures behavior while another describes the steps taken by society as a consequence of this behavior. In this sense one could say that the variables are, to a certain extent, already graded. In her thorough methodological study of prediction Simon (1971) found, after experimenting with dichotomous and continuous variables, no differences in this respect. Discussions with such experts in the field as Wilkins and Gottfredson, who have worked empirically with real data and used different methods of analysis, revealed that they also share the opinion that the dichotomizing of variables lacks practical importance.

4. The Same Stanine Scores May Conceal Differences in Raw Scores. Quensel has also criticized the use of stanine distributions. We have therefore examined the material in an effort to determine whether the same stanine scores for different sanction groups might represent different raw scores. In order to control for this possible source of error we have calculated the mean raw scores separately in the different stanine classes for the three sanction groups. The disparities uncovered in this way reach only a fraction of a decimal in almost all cases. Somewhat greater differences can only be observed in the highest stanine class, where a larger number of raw scores were brought together. The insignificant differences that do exist are caused in the majority of cases by the mean raw scores increasing within the same stanine class from CS to P and PI. However, since the differences are extremely small it is not possible to argue that the same stanine value conceals different raw scores for the different sanction groups.

As a safety measure, we drew recidivism curves based on raw scores as well. These curves resemble those calculated from stanine scores, although they become somewhat more jagged. The difference in recidivism rates is of about the same magnitude as that reported earlier.

5. There May Be Differences in the Predictive Power of the Subindexes. Börjeson has been criticized because his total risk scores were derived from variables which had all been added together. It may be that the factors differ in predictive power and that this varies between the sanction groups. Although this source of error might be more serious when it is a part of the kind of optimizing procedure used by Börjeson, we have nevertheless examined the predictive power of the present predictive instrument's subindexes. If large differences were found here, we might see, for example, that the risk scores of the PI-group were derived from a subindex with a stronger real relationship to the criterion while the P-group's risk scores were derived from a subindex whose relationship to the criterion is less strong. If so, this would go some way to explain the recidivism differences. By constructing a theoretical group risk score for each sanction group, it is possible to determine whether the obtained risk score was derived from factors which vary in relation to the true criterion. We find however that the structure of the theoretical risk group score is almost identical for the sanction groups. The sub-index for conditions of the home and upbringing is clearly responsible for the largest number of risk scores (36.3% and 35.4% respectively), while the remaining vary between 9% and 19%. The very small percentage differences between the groups' mean risk scores hardly contribute to an explanation of the recidivism differences found, even if the true relations between the individual sub-indexes and the criterion do vary somewhat.

For the sake of completeness, correlations were even calculated between the different sub-indexes and the criterion. All of the six sub-indexes have a biserial correlation coefficient between $r = .27$ and $r = .30$ with the exception of index 3, where $r = .37$. The correlations with the criterion are thus almost equally strong for each of the different sub-indexes with the exception of those covering previous maladjusted behavior. However, the effect of the somewhat better real predictive power of this maladjusted behavior index is eliminated by the fact that it represents a small part of the mean risk score (14.6% and 12.6% respectively) as well as by the insignificant difference existing between the sanction groups regarding the proportional distribution for the same index.

6. Recidivism Differences May Depend on Age Differences in the Sanction Groups. Explanations are now examined which depend on the fact that certain variables, in respect of which the sanction groups differ, are not included in the predictive instrument. To begin with, one might speculate that the reason for the different recidivism rates could be found in the different age profiles of the sanction groups. Earlier we saw that the PI-group is partly composed of younger offenders—a fact which could be expected to produce a higher rate of recidivism.

In order to examine the effect of this factor, the probation material was divided into two age groups by median value after which the previously mentioned analysis was conducted for each age group separately. This showed both the recidivism rate and the average risk scores to be greater for the younger offenders as compared with the older offenders (43% and 25% respectively and 5.2 and 4.7 respectively). Similarly, the correlation between risk category and recidivism is higher for the younger rather than the older age group (biserial r = .55 and .36 respectively). However, when the age variable is held constant, we still find the same trend as we did earlier. The recidivism rate is higher in the PI-group than in the P-group within the individual risk categories for both age groups. Since there are fewer individuals in each of the different risk categories after setting up the two age groups, the curves fluctuate more and the sub-groups become too small to be make significance tests possible. The difference in recidivism between the two probation groups is, on average, 24% for the younger age group (six risk categories) and 18% for the older group (five categories). Large differences remain, then, between sanction groups when age is held constant. Only in the case of the older group is the recidivism difference somewhat less than for the group as a whole (23% for five categories).

Although the age difference is significantly smaller between the those sentenced conditionally and the probationers, the age variable was also controlled for in this comparison. The fact that the members of the P-group are somewhat younger than the conditionally sentenced offenders, could contribute to a higher recidivism rate. The difference in recidivism between these two sanction groups reaches 9% for the younger offenders in four large even risk categories and 19% for all the comparable categories. For the older offenders the difference is 9% with the risk categories of equal size, and 15% for all comparable categories. We therefore find no differences in recidivism between age groups within the different risk categories. The size of the difference between sanction groups is about the same as that obtained earlier for the whole material (11% for four categories and 18% for seven categories).

Despite the fact that the age variable separates the sanction groups and shows covariance both with risk scores and recidivism, no difference in recidivism rate was observed between the sanction groups when the age factor was controlled for by a new analysis of the younger and older groups. Thus, the age factor, although it is not included in the predictive instrument, cannot explain the recidivism differences between sanction groups.

7. The Recidivism Differences May Be Due to Differences in Nationality. It is possible that the difference in recidivism rates between the conditionally sentenced offenders and probationers might be due to the fact that there is a large number of foreigners in the former group. The majority of these were expelled from the country and would thus, in principle, be prevented from committing new offenses registered in Sweden. However, we find that foreigners have a higher rate of recidivism—almost twice as high as that of the Swedish conditionally sentenced offenders (20% and 12% respectively).

When we repeat the previous analysis with the conditionally sentenced offenders divided into Swedes and foreigners or into the whole group and the whole group with foreigners excluded, we find great differences, particularly in the high risk groups. In the fifth risk category 50% of the foreigners recidivated as compared to 12% of the Swedes, and in the sixth category 100% of the foreigners recidivated as compared with none of the Swedes. Thus, foreigners alone are responsible for the rise in the curve for conditionally sentenced offenders which we observed earlier for the fifth and sixth risk categories—see Figure 5.2 (As can be seen in Table 5.3, no one in the seventh and eighth risk categories recidivated, and in the ninth category there are no offenders with conditional sentences). We should add that foreigners were possibly assigned risk scores that are too low since it is difficult to obtain transcripts or data from the social service authorities in their home countries. The larger number of expelled foreigners among the conditionally sentenced offenders cannot therefore explain the difference in recidivism rates. Rather they contribute to reducing the existing differences.

8. Recidivism Differences Can Be Explained by Differences in the Seriousness of the Qualifying Offense. Börjeson writes that he avoids criterion contamination by basing the measurement of independent variables on data which were available before the individual was sentenced (p. 130). Despite this claim, "the seriousness of qualifying criminality" is weighed together with diverse background factors in the predictive instrument. Börjeson's procedure in this respect has been questioned by several reviewers. Börjeson justifies his approach by saying that "from a psychological point of view" it is possible that the courts' level of punishment and not just the choice of sanction to some extent reflects their perception of the offenders' prior possibilities of readjustment and that in this way he gains better control over the decision-making bodies' selective influence (p. 109).

To avoid this criticism of criterion contamination we included previous criminality which led to earlier sentences in our predictive instrument but not the criminal activities which were responsible for the current sentence. However, we have then instead been criticized for *not* taking qualifying criminality into consideration because of the great importance the courts attach to this.

A new predictive instrument was therefore created in which the severity of the criminal act leading to the current sentence was included. This was done partly to specifically examine the importance of the variable "seriousness of qualifying criminality" and partly to examine the general significance of adding a further important variable. Like the variable "previous type of sentence", the qualifying criminality variable was divided into three parts in order to give it greater weight than the other dichotomized variables. In addition, the measurement was made as complete as possible by grading and summing for all offenses—not just for the main offense—included in the current sentence.

The relationship between risk category and criterion is almost exactly the same when measured with the new predictive instrument as it is when measured with the original instrument (biserial r = .456 and .455 respectively). The regression functions have about the same appearance as earlier. The recidivism curves for the three sanction groups correspond by and large to those of Figure 5.2. The curves are relatively parallel and do not cross each other at any point. The percentage differences in recidivism between sanction groups within the risk categories are, on the average, the same as earlier. They have, if anything, increased somewhat when a comparison is made between conditionally sentenced offenders and probationers (20% for CS/P for all comparable categories and 27% for P/PI for all risk categories).

Adding a variable to the predictive instrument, then, does not alter the result, despite the fact that the variable in question, the seriousness of the qualifying criminality, is judged to be of central importance and was given extra weight. This is an important conclusion of principle which we shall have occasion to return to later. A further analysis was performed where seriousness of qualifying criminality was assigned quite decisive significance.

The entire material was divided up by median value into a low and a high group concerning the seriousness of the current offense. As one would expect, this variable discriminates well. The total recidivism is 25% in the low group and 45% in the high group. The recidivism analysis was then repeated in the same way as before, i.e. by holding the risk categories and sanctions constant. However, the differences in recidivism between sanctions within the risk groups remain the same for both the low group and the high group set up on the basis of the seriousness of the current offense. Differences between the two probation groups within the different risk levels are just as great for both offense groups. The recidivism curve for the conditionally sentenced offenders remains on a lower recidivism level than that of the probationers for the low group, while it breaks through the latter at some point for the high group. Because there are fewer individuals in each risk category, the distribution becomes skewed, the curves more jagged and the values impossible to test for significance. We find, however, that the percentage differences in recidivism are just as large as they were earlier. In comparisons between the two probation groups, the average difference of all the risk categories reaches 31% within the low group and 29% in the high group. The corresponding differences for the CS-group and the P-group are 28% in the low group and 13% in the high group.

Thus we find that even if we build the variable "seriousness of qualifying criminality" into the predictive instrument or hold it constant by dividing the material into two groups, the results obtained earlier are still valid. The differences in recidivism between sanction groups within the risk categories have increased rather than decreased for some comparisons.

9. Recidivism Differences May Be Due to Other Underlying Factors. Are there other important underlying factors which are not included in the predictive instrument? Andenaes (pp. 126–128) asked this question in connection with Börjeson's dissertation and contended that the prediction tables only take account of information that is available in documents. He pointed out that judges generally hold the view that seeing and hearing the defendant and forming an impression of his personality is very important for their choice of sentence. Börjeson discusses this alternative explanatory model in some detail and stresses the fact that the precision of intuitive prognoses is low. This, he explains, is because assessment is performed unsystematically and without an explicit theory. Moreover, it is not only considerations of prognosis that influence the courts' decision processes. Despite the fact that Börjeson assigns relatively high values to the prognostic ability of the courts ($r = .40$ and .50 respectively), he finds scarcely any increase in the multiple correlation coefficient and therefore rejects this explanatory model. Andenæs (1978) returns, however, to the same question in his review of the present study.

It is not difficult to imagine that the courts form certain ideas of the defendant at the main hearing and that this conception influences the members of the court. But the following four conditions must be met if this argument is to be relevant for the discussion of possible sources of error in the prediction analysis:

1. The courts' decisions are affected by some factor which is not included in the social enquiry reports and sources of documented information;
2. This factor is not indirectly incorporated in the predictive instrument through covariance with other factors;
3. The occurrence of this factor varies between sanction groups;
4. This factor is directly related to the tendency of the sentenced persons to recidivate.

Although I have asked judges to give examples of such factors, no plausible suggestions have been forthcoming. Researchers with experience of index construction are also well aware of the fact that the exclusion, addition or exchange of variables has little importance for the results obtained in a subsequent analysis of relationships (Lazarsfeld's law of interchangeability of indexes).

Furthermore, the more variables a predictive instrument contains, the less important is the addition of further variables. Because the present instrument contains as many as thirty-nine variables, it would probably be extremely difficult to find new variables which would add anything of explanatory value.

10. There May Be Errors in the Criterion. Errors in the criterion are usually not discussed to the same extent as errors in the predictors although they too would reduce predictive power. Because low reliability generally does not introduce systematic errors, useful prediction can be accomplished even with fairly crude criteria (Gottfredson, p. 748).

The type of measurement used in this study, i.e. offenses recorded in the Central Criminal Register, probably does not contain random errors of measurement to any great extent. From the point of view of validity, registered offenses can be considered to result in considerably better measurement than those which are often adopted in studies of supervision, namely violation of different conditions of supervision. In several studies it has been found that the latter criterion measures the behavior of the authorities rather than that of their clients (Lerman 1975). Measuring serious offenses reduces the likelihood that what is being measured is the behavior of the police. Nevertheless, we cannot rule out the possibility that probationers under supervision may have received more attention from the police than offenders given conditional sentences. However, we cannot expect a corresponding difference to exist between the two probation groups where the recidivism differences are at least as great.

The recidivism figures we obtained for the groups studied here also seem to be representative for the country as a whole. Nine percent of offenders given conditional sentences in 1968 recidivated within a three-year period. A special analysis of probationers conducted for me by the Central Bureau of Statistics shows that 32% of all those who were sentenced to ordinary probation recidivated within a two-year period as compared with 58% of all those who were sentenced to probation with institutional treatment. Thus, the figures obtained for the districts we studied (31% and 60% respectively) correspond well with those obtained for the country as a whole. This makes it unlikely that our criterion is marred by serious random or systematic errors of measurement.

11. Recidivism Differences May Be Due to Variations in the Sanction Variable Which Were Not Controlled For. So far we have examined errors or underlying factors in respect of the prognostic and criterion variables. There is however a third information set connected with the treatment variable. As we saw in the preceding chapter, the courts may impose fines or damages in combination with the sanctions of conditional sentence and probation. This involves a variation of the sanction variable which we have not taken into consideration. Moreover, the sanction groups differ greatly concerning the extent to which day-fines were imposed together with the sanction. The proportion was greatest (57%) for conditionally sentenced offenders but almost zero for offenders sentenced to probation with institutional treatment. On the theory that fines might have an individual preventive effect and contribute to deterring the offender from committing new offenses, the greater use of fines with the conditionally sentenced offenders might provide a partial explanation for the low rate of recidivism among them by comparison with those who were sentenced to probation.

In order to study this possible error we related the imposition of fines and damages to recidivism by holding the sanction and risk groups constant. The risk scores were dichotomized to avoid obtaining too few individuals in the cells.

For the group of conditionally sentenced offenders, we find that of those who were fined 15% recidivated as compared with a mere 8% of those who were not. This difference can be seen in both the low and the high risk groups. Of the probationers who were fined 32% recidivated as compared with 29 % of those who were not. The latter minor difference is valid for both risk groups. Thus, the conditionally sentenced offenders recidivate less despite the fact that they more often fined. Indeed, the addition of fines appears to lead to an increase in recidivism rates.

When considering *fines and damages* in combination with the sanctions of conditional sentence or probation, we found the following. Recidivism is less frequent among conditionally sentenced offenders in both risk groups if they were *not* required to pay fines and damages. And we found fewer recidivists among probationers who were not fined or required to pay damages in the low risk group of offenders sentenced to ordinary probation as well as in both risk groups of those sentenced to probation with institutional treatment.

The fact that in both risk groups recidivism increases as the proportion of day-fines increases lends further support to the theory of negative individual prevention. In this connection it should be remembered that fines were chiefly imposed in those cases where the combined offenses dealt with were not especially serious.

Variation of the sanction variable to take account of fines and damages does not then explain the recidivism differences between the sanction groups. If anything, varying this variable increases the differences and thereby confirms the main conclusion concerning *negative individual prevention.*

12. Other Possible Explanations Which Could Make Recidivism Differences Illusory. There are additional error factors discussed by Börjeson. The only relevant variable for this study is *type of offense,* which is not included in my predictive instrument. It may show covariance both with the judge's choice of sanction and with subsequent recidivism. However, as we found earlier, the differences between sanction groups concerning type of offense are not great: in all groups, the majority of offenders were in the first place found guilty of larceny and in the second place of fraud.

Thus, much of the criticism leveled at Börjeson's dissertation is not valid for this study. And a further independent analysis of Börjeson's data using other statistical methods has not led to any change in his main conclusions (Mattson and Österberg 1971).

The Effects of Sanctions

After the foregoing examination it seems reasonable to think that different sanctions result in differing recidivism rates for similar comparable groups. We now attempt to find theoretical or empirical support for such a conclusion.

We shall first briefly recapitulate findings from treatment research in order to see if our result agrees with other research results and theories in the same area. Thereafter we shall undertake a detailed analysis of how probationers adjust socially during the time that they are exposed to probation treatment to see if we can find any explanations for the different recidivism rates found between the sanction groups.

This analysis is based on information available in the personal case records. Since the conditionally sentenced offenders are not placed under supervision they must perforce be excluded from this analysis.

Theories and Results in Treatment Research

By and large treatment research has shown that there are no great differences between the effects of various punishments and treatment measures. It should, however, be noted that the greater part of effect research, which has primarily been conducted in the United States, only applies to the evaluation of different treatment methods. Comparisons of the effects of different sanctions are quite rare although such research has been relatively more prevalent in Scandinavia and England. It is, of course, more difficult for the researcher interested in comparing such effects to obtain permission to conduct an experiment with different sanctions rather than with certain individual components within a given sanction. When evaluating sanctions, researchers have therefore for the most part been compelled to use prognostic methods for their studies.

The findings of the comparative studies which have been undertaken concerning different sanctions can be summarized as follows; "It seems that *measures which do not deprive an offender of his liberty* are more effective than, or at least as effective as, sanctions which do" (Bondeson 1974, 41; see pp.35–60 for a more detailed summary of treatment research).

Börjeson's doctoral dissertation (1966) culminates in the conclusion that sanctions which deprive an offender of liberty produce worse results than sanctions which do not. So far as individual preventive effects are concerned, the study resulted in a rank-ordering of sanctions as follows: conditional sentence, fines, determinate deprivation of liberty, continued probation and youth imprisonment (p. 137f).

Similar results were obtained in studies conducted by Hammond (1964, 1969): fines and a conditional sentence (absolute or conditional discharge) were much more effective than probation or different forms of institutional treatment. Probation was at least as effective as institutional treatment. One of the few true experiments undertake in this area, the Community Treatment Project (Warren et al. 1966), also demonstrated that the delinquents who were treated in the community managed better than those who were treated in an institution.

Studies of deprivation of liberty over different lengths of time are also relevant here. Several investigations using predictive instruments have shown that shorter periods of institutional treatment are at least as effective as longer periods. My own studies, which make use of a structural-functional analysis incorporating a multivariate method, have demonstrated increased *prisonization effects* with increased time in an institution, i.e. negative effects resulting from the inmates' adjustment to the prison community. Similar results were obtained from such different types of institutions as youth training schools, youth prisons, ordinary prisons and prisons for those sentenced to the indeterminate sanction of internment (Bondeson 1974). In an earlier study, I demonstrated that socialization into the criminal sub-culture of a youth training school showed covariance with subsequent recidivism (Bondeson 1968). Recidivism data collected for the thousand inmates who were interviewed in 1970 (for my 1974 study) and followed up during a ten-year period, also suggests that prisonization effects are important for the subsequent adjustment of offenders outside the institution (Bondeson 1989).

Whilst a number of studies show that sanctions involving deprivation of liberty give worse results than sanctions which do not, there would seem to be few studies which show the opposite. There are also many theories about the negative effects of life in institutions seen against the background of the official goal of rehabilitation. Clemmer (1940) described how prisoners adjusted to the prison community with its antisocial value system and Sykes (1958) described, by means of a *deprivation theory,* how prisoners, when rejected by society created a new society with other norms in order to regain their self-respect. One can also explain the criminalization process at institutions with the aid of *Sutherland's differential association theory* which asserts that criminal behavior is learned by interaction with other criminals (Cressey 1964). Goffman's theory of *total institutions* (1961) also illustrates how members of different closed organizations play various roles and how this makes their subsequent adjustment to society more difficult. On the other hand, we know much less about the effects of supervision, and the theories in this area are also less developed. However, the negative effects of supervision can, like the deprivation of liberty, be understood from the standpoint of *labeling theory* (Becker 1963, 1964; Lundén and Näsman 1973). Eysenck's fixation theory can also be considered relevant in this context (1964).

Analysis of Data from the Personal Case Records

Time to First Recidivist Offense. We saw earlier that about half of those who recidivated during a two-year follow-up did so within the first six months. Recidivism occurred particularly swiftly among those sentenced to probation with institutional treatment—39% recidivated within the first three months (Table 5.1). When we look at the probation group as a whole, we find that 24% of the PI-group and 8% of the P-group recidivated within the first three months of their non-institutional probationary period. It is during this first period that the greatest differences in recidivism rates are found between the two groups of probationers. Recidivism is about as great or twice as great for the PI-group as the P-group during the later periods as can be seen from Table 5.4.

We knew, on the basis of the total recidivism rates and risk score distribution, that recidivism was greater in the PI-group than in the P-group. However, it was unexpected that recidivism would be three times greater in the PI-group than in the P-group during the first three months of the non-institutional probationary period. What is responsible for the large difference in recidivism during these first three months? By studying certain aspects of the non-institutional probationary period we shall try to gain insight into the reasons for such sharply differing recidivism rates during this period as well as the prior role played by the probation institution.

Methods of Measurement and Follow-Up Times for Social Adjustment. In order to obtain follow-up data, content analyses were made of the information contained in the personal case records kept by the probation officers. This

TABLE 5.4 Percentage Proportions of the Sanction Groups Recidivating (first time only) during Different Periods under Supervision

	Recidivism by Supervision Period							
Sanction Group	0-3 mths	4-6 mths	7-9 mths	10-12 mths	13-18 mths	19-24 mths	Nonrecidivism	Total
P n=138	8	7	4	5	4	3	70	100
PI n=127	24	11	9	6	7	5	39	100

information is based primarily on the quarterly reports which supervisors send in to the chief probation officer. The reports deal with the circumstances under which their clients are living. The information available to the chief probation officer about the offenders may also be based on direct contact between a probation officer and a probationer or between the supervisor and social service agencies or other helping organisations.

Unlike the recidivism data, the follow-up period to which this information relates could not be delimited so that all individuals could be observed for the same length of time. Up until the date when the information was collected the probationary period was in principle at least twenty-four months for all individuals. However, some of these persons had shorter supervisory periods, either because supervision was terminated as a result of further criminality or as it was no longer deemed necessary. In a few cases supervision was terminated because the probationary period had expired.

Since under these circumstances no uniform period of measurement could be used, the follow-up observation time is identical with the supervisory period with the termination of the supervisory period. The average follow-up period was twenty-six months for the PI-group and twenty-nine months for the P-group. As these follow-up times are so closely similar, the differences in follow-up time can scarcely be considered to have any effect when the sanction groups are compared. In order to err on the side of safety, however, most of the findings are given as a percentage of the actual time (= supervisory period) each individual was followed up.

Occupational Status During the Entire Probationary Period. Occupational status has been classified into the following categories: gainful employment, studies, military service, unemployment, sickness, and institutional confinement. Table 5.5 summarizes the different forms of activity expressed as a percentage for the period during which probationers were observed.

The proportion of the gainfully employed is greater in the P-group than in the PI-group (64% and 52% respectively). Whilst 21% of the former group were gainfully employed during the entire observation period, this was true of only 6% of those from the latter group. The largest difference between sanction groups relates to the proportion who were unemployed, the average proportions being 13% for the P-group and 21% for the PI-group. The difference between the two groups concerning institutional confinement is primarily

TABLE 5.5 Occupational Status of Those Sentenced to Probation with and without Institutional Treatment during the Supervision Period (percentage)

Occupational Status during the Supervision Period	P (n=138)	PI (n=125)
Gainfully employed	64	52
Studies or retraining	6	4
Military service	4	7
Unemployed	13	21
Sick	10	5
Institutional confinement	3	11
Total	100	100

due to those in the PI-group who, to a greater extent than those in the P-group, were imprisoned or remanded in custody. Only a few of the probationers undertook military service; this was somewhat more common in the PI-group than in the P-group.

By combining the three first kinds of occupational status—gainful employment, studies and military service—we obtain a measure of the *general activity level*. Using this criterion, all probationers in both sanction groups had active occupational status for at least three months of the total observation period. Almost twice as many individuals in the P-group as in the PI-group had active occupational status throughout the measurement period (30% and 17% respectively). The general level of activity is 74% for the P-group and 64% for the PI-group. This result thus shows that the PI-group failed to a greater extent than the P-group to find acceptable forms of occupation during the probation period.

Relation of Unemployment to Recidivism. One way of measuring occupational adjustment is to study the incidence of unemployment in the two sanction groups. So that the use of varying follow-up periods should not give misleading results, the recidivism-unemployment relationship was tested for a period of at least one month's unemployment or its absence. Table 5.6 shows that the association between sanction and unemployment is highly significant with a greater proportion of unemployed in the PI-group than in the P-group (73% and 52% respectively).

When the material is split into the R-group and the C-group (recidivists and non-recidivists), we find that for all probationers, the level of unemployment is higher in the R-group than in the C-group. For the P-group the respective proportions are 17% and 11% whilst for the PI-group they are 29% and 10% respectively.

Using the incidence of unemployment among recidivists as an evaluative criterion, an almost significant association between unemployment and recid-

TABLE 5.6 Unemployment during the Supervision Period in Relation to Sanction

Sanction	Unemployed	Not Unemployed	Total
P	73	65	138
PI	90	35	125
Total	163	100	263
	χ^2 = 10.20	df = 1	p <.005

ivism in the P-group and a highly significant relationship in the PI-group is to be found (Tables 5.7 and 5.8). Thus, the incidence of unemployment and the length of unemployment is greater among recidivists in both sanction groups.

Hansson concludes "However, the most important observation in the overwhelming majority of cases, is that this unemployment is *not* a result of criminality but occurs before, or in connection with, the recidivism period " (p. 83). In the summary, he states that the association between unemployment and relapse into criminal activity "is, in time, of the cause-effect type" (p. 89).

The strong association between unemployment and recidivism and the high level of unemployment in the PI-group could thus explain the sharply differing recidivism rates between the two probation groups. The high recidivism rate in the PI-group may be due either to a diminished general capacity to adjust in society or to the negative consequences of the actual stay in the probation institution. Moreover, these factors might show covariance and enhance each other. In the next section we shall deepen this analysis and try to test both explanatory models.

Occupational Status During the First Period of Non-Institutional Treatment. Probation institutions have a special responsibility in this matter since the institution has a duty to clear up problems in the offender's social environment and help him procure employment and a place to live. If the probation institution does not prepare probationers for non-institutional treatment by arranging meaningful employment and acceptable accommodation, the PI-group runs the risk of being handicapped by comparison with the P-group at the very beginning of the non-institutional supervision. It must also be remembered that some probationers lose their jobs and homes just because they have been placed in an institution (see Chapter 7).

1. The Relation Between Unemployment and Recidivism. There is a statistically significant relationship between unemployment and type of sanction for the first three-month period of non-institutional treatment. During this period, 38% of the PI-group were unemployed for at least one month while the corresponding figure for the P-group was 24%. During the second three-month period unemployment decreased to 30% percent for the PI-group and to 19% for the P-group. Recidivism, which was 24% and 8% respectively for the first period, decreased during the second period to 11% and 7% respectively. Thus we find a connection between sanction and unemployment within and between the different time periods.

TABLE 5.7 Unemployment Related to Recidivism/Nonrecidivism in the P Group

Non-Recidivism/Recidivism	Unemployed	Not Unemployed	Total
C	45	51	96
R	28	14	42
Total	73	65	138

$\chi^2 = 4.60$ df = 1 $p < .05$

TABLE 5.8 Unemployment Related to Recidivism/Non-Recidivism in the PI Group

Non-Recidivism/Recidivism	Unemployed	Not Unemployed	Total
C	26	23	49
R	64	12	76
Total	90	35	125

$\chi^2 = 14.34$ df = 1 $p < .001$

2. ***The Part Played by the Probation Institution in Procuring Employment.*** One of the reasons for the high rate of unemployment in the PI-group is obviously that the probation institution does not succeed in helping the probationers to solve their employment problems in an acceptable way. As many as 26 of 127 (20%) of the probationers lacked work at the time they began non-institutional supervision. The probation institution or the probation services found new jobs for 43% of those sentenced to probation with institutional treatment. Only 8% returned to the same type of work they had before they were sentenced, 13 % found new employment by their own efforts, 3% entered job preparation schemes and 12% were to undergo retraining or take up additional study in some other way. Of the one-fifth of the PI-group who were unemployed on release from the institution, 73% recidivated. By contrast, only 50% of those who had work when released, relapsed into new crime.

Further evidence that the institution has not succeeded especially well in solving employment problems is the fact that 69% of those who obtained work with the assistance of the institution or the probation services, recidivated, as compared with only 37% of those who obtained work in other ways. To illuminate the part played by the probation institution plays in this failure we shall examine the kind of work found for the probationers through the probation institution.

Among the entire PI-group 65% of the jobs held required no vocational training. But for those for whom work was found, the proportion was 82%. With reservation for missing data on incomes, it was found that the work procured through the probation institution gave a 15% lower wage than the average income for the group as a whole during the observation period. Especially striking is the fact that 15% of those for whom work was procured by the probation institution or probation services, stayed less than seven days at that work, more than half stayed less than three months and only 9% stayed more than one year.

These examples clearly show that the probation institution does not succeed in solving the problem of procuring meaningful work for the probationers. However, in the institution's defence it could be argued that these were difficult clients. The institution, it might be said, failed but with "the most hopeless cases". We shall now examine the relevance of such arguments more closely.

*3. **Analysis of Occupational Status and Recidivism with Prior Work Adjustment Held Constant.*** A conceivable explanation of the result reviewed above is that the probationers who were unemployed on release from the probation institution had also failed in their earlier attempts to adjust to the work situation. Similarly, it may be that those who were found work through the institution and who subsequently recidivated to a greater extent than others, had also had difficulties in adjusting to previous employment.

In order to control for this source of error the research material has been broken down into subgroups using previous work adjustment as the criterion. Three different measures for this were used, namely work circumstances at the time of current sentence and, additionally, in combination with previous work stability with this latter measure assessed by two different methods.

When previous work adjustment was held constant we found, however, that the discrepancies we noted earlier still remain. Among the those who left the probation institution without work, 71% of the seven who were employed at the time of sentence recidivated as compared with 74% of the 19 probationers who were unemployed at time of sentence. When previous work stability is taken into consideration, the findings are that the recidivism rates for those who were unemployed on release were as follows: 100% of those who had previously adjusted to the work situation in an acceptable way recidivated as compared to 71% of those who had not. Thus, we find that irrespective of previous work adjustment, those who left the institution without work recidivated to a considerably greater extent.

If we look at the proportion of probationers who were found work through the institution or the chief probation officer's staff, we find that 64% of the twenty-five who were employed at the time of sentence recidivated as compared to 72% of the twenty-nine who were unemployed at that time. When previous work stability is taken into consideration, we find that 82% of those who had demonstrated good work stability recidivated as compared with 65% of those who had not demonstrated such stability. The high rate of recidivism for those who were helped through the institution to obtain work is thus still valid and even increases for the group who had previously shown good work stability.

Finally, if look at those who left the probation institution after having found work in some other way we find that 40% of those who had work at the time of sentence recidivated compared with 50% of those who were then unemployed. If we also take work stability into account we find that 20% of those who had previously adjusted well to work recidivated as compared with 53% of those who had not adjusted well. Of those who left the probation institution having found new employment by their own efforts, 33% of those who had adjusted well to previous employment recidivated as compared with 50% of those who were not so well-adjusted. The lowest recidivism rate, irrespective of prior work adjustment, is to be found among those who were employed in the same kind of work before and after their stay in the institution. Only one-third recidivated even among those who lacked work stability earlier.

Housing and Accommodation

Accommodation is a problem for many probationers from both sanction groups. A majority of probationers lack permanent accommodation. Frequent moves, overcrowding and poor housing are the realities confronting many of them. Almost half of those in the PI-group and one-third of those in the P-group lived in their parents' homes during the greater part of the probationary period. The next most common form of accommodation was, for the PI-group, sharing or boarding with someone else, and, for the P- group, living together with their wives. In both sanction groups there were isolated cases of persons who completely lacked a permanent place to live during the entire supervisory period.

About half of both sanction groups live in below-average or low standard apartments. The PI-group live in low standard apartments to a somewhat greater extent than the P-group. During all the observation periods, 20–30% of probationers in both groups lived in conditions that can be described as crowded or extremely crowded, i.e. at least two to three persons per room. The frequency of removal is high in both groups. The median frequency is 2.0 accommodation moves in the PI-group and 1.4 in the P-group. This means that the average probationer in the institutional group lived in three different kinds of accommodation during the two-year observation period.

It is difficult to make accurate comparisons between the two groups. Offenders in the PI-group seem to live as boarders, live under poorer conditions or move to a somewhat greater extent than those from the P-group.

However, because of the amount of missing data about the conditions of housing and accommodation there is no possibility of trying to find any meaningful relation between this variable and the data on recidivism.

Alcohol and Drugs

Information about the misuse of alcohol comes partly from the personal case records kept by the probation service and extracts from records on measures taken by administrative authorities against offenders (e.g. driving license administrations). Since both these kinds of information supplement each other, they have been analyzed in combination.

Alcohol misuse is very high in both probation groups: 52% of the P-group and 62% of the PI-group are noted as misusing alcohol on some occasion during the period of observation. Furthermore, we find a probably significant relationship between alcohol misuse and recidivism throughout the probation material ($\chi^2 = 4.02$, df = 1, p = <.05). However, alcohol misuse is high among the group who recidivated as well as among those who did not (57% and 44% respectively).

The relationship between misuse of alcohol and recidivism is thus not as strong as that between unemployment and recidivism. It is more difficult to establish the chronological order between the different actions in respect to the misuse of alcohol and recidivism, because information on the misuse of alcohol was only recorded for six-monthly periods, whereas the other information is available for three-monthly periods. When the material is divided into six-monthly periods we find that the total frequency of alcohol misuse is greatest during the first six months of freedom with 35% of the P-group misusing alcohol as compared with 49% of the PI-group.

There is an interesting reversal of alcohol misuse rates for both probation groups before and after sentence was imposed. While the PI-group misused alcohol to a somewhat lesser degree than the P-group before sentence, their frequency of alcohol misuse was considerably higher after sentence. The differences between the groups before and after sentence was imposed becomes especially clear when continued misuse is considered.

Treatment at the probation institution has obviously not led to a reduction in alcohol misuse, but seems instead to have caused it to increase. The true differences are probably greater than those noted here because the concept of alcohol misuse as used for offenders prior to sentence refers to alcohol problems over a long period but this is limited to six months when referring to post-sentence probation supervision in the community. It is not difficult to understand why the misuse of alcohol increases after a period of confinement. Worry and anxiety escalate and employment and accommodation problems are also often aggravated.

There is very little reduction in the level of alcohol misuse for the P-group during the supervisory period; it remains at about 30% or just above. On the other hand, there is a fairly sharp reduction in the level of alcohol misuse for the PI-group where the rate was only 28% for the final six-monthly period. However, we are now dealing with a biased sample as only two-thirds of offenders in the PI-group were still under supervision whereas almost all of the offenders in the P-group remained under supervision. Many of the individuals in the PI-group who are on record for previous misuse of alcohol have, either in connection with the current misuse or in other contexts committed new offenses, for which reason in some cases the sanction was revoked and supervision consequently ceased.

Despite the fact that the rate of alcohol misuse during all the observation periods, with the exception of the last, is higher for the PI-group than for the P-group, there are fewer interventions resulting from alcohol misuse within the PI-group. For example, while continued misuse during the ensuing periods is about the same in both groups, more probationers from the P-group were taken into care for alcohol misuse. One reason for this is probably that the cases of alcohol misuse in the PI-group more often led to the sanction being revoked whereupon special measures to deal with the misuse of alcohol were evidently regarded as superfluous or devoid of meaning.

Thus, from our analysis of alcohol misuse and recidivism, we are unable to find any reduction of the frequency of misuse during the probationary period for the P-group as we had been able to do for unemployment. An analysis of the relationship between unemployment and recidivism showed that recidivism decreased as unemployment became less. The frequency of alcohol misuse cannot be related recidivism in the same way as unemployment. There is therefore less reason to believe that the misuse of alcohol leads to recidivism than there is to believe that unemployment leads to recidivism.

Since both unemployment and the misuse of alcohol nevertheless show covariance with recidivism, albeit to varying degrees, we shall also analyze the interplay between these two factors and recidivism.

Alcohol Misuse and Unemployment in Relation to Recidivism. We have seen that there is a higher rate of unemployment and alcohol misuse among recidivists than among those who do not recidivate. When we combine these two variables we find that the difference is somewhat greater between the recidivists and the non-recidivists than we found when each variable was analyzed separately. For the entire probation sample, we find that only 8% of recidivist probationers were not registered for unemployment or alcohol misuse at some time during the observation period, while the corresponding figure for those who did not recidivate is 34% In addition, 53% of the offenders in the R-group are recorded as being unemployed and misusing alcohol as compared with 23% in the C-group.

When comparing the two probation groups we also find rather large differences in these combined variables. In the PI-group there were only 16% who were not recorded as being either unemployed or misusing alcohol as compared with 28% in the P-group. Forty-three percent of offenders in the PI-group were recorded as being both unemployed and misusing alcohol as compared with 30% in the P-group.

Over time there is a diminishing tendency for these two factors to present themselves in combination. The proportion of offenders affected by one or other of these factors is largest during the first six-months period—70% of the PI-group and 54% of the P-group. These proportions dropped during the second period to 62% and 42% respectively.

Even if there is an association between recidivism and the two variables unemployment and alcohol misuse, this is far from being absolute. The association can be expected to be somewhat weakened because the definition of recidivism has been limited to relatively serious offenses and also because the analysis is restricted to first-time recidivism.

However, our ability to predict is not markedly improved by combining the variables unemployment and alcohol misuse. Because the relationship between unemployment and recidivism is stronger than that between alcohol misuse and recidivism and because, over time, whilst the tendency is for both unemployment and recidivism to diminish this is not true for alcohol misuse and recidivism, it seems that unemployment leads to recidivism to a greater extent than alcohol misuse (see also the multiple regression analysis of recidivism in Chapter 8.) During the periods of unemployment alcohol consumption probably increases which may in its turn lead to increased misuse with all that that implies for further consequences.

Drug Misuse

Information about the misuse of narcotics and pharmaceutical drugs is based chiefly on what was reported to the chief probation officer in the supervisors' reports but, in some cases, information was also obtained from social service agencies or administrations that were called on to intervene because of drug problems.

The findings suggest that drug misuse is very limited although there may of course be a non-reported misuse. The largest proportion of drug misusers, 6%, was noted for the PI-group during the first three-month period of non-institutional treatment. The figure varies during the remaining periods between zero percent and 5%. The proportion of drug misusers among the P-group offenders fluctuates between zero percent to 4%, reaching a peak only after two years. In both probation groups, the majority of drug misusers are found among those who recidivated. However, the numbers were so low that no analysis was conducted of drug misuse in relation to recidivism.

The very low rate of drug misuse in both probation groups indicates that such problems were not an important cause of recidivism. The somewhat higher incidence of drug problems in the PI-group during the first period of non-institutional treatment shows that institutional treatment does not have an inhibitory effect on the consumption of drugs. Like the misuse of alcohol, the misuse of narcotics seems to be most prevalent immediately after institutional treatment, which indicates that institutional treatment instead of assisting the offenders in their readjustment to society contributes to making it more difficult.

Final Comments

It is not possible within the framework of this part of the study to expand the analysis further to find explanations for the differences in recidivism between the two probation groups. It seems probable that the failure of the probation institution to procure meaningful employment and acceptable accommodation for the probationers, contributed to the high recidivism rates among the probationers who had been sentenced to probation with institutional treatment. The fact that alcohol misuse—and to some extent even drug misuse—during the first period of non-institutional treatment was more prevalent among the probationers who had been treated in an institution, than among those who had not, also supports the theory of *negative individual prevention.*

6

Supervision—Assistance or Control?

This chapter describes supervision as it is experienced by the supervisor and the client. This may help us to find out why offenders placed under supervision recidivate to a greater extent than those not placed under supervision even when allowance is made for the poorer prognosis for the former group. The chapter also examines how the legislator's aim of individual prevention is put into practice. Does the supervisor regard supervision as being primarily for assistance or control? Does the client experience supervision as a form of treatment or as punishment?

Aims of Supervision

As was made clear in Chapter 3, the aim of the probation sanction according to the Penal Code is one of individual prevention. As explained in Chapter 1, the legislation on probation can be regarded as a combination of provisions on coercion and provisions on support. In general, supervision is viewed as an offer and the supervisor as a resource. However, the legislator has not analyzed the ends of supervision in relation to its means in any detail.

A clear and precise set of aims for supervision cannot be derived from the legislation or the preparatory discussion which preceded it. The Protective Law Commission contended that probation was a positive form of treatment. The Commission also tried to specify the content of such treatment but these suggestions were not taken up in the Penal Code.

Supervision, according to the Order in Council on Probation (SFS 1964:632), consists of two elements, control and assistance. The control function requires the supervisor to make sure that the offender fulfils his obligations in accordance with the Penal Code or in accordance with any advice or instructions given on the basis of the Penal Code. Support and assistance is to be provided through the supervisor giving assistance and support to the offender to lead a proper and law-abiding life, or—a later formulation (SFS 1973:920)—to facilitate the offenders's adjustment in society.

The aims of supervision are not made any more explicit in the brochure "Instructions for Supervisors" (1964, 1972, 1974), which raises expectations that the supervisor will "succeed" with his work although practical guidelines on how this is to be achieved are minimal. A vague goal combined with superficial instructions and great expectations can well make the supervisor feel insecure and confused. The lack of guidelines can even, theoretically, endanger legal guarantees and protection of basic rights.

Because the existing guidelines for supervision are few and generally formulated, the content and form of supervision becomes largely dependent on the personal qualifications and capabilities of the individual supervisor.

The written information given to the offender at the start of the supervision period informs him that he is required to lead an orderly and law-abiding life, to avoid bad company and in general to follow the instructions given him by the supervision board, the chief probation officer and the supervisor (the statement has since been modified). The notice of supervision also states what is expected from the client during the probationary period, the measures that may be taken with violation of the conditions laid down and what avenues are available to him for changing the conditions of supervision and any instructions given. The offender is urged to contact, and to remain in contact, with the supervisor. On the other hand no indications are given of the supervisor's obligations towards his client nor is there any mention made of the fact that the client may turn to the staff of the chief probation officer for help.

Thus, no clear supervision aims are stated in law, the preparatory work for the law or the formal instructions which are to transmit the norm of individual prevention to the supervisor and client.

Models for the Behavior of Supervisors

There are few theoretical studies on supervisory behavior. An account of some models now follows. These are then linked to some empirical data.

English Studies of Probation

Folkard et al. (1967), who studied probation for the English Home Office, used the psychosocial model outlined in Figure 6.1.

Supervision behavior is seen as a result of the supervisor's social situation and personality. Both influence the supervisor's interpretation of the demands made on him by society and his client. Similarly, the client's behavior is molded by his personality, his social situation, and his perception of his social and personal problems.

Individual treatment is defined as the attempt to exercise a direct effect on the client. Situational treatment refers to attempts to influence the client's social environment. Control is exercised when the supervisor tries to regulate his client's behavior by exhortations and disciplinary measures. Support is given when he tries to solve the client's social or personal problems by taking steps of a material, social, or psychological nature. Folkard combined these components to obtain four types of supervision: individual support, individual control, situational support and situational control. Applying this classification to data derived from case records, the following preliminary results were obtained.

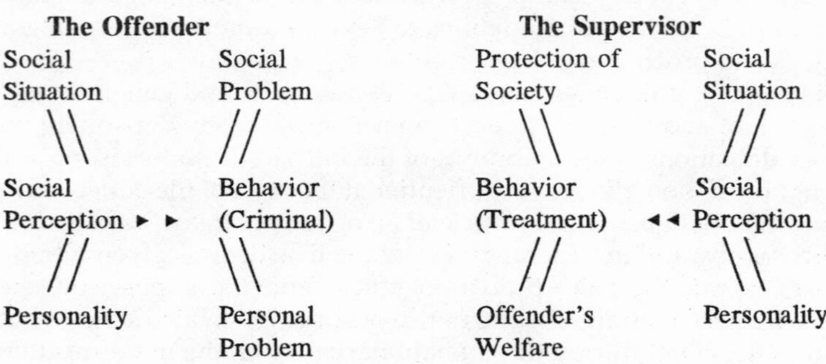

FIGURE 6.1 Conceptualized Relationships in Supervision

Older supervisors and those who were poorly educated were more inclined to use control measures. Supervision which emphasized control, especially situational control, shows the highest proportion of failures. The amount of support the clients received did not affect the outcome of supervision. These results must, however, be interpreted with caution since they are based on retrospective data.

North American Studies of Probation and Parole

Given the historical background of probation we would expect to find that different supervision methods exist (see also Tappan, pp. 564–566). Ohlin et al. (1956), from interviews with all officers in one American state, distinguished three major types of probation and parole officers:

1. The *"punitive officer"*, who defends middle-class morality, tries to force the offender to conform by using threats and punishment. His primary emphasis is on control and his aim is to protect the community from the offender.
2. The *"protective agent"* who fluctuates between the goal of protecting the community and protecting the offender. His instruments are direct assistance, exhortation, praise and blame.
3. The *"welfare worker"* who has the improved welfare of his client as his goal. This is to be achieved by the client's personal adjustment within the bounds of his ability. The community can only be protected by ensuring the client's personal adjustment since outward conformity is only temporary and can, moreover, make successful individual adjustments more difficult.

Glaser (1964) has further developed Ohlin's classification. He added a fourth type, the "political opportunist", also called "the passive officer", who is specific to American circumstances. In addition, Glaser renamed the "protective agent" to the "paternalistic officer". These four ideal types can be regarded as the product of all combinations of the two fundamental variables, assistance and control. The combinations are shown in the model of Figure 6.2.

Glaser found that welfare officers who ranked low on control and high on assistance made up 40% of the American probation and parole officers interviewed (approximately 500 federal parole officers). The paternalistic officers, who were high both on control and assistance, constituted 43% of the sample. The passive officers and the punitive officers, who ranked low on assistance, constituted 8% and 9% respectively of those interviewed.

The welfare officers had the highest proportion with an academic education, the lowest average age and the greatest number of chiefs. The paternalistic group contained the smallest proportion of officers trained in social work but with the longest practical experience of probation work. The passive officers were characterized by superior age and the punitive officers by a lack of academic education and special training.

In general, the sample was characterized by the emphasis placed on assistance—which is probably typical for the American federal system. However, we also find an emphasis on control. This may be because those under supervision were federal prison parolees. Only a very weak correlation between control and assistance was found (gamma = .08). The relative independence of the two scales which measure control and assistance justifies the cross-tabulation of supervision methods to arrive at the typology shown in Figure 6.2.

Scandinavian Studies of Probation and Parole

Hauge (1967) interviewed fifteen supervisors in Oslo, Norway, and found that they unanimously rated material assistance and help in bringing the client to insight into his own behavior as very important. Opinions differed, however, about the importance attached to monitoring client conduct. They considered direct punishment to be ineffective. Using time-studies, Hauge (1970) also found considerable differences in the supervisors' use of time and was able to show that work tasks were given different priorities by different supervisors. Thus, for example, client-supervisor contacts were reported to take from 29% to 54% of the available time. Even if the majority of supervisors agreed on the importance of influencing the client, providing assistance and attending to supervision, they had different opinions on how this should be accomplished. They lacked formulated aims for their work and were aware that the majority of clients held a negative view of supervision and were not willing to discuss their problems with correctional authorities. In addition, the supervisors reported that they suffered from a lack of co-operation with the social services and difficulties in getting disciplinary sanctions enforced within the supervising framework (see also Hauge 1968).

There are naturally certain difficulties associated with the carrying over the Anglo-American models, based as they are on professional probation and parole officers, into the Swedish system where the supervisors are usually vol-

Emphasis on Assistance	Emphasis on Control: Low	Emphasis on Control: High
High	Welfare	Paternal
Low	Passive	Punitive

FIGURE 6.2 Types of Supervisors by Emphasis on Assistance or Control

untary laymen. Nevertheless, Frej (1974) has made certain attempts to adapt her data to Glaser's typology. The findings are based on interviews with 261 supervisors. Frej found that the Swedish supervisors devoted less time to control tasks than their American colleagues. The majority reported that most of their time was spent on practical and psychological problems. Almost all of them are described as fulfilling a practical assistance function. However, certain differences between different categories of supervisors were found concerning the importance of providing personal support. The supervisors who were also social workers assigned considerable importance to this function whilst those who were also policemen emphasized its importance much less.

Skogh (1972) formulated five categories of treatment based on the models of Folkard and Glaser. Using interviews with forty randomly selected supervisors in Lund, Sweden, she attempted to determine whether the supervisors experienced a conflict between the supporting and the controlling aspects of their work. The supervisors were asked to rate the likelihood of being effective in different areas of their clients' lives by responding to four to five questions for each area. Concerning *social support,* the supervisors regarded their prospects of assisting their clients to obtain work, accommodation and financial support as relatively limited. Their prospects of helping their clients with *environmental support* (i.e. to influence them in their leisure interests and help them find new friends) were assessed as even less promising. On the other hand, they considered their chances of providing *individual support* (i.e. to win the client's confidence and discuss his personal problems), as relatively good. They considered their chances of exercising *social control* (i.e.influencing their client's choice of work, accommodation and financial management) to be relatively limited. Their prospects of succeeding in exercising *environmental control* (i.e. influencing their client's leisure activities, choice of friends and use of drugs) were perceived as even slimmer. Thus, with the exception of individual support, the supervisors assessed their possibilities of succeeding with support and control as approximately equally limited.

Skogh found the correlation between support and control measures to be strongly positive (r = .64). She therefore merged all the categories to form one treatment variable. The supervisors who, on the whole, rated the chances of supervision success as favorable were called *treatment optimists.* Those who rated them as unfavorable were called *treatment pessimists.* These groups represent the upper and lower quartiles respectively of the supervisor ratings. The treatment optimists were older, less educated, more active in associations and voluntary organizations, less experienced in probation work and they enjoyed supervising more than the treatment pessimists. The social workers deviated from this trend by showing less treatment optimism. These findings concerning treatment optimists concur with Glaser's description of the social characteristics of the paternalistic officers.

Skogh studied supervisor attitudes using scales measuring authoritarian attitudes, attitudes to control, outlook on social solidarity, attitudes to the chief probation officer and the reporting system, attitudes to friends and the sense of solidarity with individuals. The scatter of the responses was rather large and some of the supervisors' answers were contradictory. It seems likely that they found it difficult to decide what they thought about relatively complicated and abstract statements.

The different subscales were combined to form two main scales: *friendly attitudes* and *authoritarian attitudes.* A grouping of the supervisors according to their mean values on these two variables resulted in a classification similar to Glaser's. The largest group were the authoritarian supervisors (43%). This group corresponds to Glaser's punitive officers. Only 28% of these approved friendly attitudes and repudiated authoritarian ones. The supervisors scoring high on both variables (the paternalistic) and those scoring low on both variables (the passive) each constituted 15% of the sample. Skogh thought it not surprising that a majority held authoritarian views of supervision since this agrees with their official instructions. It is more surprising that 28% repudiated authoritarian attitudes since this means that their treatment ideology to a great extent is opposed to the official ideology. When attitudes were related to the assessments made of likelihood of effective supervision, it was found that the more authoritarian the supervisor's attitude, the more optimistic he was in his assessments of success with the different supervisory tasks. By contrast, treatment pessimists emphasized more such attitudes as co-operation and non-reliance on control and had a negative view of the reporting system. As with Glaser's finding, the authoritarian supervisors were older, less educated and more experienced than the other types of supervisors. There were more police and prison officers among the authoritarian supervisors than among those with friendly attitudes.

The Supervisor's Background, Education and Experience

Description of the Sample

Almost all the supervisors receiving our questionnaire were voluntary laymen who were active with our P and PI sample, in all 176 supervisors and 212 probationers—three supervisors had more than one client. Despite reminders 29% of the supervisors did not reply to the questionnaire. An analysis of their known background variables such as age, profession, etc. showed no differences between them and those replying to the questionnaire. Thus, the supervisor sample would seem to be representative of the population from which it was drawn.

The Supervisor's Social Background

In order to get a better idea of how *representative* the supervisors in our sample were, their attributes are compared with those presented in the "Report on Individual Supervisors in the Correctional System" (Ministry of Justice, Ju 1967:8), in which a sample which was representative of the national supervisor population was studied. Comparisons have been made with certain other studies, some of which stem from other periods or other geographical areas, including as far as possible the results obtained in an experiment with increased non-institutional resources carried out in the Swedish towns of Sundsvall and Karlstad. In this experiment, lay supervisors were interviewed under project circumstances which approximated to the national situation obtaining after a large scale re-organization of the prison and probation systems in 1974.

So far as the *distribution of the sexes* is concerned, men were over-represented. Of 124 supervisors, 90% were men whereas in the Report on Individual Supervisors concerning a national sample 82% were men. However, in the experiment in Sundsvall and Karlstad the proportions of female supervisors were 31% and 16% respectively. This shows that a policy of directed recruitment can change the imbalance (Frej 1974).

The supervisors' *age* seems remarkably high. The average age of our entire sample is about fifty. Only 10% of the supervisors were thirty or younger whereas 70% of the ordinary probationers and 95% of those sentenced to probation with institutional treatment were younger than thirty. In the Report on Individual Supervisors, 10% of all supervisors were under thirty years of age. In later data from Frej, the corresponding proportions were 11% in Sundsvall and 4% in Karlstad. The mean age of the supervisors in both these towns was forty-five. *Civil status* shows a clear over-representation of married supervisors in our sample—90% were married, 5% were divorced, 4% were unmarried and 1% were widowers.

The supervisors' *professions* were classified using information obtained from the chief probation officers. The dominating professions consisted of social workers, police officers and officials employed in state or municipal administration, each group comprising one-fifth of the sample. A smaller category was composed of teachers and, in addition, we found miscellaneous occupations such as professional workers, craftsmen, salesmen and housewives.

Similar results are revealed in other studies. In the Report on Individual Supervisors, 14% of the supervisors were police and 11% were social workers. Frej found the typical profession in both Sundsvall and Karlstad to be police (19% and 16% respectively). The distribution of professions among lay supervisors is clearly limited; the majority were employed by the state or the municipality. Cross-tabulation of the supervisors' professions and ages shows that there were no police officers or other public servants under thirty whilst 26% of the social workers were thirty or less.

There was a wide scatter of *education levels* among the supervisors: 17% had only an elementary education, 30% had attended a vocational training center or an adult education college, 27% had attended a lower secondary school whilst 25% had a university degree or a university education. Very few of the supervisors in Sundsvall and Karlstad had received training in social work or become qualified in a behavioral science. Cross-tabulating education and profession reveals that social workers were the category of supervisors with the highest level of education while the level of the police was usually lower secondary education and, among other public servants and miscellaneous occupations, elementary school or vocational training centers.

The supervisors also are active in some kind of *organization* to a greater extent than the average Swede. Two-thirds of the supervisors in our sample reported that they were members of one or several organizations. In another study which investigated supervisors in Lund, 71% were members of an organization, 43% had some position of responsibility within an association or organization and 25% devoted more than ten hours a month to these positions of responsibility (Jander et al. 1971). Membership in penal reform organizations was noted in only isolated cases. In this study 18% of the supervisors claimed to be total abstainers and 16% reported that they were active in religious organisations.

As many as 40% of the supervisors in our sample had had at least one *municipal responsibility* over and above their ordinary work or profession. In Sundsvall the corresponding proportion was one-third. It was far more common for the supervisors to have had responsibilities on municipal boards and committees in matters not related to social work.

Summarizing, we can say that there were appreciable differences between the supervisors and their clients in all the background variables studied here. The findings correspond well with what has been found in both nationally representative investigations and a number of other studies. From the available studies there appear to be no great differences between supervisors working for the probation service, the temperance organizations and the social services.

Previous Experience of Supervision Work and Current Supervisory Task

Number of Previous Assignments. The distribution of the number of assignments which the supervisors had previously had within the *prison and probation system* was as follows: 28% had had one to four assignments; 27% had had five to ten; 25% had had eleven to thirty and 16% had had from thirty-one to over one hundred assignments. The few women supervisors had had fewer assignments than the male supervisors. A majority of 70% had had less than ten assignments. No woman supervisor had had more than thirty supervision assignments. On cross-tabulating the number of assignments with the supervisors' professions, we find that 51% of the policemen had had more than ten assignments. Of the teachers, two-thirds had had only had one or two assignments.

Half of the probation and parole supervisors had had previous assignments for the *temperance* or *child welfare* administrations. Fifteen percent of the supervisors stated that they had had more than ten assignments for the temperance administration whilst 8% said that they had had more than ten assignments for the child welfare administration.

Caseload in Current Assignments. Of the supervisor respondents in the present study, 71% had one to five cases (with a fairly even distribution over this range) in their current assignments. No supervisor had more than fifteen cases. At the time of the study, 10% of the supervisors had no actual assignment. In addition to these current probation assignments, it is likely that a considerable number of the supervisors had been assigned cases by the social or mental health services.

At the time of this study there were no official recommendations about the number of cases a supervisor should have. In certain districts, however, three to five cases had been informally established in collaboration with the social services as the maximum permitted number. On analyzing the supervisors' current caseload by the different professions, we find that the police officers had the greatest number of cases and teachers the least. As many as 25% of the police had more than five current cases. Among social workers 18% had more than five current cases and 22% had exactly five. In the Report on Individual Supervisors the finding was that 95% of supervisors had from one to five cases. *Summarizing*, we can say that the supervisors in our sample had had a fairly considerable experience of supervision both within the probation and social service fields. In general, they had more current cases in the former field than the latter.

Recruitment and Training of Supervisors

Information Campaigns. Combined recruiting and training courses are arranged both by chief probation officers and by the supervisors' association. Participants for these courses are recruited through *inter alia* announcements placed in the daily newspapers. Attempts have been made to focus recruiting efforts on associations and organizations.

At the time of the present research there were about 10,000 voluntary supervisors working for the probation and parole services. One finding in the Report on Individual Supervisors was that there was a fairly large turnover of supervisors and a questionnaire inquiry showed that one-third of the supervisors were on their first supervision assignment. This suggests that there ought, therefore, to be a possibility of guiding the choice of supervisors through new recruitment. It was also found that one-third of the these supervisors who were on their first assignment at the time of inquiry did not wish to continue working as supervisors.

The committee conducting the inquiry proposed *inter alia* that the fee payable for supervision be increased from 25 to 50 Swedish crowns per month (approximately 3–7 US$). The higher fee, it was argued, would stimulate recruitment and justify making greater demands on the supervisors.

It appeared from the above-mentioned report that a common method of recruitment was to ask the supervisors currently in service to propose a suitable candidate from their circle of friends or colleagues whom they believed would be willing to undertake a supervision assignment. In order to obtain a broader recruiting base the committee of investigation urged the importance of dispelling public ignorance by disseminating information on the correctional services and, in particular, on the aims and work methods of non-institutional treatment.

The Protective Law Commission had also urged information campaigns which the Swedish Prison and Probation Administration considered should be focused on youth organizations in order to broaden recruitment. Thus, the authorities have long been aware of the problems of recruitment and have attempted to improve it without, however, any great success in securing change. No systematic evaluation of the information and recruiting campaigns has been undertaken.

Amount of the Fee for Supervision. Financial compensation, although perhaps not the decisive factor, is nevertheless an important aspect of the recruitment of supervisors. It was decided in Sweden in 1919 that supervisors would be remunerated. Since 1968 the remuneration has been 50 crowns (approximately 7 US$ per month, of which 15 crowns (2 US$) are regarded as reimbursement of expenses in connection with supervision and is not therefore subject to tax. That the remaining part of the remuneration is in principle taxable, and that with the present tax-system the net income from a supervision assignment is in many cases extremely small, has been the subject of criticism. Under certain circumstances such expenditures as extra travelling expenses or lost work income due to the assignment can be reimbursed.

The committee set up in 1973 to plan a radical re-organization of the prison and probation system pointed out that the sum required for a doubling of the supervisors' fee would be sufficient to employ 220 new professional probation workers (SOU 1972:64). It therefore proposed no increase of the supervisors' remuneration but recommended that increased resources be made available to compensate supervisors incurring special expenditures in connection with the their assignment. The Minister of Justice, when presenting new legislation on the prison and probation system, stated that he shared the committee's views (Prop 1973:1, Appendix 4, 128–129).

We found that 52% of supervisors considered the remuneration too little, 41% considered it adequate and 6% thought that it should depend on the degree of difficulty of the cases supervised. No-one thought the sum was too large. Only one-third of the police officers and social workers were satisfied with the present remuneration. It was primarily the supervisors belonging to the category of miscellaneous occupations who were satisfied. It is likely that the amount of the remuneration affects both the breadth of the recruitment base and the composition of the groups which show interest in supervision work.

How and Why People Become Supervisors. To the question of how they became a supervisor for the first time, 60% of the supervisors in this study answered that they were contacted by probation staff. Only 7% made contacted probation staff of their own volition. Five percent of the supervisors reported that they already worked in the prison and probation field. One-quarter obtained their first supervision assignment in some other way. It was primarily social workers, police officers and teachers who were contacted by the chief probation officer's staff at time of first assignment.

To the open question "Why did you become a supervisor?" half of the supervisors replied that they wanted to help their fellow human beings. Twenty-seven percent answered that working with supervision was a consequence of their profession, 8% that they were requested to accept the assignment and 6% that they knew the client. Almost half of the social workers answered that they became supervisors because of their professional calling.

The courts and probation committees appoint supervisors from among the persons who are adjudged suitable by the chief probation officers. This does not exclude the clients themselves from choosing people from these categories as supervisor. These persons may be the only socially established people the client has come in contact with.

To the question of whether the client knew the supervisor prior to the start of supervision, slightly less than one-tenth of the supervisors reported that they knew the client well. The proportion was highest among social workers and teachers. One-third of the supervisors replied that they knew who the client was—here the proportion of police officers is especially large (67%). Overall more than half of the supervisors did not know the client before they accepted the assignment.

To the question whether the client had asked for the person in question to be the supervisor, one-quarter of the supervisors answered that this had been the case. The proportion of affirmative answers was considerably greater among the police officers (50%) and somewhat greater among social workers and teachers than the other categories.

Membership of Supervisor Associations. The associations which were started in the 1960s and which, in general, are common to supervisors from all the different social service fields, arrange courses for both new and experienced supervisors in collaboration with the adult education organizations. They also arrange information meetings where members are given the opportunity to discuss current problems informally.

Forty-three percent of respondents said that they were or had been members of a supervisor association. Membership in these organizations was more common among the police officers (54%) than among the other professional categories. Since the older supervisors were more often members than the younger officers (56% of the supervisors aged group 61–70 were members of associations as compared with 23% of those under 30 years of age), the age factor could provide an explanation for the large proportion of members among the police.

Among the supervisors who were or had been members of a supervisor association, as many as 83% thought that the association had been helpful to them in their work.

The Training of Supervisors. What training do the supervisors receive for their work? As was mentioned earlier, each supervisor receives a copy of "Instructions for Supervisors" which is distributed by the Swedish Prison and

Probation Administration. In it, the supervisors' duties are described in broad outline. The Administration also provides training programs which take up subjects considered useful for supervisors, e.g. supervision practice, work of the employment bureaux, social service assistance and alcohol and drug problems. Many supervisors had already gained knowledge of some of these subjects through their professional activities but this could not be expected of the majority of newly recruited supervisors.

We also studied to what extent the supervisors had participated in some form of training for supervision including in this their own professional training, for example, in social work. Of the questionnaire respondents, 55% stated that they had taken part in some form of training for supervisors. A large proportion of police officers (54%) had not taken part in any form of training.

In the Report on Individual Supervisors it was stated that 31% of the supervisors had taken part in some form of training. This suggests that a certain improvement had taken place by the time the present research was conducted. Since as many as 45% of the supervisors studied here had not taken part in any training courses for supervisors, it was hardly surprising that 59% expressed a desire for supervision training. In the heterogeneous group of miscellaneous occupations, the proportion was as great as 73%. But the police officers, who had participated to the least extent in training for supervisors, had the lowest proportion desiring additional training (50%). Supervisors can be given information by the chief probation officer about the carrying out of their assignment. One-quarter of the supervisors in this study reported, however, that they did not receive any instructions from their chief probation officer.

Thus, despite a narrow recruitment of supervisors, a large proportion had not received any special training for supervision work. The re-organisation of the prison and probation systems which was undertaken in 1974 involved a considerable increase in the number of professional probation staff and hopefully will lead to a greater investment in the recruitment and training of voluntary supervisors.

The Supervisor's View of the Probation Services and Crime Prevention

There are several reasons why the supervisors' views on non-institutional treatment should be studied. Through their supervision experience they have obtained a special insight into the way in which probation functions. Their views of the prison and probation system and the resources available for their work may at the same time be provide insights into the way in which the various supervisor groups assess this part of the public sector. Moreover, we may expect their attitudes towards their own work to affect their actions in a variety of practical situations. Their view of individual prevention also tells us something about their degree of treatment optimism which in its turn can guide their own behavior.

The supervisors answered questions about their opinions of the aims of supervision, the resources available for non-institutional treatment, their personal experiences of supervision, what they would like to change in supervision work and their views on Swedish criminal policy. We also asked for their views on the individual and general preventive effects of supervision.

Questions and Answers About Aims

The majority of supervisors believed that the offender must, in some way, become more integrated in society and that the supervisor should assist him in this process of adjustment. Examples of answers to a question on aims were: "The client will become law-abiding and useful to society in his life-style", "Getting the client to accept society's norms", "Integrating the client into society as a competent citizen", "Social adjustment and coping satisfactorily like the rest of us; making the client willing to work".

To a follow-up question about whether the supervisors believed that there were resources available to attain the aims of supervision, 51% answered "yes" and 43% "no", while 6% left the question unanswered. The supervisors who only had one or two supervision assignments thought that the resources were insufficient to a greater extent than other supervisors (66%).

When asked to say in what way they considered that resources were available or lacking there was an interesting difference in the aspects emphasized between the affirmative and negative answers. Those who believed that *resources were available* concentrated primarily on the micro-relationship between the supervisor and the offender. They called attention to the *supervisor's individual resources* such as his personality and ability and emphasized the importance of altruism, engagement, perseverance together with the supervisor's contacts and connections.

Those who believed that *resources were not available* for reaching the aims of supervision, pointed to the macro-level conditions such as a lack of *community resources*. They emphasized the difficulty of getting work and accommodation, solving financial problems and hostile or indifferent community attitudes.

The Resources Available for Non-Institutional Treatment

A direct question put to supervisors was whether they considered the resources of non-institutional treatment to be sufficient or insufficient. As many as 73% said that they thought the resources were insufficient, only 13% believed them to be sufficient whilst 12% left the question unanswered. Of the twenty supervisors who had more than thirty probation or parole assignments, only one thought that resources were sufficient.

Among the spontaneous comments to this question primary emphasis was given to complaints about financial and staff resources. Other criticisms refer to the difficulty of finding time for supervision, the lack of adequate and conscious treatment planning, the lack of treatment facilities and the difficulty associated with getting assistance from the various social agencies.

The supervisors who considered the resources of non-institutional treatment to be *sufficient* had only vague justifications for their views, e.g. belief in "the right person for the job" and "teamwork".

Satisfaction with Supervision Work

A direct question was put to them about how satisfying they found supervision work. Altogether 59% found the work satisfying and of this group 9% found it extremely so. Twenty-seven percent expressed no clear opinion whilst 14% stated that they found the work unsatisfying.

The police officers experienced their supervision work as satisfying to a greater extent than others (67%), while social workers felt dissatisfied (26%) to a greater extent than others. The degree of satisfaction felt in work is partly a function of the expectations entertained. It seems likely that the social workers have greater treatment expectations than the police officers and therefore experience a sense of failure to a greater extent when the client's adjustment in society does not succeed.

Difficulties of Supervision

Many different problems were revealed in the responses to an open question concerning what the supervisors experience as the most difficult part of their work.

Difficulties which related to *the offender's social situation* included alcohol, obtaining work, procuring accommodation and meaningfully occupying leisure time.

Among the difficulties about the *relationship between supervisor and client* was the general psychological problem of contact, of establishing a feeling of trust between supervisor and client, in motivating the client and getting him to want something, of travelling over long distances, in contacting the client and fears that the client would relapse into crime.

Difficulties which related to the *community in general and authorities in particular* included poor co-operation with social service agencies, the lack of financial resources, unsatisfactory contact with the police and lack of psychologists or doctors to provide support. Other problems mentioned included a clash of loyalty as between the client and society, massmedia denigrations, the overly severe demands made on the offender by the supervision boards and lack of understanding on the part of the community.

Reform Suggestions

The supervisors were asked if they wanted to change supervision in any way and, if so, to specify what they would like changed. Thirty-one percent answered that they did not want to change anything and a further 5% left the question unanswered. The remaining 64% wanted to see changes.

Some of the problems, such as the collaboration between authorities and individual supervisors and the lack of economic and staff resources, have already been discussed. Other things which they wanted to change may be illustrated by the following quotations: "Better contact between supervisor and the authorities—not least the police who fail to inform us when a client is taken into custody", "Half of the probationary period ought to be abolished and the client helped instead", "The duty to report should be changed", "The client, not only the supervisor, should report problems to the chief probation officer", "Prejudice against having an offender in a municipal or public service". Several of these suggestions seem well-founded and worthy of consideration. Social workers and teachers made the most suggestions and the police and other professions made least. There was a tendency for those with many case assignments not to make reform suggestions while those with few assignments more often made several.

Attitude to Swedish Criminal Policy

Supervisors were asked if they were, on the whole, satisfied with Swedish criminal policy. A slight majority—51%—stated that they were not satisfied, 44% declared that they were fairly or completely satisfied and 5% left the question unanswered.

The teachers and social workers were dissatisfied with Swedish criminal policy to a greater extent than other professional groups. The younger supervisors expressed the greatest discontent. Two-thirds of supervisors under forty expressed dissatisfaction.

The Supervisor's View of Crime Prevention

To the question "Do you believe that supervision can keep a person from committing new offenses?", 58% answered "yes", 25% "no" and 15% said that they did not know. The question posed is a leading one yet there is only a relatively weak majority expressing belief in the individual preventive effect of supervision. The trend is for the more experienced supervisor to perceive possibilities of supervision more positively. Thus, among the ten supervisors who had had more than 51 assignments, all believed that supervision could prevent the commission of new offenses.

Another question was: "Imagine that your client had no supervisor during the probationary period. How do you think he would manage?" Sixty percent of the supervisors answered that they believed their client would not make out as well as with a supervisor, 35% believed he would manage just as well and 5% that he would manage better.

The proportion of supervisors who believed that supervision can keep a person from committing new offenses was thus almost the same as the proportion who thought that their client would not manage as well without a supervisor (58% and 60% respectively). Such a pattern of answers indicates a certain degree of reliability. However, we should note that the latter question referred to a specific client and that the answers could be expected to be influenced by the way in which this client was coping during the probation period, which in turn may result in differences in the individual answers. In substance, we can discern a prevailing uncertainty as to the effectiveness of supervision as a tool in criminal policy.

To the question "Do you believe that people are kept from committing crime because others are punished?", 27% answered "yes", 59% "no" and 11% that they did not know. Thus, only a minority of supervisors seem to embrace a general prevention theory as formulated in the question.

Those with the greatest confidence in general prevention were the police officers (42%). Teachers and civil servants show the least amount of confidence (0% and 20% respectively). The social workers responded with the largest number of "don't know" answers (26%) (none of the police officers expressed any doubt). Those with less education tended to dissociate themselves to a greater extent from the notion of general prevention. Similarly, the older supervisors tended to believe in general prevention theory to a lesser extent than the younger supervisors. There is covariance between education and age such that the older supervisors are generally the less educated. Ek and Hultén (1971, 1975) theorizing that the general prevention ideology is part of an acknowledged system of norms embraced by the upper strata of society, expected for this reason to find such a relationship.

The greatest agreement was found between those who believed neither in the individual nor in the general preventive effect of supervision. Of those agreeing with general prevention, a majority believe that supervision has an individual preventive effect. On the other hand, a majority of those who believe in the individual preventive effect of supervision, do not believe in general prevention. Thus, considerably more supervisors express confidence in the individual preventive effect of supervision than in general prevention.

Summarizing Comments

Roughly speaking, we can divide the supervisors into two main groups. Somewhat more than half thought there were resources available for attaining the aims of supervision, were satisfied with supervision work, were on the whole pleased with Swedish criminal policy and believed in the individual preventive effect of supervision. It was chiefly the police officers and the older supervisors who were satisfied with these aspects of the present system. The social workers and the younger supervisors were the most critical. The professional social workers were to a greater extent young and highly educated.

The results of our study seem to correspond well with Ohlin's and Glaser's *models for the behavior of supervisors.* The largest group of supervisors may be described as protective or paternalistic and the next largest as welfare supervisors. It seems, however, that the protective supervisor has something of the punitive officer's "middle-class morality" while the welfare supervisor is somewhat less of a diagnostician than the supervisors in the American theoretical models. We find, just as Glaser did, that the protective supervisors were the less educated and, in particular, lacked training in social work. However, they were well experienced in practical supervision work. The social worker category of supervisors had more often an academic education than the other categories and they were younger. Furthermore, we found, in conformity with Skogh, that the treatment optimists and the authoritarian supervisors were poorly educated compared with the other groups of supervisors and that they were older and more experienced than the other types. A large proportion of these supervisors were police officers.

Double Loyalty

In this section, a description of the supervisor's loyalty conflicts is used to further illustrate the previously outlined models for the behavior of supervisors.

Analysis of the Loyalty Conflict

The supervisor must on the one hand represent society and its established norms, and, on the other hand, stand at the side of the offender and safeguard his interests. Having a position midway between the probation agency and the client, the supervisor risks coming into a conflict situation which can jeopardize his chances of fulfilling the aims of supervision. It is this situation and its ensuing difficulties that one of the supervisors referred to as "the double loyalty one feels towards society and client".

Gordan writes in a handbook for supervisors (1967): "If the supervisor is to convince his client of the value of social adjustment and the possibility of liking and trusting a socially well-adjusted person, he must be able to represent society in the way we want the client to learn to see it" (p. 92). The word "we" in this quotation suggests that Gordan identifies with the control policy of the state and that he proceeds from unitary social values, taking it for granted that the supervisor will do the same. Further, Gordan stresses that: "Loyalty towards the probation agency is a prerequisite for the agency to take the risk of relying upon the supervisor and entrusting him with a mission for which the agency remains entirely responsible." But at the same time he points out that "loyalty towards the client is a prerequisite for his trusting the supervisor and being willing to co-operate with him" (p. 92). Nevertheless, Gordan does not seem to think that these conflicting demands present any real problem: "Even if these demands for loyalty can occasionally constitute a conflict for the supervisor, they should not prove irreconcilable in the long run" (p. 92).

These quotations illustrate the supervisor's central problem. Can he reconcile the demands for control and support? Many experts maintain that the two aims of supervision are incompatible and that a conflict of loyalty is therefore inevitable. Comprehensive sociological research has demonstrated how difficult it is to combine punishment and treatment (see, for example, Galtung 1961; Cressey 1961). Others, like Gordan, contend that control and support are not incompatible. To the extent that the supervisor eliminates support and keeps exclusively to the control aspect of his work, he will obviously experience no conflict. The same holds if he re-defines support to include control. Because the concepts are vague, they invite such shifts in meaning.

As mentioned earlier, the supervisor, according to the Order in Council on Non-Institutional Treatment, is required to undertake control and support functions. The control function is specified in detail and is, moreover, the only thing that can be supervised. This means that the supervisor formally fulfils his obligations if he meets the demands raised by the control aspect of his work by maintaining contact with the offender and reporting on this contact to the chief probation officer.

The instructions concerning the support function are unclear and incomplete. Within the broad framework of the directives, the supervisor is forced to set up his own aims for supervision and to define the means of attaining them. To the extent that the supervisor is uncertain about what the expectations of the authorities require, and to the extent that he is subjected to different expectations and demands from his client, he may feel unsure about how he should act and thereby come into a conflict situation.

I showed in Chapter 2 that the double purpose of supervision is reflected in the form and content of the organisation. The formal structure (i.e. the Swedish Prison and Probation Administration, the supervision boards and the chief probation officers) is responsible for the control function, while the more informal structure (the voluntary supervisors) supplies the support function.

Seen historically, non-institutional treatment has its roots in relief work largely based on voluntary efforts. This has been maintained in the continued policies which treat individual involvement on an idealistic basis as more or less essential for the realization of non-institutional treatment. Belief in the significance of idealism is reflected in, *inter alia,* the supervisor's poor financial recompense for his work.

As a rule, the voluntary supervisors work outside the formal administration and are relatively isolated. They experience the both the demands of the administration to act in its interests just as they experience the demands of the client to safeguard his interests. In certain situations a conflict between the interests of society and the client can or must ensue. It is in this structural context that the loyalty conflict should be seen.

Double Loyalty Issues

Despite the semantic difficulties which arise we have nevertheless tried to construct some questions which could illuminate the loyalty conflict. These questions will also be dealt with later in connection with the comparisons drawn between separate pairs of supervisors and clients.

The Supervisor's Position Between the Administration and the Client. A first question was: "How do you experience your position as a supervisor? Do you consider that you are primarily on the side of your client or primarily on the side of the chief probation officer and the supervision board?"

A majority of 70% reported that they considered themselves to be on the side of the client and only 7% answered that they were on the side of the administration. In addition to these responses 12% claimed that they were on both sides and a further 8% made other comments to the question or gave other types of answer. In terms of profession, the client-alternative was most common among social workers (89%) and least common among police officers (58%). Public servants and those with miscellaneous occupations answered somewhat more often that they were on the side of the chief probation officer and the supervision board. None of the supervisors aged 31–40 were on the side of the chief probation officer and supervision board.

To the normative question "What position do you think a supervisor *should* take, should he be on the side of the client or on that of the chief probation officer and the supervision board?" a somewhat smaller number of supervisors than was found with the previous question answered "on the side of the client" (61% as opposed to 70%). The same proportion of supervisors answered "on the side of the chief probation officer and supervision board" with both questions, namely 7%. However, a greater number of supervisors constructed their own alternative—"on both sides" (19%)—or gave other answers (10%) to the latter question. Thus, as many as one-third responded with other kinds of answers than the given alternatives or abstained altogether from answering the question.

The simplified formulations used cannot entirely explain the obvious difficulties the supervisors had in answering the questions. The displacement in the distribution of answers between the two questions suggests something of the nature of the loyalty conflict. A certain discrepancy exists between the supervisor's personal attitude and the way in which he perceives the norm for the same behavior. There is also some uncertainty in the perception of the norm, i.e. varying expectations as to whose interest the supervisor should represent. The answers give scant support to Gordan's theory that the seemingly incompatible demands become reconciled over time.

Reporting on and Giving Information to the Client. Another question which touches on the double loyalty issue is whether the supervisors consider it their duty to report all that they know about client misconduct to the chief probation officer. While 20% of the supervisors did consider it their duty to report everything, 77% did not. Even if the question is generally formulated and does not necessarily tell us anything about the supervisor's actual behavior, the distribution of answers clearly demonstrates that the supervisors are more inclined to see themselves as the client's defender than as his prosecutor.

The same picture also emerges from other research. In a study of supervisors in Lund, 77% said they did not report all the client's misconduct to the chief probation officer (Jander *et al.*, p. 43). The researchers point out that the misconduct concerned was of such serious nature that it came to the attention of the authorities in any case since it included offenses reported to the police or actual prosecution.

In another study of professional probation officer attitudes, 79% rejected a statement that supervisors are morally bound to report the offenses which their clients relate to them (Hagström et al. 1971). This negative attitude to the obligation to report was expressed primarily by ordinary probation officers not holding chief positions, that is, by those with an academic degree, women officers, those who had not been on the job for very long and those who worked in big cities.

The answers given seem to well illustrate the supervisor's loyalty conflicts. In their desire to protect the client's interests the majority of supervisors appear even to misinterpret society's demands concerning their obligation to report on their client's (mis)behavior. They seem also to be supported in this by professional working probation officers.

The supervisors asserted that they found it difficult to work together with the client in a relationship built on mutual trust if they were seen by the client as "spies". The majority of supervisors feel that the role of friend and confidant is incompatible with the obligation to report on the client's misbehavior.

Should the Client Read the Supervision Report? One way to lessen what the client experiences as "secretiveness" and thereby preserve good relations, would be to allow the client to read the supervision report before it is sent to the chief probation officer. Supervisors were asked what they thought of this proposal. Sixty-one percent agreed with it whilst 37% did not. Thus although supervisors are divided on this test of open co-operation a majority believe that the client should be given an opportunity which is usually denied him. Certain changes have taken place in this respect during recent years but, according to the probation staff in Malmö the majority of supervisors still keep their reports to themselves. The answers to our question clearly demonstrate the existence of a loyalty conflict.

The teachers, social workers and police officers thought that the client should be given the opportunity to read the supervision report to a greater extent than the public servants and other occupational categories (75% and 49% respectively). The former groups presumably take a more professional stance on the writing of reports. That police officers expressed liberal ideas in this matter is probably because they are well accustomed with the right of suspects to read their reports and that preferably suspects should always do so.

Thirty-eight percent of the supervisors who only had an elementary school education thought that the client should be allowed to read the report but this proportion reaches 78% among the supervisors with an academic degree.

There is covariance between the answers to this question and age in that the supervisors aged 35 or less take the most positive view of this proposal (86%).

The Client's Right to Participate in the Decision-Making Process. The last question dealt with participation in the supervision relationship. The question reads: "Do you think the client should take part in the making of decisions which concern supervision?". Thirty-seven percent of the supervisors answered "Yes, in all such decisions", 51% answered "Yes, in certain of such decisions" and 9% answered "No, not at all". Thus, the supervisors' responses vary from just over one-third who were willing to give the client the right of participation in all questions to slightly less than one-tenth who did not want him to have any say at all in decision-making.

Teachers and social workers had the most positive attitude to giving the client the right of participation and the category of miscellaneous occupations the most negative. Police officers and public servants come in between these two extremes.

Final Comments. Double loyalty seems to be a truly experienced reality for the supervisors. The majority of supervisors took the clients' part but at the same time had doubts about allowing them insight into, and control of, supervision. But the supervisors are not a homogeneous group. Their attitudes to the issues dealt with here have been related to background variables such as profession, education and age. Throughout we can see a trend for the supervisors with better education and lower age to be more inclined to give the client more participation possibilities and to dissociate themselves from the formal requirements of their work. Just as in the previous section, we find that social workers are the most, and police the least, client-oriented professional category.

The Association Between Control and Support in Supervisor Behavior

We have earlier seen that Glaser found no relation between the controlling and supporting behavior of American federal professional parole officers. On the other hand, Skogh found a fairly strong positive relationship between control and support in the attitudes of Swedish voluntary lay supervisors working with probationers. The difference in the findings from these two studies may be explained either by the varying degree of supervisor professionalism or the varying degree of severity of the offenses committed by the supervised offenders or by both factors. The explanation may also be that Glaser measured behavior and Skogh measured attitudes. Nor can the possibility that chance factors played some part be excluded, not least in the small sample of supervisors studied by Skogh.

The attempt has also been made in the present study to investigate the relationship between control and support as exercised by the supervisors. Great difficulties are associated with operationalizing the concepts in an unambiguous way so that they can be compared with earlier studies. Probably, more satisfying measures have been obtained for control than for support. *Support* has been defined more in psychological terms as whether the supervisor has confidence in the client, whether the supervisor considers himself to be on the client's side or believes that the client perceives the supervisor to be on his side.

A *control index* was created with four questions which asked the supervisor if he checked whether his client was diligent so far as work was concerned, what his client did in his leisure time, how his client managed his finances and whether his client used alcohol. By simply adding the number of "yes" answers, several response categories of approximately equal size were obtained for ascertaining the number of supervisors answering "yes" to none, one, two three or all four of these items.

This study shares with earlier studies the weakness of only focusing on the *supervisor's* answers about the control and support aspects of supervision. By not including the clients' assessments of these aspects certain sources of error may have been introduced. We shall return to this matter later.

It should be said at once that we did *not* find any statistically significant association between the various measures of control and the various measures of support. Such trends as we were able to discern will, however, be indicated.

Not surprisingly there is some covariance on several variables between the supervisors who control their client and those who lack confidence in their clients. Those who control their client to a greater extent than other supervisors feel that they are on the side of the chief probation officer. However, these supervisors believe that the clients perceive them as being on the clients' side. The supervisors who use only limited or no control consider themselves to be on the client's side but believe that the client perceives them to be on the side of the administration. This seemingly paradoxical result can probably be explained by the fact that the controlling supervisors are, to a greater extent than other supervisors, treatment optimists. As we saw earlier, treatment optimists are characterized by long experience, less education and a somewhat authoritarian attitude. In this category we find the paternalistic supervisor who, to a high degree, assumes a "middle-class philosophy" and has greater difficulty in objectively placing himself in the client's situation. The more professional social worker takes a stand for the client but at the same time realizes that despite this the client is suspicious of the help he can offer.

Another index, which was also presumed to measure a dimension of control, even if less rigorously, used questions about whether the supervisor had had any *contact* with the client's family, parents, employer and teachers. This index also produced a relatively good dispersion of answers over the different values. We find here that the supervisor who makes many such contacts harbors a somewhat greater trust for his client. As this finding suggests, we might logically expect this index of control to be more intermingled with support than the previous index which concentrated purely on control. This latter finding also shows that the previous result, where a relationship was found between control and lack of trust, cannot be explained by the client having greater handicaps. Such a handicap factor could be expected to show an association between "many contacts" and "inferior trust", which is not the case. However we find, as we did earlier, that the supervisors who contacted many people in the client's surroundings considered themselves to be on the side of the administration although this relationship is very weak. On the other hand, there is an almost significant association between "many contacts" linked to a belief that the client perceives the supervisor as being on his side and "few contacts" linked to a belief that the client sees the supervisor as standing on the side of the administration. Thus, we find the same result as we did in the case of the pure control question, i.e. that controllers are treatment optimists. As we shall see later, they also misinterpret the client's attitude.

The various questions on control show covariance in a way that can be expected if they are more or less reliable. The supervisors who believe they are on the side of the administration think, for example, that it is their duty always to report on their client to the chief probation officer. We also find a relationship between checking on the client in various ways or between contacting people in his surroundings and meeting the client more often or taking a little more time with him. This finding might possibly be interpreted to mean that even the meetings between client and supervisor have a controlling character. Another interpretation is that the more active supervisors contact both the client and people in his surroundings to a greater extent than the less active supervisor irrespective of whether the contact is made with the aim of checking on the client or not.

We stress, however, that all the relationships found are very weak. Therefore, we could say with Glaser that we did not find a simple connection between control and support. In some cases there is a weak negative association and in others a weak positive association. Thus, we do not find support for Skogh's conclusion that the relationship between control and support is strongly positive.

The trends we can discern in our data, then, are that the controllers have less confidence in the client and that they believe that the client perceives them to be on his side. The supervisors who control less have a more realistic perception of the clients' assessment of their position. Among the controllers we find the protectively-minded supervisors who are older and have longer experience but shorter training than the other supervisor types. Among those who control less, we find the supervisors who were earlier classified as welfare workers; they are younger, less experienced and have gone through longer training.

The above analysis shows how difficult it is to base judgments of the way in which the control and support aspects of supervision are in fact perceived by clients solely on the responses of the supervisors. We continue, therefore, with a dyadic analysis in which the supervisors' and clients' answers are related to each other.

Dyadic Analysis of Supervisors and Clients

Even if the supervisors' social backgrounds and attitudes are of great importance it must be remembered that supervision consists of an *interplay* between supervisor and client. An analysis of this interaction is therefore essential in order to discover what prerequisites exist for a meaningful dialogue.

In general we may say that greater similarity between supervisor and client concerning background variables and attitudes leads, at least up to a certain point, to better possibilities for good *communication.* If their understanding of one another increases, the possibility of exercising *influence* probably increases also. The opposite is also true—the greater the differences, the more limited are the possibilities of communication and the exercising of influence. These general laws of social psychology have been shown to be valid in a variety of situations (Krech et al. 1962).

In the following *dyadic or pairwise analysis,* each supervisor's responses are compared with those of his client. Through these pairs of respondents (*dyads*), we can analyze the supervision process simultaneously from both the supervisor's and the client's perspective. The questions put to supervisors referred to a named client. The replies to identical questions given by supervisors and their clients were cross-tabulated dyadically on several variables. Because the groups were relatively small, statistical measures of association have not been calculated.

Lack of space prevents the presentation of the original tables. In the majority of cases, however, there are illuminating differences between the two groups even in the *marginal* frequencies. On occasion percentage agreements between the dyadic values will be presented as a supplement to the frequencies.

Description of Sample

For various reasons, 51% of the 212 *clients* making up our research population did not reply to the questionnaire used. But reckoning non-response only among those who in fact received our questionnaire reduces the proportion of dropouts to 42%. (At least three attempts, and often considerably more because of changes of address, were made to reach clients.) Since contacting persons who are under supervision or who have completed supervision or reminding them of their sentence can be ethically doubtful, we could not consider disturbing them further.

A comparison between responding and non-responding clients on background variables taken from the case records show no differences, however, between the two groups—not even in such important variables as age, total risk points and seriousness of all offenses. The only differences which could be determined apply to recidivism itself. This is somewhat greater in the dropout group in which a larger proportion had had their sentences revoked and been subjected to sanctions depriving them of their liberty (15% difference). The latter situation can be seen as a factor which made their participation more difficult or caused diminished interest in our study. Despite the large dropout the sample seems to represent the parent population fairly well.

In our dyadic analysis we proceed from a sample of eighty-one pairs of supervisors and their clients. When we compared the distribution of answers for the total study sample of one hundred and four clients with the eighty-one clients from the dyads, we found that throughout the differences were at most a few percent in the individual answer categories. On further checking to see if there are any differences between the P-group and the PI-group no real differences between the two groups emerge.

A similar comparison was made between the one hundred and four supervisors in the total sample and the eighty-one in the dyads. The differences in the answer distributions were seldom more than a few percent. The extra amount of missing data—inevitable with dyadic analysis—does not seem to have involved any loss of representativity for the dyadic sample.

Over and above what these statistical analyses tell us, it might be said that the clients in the dyadic study possibly constitute a positive sample of offenders since their rate of recidivism is somewhat lower. It may be that the supervisors too constitute a positive sample if we make the assumption that the more authoritarian supervisors tend to refrain from taking part in a scientific investigation (see, for example, Adorno et al. 1950).

Age Comparisons Between Supervisors and Clients

Age is an important background variable because it is an expression of different experiences and is related to different attitudes. We have already observed the importance of the age variable for the supervisors' attitudes and ideas.

Factual Age Differences. As mentioned earlier, the median age of the supervisors was fifty. For the offenders in the dyad group it was twenty-seven. Two-thirds of the offenders were thirty or younger but this is true of less than every tenth supervisor. The difference in age between the supervisors and their clients is not only a statistical fact but also socially significant. The difference is a whole generation.

Because the gap in ages between the two groups is so great, there can scarcely be correspondence between paired individuals. Seven supervisors who were under thirty had clients who belonged to the same age group but the majority of clients under thirty had, of course, supervisors who were considerably older.

Preferred Age Differences. The offenders were asked what age they would prefer their supervisors to have. Only 9% of the clients said that supervisors ought to be over fifty although 47% had a supervisor who was in this age range. The most preferred age for supervisors lay between thirty and thirty-nine years (suggested by 37% of the clients). But only 17% had a supervisor in this age group. Seventeen percent of the clients wanted a supervisor who was thirty or younger. Only 9% had a supervisor in this age range. As we might expect, the client's dissatisfaction increases with the age of his supervisor. It might be said that while the client had as a rule a supervisor who could be his father, he wished instead to have a supervisor who could be his elder brother.

The age differences between supervisor and client are so great that it would be impossible with the present recruiting situation to comply with the clients' wishes. The fact that the clients were not only considerably younger than their supervisors but also wished that their supervisors were much younger, suggests that there is not only a factual generation gap between the two groups but also that this is perceived and experienced as creating an oppositional and difficult relationship.

The supervisor-client relationship often includes a superior-inferior relationship and the age difference probably accentuates this further. The risk is thereby increased that the supervisor will be experienced as a guardian. This probably makes the development of a trusting relationship between partners who are to a certain extent on an equal footing more difficult. Yet such a relationship seems to be one of the conditions for supervision to be effective.

Interaction Between Supervisor and Client

Frequency of Contact During First and Last Year of Supervision. The handbook "Instructions for Supervisors" states that the need for contact is greater at the beginning of supervision than later since the supervisor and client must get to know one another and there may be various practical problems to solve. Thus, it may be a question of one or more contacts per week in the beginning but no more than once or twice per month later in the supervision period.

Supervisors and clients were asked to say approximately how often they met during the first and most recent years of supervision. Table 6.1 shows that 24% of the supervisors and 21% of their clients reported meeting once weekly or more often during the *first year of supervision.*

If the statement in "Instructions for Supervisors" can be considered a recommendation, then only a minority of supervisors live up to its somewhat vaguely formulated norm. The median meeting frequency stated by supervisors was once every three weeks whilst their clients asserted it to be once a month. Excluding the missing data from the supervisors makes the median frequency once every two weeks. Substantially more of the clients than the supervisors answered that they met once every second, third or sixth month, sporadically or never during the first year.

Contact between supervisor and client is a prerequisite for treatment and it is reasonable to think that a supervisor would need to meet his client several times a month initially in order to produce any positive results. Because the first period is generally considered to be the most difficult, the frequency of contact reported by the supervisors must be regarded as low. According to the clients, the majority of them meet a supervisor at most once a month during the first period of supervision when the meetings may be seen as being more of controlling than supportive character.

Supervisors as well as their clients reported that they met less often during the final year than during the first year of supervision. Fifty-five percent of the supervisors and 46% of the clients stated that meetings took place once a month or more often (corresponding figures for the first year of supervision were 70% and 57% respectively). Thus, while the supervisors report a greater contact frequency than their clients for the first year, this difference decreases during the final year.

Desired Contact Frequency. Supervisors and their clients were asked if they wanted to meet more often, about as often or less often than they in fact do. Two-thirds of both groups stated that they were satisfied with meeting as often as they did. Among the remaining one-third, a majority of the supervisors would like to meet more often and a majority of the clients would like to meet less often. This latter finding could be interpreted as indicating that the clients, to some extent, want as little contact as possible but feel forced to have contact with their supervisor while the supervisor is more keen to maintain contact in order to carry out his task satisfactorily.

Duration of Contact. One question dealt with the length of time that meetings usually take. As Table 6.2 shows, 13% of the supervisors and 31% of the clients reported a duration of fifteen minutes or less. Forty-two percent of the supervisors and 37% of their clients reported meetings lasting half-an-hour. We find that the greatest time difference concerns the very short periods: 2% of the supervisors and 19% of their clients claimed that they met for less than

TABLE 6.1 Frequency of Contact during First and Last Years of Supervison According to Supervisors and Clients (percentages)

	First Year		Last Year	
Response	Supervisor	Client	Supervisor	Client
Daily	4	6	0	0
Once/week	20	15	10	10
Once/2 weeks	22	15	11	7
Once/3 weeks	10	4	12	7
Once/month	14	17	22	22
Once/2 months	4	9	10	12
Once/3 months	1	11	4	7
Once/6 months	0	4	2	5
When necessary	2	0	0	0
Sporadically	1	11	0	0
Other	0	0	16	12
Never	0	6	11	14
Missing data	22	2	1	2

TABLE 6.2 Duration of Contact According to Supervisor and Client (percentages)

	Time Supervisor and Client Meet	
Response	Supervisor	Client
Less than 15 minutes	2	19
15 minutes	11	12
30 minutes	42	37
1 hour	25	15
1-2 hours	7	9
2-3 hours	1	0
More than 3 hours	0	0
Other answer	9	9
Missing data	2	0

fifteen minutes. Meetings which take 15 minutes or less probably do little for the client in the way of treatment but could instead be said to have the character of fulfilling the client's duty to be there. Even for a superficial discussion of personal problems 30 minutes must be considered a minimum. But the majority of supervisors and clients responded they met for half-an-hour at most. This suggests that the meetings in a large number of cases had a controlling rather than a supportive function.

Initiation of Contact. If the contact is to seem natural both partners ought to be able to initiate a meeting. Table 6.3 shows that 72% of the supervisors and 52% of their clients consider that their meetings *ought* to function in this way. On the other hand, only 46% of the supervisors and 38% of their clients report that the two parties *in fact* initiate meetings equally often.

The supervisors report that it was considerably more common for them to initiate contact than the clients. But the clients claim that they took the initiative somewhat more often than their supervisors. Among those who do not think that supervisors and clients should initiate meetings equally often, a majority of supervisors consider it to be the client's responsibility while a majority of clients believe it to be the supervisor's responsibility. The of agreement in this response pattern points to a fundamental problem in the communication process.

The notice of supervision which the client receives at the beginning of the supervision period informs him of his duty to keep in contact with his supervisor. He is not, however, informed of his supervisor's obligation to keep in contact with him. Consequently, the fact that as many as one-fifth of the clients actually believe that they alone ought to initiate contact with their supervisor can partly be explained by the information received initially by the client.

The Factual and the Desired Place of Meeting. According to the "Instructions for Supervisors" it is impossible to provide general recommendations about the place for the meetings between the supervisor and client but the supervisor must ensure that his contact with his client does not lead to unauthorized persons finding out that the client has been placed under supervision.

Asked where they usually meet, 40% of the supervisors replied that the meetings took place in their own home or at their place of work and 37% said that it took place in the client's home. As can be seen from Table 6.4 the corresponding figures for the clients are 50% and 31% respectively.

Asked where they would prefer to meet, 38% of the supervisors answered at their home or place of work and 35% answered at the client's home. Forty-one percent of the clients answered that they wanted to meet in their supervisor's home or place of work and 33% answered that they wanted to meet in their own home.

If one assumes that the client is in need of support and contact, then the most natural place for the meetings between supervisor and client would be the client's home. The supervisor could thereby see how his client lives and could, relatively undisturbed, talk with the client about his problems in a place where the latter probably feels most comfortable and unconstrained. Meetings at the supervisor's place of work generally occur in a state or municipal office where the client probably finds it more difficult to feel uncon-

TABLE 6.3 Who Took the Initiative to Meet Most Often and Who Ought to Have Taken the Initiative to Meet? (percentages)

	Who Took the Initiative?		Who Ought to Take the Initiative?	
Response	Supervisor	Client	Supervisor	Client
Supervisor	41	27	7	28
Client	14	31	15	20
Both	46	38	72	52
Other	0	1	2	0
Missing data	0	2	4	0

TABLE 6.4 Where Do Supervisor and Client Meet and Where Do They Want to Meet? (percentages)

	Where They Meet		Where They Want to Meet	
Response	Supervisor	Client	Supervisor	Client
Supervisor's home	20	22	23	22
Supervisor's workplace	20	28	15	19
Client's home	37	31	35	33
Client's workplace	0	1	0	1
Other place or places	22	14	26	22
Missing data	1	4	1	2

strained. Even if the aim of contact is control rather than support, the client's home still remains the most natural place to meet. If visits to the client's home are perceived as an encroachment, the supervisors can choose some neutral place for their meeting.

There is a difference of opinion among the supervisors and to some extent between the clients and their supervisors, about where they actually meet and where they want to meet. The fact that the proportion of supervisors stating that they meet at the client's home is higher than that of clients stating that they meet there can probably be explained by the supervisor's believing that he fulfils his task better in this way. Both groups, particularly the clients, would prefer to meet less often at the supervisor's place of work than was the case in reality. It is, however, noteworthy that a somewhat larger number of supervisors prefer to meet at their own place of work or home rather than in the client's home; this is true both for the factual as well as the preferred pattern of contact. One interpretation of this may be that many of the supervisors want to get the visit out of the way as quickly and as easily as possible. A partial alternative explanation is that they adjust to what the majority of clients want, that is to make the visit as impersonal as possible.

Obviously we cannot exclude the possibility that the client is afraid that people in his neighborhood may find out that he is under supervision if his supervisor visits him at home. However, those who are closest to him would probably already know about the supervision and it need not be evident to those not directly involved that the person visiting the client is a supervisor.

The supervisor and client contact pattern suggests that there is some tension in their relationship. The dominating impression is that they try to meet as little as possible, that each of them often thinks the other should take the initiative and that they want to meet in as formal a setting as possible. If we assume that the client is in need of contact and that the supervisor brings about treatment during this contact, then the opposite should obtain. Even from the point of view of control, we would expect the supervisor to meet his client, to take the initiative and to visit his client at home to a greater extent than he does.

Contacts in the Social Environment

Contact with Family, Parents and Employers. Asked whether the supervisor has made contact with the *client's family,* 58% of the supervisors said "yes" as compared with 34% of their clients. Agreement within pairs is very low among those who answered "no" or said that the client in question does not have a family.

Asked whether the supervisor has made contact with the *client's parents,* 65% of the supervisors answered "yes" as compared with 51% of their clients.

The question of whether the supervisor has made contact with the *client's employer* was affirmatively answered by 34% of the supervisors and 21% of their clients. No less than 18% of the clients answered that they did not know if their supervisor had made any such contact. This is remarkable since the supervisor should not contact the client's employer without the client's consent.

Throughout the supervisors report a higher frequency of contact with the client's surroundings than their clients do. It may be that the supervisors report too many contacts or that they make such contacts without informing their clients. A supervisor should not, however, make such contacts behind his client's back if their work together is to be built on mutual trust.

No advice is given in the "Instructions for Supervisors" on how they should proceed when making contact with people in the client's surroundings—the supervisor has to use his own judgment. The supervisors must, however, observe their pledge of confidentiality. In principle, the client should be informed of any contacts made on his behalf before they take place. The comparison made between the answers given by the supervisors and their clients suggests that this was not always the case.

Desired Contacts with Family, Parents and Employers. What do supervisors and clients think is the ideal procedure for making contacts with the social environment? Seventy-four percent of supervisors but only 31% of their clients think that contact should be made with the *client's family.* Almost one-fifth of the supervisors left the question unanswered.

As many as 80% of the supervisors but only 28% of the clients believe that contact should be made with the *client's parents.* The clients who answered this question affirmatively also had supervisors who answered affirmatively. This agreement between answers could imply that some communication had taken place between supervisor and client on this matter. But since the agreement between answers is so low in general, this possibility is not very likely.

To the question of whether they think the supervisor ought to contact the *client's employer*, 27% of the supervisors and 11% of their clients answered affirmatively.

Once again the clients want contact to be made with people in the client's social environment to a lesser degree than the supervisors. The differences become even greater with respect to ideal and actual behavior. When the factual circumstances are compared with the desired circumstances we find that the supervisors want to have even more contact with the client's family and parents while the clients want less contact to be made with everyone. Thus, once again we can observe asymmetry in the factual relations but also, to a considerable degree, in the opinions on how these should be managed.

The main reason for the different answers given by supervisors and clients is probably that the supervisors regard the above-mentioned contacts primarily as offers of help while the clients see them as attempts at control. Another explanation as to why the clients do not wish the supervisors to make contact with persons in their social environment could be that the clients are afraid that people in their surroundings will get to know that they have been placed under supervision with the risk of consequent stigmatization.

Problem Areas

Supervisors and clients were asked to answer questions on the problems which the clients experienced during supervision, whether the clients took these problems to the supervisor and whether he was able to help them find solutions to these problems. Nine different areas were named—financial matters, work, accommodation, alcohol, drugs, leisure, sickness, family and driver's license—and a final possible problem area was left open.

As can be seen from Table 6.5 the supervisors have consistently reported the presence of various problems to a greater extent than their clients.

According to the supervisors, the proportion of clients who came to them with these problems was somewhat less than the proportion with the problems. The supervisors assert that they have been able to help nearly all the clients who asked for help. But according to the clients' the proportion turning to their supervisor for help, and especially the proportion who considered that they were helped by him, is markedly less.

The supervisors and clients were, however, in agreement that most help was given where the supervisor was able to provide a service. Supervisors and clients consider that *financial matters* constitute the greatest problem. The majority of clients had experienced problems with their finances, had turned to their supervisors for help and had been helped to a greater extent than was the case with other problems.

Sixty-eight percent of the supervisors and 53% of the clients reported that financial problems caused most difficulty during the supervision period. The dyadic agreement is unusually large here—42% for affirmative responses and

TABLE 6.5 Information According to the Supervisor and His Client about Which Problems the Client Has, whether the Client Approached the Supervisor and whether the Problems Were Solved by the Supervisor (percentages)

		Client's Problem		Asked for Help		Received Help	
Problem Area		Sup.	Client	Sup.	Client	Sup.	Client
1	Finances	68	53	57	38	51	24
2	Work	46	17	46	14	20	11
3	Accommodation	26	25	37	17	36	7
4	Alcohol	44	15	22	7	21	7
5	Drugs	1	1	1	1	1	0
6	Leisure	17	2	5	0	6	0
7	Sickness	16	16	11	6	7	2
8	Family	18	11	19	4	15	2
9	Driving license	3	2	7	4	4	2
10	Other	22	5	12	5	12	6

63% in total. Fifty-seven percent of the supervisors but only 38% of the clients report turning to the supervisor for help with financial problems. Here the dyadic agreement of affirmative answers is 32% and 69% in total. Fifty-one percent of the supervisors but only 24% of the clients believed that successful help had been given. Dyadic affirmative answer agreement is 21% and 68% in total.

Most offenders sentenced to probation are poorly educated and if they have work at all it is badly paid. They are therefore in a poor financial situation from the start. In addition, many owe legal expenses, fines and damages. The probation organisation has, however, limited financial resources at its disposal. Consequently, the clients must turn to the social service authorities when they need financial assistance. The supervisor can act as an intermediary with such contacts, he can help the client plan financially and he can contact creditors and seek postponement of any payments due. Supervisors are warned in the "Instructions for Supervisors" against themselves lending money to clients.

The next most important problem areas are *work* and *accommodation*. Forty-six percent of supervisors but only 17% of their clients reported that the greatest problem was work. Twenty-six percent of the supervisors and almost the same proportion of clients stated that accommodation caused serious difficulty. The supervisors stated that all the clients with work difficulties had turned to them for help but the proportion of clients agreeing with this statement was considerably less. The proportions of supervisors who claim that their client came to them with accommodation problems and who say they were able to give help is greater than the proportion of clients agreeing with these statements. The dyadic agreement between supervisor and client on affirmative answers is on average 10%, but the total agreement reaches 60 to 80%.

Since the clients generally have a low level of basic education and often lack vocational training they have great difficulties when seeking work. Those who are offered a job must often take it even if they are not particularly suited for it or happy with it. The supervisors may have contacts who can help in providing a job and they may also support the client in his contact with the employment agency.

In general, if the offender has no place to live he must, possibly together with his supervisor, turn to the local housing authorities. The chief probation officer has also certain possibilities to arrange accommodation. In addition, the municipal social services can provide hostel accommodation to some extent and in certain towns there are also halfway houses.

After these practical difficulties, *alcohol* seems to be the most prominent of client problems. Among the supervisors, 44% held this view as compared with 15% of their clients. Half of these supervisors also stated that the client came to them with this problem—a statement with which a far smaller proportion of the clients agreed. Almost as great a proportion of these supervisors thought they were able to help the client with his alcohol problem—a view which was shared by only a relatively small proportion of the clients. For all three questions on alcohol problems, the supervisors have a substantially higher frequency of affirmative answers than their clients. The agreement of affirmative answers within dyads is also very small.

Only one supervisor and one client reported on the presence of *drug problems.* When the present research was undertaken in 1970 drug use was relatively rare.

A fairly common problem reported by both supervisors and clients is *sickness.* The supervisors are naturally only able to provide limited help in these cases.

Leisure was regarded as a problem area by many supervisors but scarcely mentioned by their clients. Some supervisors stated that their clients came to them for help with the problem and that they were able to assist them but no client stated this.

Supervisors and clients reported problems in *client family relationships.* Fifteen percent of supervisors thought that they had been able to help their client with this problem but only 2% of their clients agreed with this assessment.

Although correctional officials had informed us that many clients had their *driver's license* suspended after sentence or had difficulties in regaining it, only two supervisors and two clients reported such problems.

Throughout the supervisors have consistently reported more problems than their clients. It was not possible to determine whether the differences were due to the supervisors' desire to assert the importance of their work or to the clients' use of defence mechanisms and denial of their problems. Both factors can, of course, operate at the same time.

The clients were also asked to say whether they had *approached the chief probation officer* with any of the above-mentioned or similar problems. Once again, the greatest problem named was the financial situation (16%) followed by accommodation (7%). Apart from these difficulties only a few reported other problems. Obviously therefore probationers do not turn to the chief probation officer with their problems to any great extent. When they do they mostly want help with financial matters. The assistance which the chief probation officer can be expected to provide is service-oriented to a greater extent than is the case with voluntary supervisors.

These findings may mean that the clients' greatest problems are of purely practical nature but it may be that they find this type of problem easiest to talk about. Both interpretations could be valid. It is, however, obvious that the clients have problems with their financial situation, work and accommodation and that the supervisors can help them. At the same time, we see that the clients would rather go to their supervisors than to the professional probation staff with problems of a more personal nature.

When our findings are compared with those from the Sundsvall project, we find relatively good agreement. There, too, the clients reported the greatest problem to be their financial situation (Kühlhorn 1975:1, 41; cf. 1979:5).

Special Conditions

Apart from having to comply with the general conditions already described, special conditions may be imposed by the court at time of sentence. During the probationary period a supervision board may decide on new conditions or revoke earlier ones. According to the preparatory work on the Penal Code, the aim of these conditions is to provide the offender with measures of support which can facilitate his adjustment in society. The condition to pay damages need not, however, be justified by reference to individual prevention.

The Use of Special Conditions. When conditions are imposed, both the offender and his supervisor should be notified in writing. We asked if the offender had received notice of conditions when he was sentenced and, if so, what they were. Fifty-three percent of the supervisors and 69% of the clients reported that no such notification had been received. In many cases with imposed conditions only one condition was named although there were in reality up to five imposed conditions.

The agreement between answers from the various dyads is only 49%—a low agreement level for a question concerning knowledge of facts. It is essential that both parties have proper information about these special conditions. Non-compliance by the offender lays him open to blame and the supervisor is responsible for checking that the conditions are being followed.

Supervisors as well as clients reported the most common condition to be *abstention from alcoholic beverages* (supervisors 17%; clients 11%). It is difficult for alcohol misusers to abstain totally and such a restriction is seldom especially effective. Yet, violation of this condition could result in the probationer being subject to coercive measures taken by the temperance authorities. Conditions regarding abstinence from alcohol have been abrogated since a law on certain changes in the Penal Code came into force in 1974.

The second most common condition, named by 10% of the supervisors and 7% of the clients, concerns *employment.*

The condition *to pay damages* comes in the third place. Seven percent of the supervisors, but only 1% of the clients, mentioned this condition.

Other conditions mentioned by the supervisors, but not clients, concerned undergoing some form of treatment (2%) and residence (1%).

Payment of Damages and Insurance. The payment of damages may be ordered to give the sanction increased severity. But this is a condition which easily becomes one that the probationer cannot fulfil. In addition he often has other debts, e.g. alimony, fines and legal expenses. If he does not pay the damages this may be held against him when termination of his probation comes up for consideration. It has happened that supervision boards have been known to refuse termination as long as the damages remain unpaid. However, there has probably been an easement of these restrictions following recommendations by the Committee on Correctional Reform.

A question was put about whether damages should be paid through some kind of insurance. One-third of the supervisors and half of their clients answered that they thought damages should be paid in this way.

Breach of Conditions. That conditions are not easy to follow is seen from the fact that 69% of the supervisors believed their clients to have violated a condition. Forty-five percent of the clients with conditions reported that they had violated at least some of them. Breach of conditions appears therefore to be relatively common.

Reporting to the Chief Probation Officer. Almost two-thirds of the supervisors stated that they would report a violation of conditions to the chief probation officer. Half of the clients believed that their supervisor would report a violation. Reporting of violations is a reality and experienced as such—a situation which probably contributes to oppositional relations between supervisor and client.

Measures of Support or Punishment. According to the legislator, special conditions are intended to provide support. However, every sixth supervisor and more than half of their clients, regarded conditions primarily as punitive measures. The legislator has obviously failed to achieve his purpose. Imposing conditions demonstrates how difficult it is to combine assistance and control in supervision.

Committee on Correctional Reform. This Committee recommended a reduced use of conditions (SOU 1972:64). It considered that conditions imposed by the courts were often unrealistic, without real treatment content and did not have the desired control or treatment effect. Yet non-compliance could lead to serious sanctions.

Reporting—Its Importance for Supervisor and Client

Supervisors must report quarterly on their clients to the chief probation officer using a printed form informing the chief probation officer by personal or telephone contact. The supervisor may also propose measures to be decided on by the supervision board.

The primary purpose of reporting is to create a basis for taking suitable measures. Even if the intention is good, this does not mean that the client will experience reporting positively. Supervisors have probably tended to record negative rather than positive things about their clients since the former is of greater interest for the controlling authorities. The clients can therefore perceive these reports as repressive control instruments. The client has not been asked to recount his needs or comment on the supervisor's treatment plan or lack thereof.

A 1972 circular instruction from the Swedish Prison and Probation Administration emphasized drawing attention to both positive and negative sides of the client and stated that "since many clients mistrust these reports, the supervisor and his client should preferably discuss its content" (Circular 31, p. 9). However, it is not certain that this proposal will overcome the client's suspicious attitude. What should the supervisor do when, having discussed the report with his client, he finds that they cannot agree? In any case, the client's suspicion may be directed more towards the receiver of the report than its sender.

In answer to a question whether it was desirable for the client to read through the report, 73% of the clients replied positively but only 58% of their supervisors. That as many as 42% of the supervisors were against their clients reading the report suggests that the supervisors find themselves in a position between the administration and the client where different considerations of loyalty can come into conflict. That 25% of the clients were against reading the report may mean that they lack interest or that they feel powerless and resigned.

The question of reporting shows that the contact between supervisor and client is not one of complete co-operation and trust. Reporting, with or without the client's participation, probably does not contribute to good relations.

Perceptions of Supervision

The Client's Right to Participation in Decision-Making. Should the client take part in the decision-making in matters which concern his supervision? Thirty-five percent of the supervisors answered "yes, in all matters", 56% "yes, in some matters" and 9% "no, not at all". The corresponding figures for the clients were 49%, 37% and 13%. Agreement between supervisor and client views was relatively good since 91% of the supervisors and 85% of clients thought that the client should have a say in all or some matters. However, dyadic agreement was only 44%. That pairs of supervisors and clients differed on such a central question probably leads to tension in their relationship.

It is surprising that the clients were not willing to a greater extent to participate in such decision-making. This lack of thoroughgoing interest in what should be important to them, may result from passivity or resignation in a control situation. If so, the rehabilitative aim of reinforcing the probationer's self-confidence, self-respect and dignity appears not be met to any great extent.

Length of Probationary Period. The probationary period is three years. The supervision board may terminate supervision before this time if it is no longer considered necessary. In all, 34% of the supervisors and 71% of the clients thought that the probationary period is too long. No-one thought the period too short. The dyadic agreement was only 43%.

Those answering "too long" were asked to specify a desirable length of time. Of the supervisors responding 23% thought that it should be one year, 40% that it should be two years and 23% preferred variation from case to case. Among responding clients 58% would prefer the period to be one year, 25% preferred up to two years and 8% wanted variation from case to case. Thus, the clients wanted a shorter probationary period to a greater extent than their supervisors. The great differences between the two groups once again demonstrates a latent tension in their relationship.

The Committee on Correctional Reform proposed in its report (SOU 1972:64) that the probationary period be two years and that supervision be reviewed after one year so as to decide whether to terminate it or instead offer the client a contact person. The latter might be retained for a third year but would have neither a control function nor a reporting responsibility. He would function only as a counsellor on personal and social problems. In the subsequent law which came into force in 1974, the supervision period was reduced to one year but the same probationary period was retained. The supervision board could decide to extend the supervision period if it thought there were special reasons for an extension which, however, cannot be longer than the probationary period.

Encroachment on Personal Freedom. Supervisors and clients were asked whether they considered supervision to be a considerable encroachment on the client's personal freedom. Ten percent of the supervisors believed it to be so as compared with 38% of their clients. This is a sizeable discrepancy of opinion. The dyadic agreement is only 4%.

Public Attitudes. How do the supervisors and their clients perceive the public's attitude to probationers? Sixty-seven percent of the supervisors believed that their clients were treated by the general public in the same way as before sentence and as much as 63% of the clients agreed with this. Twenty percent of the supervisors thought their clients were treated worse than other people in society and 29% of their clients were of the same opinion. The marginal distributions suggest that the supervisors and the clients had approximately the same views concerning this matter, but the dyadic agreement does not exceed 52%. The responses support a theory of stigmatization in that almost one- third of the clients felt labeled by their sentence.

Double Loyalty

The Supervisor's Position Between the Administration and the Client. Earlier in this chapter we observed that 70% of the supervisors considered themselves to be on their client's side, 7% felt that they were on the side of officialdom and 12% that they were on both sides. When the supervisors were instead asked how they *believed their clients viewed* their position, the proportion answering "on the client's side" fell to 63%, for "on both sides" to 5%, while the proportion answering "on the side of the officialdom" increased to 21%.

As can be seen from Table 6.6 the distribution of supervisors' beliefs about their clients' view approximates closely to the distribution of the *clients' responses to the question of whose side they believe their supervisor is on.* Sixty-two percent of the clients answered that supervisors were on the client's side, 7% that they were on both sides and 23% replied that they were on the side of officialdom.

Although the marginal distributions are much the same, dyadic agreement is only 50% (i.e. the sum of the diagonals 42 +7 +1 percent). Without the dyadic analysis we might have thought that the supervisors' perception of their clients' view is very good. The lack of agreement in answers from pairs indicates that there is often a considerable social psychological distance between the supervisor and his client.

It can be seen from Table 6.7 that there is a certain dissonance between supervisor and client concerning the answers to the question of where it is thought the supervisor *ought* to stand. While 59% of the supervisors think that they should be on the client's side, 81% of their clients feel that this ought to be the case. Dyadic agreement increases to 58% for this normatively formulated question.

Confidence Between Supervisor and Client. To the question of whether the supervisor had confidence in his client, 46% answered "yes, completely", 48% "yes, to a certain extent" and 6% answered "no, not at all". To the question "Do you think your supervisor has confidence in you?", 41% of the clients answered "yes, completely", 51% answered "yes, to a certain extent" and 6% answered "no, not at all". The marginal figures suggest good agreement with 94% and 92% respectively answering that confidence exists either completely or partially but again the agreement within pairs is considerably less with only 53% concordance between supervisor and client as can be seen from Table 6.8.

To the question of whether the clients have confidence in their supervisors, 52% of the clients answered "yes, completely", 32% answered "yes, to a certain extent" and 16% answered "no, not at all". To the corresponding question "Do you think your client has confidence in you?" 46% of the supervisors answered "completely", 52% "to a certain extent" and 1% answered "not at all". The supervisors overestimate, therefore, the confidence their client have in them. Nor is dyadic agreement very great at 49%. In all cases where the client claimed that he did not have confidence in his supervisor, the supervisor believed that his client completely or partially had confidence in him (see Table 6.9).

The question posed about the supervisor's position may be criticized as creating a false dichotomy since the chief probation officer and supervision board do not necessarily represent polar opposites of the official society and the controlling authority. In the second question arises the problem of how to define the concept of "having confidence in someone". Disregarding such semantic complexities, however, we find it interesting that both questions produce broadly the same picture. Since the possible errors are different for the two questions, their consequences are probably not serious.

TABLE 6.6 Supervisor and Client Perceptions of Supervisor's Position (percentages)

Supervisor's Response to the Question: On Whose Side Does Your Client Think You Stand?	Client's Response to the Question: "On Whose Side Does Your Supervisor Stand?"					
	Client	Employer	Both	Other	Missing Data	Total
Client	42	12	5	2	1	63
Employer	11	7	1	1	0	21
Both	4	0	1	0	0	5
Other	2	2	0	0	0	5
Missing data	2	1	0	2	0	6
Total	62	23	7	6	1	100

The distribution of answers from the supervisors and their clients shows that their relationship is in no way characterized by complete mutual confidence. Moreover, the dyadic analyses indicate that the their cross-perceptions of each other are discordant, which suggests frequent miscommunication. The difficulty one party has in judging the other's views probably creates uncertainty and distance in the supervisor-client relationship.

The Effect of Supervision and Crime Prevention

As we saw earlier, supervision is meant to be a positive form of treatment even if, in principle, there are no special methods for implementing it. The shaping of treatment is therefore to a large degree dependent on the individual supervisor. The supervisor's faith in supervision as a form of treatment, his appraisal of it as a means of resocializing offenders and his view of his own role, are all factors which come into play. His general evaluation of supervision is likely to affect the assessment of his own role as supervisor and vice versa. These evaluations may also influence his judgment of his client's possibilities and be, in turn, significant for the client's assessment of his own possibilities (cf. Mead's concept of the looking-glass self 1934).

The Importance of the Supervisor in the Individual Case. To the question of how the supervisors believed their client would manage without a supervisor during the probationary period, 65% answered "worse", 28% answered "just as well" and 1% answered "better without" with 4% saying that they did not know (see Table 6.10).

When the question was put to the clients the distribution of answers looks somewhat different. Nineteen percent of them answered that they would manage worse without a supervisor, 68% thought they would manage just as well and 14% believed they would manage better on their own (see Table

TABLE 6.7 Supervisor and Client Perceptions of Where the Supervisor Ought to Stand in Relation to the Administration and Client (percentages)

Supervisor's Response to the Question: "On Whose Side Ought a Supervisor to Stand?"	Client's Response to the Question: "On Whose Side Ought Your Supervisor to Stand?"				
	Client	Employer	Both	Other	Total
Client	51	4	2	2	59
Employer	7	0	1	0	9
Both	16	0	5	0	21
Other	6	1	0	2	10
Missing data	1	0	0	0	1
Total	81	5	9	5	100

TABLE 6.8 Supervisor's Confidence in Client and Client's Perception of This (percentages)

"Do You Have Confidence in Your Client?"	"Do You Think Your Supervisor Has Confidence in You?"				
	Completely	To Some Extent	Not at All	Missing Data	Total
Completely	25	17	1	2	46
To some extent	15	28	5	0	48
Not at all	1	5	0	0	6
Missing data	41	51	6	2	100

6.10). Thus, we see that more than three times as many supervisors as clients believed the latter would be worse off without a supervisor. Dyadic agreement is also only 37%.

This lack of concordance of opinions probably rightly reflects the different positions held by supervisors and clients as well as the different roles they play in the supervision relationship. The supervisor naturally wants to believe in his function—a fact which may lead him to overestimate his own importance. Alternatively, the supervisors' response may mean that they under-

TABLE 6.9 Client's Confidence in Supervisor and Supervisor's Perception of Client Confidence in Him (percentages)

"Do You Think Your Client Has Confidence in You?"	"Do You Have Confidence in Your Supervisor?" Completely	To Some Extent	Not at All	Total
Completely	28	9	9	46
To some extent	23	21	7	52
Not at all	0	1	0	1
Missing data	0	1	0	1
Total	52	32	16	100

TABLE 6.10 Supervisor and Client Views of How the Client Would Have Managed without a Supervisor (percentages)

Supervisor's Response	Client's Response Better	As Well	Worse	Total
Better	1	0	0	1
As well	4	21	4	28
Worse	7	43	15	65
Don't know	1	2	0	4
Missing data	0	1	0	1
Total	14	68	19	100

estimate their clients' ability to manage on their own. The client, on the other hand, is probably inclined to underestimate his supervisor's importance. He may, for example, lack insight into his own situation. From a psychological point of view, however, the client would benefit from believing in himself and developing his personal resources.

Reliable data is still not available to settle the question of whether the supervisor or his client makes the more realistic assessment of the importance of supervision. However, there is an abyss between supervisor and client concerning the assessment made by each party the other's role and abilities.

The Individual Preventive Effect of Supervision. To the question whether they believed that supervision could hinder the commission of new offenses 62% of supervisors answered positively. The proportion answering negatively was 21% while the proportion of those who did not know increases to 15%.

However, only half as many clients believed that supervision could hinder the commission of new offenses for 31% responded affirmatively, 47% negatively while 20% did not know (see Table 6.11).

Dyadic agreement is also limited, reaching only 33%. The largest individual category of dyads (33%) is composed of supervisors who believe supervision has an effect on crime prevention and clients who do not think so.

The varying opinions seen above may be a natural manifestation of the different positions held by supervisors and clients in the supervision relationship, of their different life experience and of their different frames of reference and norm systems. The lack of agreement in such fundamental questions as the general and specific value they place on supervision naturally makes collaboration between supervisor and client more difficult.

Belief in General Prevention. A broadly formulated question on general prevention was put to supervisors and their clients. The responses are shown in Table 6.12.

More than three times as many supervisors as clients believed that people refrain from committing crimes because others are punished.However, only a minority within each group answered in this way—31% of the supervisors and 9% of their clients. A majority of both supervisors and clients (54% and 80% respectively) repudiated the theory of general prevention. Only 11% of the supervisors and 7% of their clients responded with a "don't know" answer. Dyadic agreement is somewhat greater than it was for responses to questions on individual prevention but nevertheless only reaches a total of 50%.

Summarizing Comments

The dyadic analyses show that the supervisors and clients, in many respects, stand at a distance from one another. They are separated by a generation in age. The greater proportion of supervisors belong to the middle classes and their clients to the lower social classes. There is great psychological distance between the two groups in their attitudes. The supervisors have much difficulty in correctly comprehending their clients' views. Differing points of view and inaccurate perceptions may well make for difficulties of communication and collaboration between supervisor and client. The mutual confidence upon which treatment should be based seems to be lacking to a great extent.

Recidivism Related to Supervision

The last step in our analysis is to relate recidivism rates to the supervisors' personal and social characteristics and the subjective experience of supervision by clients and supervisors.

We have already seen that supervisors do not form homogeneous groups and that they supervise in different ways. It is this variation that makes possible the study of client readjustment under different conditions. However, it is not always easy to interpret the associations found causally. In the first place, certain clients may have been placed with certain supervisors. An attempt has

TABLE 6.11 Views Held by Supervisors and Clients on whether Supervision Has an Individual Preventive Effect (percentages)

	Client's Response				
Supervisor's Response	Yes	No	Don't Know	Missing Data	Total
Yes	22	33	6	0	62
No	4	6	9	2	21
Don't know	5	5	5	0	15
Missing data	0	2	0	0	2
Total	31	47	20	2	100

TABLE 6.12 Views Held by Supervisors and Clients as to the Effect of General Prevention (percentages)

	Client's Response				
Supervisor's Response	Yes	No	Don't Know	Missing Data	Total
Yes	5	23	1	1	31
No	4	44	5	1	54
Don't know	0	10	1	0	11
Missing data	0	2	0	1	4
Total	9	80	7	4	100

been made to take this into account by classifying clients according to prognosis. The material has been analyzed both in its entirety and after having been divided into two equally large groups on the basis of the clients' risk scores as calculated in the prediction study. Secondly, certain questions may be difficult to interpret because a relapse into crime, which may have happened before our questionnaire was answered, may have affected the responses. The supervisors' answers may then be *post facto* rationalizations just as the clients' answers may be defense mechanisms.

To start with, we should point out that recidivism among the clients we study in this section is lower than that revealed in the recidivism study described earlier. The first reason for this is that those sentenced to probation with institutional treatment were only included here if sentenced during the first year (1967) whereas the cases in the recidivism study comprise a two-year cohort. The second reason is that the missing data from the questionnaire is greater among those who recidivated and had their probation revoked. We thus come down to a level of recidivism which is more characteristic for probationers with the exception of those sentenced to institutional treatment (33% of the sample where the supervisors are the starting point and 31% where the point of departure is the clients).

Recidivism will first be related to supervision as it can be described through the supervisor's personal and social attributes. Thereafter, recidivism will be related to the supervision as described by both supervisors and clients. Thereafter a comparison is drawn between the results of both studies. The reader who wishes to avoid a mainly statistical analysis can go directly to the summary at the end of the chapter

Attributes of Supervisors and the Supervision Process as Described by Supervisors

A total of forty variables, judged to be essential for either a theoretical or empirical analysis, were studied. From the point of view of treatment it must be considered unsatisfactory that *only a few of the variables correlate significantly* with the clients' tendency to relapse into crime. To put it bluntly, there are no great differences between the different types of supervisors and supervisor styles on the one hand and the clients' tendency to recidivate on the other. This conclusion is in agreement with the findings from the systematic summaries made of reliable studies in treatment research (Lipton, Martinson and Wilks 1975).

Supervisor Characteristics. Considering the relationship found earlier between certain background variables and supervisors' attitudes, it is surprising to see that the supervisor's *sex, age and education* scarcely differentiate our data concerning the recidivism of the clients.

The very weak trends we discern are:

1. Among the clients of the small number of women supervisors in our study, there is a somewhat higher recidivism rate for those whose prognosis is good and a lower recidivism rate for those whose prognosis is poor.
2. The few supervisors under thirty had better recidivism results with clients in higher risk groups and less satisfactory results with those in lower risk groups.
3. The supervisors whose education was limited to elementary school also had poor recidivism results, especially for clients from the high risk groups.

Whether the supervisor had undergone *training for supervision* shows scarcely any association with the readjustment of clients although there is a tendency for the clients of supervisors who had received training to recidivate less than the clients of those who had not (31% and 37% respectively). The difference increases somewhat for clients in the high risk groups.

So far as the *professions* represented among the supervisors are concerned, we are unable to discern any significant relationship between these and recidivism. However, we do find one clear trend, namely that there are more recidivists among the clients of police than among those of social workers (42% and 26% respectively, p = <.09 with a one-way test). Both groups have the same number of clients with high risk scores so differences in prognosis cannot explain the difference. We also find the same recidivism result for both professional categories within the low and high risk groups: recidivism among police officers' clients in the low risk group is 36% as compared with 21% for the clients of social workers in the same risk group, while the corresponding figures for high risk group are 47% and 29% respectively. Earlier we noted that there is a *role conflict* concerning the support and control aspects of supervision among the police officer supervisors. The high recidivism rate among the police officers' clients does not necessarily mean that the police are bad supervisors but rather that they are good policemen. Because of the detective nature of their work it may be that the police can more readily discover and investigate possible criminal activities among their clients or past information to their colleagues who are undertaking investigations. But just because they may be considered good police officers in these activities they are less successful as supervisors. How could a client approach a police officer in confidence when he knows that if he tells him, for example, about a previous crime for which action has not been taken, the officer is obliged to register this information and his sentence may be reversed or his liberty curtailed as a consequence?

The variable *previous number of probation or parole assignments* presents two opposing trends: supervisors with a very large or very small number of previous cases had clients who recidivated to a lesser extent than clients of other supervisors. The clients of the few supervisors who have not previously had any cases, have a zero recidivism rate. The recidivism rate is 30% among the clients of supervisors who have had 1–3 previous assignments, and 28% among the clients of supervisors who have had more than thirty-one cases. On the other hand, the recidivism rate for clients of supervisors who have had four to ten previous cases is 47% and 38% for those who have had eleven to thirty cases. As we might expect, the inexperienced supervisors were more often assigned clients with better prognoses. However, these supervisors have also obtained good results with clients whose risk group is high. This supports earlier discoveries that experience of supervision is not always an advantage. Nevertheless, we cannot exclude the possibility that these supervisors may have picked or been assigned clients for whom they had especially good possibilities of providing help.

The group of supervisors who had previously had some thirty assignments worked with a larger number of clients with high risk scores but despite this their clients recidivated to a lesser extent and the recidivism rate is lower even among the clients in the high risk group. While the discrepancy between supervisors with different numbers of cases almost disappears in the low risk group, the curvilinear relationship observed earlier becomes stronger in the high risk group. Experience seems to lead to a certain amount of competence and this experience seems especially important for the more complicated cases. The conclusion would seem to be that both the completely inexperienced and the professional supervisors are the most successful in helping clients to readjust.

Supervision as Described by the Supervisors. The *number of meetings during the first year* of supervision shows a significant relationship between frequent meetings and high recidivism rates. This somewhat unexpected result might be explained by the fact that supervisors meet more often with clients with poor prognoses. When we hold the risk scores constant, we find however that the *relationship is strengthened in the low risk group*: 88% of the clients whose risk score is low and who meet their supervisors once or more a week relapse into crime as compared with 33% of those who meet their supervisor once a fortnight and 14% of those who meet every third week. The recidivism rate is zero for those clients who meet their supervisors from once per month to once per quarter or even more sporadically.

The opposite relationship exists for clients with *high risk scores,* namely a covariance between low frequency of contact and high recidivism. While there is a clear positive correlation between number of meetings and the size of recidivism in the low risk group, the association is somewhat weaker in the high risk group. The results indicate that the more often client and supervisor meet, the less successful the outcome of treatment for clients with good prognoses. On the other hand, frequent contact between supervisor and client seems to be beneficial for clients whose prognosis is poor.

The *frequency of meetings during the last year of supervision* is perhaps a somewhat doubtful indicator as clients may have recidivated prior to answering the questionnaire. On the whole this variable also indicates a significant relationship between high recidivism and more frequent contact between clients and supervisors. Even within the low risk group the relationship is significant, and we can discern the same trend in the high risk group. Thus, even the clients whose prognosis is poor seem to find it difficult to benefit from an intensive contact after a long period of supervision.

The question of *how long the meeting usually lasts* also revealed a relationship between long meetings and high recidivism. This relationship exists in both the low and the high risk groups but is especially evident in the former. Recidivism is twice as prevalent in the low risk group among clients who meet their supervisor for one hour or more, as among clients from the same group who meet for a maximum of fifteen minutes (37% and 18% respectively).

The question of *where to meet* also shows an association with recidivism. Recidivism is lower among the clients who meet their supervisors in their own homes (32%) than among those who meet in their supervisor's home (48%) or at his workplace (41%) or somewhere else (40%). It is particularly low among clients who meet their supervisors in different places (4%). It may be that when client and supervisor meet in the client's home, the supervisor shows a great deal of interest in his client, and that when they meet at different places he shows greater imagination which, in turn, may lead to a more personal supervision relationship. The result is the same in both low and high risk groups; it is noteworthy that among the clients whose supervisor meets them in different places, only one of eleven clients in the low risk group and none of the twelve clients in the high risk group, relapsed into crime.

There is a significant association between recidivism and the person who, according to the supervisors, *initiated the meetings.* Recidivism is highest among the clients who themselves initiated contact (53%), intermediate among those whose supervisor took this initiative (38%) and lowest when both supervisor and client initiated contact (19%). Where contact was made on a mutual basis, the supervisor and client seemed to have a somewhat more equal relationship leading to a better outcome. Recidivism is lowest in low as well as high risk groups when both the supervisor and the client initiated contact. In the low risk group we find that recidivism is highest when the supervisor initiated contact (42%) and that it is actually four times higher than when both parties initiated contact (11%). In the high risk group we find that recidivism is greatest when the client initiated contact (62%). This is twice as high as when both parties took the initiative (27%). These results again seem to suggest that the supervisor's activity is directly detrimental to clients whose prognoses are good. Furthermore, it is obviously not enough for the client with a poor prognosis to fulfil his obligations and contact his supervisor.

We now describe the relationships which, although not statistically significant, may have *social significance.*

To the question whether the client *asked for the supervisor he got,* the lowest recidivism rate was found among the clients whose supervisors responded affirmatively (28%), intermediate among those supervisors who answered "no" (34%), and highest among those whose supervisors said that they did not know (39%). In the low risk group we find very few recidivists among the clients of supervisors who answered "yes" (17%) and many in the high risk group among the clients of supervisors who said that they did not know (47%). Once again it would seem that personal interest, as revealed by the fact that the supervisor was selected by his client, has a positive effect on recidivism rates and the lack of such interest a negative effect. There are no great differences in recidivism rates among clients whose supervisors think the probationary period is too long or just right, but the follow-up question, *"how long should the probationary period be?"* produced a clear trend. The lowest recidivism rate is found among the supervisors who replied that the probationary period ought to vary in accordance with the client's individual needs (18%). This trend is apparent in both the low and high risk groups (15% and 22% respectively). These results could mean that supervisors who do not want general time limits but think length of the probationary period should be dictated by specific needs, are personally more interested in their clients. Supervisors who commend individualized treatment by varying the probationary period may also be said to advocate a purely individual preventive view of supervision and favor support more than control.

On the whole, there are only slight differences in the recidivism rates of clients with and without imposed *conditions.* There are, however, considerably more recidivists in the small group who received three or more such conditions (60%, n = 5). However, with the risk group held constant we find it interesting that the recidivism rate of low risk group clients with conditions is greater than that of those without conditions (33% and 24% respectively) but less in the high risk group (31% and 44% respectively). This may mean that the conditions are detrimental to those who do not need them and beneficial to those who are most in need. The findings suggest that conditions should be used with restraint but not that they should be abolished.

A slight association was found between recidivism and whether the supervisors had said that they would *inform the chief probation officer* if their client violated any of the conditions laid down. Recidivism is greater among the clients of supervisors who claimed they would report their client than among the clients of supervisors who said they would not (33% and 26% respectively). The difference is the same in both risk groups. The results indicate that it may be beneficial for the client if his supervisor takes the client's part and refrains from reporting since he might thereby risk losing the client's confidence.

Recidivism is lowest among the clients of supervisors who answered "yes, completely" to the question whether they *have confidence in their client* (24%), and highest among the clients of supervisors who answered "no" (44%). This almost significant difference becomes clearly significant in the high risk group (16% and 80% respectively) but almost disappears for the low risk group. We should not rule out the possibility that the supervisor's confidence in his client could have been affected if his client had recidivated. However, the result shows that this cannot be the only explanation. It seems that the confidence supervisors have in their clients is important for their chances of rehabilitation, especially for clients with a poor prognosis.

While there is scarcely any difference in the recidivism rate among clients of supervisors who say that they are on the client's side only or chief probation officer's side only, and among the clients of those who claim to be on both sides, we do find a more distinct association between *the supervisor's perception of the way in which they are viewed by their clients* and the client's readjustment. There is greater recidivism among the clients of supervisors who believe their client sees them as standing on his side (36%) as compared with those who believe that the client sees them as standing on the side of the chief probation officer and the supervision board (26%) or on both sides (0%). The greatest recidivism is however found among the clients whose supervisors did not answer the question at all. When the sample is divided up into risk groups, the difference is reinforced somewhat in the low risk group but almost disappears in the high risk group. On the whole we find that this form of treatment optimism, which here can be seen in the supervisor's false belief that his client considers him to be on the client's side, has a negative effect on treatment. We noted earlier that such treatment optimism is most common among the protective supervisor types. Thus, it seems that it is especially those clients whose prognosis is good who react negatively to a paternalistic attitude.

We also found a tendency for recidivism to be greater among clients of supervisors who did not *believe supervision represents a considerable encroachment* on the client's personal freedom (34% as compared with 25% for the others). However, this relationship is valid for lower risk group clients only. Thus, even this result suggests that the supervisors' false treatment optimism can be detrimental (many more clients than supervisors consider that supervision represents a considerable encroachment).

The follow-up question of *whether the supervisors believe their client experiences supervision as a considerable encroachment* showed the following tendency: there are fewer recidivists among the clients of the supervisors who responded with a "don't know" answer, especially in the low risk group. We may interpret this to mean that a less dogmatic stance from supervisors is beneficial to treatment. The same trend, i.e. fewer recidivists among the clients of supervisors who are not dogmatic and who respond to a complicated question by saying that they do not know, has been observed in the responses given to many other questions (e.g. those dealing with individual and general prevention). There are glimpses here of supervisors with non-authoritarian personalities who, armed with a better education, have a better capacity to make objective diagnoses. This personality is found to a high degree among the category of "welfare supervisors".

There is ample evidence that an uncritical attitude and an unmotivated acceptance of things as they are can be detrimental. There are more recidivists among the clients of the few supervisors who believe the *resources available to non-institutional treatment are sufficient* than among the clients of supervisors who consider them insufficient (45% and 33% respectively). This finding applies to both risk groups. The question of *how supervisors perceive their work* yielded the following result: 50% of clients in both risk groups whose supervisors were "very satisfied" recidivated. Even those who said they were "very dissatisfied" have more than the average number of recidivists among their clients (39%). Once again we have a result which implies that unfounded treatment optimism is detrimental.

There are fewer recidivists among the clients of supervisors who are *satisfied with Swedish criminal policy* than among the clients of supervisors who are not (25% and 41% respectively). We find this relationship, which is almost statistically significant, in both risk groups. Similarly, there is greater recidivism among the clients of supervisors who believe that resources are available for reaching the goals of supervision than among the clients of supervisors who think such resources are lacking (29% and 39% respectively). This seems to express another form of treatment optimism which is less unfounded and unrealistic and which may induce supervisors to produce better results.

The tendency that supervisors who are actively interested in their work have greater success in their treatment efforts is also revealed in the responses to the question of whether *supervision should be handled by fulltime workers or volunteers*. Recidivism is greater among the clients of supervisors who chose the fulltime worker alternative than among the clients of supervisors who chose "volunteers" (41% as compared with 31%). It is surprising that approximately one-quarter of the supervisors, themselves volunteers, should recommend only fulltime workers. Because the proportion of responses is almost exactly the same in both risk groups, the results seem to reflect the supervisor's belief in their own work and its consequences.

Supervision as Described by Clients

In order to assess what supervision means to the clients, we also related some of their answers to recidivism. Because of many missing data from clients the analysis is limited to ten central questions. Recidivism is defined as offenses recorded in the Criminal Register. Just as with the analyses of supervisor data, the clients have been divided into risk groups on the basis of the prediction categorisations.

Scarcely any significant association between the quality of supervision and recidivism was found but the trends which were uncovered will be described briefly.

Contact frequency as reported by clients follows the same trends as those revealed in the material obtained from the supervisors and shows reversed tendency in the different risk groups. Thus, recidivism is high among clients in the low risk group who more often meet with the supervisor (contact frequency: once per week = 43%; once per fortnight to once per month = 15%, every second month or more seldom = 17%). It is low among clients in the high risk group (21%, 41% and 50% respectively).

The question of *desired contact frequency* scarcely differentiates the material as a whole but we do find different trends within the risk groups. The majority of clients in both groups want to maintain the same level of contact with their supervisors. But recidivism is highest among the clients in the low risk group who wanted to meet with their supervisor less frequently and lowest among clients in the high risk group who would prefer to meet with their supervisor more frequently.

The question of who *takes the initiative to meet* showed that the total recidivism rate is lowest when both parties take the initiative. In the low risk group recidivism is greatest when the supervisor takes the initiative, and in the high risk group recidivism is greatest when the client does so.

Half of the clients in the low risk group claimed that they had *approached their supervisor with their problems* irrespective of whether they relapsed into crime or not. The majority of clients in the high risk group had taken their problems to their supervisor and recidivism among these clients was considerably less than among those who had not seen the supervisor and discussed their problems. Supervision would therefore seem to have a positive effect for high risk clients but not for the others.

We find a similar covariance between recidivism and the clients' view of whether they *were helped* or not. In the low risk group those clients who in a higher degree consider they received help from the supervisor, clearly recidivated more often. We find the opposite, albeit weaker, trend in the high risk group. The supervisor's help, then, seems objectively to have a detrimental effect on clients who are not poor risks even though they can subjectively believe they were helped. It may be that in these cases the supervisors take upon themselves a responsibility which their clients are not only ready to accept but also need for their continued development. We could refer to either an infantilization or a stigmatization theory for explanations of these results. For the clients with the most negative backgrounds, on the other hand, perceived help can be beneficial to their attempts at readjustment.

The question of *whose side the client thinks his supervisor is on* reveals a very weak general trend: there are fewer recidivists among clients who believe the supervisor is on their side. But here as well, we find opposing tendencies in the different risk groups. In the low risk group recidivism is greater among the clients who believe the supervisor is on the client's side, while there are clearly fewer recidivists among the clients in the high risk group who believe the supervisor is on the client's side. Once again it looks like perceived support may be detrimental for the clients with less negative backgrounds and beneficial for those with more negative backgrounds

Similarly, we find that clients who say they *have confidence in their supervisor* recidivate to a somewhat smaller extent than those who do not. This result can be found in both risk groups, although it is somewhat clearer in the high risk group. The number of clients who do not have confidence in their supervisors is also much greater in the high risk group. Thus, it would seem that in the majority of cases the rehabilitation of a client is facilitated by his having confidence in his supervisor and this applies above all to the clients with the most negative backgrounds.

In part, similar trends may be discerned in the responses to the question of whether the client considers supervision to be a *considerable encroachment on his personal freedom.* There is an almost significant association between high recidivism and the perception that supervision encroaches on personal freedom. This association is clearly significant in the high risk group but it almost disappears in the low risk group. An explanation for the total result could be that the supervisors and other authorities are more active in their dealings with clients in the high risk group as these persons may be considered to have more problems than others which in turn may lead the clients to feel a sense of encroachment. We also find that more clients in the high risk group feel supervision is an encroachment. But, since the differences are reinforced in the high risk group, this could hardly be the explanation. Among the clients with a more negative history 68% of those who had recidivated considered supervision to be a considerable encroachment as compared with 23% of those who had not recidivated. Insofar as the concept "considerable encroachment on personal freedom" can be interpreted as a perception of more control, we find that when the clients with a negative history experience such control, the likelihood of recidivism increases.

We should, once more, underline the fact that the causal analysis performed on the individual questions is somewhat uncertain as underlying factors may have affected both the dependent and independent variables. On the other hand, if several responses point in the same direction and are, moreover, supported by a theory, the degree of certainty increases. The fact that high recidivism rates can result from feelings of encroachment by the supervisor, can also be explained by a stigmatization theory or Eysenck's fixation theory.

There is a slight tendency in the client's responses to the question *"Do you think your supervisor has done his best to help you?"* for those who answered "no" to recidivate to a greater extent than others. However, the majority said that their supervisor did what he could to help and here once again we can discern different trends in the two risk groups. There are fewer recidivists among the clients in the high risk group who think their supervisor did what he could to help them. On the other hand, there are more recidivists among the clients from the low risk group who say that their supervisor did what he could to help. Thus, the supervisor's efforts seem to have a positive effect on the clients in the highest risk groups and a negative effect on those in the lower risk groups.

There is a general tendency for the clients who said they would have *managed better without a supervisor* to have a higher recidivism rate. Again we find rather opposing trends in the two risk groups. Many clients in the high risk group said they would have managed better without a supervisor and there are more recidivists among these clients. Of course, the clients' answers could be rationalizations, i.e. attempts to place the blame for their failures on their supervisors. However, the most common answer, even in the high risk group, is that they would manage *just as well* without a supervisor. This answer is also the most common one among those who do not recidivate. Thus we could say that there is some evidence against the rationalization interpretation. Usually, those who said they would have managed *worse* without a supervisor belong to the group who managed well. There is a tendency in the low risk group for those who claimed that they would have managed just as well without a supervisor to belong to the group who did not recidivate, while those who answered that they would not have managed as well without a supervisor are found among those who recidivated. The difference between risk groups lies mainly in the less frequent, extreme categories which makes interpretation difficult. In both risk groups the most common answer is that the client would have managed just as well without a supervisor and in both groups this answer is somewhat more common among those who did not recidivate. The fact that more clients who recidivated in the high risk group think that they would have managed better without a supervisor, may be a rationalization but it could also be a realistic assessment of the situation. We can hardly resolve the issue on the basis of the present data. However, the observed tendency in the low risk group (i.e. many of those who think they would not have managed as well without a supervisor actually recidivated) seems once again to indicate that help, as experienced by the client, is not necessarily the same as real help. There are traces here of the same pattern which has been seen in the replies to other questions.

Asked whether supervision *can restrain people from committing offenses* the number of clients replying "yes" and "no" was the same in both the recidivist and non-recidivist groups. Recidivism is somewhat greater among the clients in the low risk group who answered "yes" than among those who answered "no". However, the highest recidivism rate is found among clients who said that they did not know. This trend is reversed in the high risk group, i.e. the highest recidivism rate is found among the "yes" responses and lowest among the "don't know" responses. We can thus assert that in general the clients did not give answers which excused their failure. One could think that clients who had recidivated might be inclined to think that if supervision had not helped them refrain from new offenses, it would not hinder others either. But we cannot trace any such rationalizations in the answers given.

Comparisons Between Supervisor and Client Descriptions

It was earlier stated that there was a statistical association between supervisors' answers on *frequency of contact* during the first year of supervision and high recidivism. The association was strongest in the low risk group and reversed in the high risk group. The contact frequency reported by clients follows the same pattern.

We find a clear tendency among both supervisors and clients for those who said that both parties took the *initiative to meet* to show lower recidivism. According to supervisors and clients alike, recidivism is greatest among the clients from the low risk group when the supervisor took the initiative, and greatest in the high risk group when the client took the initiative.

We found a somewhat higher recidivism rate among clients of supervisors who believed their client felt they were on the client's side. A similar tendency appears in the client sample. In both cases the association is stronger in the low risk group.

Recidivism increases as the client's *confidence in his supervisor* decreases. Because the supervisors misperceive the degree of confidence the client has in them this variable does not discriminate. On the other hand, there is covariance between the supervisor's confidence in his client and recidivism. This confidence seems to be especially important in the high risk group where the association in both cases is strongest.

Recidivism was high among clients who believed that supervision represented a considerable *encroachment on their personal freedom* especially in the high risk group. But among the supervisors there were no clear differences, neither when they assessed supervision's encroachment on freedom nor when they estimated their client's views of this question. The trends which can be seen concern supervisors who replied that supervision does not encroach on the client's freedom (in which case we find high recidivism among their clients) and those who said they do not know how the client feels about it (in which case we find low recidivism, especially among clients in the low risk group).

The question whether *supervision can restrain people from committing offenses* scarcely differentiates any of the groups.

In short, the answers to questions which are common to both supervisors and clients provide a somewhat similar picture. This suggests satisfactory reliability.

Summary of Supervisor Styles, Client Categories and Treatment Effects

The relatively high recidivism rates among probationers indicates that the legislator's aims concerning individual prevention have not been realized. We now examine whether more or less emphasis on the support and control aspects of supervision would have any significance for the client's readjustment in society.

Earlier we noted that the supervisors are fairly homogeneous as far as social class and age is concerned, yet they nevertheless display different styles of supervisory behavior. Broadly, the paternalistic (or protective) supervisor, is characterized by relatively high age, long experience and little training in social work. This supervisor type places emphasis on the control aspect of his work. The punitive type of supervisor offers little assistance and emphasizes control. Authoritarian attitudes and a false treatment optimism are found among both paternalistic and punitive supervisors. The welfare supervisor, who stresses support rather than control, is characterized by younger age and better education. Police and social workers—both common professional categories among the voluntary supervisors—may be seen as characteristic types of different supervisor categories where control is emphasized to a greater extent by police and to a lesser extent by social workers.

The effect of supervision seems to vary not only according to the degree of control or support which is emphasized in the supervisor's behavior but also with client type. Because the content of supervision varies with different clients and supervisors, one would expect its outcome to vary depending on how it is organized and experienced by both parties. Since the concepts "control" and "support" are somewhat obscure and we are forced to take account of the way in which the client perceives them, the results can be difficult to interpret.

As in the English probation studies, contact which can be classified as *control* seems to yield the largest number of failures. For example, police have the highest and social workers the lowest recidivism rates among their clients even when allowance is made for the clients' prognoses. More frequent contact between supervisor and client, measured by number of meetings or length of meetings, shows covariance overall with high recidivism rates. The fact that this association is stronger in the low risk group suggests that clients perceive this contact as control, an unnecessary intrusion, and therefore react negatively. The fact that the association disappears or even is reversed in the high risk group, may be interpreted to mean that more clients in this group actually need help and therefore find the contact supportive. This interpretation receives support from the finding that there is a high rate of recidivism among the clients in the low risk group who would prefer less contact with their supervisor, while in the high risk group there is greater recidivism among the clients who would prefer more frequent contact.

The supervisors who possess a *false treatment optimism* (the inaccurate beliefs that their client perceives them as standing on his side or the belief that their clients do not see supervision as a serious encroachment on personal freedom) also shows poor treatment effects. Similarly, the supervisors who find the non-institutional resources sufficient or who find their work satisfying, also show poor results. This form of treatment optimism seems particularly detrimental for clients in the low risk groups.

The supervisors who assume a *suppostive attitude* (as manifested, for example, in their expressed confidence in their client) seem to get better results, especially with the high risk group. There is covariance between supervisors who take the client's part and do not always report his violations and low recidivism. Supervision based on purely individual prevention (supervisors think the probationary period should be adjusted to the client's individual needs) seems to succeed more often in rehabilitating clients.

The supervisor who assumes a more *informal and friendly style,* also seems to obtain better treatment effects. Concrete expressions of this may be that both supervisors and clients initiate contact or that they meet at different places. Similarly, a more personal relationship (for example, the client explicitly desires to have a particular supervisor assigned to him) leads to better results.

To the initial question why supervision does not have a more *positive* individual preventive effect, one can answer that, given the general lack of contact between supervisor and client and the lack of resources available to them, it seems understandable that supervision designed to provide support and assistance does not have any great impact. Even every third supervisor believes his client would manage as well without a supervisor as with one.

To the question of whether supervision might have a *negative* individual prevention effect, it would seem that this may well be the case for certain clients. Slightly more than every eighth client thinks he would manage better without a supervisor and we find more recidivists among these clients. This figure might be regarded as high bearing in mind the indoctrination that takes place but it may also be seen as the client's attempt at rationalization. However, the fact that a high degree of contact between supervisor and client was detrimental to the rehabilitation of clients in the low risk group provides some support for the theory of negative individual prevention. Furthermore, we find that the *stigmatization theory* helps explain the observed situation where exaggerated activity from the protective or overprotective supervisor leads to negative treatment results.

Further support for a stigmatization theory is found in the beliefs of every fifth supervisor that his client was treated more unfavorably after sentence than ordinary people and of every third client that he was treated better before being sentenced than after. Apart from those objectively reporting such experience we suspect that many more clients subjectively fear the reactions of people in their surroundings. Furthermore, a large number of clients say they find supervision a considerable encroachment on their personal freedom and there tend to be more recidivists among these clients, especially in the high risk group. At the same time, this latter finding seems to contradict the theory of individual deterrence.

The infantilization theory also finds support in the data in that those who need support the least are most harmed by it. The clients in the low risk group who recidivate most are those who say they have been helped. This negative effect of treatment may be interpreted to mean that the supervisor took responsibility away from his client and thereby rendered his adjustment in society more difficult. Both stigmatization and infantilization can be seen as fixation in the sense Eysenck uses this term.

That the recidivism rate is higher among probationers than among offenders given conditional sentences may thus be explained by the fact that supervision is detrimental to the rehabilitation of certain groups of clients.

7

Institutional Treatment—Punishment or Treatment?

In this chapter shall describe the social structure of a probation institution and try to find data which can help us understand the observed differences in recidivism rates between those who were sentenced to probation with institutional treatment and those who were not. Another related purpose is to determine how the legislator's intentions concerning individual prevention are put into practice.

In order to ascertain if a probation institution may be described as a treatment facility or an ordinary prison we conducted a structural-functional analysis of such an institution. Starting from a theory that an institution is a social system we studied the goals, values, structures and activities of the institution as well as its relation to the outside world and change possibilities. This theoretical framework allows us to study the perceptions of both staff and inmates of the goals of treatment, the value they attach to them, interaction between both groups and their attitudes towards each other, the content of the treatment program and the probationers' "careers" at the institution. Finally, we discuss the institution's openness for change.

What we describe here is a completed chapter in the brief 10-year history of probation institutions. The way in which these institutions were created and their subsequent development is of interest for the sociology of law. With the re-organization of the prison and probation systems in 1974 a further estrangement from the legislator's intentions occurred since the sanction of probation with institutional treatment remained unchanged but, at the same time, the probation institutions became open neighborhood prisons. Moreover, in 1983 probation with institutional treatment was completely abolished. Instead the court could order that probation be combined with imprisonment for at least fourteen days and at most three months.

Description of Sample and Method

The institution studied was in the southern region of Sweden which covers the jurisdictional area of the courts covered in the present research. The account given here of the institution is based in the first place on *standardized interviews* of staff and probationers conducted by sociology students and in the second place on *participant observation* by a sociologist with a law degree. Comparisons were also made with the findings of other studies, in particular, my own research on correctional institutions (Bondeson 1974; 1989). The annual reports of the probation institution under study were also examined in order to check and supplement our other data. The report generated has been discussed with the governor of the institution and questions were put to him about more recent developments. This material is supplemented with the *responses* to a survey of the probationers who had been subjected to institutional treatment.

The Institution as a Social System

A probation institution may be described as a *social organization* the activities of which are co-ordinated by a management whose task is to realize one or several goals while observing a set of laid down rules and utilizing all available resources.

Each organization creates its own world which to a greater or lesser degree determines the activities of its members. The organizations which to a high degree decide over the actors of the system have been designated *total institutions* by Goffman (1961). Prisons, reformatories, mental hospitals, hospitals, homes for the aged, army barracks, isolated work places such as ships and monasteries are given as examples of such organizations. Probation institutions can be seen as examples of such total institutions where the actors must conduct all their activities throughout each and every day within the same physical space. Because the probation institutions use coercive control they may also be regarded as *coercive organizations* in the sense that Etzioni (1961) uses that term. Insofar as the institution uses normative control, based on symbolic sanctions, to a greater extent than coercive control, it may be said to develop towards being a *normative organization.*

Aims

The new sanction which was introduced at the time of the entry into force of the Penal Code made it possible to prescribe treatment in an institution in the initial phase of probation. The reason given for this sanction was individual prevention (see Chapter 3 for a review of the legislator's intention). The legislative text provides that institutional treatment shall be included in an offender's probation if it is "considered necessary for his correction or otherwise". The Minister of Justice clarified this as follows: "In the legislative text emphasis is placed primarily on considerations of individual prevention. Institutional treatment aims at making probation a more effective sanction than it would otherwise be and probation as such may not be resorted to except when justified by considerations of individual prevention" (Prop 1962:10, C299).

The treatment content of the new sanction form is not specified in detail, but the Protective Law Commission asserted that "the short period of treatment should be used to influence the probationer psychologically and pedagogically so that he gains insight into how important it is for him to refrain from committing crimes in the future" (SOU 1956:55, p. 145). The Minister also emphasized that institutional treatment should be above all a preparation for the longer period of treatment in the community.

Four new institutions were constructed presumably because it was desired to make a clear difference between the probation institutions and the ordinary prisons. The new institutions were open, small and were relatively well equipped and well staffed.

Values Held by the Staff

Because the aims of an institution will primarily be mediated by its staff, one of the tasks of this study is to examine staff values. The aims expressed by the institution's management or the ideology embraced by management can be expected to color the work of the institution both in terms of staff conduct as well as probationer reactions. Value judgments are manifested primarily in the strategies adopted by the management of the institution (Street et al. 1966).

The Purpose of Institutional Treatment

The following question was put to the staff: "What do you think is the purpose of probation with institutional treatment?" The majority responded in accordance with the official aims. Of the twenty-three answers received (the same person may have chosen more than one alternative) twelve deal with preparing the probationer for treatment in the community and arranging work or accommodation for him on release. Six answers range over the alternatives of trying to induce the probationer to discontinue his criminal activities and to realize the seriousness of his situation. Two answers emphasized work training while three named other aims. None of the staff members considered the object of institutional treatment to be punishment. Thus, the staff gave expression to the official ideology.

Assessment of the Probationer Population

A large majority of staff members thought that the probationers who came to the institution should not be there. There were only two who thought that the clients were by and large the right ones to have been sent to the institution. Five persons thought that they had too serious criminal histories to justify placement and the staff as a whole held the view that their offenses were too serious. Several persons pointed out that the courts had a mistaken view of probation with institutional treatment. They stressed the fact that the institution should be a place for first-time offenders but that it was used instead as a "last attempt at rescue" or even in some cases the offender's last chance before internment. One person said that some of the probationers were really mental patients. It was also said that those who have the right circumstances outside the institution ought to be sentenced to probation without institutional treatment.

Thus we find a great deal of criticism of the courts' practice in imposing probation with institutional treatment. To the extent that the courts' application of this sanction differs from, or is perceived as differing from, what is laid down, the staff's chances of carrying into effect the stated aims are rendered correspondingly remote.

Attitude to Mixed Categories of Inmates

One of the prerequisites for the new probation institutions—the separation of the probationers from other prisoners—had not been realized. Because of unused capacity in the probation institutions other types of prisoners—for instance those who had been granted study release, those sentenced for drunken driving, conscientious objectors and certain privileged inmates—were also allocated to them.

However, the staff did not express any dissatisfaction in response to a question of what they thought about the fact that probationers and prisoners were placed together in the same probation institution. Four persons thought that this was no problem mainly because the different groups did not mix. Seven persons stressed the positive influence which offenders convicted of drunken driving had on probationers. Of these, four thought at the same time that prisoners on study release had a negative effect on probationers and a further two said that such prisoners created irritation because of their greater freedom. Only the governor asserted that the two groups had different needs and that it was therefore unwise to mix them.

Perception of the Probationers' Possibilities of Resocialization

The therapeutic efforts of the staff are, to a certain extent, governed by their assessment of the probationers' chances of readjustment. A common answer to the question of what the staff thought of the probationers' ambition to lead a law-abiding life, was that they had no such ambition. Some of those interviewed thought that "deep down " all probationers wanted to live in accordance with the law but, as a workshop foreman expressed it, "the financial demands made on them are too great". The governor stressed the fact that the institution is authoritarian in nature and that it cannot bring about positive changes. He said that "some of the probationers are not wholly damaged" and that they perhaps had some possibility of subsequent adjustment in society.

Half the staff believed that only about 30% of the probationers would manage without committing offenses in the future. Only one person estimated that more than 50% would manage adequately. One of the governors said that the probationers would manage neither better nor worse than the inmates of other correctional institutions.

The staff's estimation of recidivism is quite realistic although it was not then known that about 60% of the probation clients recidivated. The pessimistic view of their chances of resocialization could therefore be regarded as elements in an ideology which could lead to, and at the same time excuse, reduced treatment efforts. There is a real risk that this is true if the answers are interpreted to mean that either the punishment was too lenient or probationers lack the fundamental psychological prerequisites for subsequent adjustment. Such ideas were expressed in discussions with the staff.

The Value of Order and Surface Calm

From the staff's point of view, peace and quiet are prerequisites for the smooth running of their organization. While order is at most a means of reaching some goal it can, in coercive organizations, become an end in itself (cf. Merton's analysis of displacement of aims 1957, 199).

The motto for probationers was *"look after yourself"*. As an example of this the case was cited of a university student who had been sentenced for refusing military service and who wanted to help some immigrant probationers with language instruction. He was refused permission to do this on the grounds that he should look after himself.

The common use of *medication* at the institution can also be interpreted as a sign that order and surface calm has become an aim in itself. From interviews conducted with the probationers it appeared that seven of thirteen were regularly given sedatives. Two of them had not even asked for medication—it had simply been prescribed. The staff were well aware of the extent to which medication was used. Nine of the staff members interviewed estimated the number of inmates who were given sedatives to be about half the population—an estimate which was in agreement with the probationers' responses.

Custodialism

The staff members were asked to respond to an instrument for measuring custodialism developed by Olsson who, under my supervision, wrote a report on the staff of two probation institutions (1971). The scale is a modified version of the one developed by Gilbert and Levinson (1957). These researchers use the concepts *custodialism* and *humanism* to describe two opposing ideologies held by staff members of mental hospitals in the United States.

The *custodial* orientation has the traditional prison as a model with the main aim being the containment of prisoners. The custodial prison officer, truly a guard, sees prisoners as being different from normal human beings with behavior which is both unpredictable and dangerous. He believes that he cannot understand the inmates nor relate meaningfully to them. The custodial ideology is characterized by detachment, mistrust and a pessimistic view of rehabilitation. The *humanist* prison officer, on the other hand, believes that criminality is caused by social and psychological factors and is relatively optimistic about the inmates' chances of resocialization in a democratically organized environment made more like a therapeutic community. The custodial and humanist officers may be seen as *ideal types* in Weber's sense of the term. The majority of staff members are found somewhere between these two polar extremes on the scale.

The answers showed the two governors and the assistant governors to be thoroughgoing humanists. The mean values of the questions answered by this category of staff were higher than those for the basic grade prison officers at the probation institution and at two prisons studied earlier.

This phenomenon of finding a humanist ideology among the higher echelon staff and that custodialism is more common at the lower levels, is typical for *hierarchic organizations*. Johansson (1966) also found, in his study of staff in Swedish mental hospitals, that the groups whose position was lowest in the hierarchy were most custodial in attitude (see also Israel and Johansson 1965).

However, it is not possible to exclude the possibility that over and above position in the organization, educational factors play a part. The better educated staff know how they should answer—which does not necessarily mean that they actually possess the attitude in question.

When comparing attitudes held by staff in the open, treatment-oriented probation institution and the staff of two closed, traditional prisons we do not find great differences in the answers given. However, three of the questions show that the staff of the probation institutions deviate in the direction of greater humanism. Some of these differences in attitude can at least partly be explained by the differences in organization at the two types of institution.

The Social Structure

An organization is built around both a formal and an informal structure (Roethlisberger and Dickson 1939). *The formal structure* consists of an organization plan, rules for the recruitment and training of staff and other rules which regulate activities, the organization of member groups, decision processes, etc. *The informal structure* refers to the things which occur within the organization but outside the formal structure. Communication patterns, social interplay, ways of following rules and regulations are primarily to be found within the informal structure.

General Physical and Social Structure

All four probation institutions in Sweden were built on the same lines. The institution is classified as open even though it is surrounded by a high wire fence. Along the fence are floodlighting posts. Within the institutional perimeter there are an administration block, two pavilions for inmates, a kitchen and dining room, a work shop, a warehouse and a "little house" containing some recreational equipment. The two identical pavilions each house twenty inmates. Both have a lounge with a pantry and an entrance in the middle of the building as well as ten bedrooms and showers and a bathroom at each end. The dining room building has one for the staff and one for the inmates. The kitchen is modern and the work shop is relatively well equipped. Within the grounds there is a gravel area for football and, more recently, a miniature golf course has been made.

In respect to *power structure*, we shall, at this point, only mention that the decision process is centralized. We may therefore describe the institution as authoritarian rather than democratic.

When considering the probation institution as a social organization, two *member groups* can be distinguished: staff and inmates. Typical for coercive organizations where people are more or less divided into castes or classes is that the word member is not included in the terminology (Levinson and Gallagher 1964). However, in a treatment institution, both member groups should be working together in an effort to realize the organization's aims.

Whether the concept "member" can be used to describe participants who are brought into a system by force is open to debate. Here, the term is used neutrally to describe the actors in a system without presuming any common interest between the various member groups. Thus, I do not proceed from the position that harmony exists between the different groups' interests (see Abrahamsson 1975, 144–147, for criticism of the concept "member" in respect of assumptions of harmony). In order for treatment institutions to be truly therapeutic there probably must be a presumption that recruitment is voluntary and that the "treaters" and the "treated" share a common interest, i.e. that something should be cured or changed (cf. a hospital or therapeutic community).

Staff

The Protective Law Commission suggested that probation institutions be furnished with "well-qualified personnel who, from the point of view of treatment, could make good use of the short time at the probation institution" (SOU 1956:55, 144).

Education. Four of the fourteen people interviewed had academic qualifications—the permanent governor, the substitute acting governor and the two assistant governors (one had a bachelor's degree in social work and the other a master's degree). The other staff members had gone through elementary school; two had sat for the lower secondary school leaving certificate, one had gone to a school of economics and one had attended an adult education college. In general, the various staff groups had attended the training courses necessary to qualify them for their respective positions. However, on considering the qualifications obtained after completed basic education it is apparent that there is little difference between personnel working in the probation institutions and in traditional prisons. Only two persons with higher education were present at the institution at the same time, i.e. the governor and one assistant governor.

Temporary Staff. The higher positions are often held by temporary personnel. The office of governor as well as the positions of the two assistant governors were, for example, all held by temporary personnel at the time of the interviews. The office of governor and/or one or both of the two assistant governor posts had been held by temporary personnel since 1967. The governor post was chiefly filled on an acting basis by the institution's permanent first assistant governor while personnel with completed or partial academic degrees and a prison officer under training, filled the assistant governors' positions during vacancies. It seems that long-term temporary posts, despite the extensive vacancies, were not advertized as vacant. Instead, the regional administration had chosen and appointed substitutes. These rather insecure conditions of employment and, in particular, the lack of continuity, were said to a large extent to have subdued any ambitions the assistant governors might have had of contributing to a more progressive development of work at the institution.

Recruitment. Probation institution staff were, to a large extent, recruited from other correctional institutions. The fourteen people interviewed had an average of nine years service behind them. Two had worked for over twenty years in corrections and a further three for more than ten years. Altogether twelve persons had worked for more than five years in this field. The two assistant governors, on the other hand, were relatively new and had worked less than one year in corrections. Neither of them had been at the institution for more than six months. Seven persons had been at the institution since it was opened.

If there had been a real ambition to realize the treatment aims expressed in the preparatory work to the law, the probation institutions should not have been filled with staff transferred from traditional prisons. These persons, who in several cases had many years of service in corrections behind them, had been trained in a more custodial prison climate than that existing today. There is an obvious risk that these persons take habits, behavior patterns and values with them from their previous jobs. The bureaucratic rules governing staff policy within the Swedish Prison and Probation Administration have been prejudicial to the realization of the treatment notion for an analysis of bureaucracy (see Weber 1956).

Division of Work. In reply to the question about which tasks take the most time, the staff reported that administration, supervision of work and general supervision tasks were the most time consuming. The acting governor said: "One must devote the most of one's time to the staff. If the institution is to function, then the staff must function also". The basic grade officers replied "make sure that the inmates follow the rules, keep to the timetable laid down, keep themselves clean and make sure that the cleaning squad cleans the place properly". Only three persons held that contact with probationers took the most time.

In response to the question what *ought* to be their most important task a majority of the interviewed staff members said however that it was talking with the probationers. One basic grade officer declared that "it is most important to mix with the probationers, teach them a little about life, about social norms, such as washing themselves and making their beds".

Thus, we can suppose that the staff experience a conflict in their work. The majority of them devote most of their time to administrative and traditional supervisory tasks while thinking they ought to devote most of their time to talking with the probationers.

The Inmates

Recruitment and Composition of the Inmate Population. *The number of probationers* has never been sufficient to fill more than one of the pavilions. According to a decision by the Swedish Prison and Probation Administration, ten of the forty places were reserved for so-called "study prisoners" (i.e. prisoners transferred from ordinary prisons who had been granted study release). The number of occupied places at the institution varied between ten and twenty for probationers and between ten and fifteen for prisoners. During the week of our field work, thirteen probationers and from seven to ten prisoners were at the institution. The staff thought that there were too few probationers at the institution at the time of our interviews (i.e. when it was only half full) and thought that the optimal number would be between twenty and thirty. The term "inmates" refers to *both* probationers and prisoners.

Eight of the probationers were 19–21 years old, two were between 24 and 27, and three were 40–41 years. According to the Protective Law Commission probation with institutional treatment was primarily intended for young offenders. That three of thirteen were over 40 at the time of our interviews can be said to conflict with one of the prerequisites for institutional treatment.

A question on *education* revealed that none of the probationers had had more schooling than the first nine compulsory years. On the other hand, the majority of them, ten of thirteen, had had some kind of *vocational training*. As to the probationers' *work and accommodation* before commitment, eleven of thirteen reported that they had a place to live and six that they had a job. The answers to this question indicate that the courts did not find the occupational status of half of the probationers reason enough to refrain from depriving them of their liberty.

The *dominant offense* in the current sentence for which a clear majority of probationers were sentenced, was an offense against property. The second most common type of crime was fraud. None of them were sentenced for drug related offenses.

Concerning *previous measures and crime* we found that all the probationers, with the exception of those around forty years of age, had had contact with the child welfare authorities. Four, including two of the forty-year-olds, had had contact with the temperance services. Nine had had some kind of alcohol or drug problem. Eight had been convicted before.

Most noteworthy is perhaps the fact that half of the probationers had previously been committed to some institution. Two of these seven had spent more than two years at institutions and three over five years. Three probationers had earlier been in prison and one had been committed to a youth prison. One had spent more than five years in prison. The annual reports show that the percentage of probationers who had previously been in prison increased somewhat during 1967–1970. This judicial practice does not accord with the proposal made by the Protective Law Commission that those sentenced to probation with institutional treatment should "as a rule be first-time probationers" (p. 146).

A recommendation concerning *remand in custody* which was proposed by the Protective Law Commission does not seem to have been followed by the courts either: "If an offender who has been held in remand in custody is sentenced to probation, it should be possible to avoid imposing treatment at an institution unless the remand has been of only short duration" (SOU 1965:55, 144). All but one of the probationers interviewed had been remanded in custody in connection with their current sentence. The average period on remand was twenty-nine to thirty days. One probationer reported that he was detained for sixty days and another that he was held for 105 days.

Different Categories of Inmates. Even though offenders *sentenced to imprisonment* were not included in our population they were a part of the institutional group. They can be divided into different categories. The "study prisoners" were, as a rule, serving relatively long sentences. Conscientious objectors were usually serving a one-month prison sentence. Both these groups were often considered troublesome by the staff because of their political convictions and their willingness to make criticisms and demands concerning conditions at the institution. A third group was composed of drunken drivers. A fourth group consisted of people from the higher social classes, for example, private business men able to continue their activities during their stay at the institution. The two latter groups were reported to be well-respected by the staff because of their age, social position and willingness to cooperate. Obviously, the prisoners were a heterogeneous group and together with the probationers represent a vast spectrum of different conditions and needs.

Probationers who were serving a sentence of only about one month, tried chiefly to make the time pass and were, therefore, less interested in the conditions of confinement. The "study prisoners" lived under the pressure of trying to adjust to a life of semi-freedom and felt they were under a constant threat of being transferred if they did not behave themselves.

It is likely that unnecessary misunderstandings and irritation arose among the groups because they were not suitably informed of each other's position and conditions at the institution. Two of the probationers did not even know that there were offenders sentenced to imprisonment at the institution.

The majority of probationers felt that the conditions were better for the prisoners because they were granted town passes. While three probationers were positive to the situation with prisoners at the institution, twice as many were negative. Whilst the staff did not consider the mixing of offender categories a problem, the probationers obviously found it a strain.

Mixing probationers with prisoners is clearly contrary to the legislator's intention. The Protective Law Commission emphasized the importance of not placing probationers, who were presumed to be first offenders, together with recidivists (p. 146). The Minister concurred in principle with this requirement: "An essential feature of this form of custody is that, as far as possible, the probationers be kept separate from other types of offenders" (Prop. 1962:10, C300).

Division of Work. A division of work can be observed among the inmates. The working day was devoted to making wooden loading platforms in the workshop. The majority of probationers continued with this activity until they were released. However, some were given the opportunity to "advance" to kitchen work where they assisted in the cooking and washed dishes. In addition, one or two inmates were needed to clean the administration building and the pavilions. There were also occasional opportunities to work as a painter or tending the garden.

The probationers rated the various jobs in the following order: kitchen work, painting and gardening were placed at the top of the hierarchy while nailing industrial loading platforms together and cleaning were placed at the at the bottom. The inmates with high status in outside society were assigned the "best" tasks and those with low status were allotted the "worst" tasks (see also Israel, SOU 1963:24). The "good" jobs were given chiefly to drunken drivers, the majority of whom had better positions in society than the average inmate, and to the older probationers.

The job of nailing together loading platforms was obviously not popular. This was later supplemented with occupational therapy in the form of assembling toys which at least had the advantage of being less noisy. It was difficult for the many emotionally unstable probationers to put up with noisy work.

Power Structure

The power structure of the probation institution may be described as *authoritarian.* The decision process was centralized as the governor alone was responsible for all operational decisions. The governor was, in his turn, subordinate to regional management. Application by prisoners for home leave had, in certain cases, to be made to the regional director.

Staff members were given the opportunity to put forward their views during the morning meetings. Inmates usually had to express their opinions in individual discussions. Attempts had been made to create an *inmate council* but this did not last long. The "study prisoners" made an attempt in the spring of 1971 to help the inmates gain participatory influence but this initiative was said to have been opposed by institutional and regional officials. In the summer another attempt was made and resulted in the formation of an inmate council with four representatives from the inmates and four from the staff. The council met regularly for a while and discussed different issues but had no authority to make decisions. It was started under the direction of the permanent governor but was discontinued in the fall of the same year. The acting governor announced that the council was discontinued because the inmates lacked interest in it. It seems that a prerequisite for the success of such an enterprise is the active support of staff, as the inmates are, at times, only mildly interested.

In answer to the question "How much say do the inmates have in the running of the institution?" eight of thirteen probationers answered that they had little or no say. All of those with "good" jobs who belonged to the older age group thought that the inmates had quite a lot of say. The answers given by the probationers at this institution differed little from those given in interviews at correctional institutions for juveniles (Bondeson 1974, 455–456). When the same question was put to the staff, twelve of fourteen answered that the inmates had little say. In response to a question about whether the inmates could put forward their own views, the staff said that they might do so in a personal capacity but, as one assistant put it, "action is seldom taken".

Relations Between the Various Staff Groups

It is characteristic of coercive organizations with some treatment elements that certain staff groups take charge of the custodial tasks while other staff groups take charge of the more treatment-oriented tasks. This division of labor often leads to tension and conflict between the various staff groups (see Cressey, 1960; 1961).

In response to the question "How do you think your colleagues find the treatment of probationers at this institution?" all custodial staff said that they believed their colleagues shared their own views. One of the foremen replied that he thought his colleagues' opinions as to treatment were positive, another that he knew nothing of the views of his colleagues and the third foreman gave a description which seems somewhat critical: "There must be order. The probationers are only at the institution to work. Some of the staff think we should be stricter." The treatment staff generally show less conformity in their answers. One of the governors asserted that the staff members had divergent views, two assistant governors believed that the staff thought that "the probationers are treated too well" and one assistant governor claimed that "a minority of staff members are not willing to help".

It is characteristic of authoritarian organizations that the staff try to conceal their conflicts. If they allow the conflicts to surface there is a risk that they would feel the necessity to re-examine the power structure and way of working at the institution. This situation is well illustrated in the answers to the foregoing question in which the staff groups either conceal or reveal disagreements depending on how much sympathy they feel for the authoritarian organization. The custodial staff have, almost without exception, tried to conceal—or at least avoid confessing—disagreements, while the managing and treatment staff were more inclined to reveal them.

The question "Are there any differences of opinion between staff and management as to how the institution program should be designed and how the probationers should be treated?" yielded a clearer picture of the existing disagreements. One of the governors said quite openly: "There is a clear line of distinction. It comes also as a part of one's training. I am a social worker and the basic grade custodial staff have another kind of training. The majority of them started work in the repressive correctional system which emphasized good order and discipline". The other governor said somewhat more cautiously: "Some of the basic grade officers think the probationers should be more strictly treated." One of the assistant governors expressed the prevailing conflict of opinion in the following way: "The basic grade custodial staff are more restrictive. Some of them come from the central prison and they only act as guards." The second assistant governor emphasized the conflict aspect: "There is always trouble between the basic grade staff and the assistant governors. The former want to nail the latter. The probationers are either forgotten or they are get squeezed between management and custodial officer staff." The third assistant governor called attention to the conflicts within staff groups: "The question is whether the probationers are to be treated conservatively or humanely. There are controversies between groups and individuals, some people don't talk to each other." He added: "There are both conservative and radical custodial officers but top management takes the side of those who want to emphasize the custodial aspects in the treatment of the probationers".

It can thus be seen that even in the probation institution *opinions differ between the professional treatment staff and the traditional custodial officer staff.* A number of studies have shown how specialists, psychologists and social workers, because of their placing emphasis on individual treatment, easily come into conflict in an authoritarian system with staff groups more oriented towards guarding. If management "takes the side of those who want to emphasize the custodial aspects in the treatment of probationers" then this may be seen as a further sign that the probation institution is most comparable with traditional prison establishments.

Communication Between Staff and Probationers

Need of Information. Despite the small size of the institution, there were considerable communication problems. Both staff and probationers complained about the lack of information. The lack of satisfactory communication was made clear by half the staff who considered that they were not well enough informed of the various matters concerning their work at the institution.

Naturally enough, the probationers had an even greater need for information as they, by comparison with the staff, stayed only a short time at the institution. On arrival at the institution, the probationers were given complete information about the rules which must be obeyed but they considered that information about treatment was insufficient. They felt that they were not properly informed of such things as group discussions, study activities, work furlough and leisure activities. For example, the majority of them did not know that they could obtain equipment for sports training. One probationer thought that he was not allowed to take part in group discussions "because one should be there only for the last ten days". Another probationer declared that he had not been given work furlough because such a release could be granted only after three weeks in residence. Lack of information or incorrect information can have the unintentional effect that the probationers do not utilize the treatment resources which actually are available to them.

Pattern of Interaction According to the Staff. The probationers had the *possibility* of talking to the staff at almost any time because there were so many staff members. The basic grade custodial officers reported that they had long daily conversations with the probationers. The assistant governors said that they had long conversations with the probationers twice per week.

Each of the staff members questioned, with the exception of one custodial officer, felt that the probationers *needed* contact with the staff. The custodial officers believed that none of the probationers, or only very few of them, desired as little contact as possible with the staff. On the other hand, the two assistant governors thought that there was a conflict between the probationers' objective need of contact with the staff and the way they subjectively perceived the necessity of such contacts; the assistant governors believed that half the probationers did not want these contacts.

The staff gave various answers to the question whether they had the possibility of *meeting* the probationers' need for contact. Four persons felt that they lacked time and therefore could not satisfy the probationers' contact needs. Seven thought that the possibility ought to exist as there were quite a lot of staff with treatment and not control tasks. One assistant governor answered that "time exists and possibilities exist but they are not utilized because of lack of interest and laziness".

The custodial officers, who more than any other staff group were responsible for the personal contact with the probationers, had varying and rather pessimistic opinions about their chances of satisfying the probationers' contact needs.

Pattern of Contact According to the Probationers. The probationers' answers to the same questions produce a somewhat similar picture. The staff reported discussions with probationers as being somewhat more frequent and of longer duration than the probationers did.

The probationers said that they spoke more with the custodial officers than with the assistant governors. On the other hand, four of them reported that they almost never talked to the custodial officers, no more than was absolutely necessary. A majority of probationers said that they talked with the assistant governors at least once a week. However, three of them reported that they almost never talked with the assistant governors.

If the conversations occurred more often between custodial officers and probationers than between them and the assistant governors, they were, on the other hand, longer with the assistant governors. Ten probationers thought that their discussions with assistant governors were usually long. Just as many noted that their conversations with the custodial officers were short.

Eleven of 13 probationers reported that they did not want to speak more with the staff than they in fact did. The two probationers who did want to talk more with the staff were among the four who felt that they had little chance of refraining from committing further offenses when released. Thus, those who needed help to get along outside the institution seem to be the ones who had most difficulty establishing the contact they needed. But the present staff seemed unable to establish the contact these probationers wanted. Of the four who felt they lacked prospects, each said he would take his problems primarily to the other probationers or to a psychiatrist or psychologist. Almost all the other probationers said that they would choose someone from the management staff if they had some personal problem they wanted to discuss.

The Probationers' Attitudes to the Staff

Two questions were put to the probationers: "What do you think of the custodial officers at this institution?" and "What do you think the other probationers think of the custodial officers?" Table 7.1 shows the answers obtained.

TABLE 7.1 Probationers' Attitudes to Custodial Officers: Own Attitudes and Assessment of the Attitudes of Others (absolute numbers)

	"Screws" Only	Both "Screws" and Ordinary People	Ordinary People	No Opinion	Total
Own attitude	1	7	5	0	13
Assessment of others' attitudes	6	2	1	4	13

In order to establish to what extent the probationers regarded the staff as controllers, the inmate *argot* was used. The Swedish word *"plit"* is a derogatory term for a prison officer who runs around locking and unlocking doors (cf. the English argot term "screw"). "Plit" has disagreeable connotations for the inmates and this has been confirmed by an Osgood test where with fifteen different pairs of adjectives the word "plit" produced higher negative values than the words for both guard and prison officer (Bondeson 1974, 145; Bodin 1971). In Table 7.1 the word "screw" is used for "plit".

In Table 7.1 the distribution of answers between the two questions differs considerably. Only one of thirteen probationers regards the custodial officers as "only screws". On the other hand, as many as six of thirteen—or six of the nine who had an opinion here—thought that the other probationers see the custodial officers as "only screws". Thus, we find that the probationers misperceive the attitudes of their fellows.

Group Pressure and Pluralistic Ignorance

The difference between private and public attitudes has been called *pluralistic ignorance* in accordance with Allport's terminology. However, the concept has come to be used for a somewhat different phenomenon (see Bondeson 1974, 147–148 for a more extensive review of this). "Pluralistic ignorance" is used by criminologists to describe the situation observed in penal institutions where a greater proportion of inmates express the norms of the prison subculture on the basis of what they believe—wrongly—to be their fellow inmates' attitudes rather than their own values.

The phenomenon of "pluralistic ignorance" is interesting because it uncovers *the perception of a group norm.* Whether the perception is correct or incorrect the perceived group norm exerts *pressure on the group.* It is this social pressure, rather than the psychological perception in itself, that should interest the student of social organizations.

In my previous study of different correctional institutions it was shown that just over one-quarter of the inmates regarded the custodial officers as "only screws" while just over one-third thought that the other inmates regarded the custodial officers in this way. "Pluralistic ignorance" or, to use the term I prefer, *perceptually strengthened norms,* was observed at every kind of correctional institution. I also found that at institutions where a low proportion of inmates individually regarded custodial officers as "screws" there was the greatest increase in the proportion of inmates believing that their fellow inmates saw them as such. On the other hand, at institutions with a high proportion replying affirmatively to the question on individual attitudes there was a low proportion replying affirmatively to the perception question. However, nowhere was the difference so great as it was at the probation institution. Only 8% of the probationers answered the individual attitude question with "only screws".

But the proportion answering the perception question with "only screws" at the probation institution was 46% if we count all the answers. While the difference in the proportions between the two sets of answers was 13% at training schools and only 2% for those sentenced to internment, the difference was at least 38% at the probation institution. If we count only the answers in which an opinion was expressed, as was the case at the other institutions, the figure is 59%.

Probably the explanation lies in the character of the social organization under study here. The same pattern which we found accentuated at the probation institution, could also be observed at the most therapeutic of the institutions studied in the earlier research. It seems that a coercive organization with some elements of treatment can create positive attitudes among some of its inmates but at the same time each of these offenders believes he is the only one with a positive attitude towards the staff. In other words, treatment is not so dominant that it succeeds in changing the social atmosphere sufficiently for all inmates to realize that a majority of them share positive attitudes towards the staff. On the contrary, the coercive element is such a dominating feature that inmates believe the majority of their fellow inmates to hold negative attitudes. Two characteristic features of *coercive organizations* are, firstly, that those whose job it is to treat are not accepted and, secondly, that communication does not flow easily through the rigid hierarchy. As a result of this second feature, inmates easily perceive a group norm wrongly and later get no opportunity to correct this misperception because the various individuals are forced to assume various defensive postures because of what they believe to be the social climate.

The Probationers' Mutual Relations

Seen from the staff's point of view, the probationers' contacts with each other are in general superficial. One custodial officer characterized them in the following way: "They know nothing about each other, don't know each other. They don't even know one another's name." However, when we listened to the probationers themselves we were more inclined to believe they had good mutual relationships. When we asked how they would describe the cohesiveness of their group, twice as many thought that it was strong as thought it was weak. While two-thirds thought there was strong cohesion among probationers at the probation institution, barely half the inmates studied at thirteen other correctional institutions shared this view (Bondeson 1974, 164).

To the follow-up question, "How cohesive *should* the probationers be?" six answered that things were all right as they were, five that the probationers ought to act more as a group and two that they ought to act more as individuals. Because so many felt that there already existed strong group cohesion it is natural to find fewer probationers who believe they ought to act more as a group. When drawing comparisons with the institutions studied earlier, we find the greatest similarities between the probation institution and ordinary youth training schools where the majority of adolescents felt they had strong group cohesion and a minority that they ought to act more as a group.

Despite the short time spent at the institution and the large age variation, group cohesion seems stronger in the probation institutions than in most of the other correctional institutions. Inmate cohesion and solidarity have been regarded as defense mechanisms, a way for the inmates to reduce the pressures contingent upon incarceration and society's condemnation and at the same time increase their own self-esteem and group status (Sykes 1958).

The Institution's System of Rules

The rules of an institution are interesting because of the norm system they reflect and because they reveal a great deal about the activities which are normally governed by the rule system.

The Protective Law Commission found it difficult to specify the content of treatment which should be available at probation institutions. It did, however, state clearly what the institutions should *not* strive to achieve: "It ought to be especially emphasized that the proposal does not mean that probation institutions should introduce treatment which has been described in discussions of criminal policy as a short sharp shock, nor that iron discipline be maintained among the probationers nor that the routine at the institution should follow an exact schedule" (pp. 145–146).

Every bureaucratic organization has need of a system of rules. It is therefore the content of the regulations and not the mere existence of a rule system which characterizes a social organization. The rules and regulations concerning the activities of the probation institution fill various functions. The following description keeps relatively close to Tajthy's account.

There are, first of all, a series of rules which are designed to ensure the physical presence of inmates in the institution—prohibited areas, the locking of internal and external doors at specified times. Somewhat similar rules determine the framework for co-existence—the time to get up, to eat, to go to bed, etc. Other rules strictly forbid certain activities, for instance, visiting each other's rooms after 10 P.M. tattooing and gambling. There are rules which require the inmates' active participation in work and rules which make the work of the staff easier. Thus, the custodial officers were empowered to decide whether inmates might watch television after 10 P.M. This rule was amended so as to require inmates to apply in writing to the governor in advance. The new rule led to a reduction of extended television watching and made the staff's job easier.

Some rules live on tenaciously. Letter censorship, for example, is not normally carried out but exists nevertheless as a potential control possibility. Censorship does not exist but the governor makes spot checks on letters. Of special interest are rules which have lost their original function. Sundin provides the following description of probation institutions:

> When they (the probation institutions) were opened, the area around the buildings had not yet been cleaned up so signs were placed at the entrances of the administration buildings requesting inmates to take off their shoes before entering. The signs were later taken down at some of the institutions when they were no longer needed but were left in place at other institutions even though the area was clean. The staff entered the administration buildings with their shoes on while the inmates were obliged to remove theirs at the entrance. What was left was a ban which had no other function than to mark social distance (p. 78).

The institution studied here had the above-mentioned sign left up at the time of our investigation. Inmates removed their shoes at the entrance. Yet other rules have a suppressive effect on inmates. When probation with institutional treatment was first introduced, probationers were permitted to wear their own clothes at the institution. Two years later, however, the habitual green prison clothing was brought into use on the grounds that when probationers have access to their own clothes the risk of their escaping increases and that anyway inmates have problems washing their own clothes. Since there had scarcely been any escapes from the institution studied here and that laundry problems are solvable, it could be said that the institution too easily gave up the idea of reducing social differences between staff and probationers by not using prison clothing.

The limiting of telephone calls and visits was also justified on rational grounds but had nevertheless a demoralizing effect on inmates.

The ensemble of the many rules governing life at the probation institution showed a guardianship mentality and instead of increasing a sense of personal responsibility actually reduced it. The authoritarian character of the institution is revealed in the staff's view of orderliness, cleanliness and hygiene. They tried to teach probationers social norms with the help of regulations and detailed instructions about what is meant by socially acceptable behavior.

Through the detailed rule system outlined above probationers can feel degraded to the position of people who lack the capacity to judge the simplest of actions. The staff seem to base their actions on an ideology which affirms that teaching probationers conformity to certain rules also changes their behavior patterns in other respects. The danger is, however, that the learning of social skills becomes reduced to the learning of such relatively unimportant matters as straightening the sheets and keeping wooden shoes in the cupboard.

However, the staff do not always keep strictly to the regulations. The degree to which obedience to the rules is controlled, varies from custodial officer to custodial officer and even for the same custodial officer at various times depending on his mood. The regulations may be applied more stringently to one inmate than to another depending on the relations existing between inmate and custodial officer.

As can be seen from the above description, the regulations which applied indicate that the institution was an authoritarian, coercive organization rather than a democratic institution oriented towards treatment. Sykes (1958, 35–37), who has described the rule system of American prisons in detail, asserts that for the custodial staff "maintaining good order" seems to be the most important device ever discovered when it comes to preparing the prisoner for following the rules of society after release.

The probation institution can hardly be said to have taken to heart the Protective Law Commission's warning that treatment should consist neither of a short sharp shock nor adherence to a routine based on an exact schedule.

Institutional Activities

Daily Routine

Work. The main job at the probation institution was making wooden loading platforms. Inmates worked on a piecework basis. When asked if they thought that there was any difference between the work situation at the institution and outside, nine of thirteen probationers responded that the conditions at the institution were worse than outside. Seven asserted that the coercion used in the job at the institution made it different from work outside. Four pointed out that their wages were much lower, "slave wages", for the work they did at the institution.

A majority of the staff, eleven of fourteen, also thought that the work done by inmates at the institution was monotonous and without meaning. The two governors and one of the foremen were especially skeptical about the work describing it as "negative and deadly", "Sisyphean labor" and "dreadful". The other two foremen, on the other hand, considered the work good and thought that it provided training.

The staff agreed that the probationers needed vocational training but the majority asserted that it would be difficult to arrange because the period of stay was so short. Nine nevertheless thought that the planning could be better, four that aptitude tests could be used more often and three that vocational training could be started at the institution and completed in the community after release.

Education. Education was provided on three mornings per week through an adult education organisation. It included mathematics, Swedish, English and civics. The studies were mainly similar to those undertaken during the last few years of elementary school. Inmates received a small sum for each hour they took part, but they had to pay about seven times that amount to enrol for each subject. Those who worked in the kitchen were not permitted to take part in the courses because, it was said, their work shifts could not be fitted in with morning education classes.

At the time of this research only three probationers were taking part in these courses. Two probationers who did not participate would have liked to, one of them being prevented because he worked in the kitchen. One of those who did participate explained why so few probationers took part in the courses: "You get less pay. You get twice as much for working in the workshop as you do studying. Also the guys don't think they can handle it. You have to go to the assistant governor and he decides if you can study. The staff think the guys choose education to get away from the workshop. This is partly true, but it is still better to learn something than to stand and hammer in nails all day".

Half of the staff think the education courses could be more comprehensive. Those who consider them unsatisfactory think that the number of subjects and hours of instruction could be increased. Moreover, they thought that different groups should be formed for different educational levels so that individual needs would be better catered for.

The annual reports also urge extended theoretical instruction at the institution. "Many inmates have alarmingly little knowledge which has little to do with lack of intellectual ability and more with lack of schooling" (1973/74). Subsequent intensified instruction was commented on in the following way: "This instruction cannot possibly fill the gaps in knowledge. The majority have not enough knowledge to continue with local adult education. Some kind of preparatory courses should be arranged within the framework of ordinary probation in collaboration with some educational organization" (1974/75).

Group Discussions. Group discussions were not organized on a regular basis. This activity was not functioning at all during the time prior to our field work at the institution. At the time of the study, nine probationers took part in group discussions. The four probationers who did not take part wanted to but they had not been offered the chance to take part. The discussions took place three times a week for an hour during working hours. They were led by one of the staff, usually an assistant governor. Life at the institution was the most frequent topic of discussion or the probationers might want some kind of information, e.g. about social welfare, supervision, work opportunities and the like.

Leisure Activities. During the week, the inmates had about three hours every day between the evening meal and locking-up time in which they could move freely about within the institution. Activities were usually not organized so the inmates were left to find things to do. Recreation possibilities depended on the season and weather. As they could not be outside during most of the year, the inmates usually stayed in their pavilions. There they slept or played cards until the TV-programmes started. When the weather permitted a varying number of inmates played football. However, many soon lost interest because they were so unfit. Croquet was introduced during the time we were there and this game was a success. On the weekends and holidays, however, these activities were insufficient.

All the staff members, except one custodial officer, agreed that there were insufficient leisure activities. Five said that the lack of financial resources was to blame and four blamed the lack of staff resources. One of the governors believed "the staff are afraid of breaking with tradition" and this prevented the development of more comprehensive activities. One of the assistant governors thought that "inmates could be taken to the theater or swimming, but no-one (on the staff) wants to make the sacrifice" and added: "some of the staff are opposed to such activities". Another assistant governor noted that "management lacks interest and energy".

Outside Contacts. Probationers were only permitted to leave the institution on work furlough or when visiting a hospital. They could receive visitors every second Sunday between 1 and 3 P.M. They had limited opportunities to make and receive telephone calls but they could write as many letters as they wished.

Half the staff considered the probationers' contacts with the world outside the institution were satisfactory and half thought they were not. Several of the staff members reported that they wanted "more ordinary people to visit the institution such as union representatives, employers, various interest groups and everyone with an idealistic involvement would be welcome". Others thought time was too short and expressed a fear of disturbing the routines. According to one person, "it is not good to have too many people (from outside) running around here".

The Probationers' Careers at the Institution

Goffman (1961) talks of an inmate's *moral career* when he describes the progressive changes that take place in him with respect to his view of himself and of significant others in his life. He becomes the victim of a humiliating process which Goffman calls the *mortification process.* This process denotes, among other things, the situation in which inmates are stripped of their personal belongings and their civilian roles and are subjected to exposure through censorship and search.

Sentence. It was by no means uncommon for probationers not to know what the sanction means. It was said to be quite common for the probationers to stay a long time at the institution before they realized what probation with institutional treatment implied. One custodial officer said: "I don't think they understand what it means—99% don't know. Information from the courts, and even from us, is too poor".

How do probationers perceive the *intention* behind probation with institutional treatment? Five answered that the intention was to prepare the offender for treatment in the community and to arrange work and housing. Five thought the intention was to get the offender to terminate his criminal activities or to get him to understand the seriousness of his situation. Three had different answers, one of whom said that the idea was to give them work training. It is remarkable that none of them thought the intention was to punish the offender.

There is relatively good agreement between the views held by probationers and those held by the staff as to the intention behind the sanction. The slight difference which does exist, can be seen in the somewhat more frequent answer given by staff that the sanction prepares probationers for non-institutional treatment and by probationers that attempts are made with the sanction to terminate criminal activity. On the other hand, half of the staff thought the probationers regarded the sanction as punishment when in fact none of them did.

Reception Procedures. When the probationers arrived at the institution he was received by a custodial officer who filled in different forms registering reception at the institution. Thereafter his civilian clothes were exchanged for a pair of green trousers, two green or brown shirts, a thick grey jumper, a green jacket, a pair of black wooden shoes, two undershirts, two pairs of underpants, two pairs of socks, one pair of nylon socks and a pair of blue overalls for work. After this *ritual* the offender had become stripped of his civilian role and assigned a *prison role* for some time to come (see Garfinkel 1956, regarding rituals and degradation ceremonies).

Treatment Board. In principle, the activities and treatment of the probationers should be determined by a treatment board. These boards however, did not function as intended. Only one of the thirteen probationers said that he had been before a treatment board which was supposed to review his treatment program. According to him, they discussed hygiene during this meeting.

If the treatment board does not function, how then is treatment planned? As we saw earlier, the majority of probationers are put to work nailing loading platforms from the first working day, and thus the occupational problem is solved. The other matters which should be discussed by the board, such as preparation for non-institutional treatment, were discussed in subsequent conversations between the probationer and an assistant governor.

Discussions with Assistant Governors and Preparation for Non-Institutional Treatment. The assistant governors' main tasks were to keep case records and send probationers out into the community with jobs and a place to live.

Eleven of the interviewed probationers said that they had a place to live and six that they had jobs when they were committed. Two said they lost their homes as a result of being committed and one lost his job. When asked what they wanted on release, the majority said they wanted an apartment and a good job; there were just as many "good job" answers as there were "apartment" answers.

The assistant governor and the probationer discussed job opportunities on the work market and which jobs to seek. However, steps were not taken to arrange work and accommodation until about two weeks after the probationer's arrival at the institution. One of the assistant governors asserted that work and accommodation cannot be found earlier because the probationers must be at the institution for at least one month. He believed it to be impossible to look for a job before the probationer can start working as in the majority of cases the employer wants the probationer to start work immediately. Opinions differed between the governors and assistant governors as to the number of probationers for whom they arranged work and accommodation and ranged from "about half" to "a few".

In the same way, we found divergent data on the extent to which the National Labor Market Board (Arbetsmarknadsstyrelsen) was used when looking for work. The two governors asserted that a representative from the Board visited the institution once a week while one of the assistants said that the institution no longer had any contact with the Board and another that there had not been a representative at the institution for over a month. Only one of the probationers who had been there over a month, said that he had met with a representative from the Board. Information on how often aptitude tests were performed varied but the interviewed probationers had not been tested.

According to the assistant governors and governors, probationers had little chance of getting the work they wanted. If the probationer has "some special training, the chances are good", but otherwise it was "almost hopeless". They pointed out that the "job market is tough, especially for those who have been confined in an institution". The assistants wished the "employers' attitudes could be changed for the better" and that "contact with unions and the man in the street could be arranged".

Work Furlough. If an probationer needed to meet a prospective employer personally, he could be granted a work furlough. The furlough might last for a couple of hours or a whole day. The probationer either went alone or was accompanied by a custodial officer who drove him. These furloughs were granted, as one assistant expressed it, "only in the final stage". The staff held the opinion that enough furloughs were granted. However, only two of the thirteen probationers had been granted a work furlough and three had been refused such furloughs.

Psychiatrists and Psychologists. The consulting psychiatrist should be at the institution once a week. The majority of probationers had visited him for "nervous upsets". The most common treatment given was the prescribing of strong tranquilizers.

The psychologist post was vacant at the time of this study. According to the annual report of 1971/1972, a psychologist who had been appointed after we were there, left the institution because the staff were unhappy with the way he conducted a so-called community meeting. After a further period the next psychologist had to devote a great deal of time to the staff. None of the consulting psychologists seems to have had individual contact with the probationers.

The Probationers' Adjustment to the Institutional Life. Many of the probationers sentenced to institutional treatment reacted to the pressures of prison life by *playing it cool*—to use Sykes's terminology. They were often worried and anxious but tried to hide these feelings behind a tough attitude. They tried to endure the relatively short period of confinement and strove to avoid making their problems worse. There were very few escapes from the institution. According to the annual reports, there were usually only a couple of escapes per year. The most common reasons given by the staff for these escapes were: "broken relationships outside the institution", "a prospective employer refused him a job during a work furlough" and "had a row with the staff".

Release. Probationers may be released from the probation institution after the supervision board has so decided. The board met once a week at the institution and assessed whether employment and accommodation problems had been satisfactorily resolved. It had become the practice to release probationers after just over a month's stay, i.e. informally a definite period for confinement had been accepted.

Chances of Not Resorting to Crime. The probationers were asked to rate their chances of surviving without committing further offenses after release. Nine thought their chances were good, while four believed they had little chance. Thus, we see that they assessed their future social situation less pessimistically than the staff did. On the other hand, the staff made more realistic judgments of recidivism rates than the probationers. Like the inmates interviewed in different correctional institutions (Bondeson 1974, 315ff.), probationers overestimated their chances of coping in the community.

The Effect of Confinement on the Probationers. More than half the probationers mentioned the following *positive* consequences of institutional life: they get a good place to live when they get out, they live a protected life at the institution and they get medical care at the institution.

More than half them said they experienced *negative* effects from their confinement: nervousness, loss of confidence in others, dependence, apathy and laziness, they wanted to "hit back" when they got out.

Survey Data. I have made a special analysis of the questionnaires completed by probationers sentenced to institutional treatment in the original sample. This group totals thirty-four people. To the extent that they do not constitute a representative sample because of missing data in questionnaire responses the sample probably has a positive bias. These respondents have, besides answering the questions analyzed in the section on supervision, also answered questions concerning institutional treatment.

When asked if the institution arranged work for them, 12% answered "yes". Only 3% said they were happy with the work obtained for them. Only 6% reported that the institution had found them a place to live.

The majority of them had participated in group discussions at the institution, but 82% thought them of no value. As many as 56% claimed that they had never spoken to a psychiatrist or psychologist at the institution. One-fifth of those that had done so reported that their meeting with the psychiatrist or psychologist was useful.

One-quarter of the probationers sentenced to institutional treatment said that they had received a visit from their supervisor, and somewhat more than one-quarter said that they had had telephone conversations with their supervisor while they were at the institution. These proportions may be considered to be high bearing in mind that this was several years before the re-organization of the prison and probation systems which emphasized such contacts with the outside world.

When asked how they were affected by the probation institution, the majority answered that the experience had been neither beneficial nor detrimental

(62%); a somewhat greater proportion thought that it had been detrimental rather than beneficial (18% and 12% respectively) and a few thought it had been both beneficial and detrimental (9%). When the direct question whether they thought the experience had been detrimental to them was put, one-quarter answered affirmatively.

What advantages had they received from their stay? Nobody believed the work training had been of any value, 3% found the vocational training useful, 9% said they had become more fit, 18% had formed a better attitude to society, while 41% felt they had learnt to understand themselves better.

When the probationers were released they often tried to conceal the fact that they had been at a probation institution. One-third tried to hide it from their friends, almost half tried to hide it from their employers and just as many tried to hide it from their workmates. These results lend considerable support to the stigmatization theory.

Thus, the somewhat dismal picture of the treatment situation at the probation institution which emerges is about the same in the interview data as from the survey data.

Relations with the Outside World

The probation institution is governed in varying degrees from the outside—by the penal system's higher management and by the surrounding social system. Theories of open systems which emphasize interaction with the environment as an important factor for the survival of the organization seem at least partially applicable for describing the probation institution (Katz and Kahn 1966; Buckley 1967).

The *higher management system* consists of the Swedish Prison and Probation Administration, the Ministry of Justice and ultimately, Parliament. Institution management cannot decide, for instance, on changes which affect the budgetary framework, the modification of the industrial program or the provision of full-time educational and training courses or the appointment of a psychologist, a recreation organizer or a study supervisor. Restrictions of this kind have made it difficult to establish an atmosphere of rehabilitation at the institution. The governor, who had had great expectations of institutional treatment's possibilities, resigned from his post in the fall of 1971 after many setbacks.

The institution was also affected by the *surrounding social system.* Restrictions on town passes for "study prisoners" were the result, among other things, of certain local authorities expressing disapproval of "drug pushers running around loose in the community claiming to study". In the same way, public opinion as expressed in letters to editors, can have an inhibitory effect on reforms.

It is noteworthy that the institution studied here did not have any contact with the other three probation institutions which were established at the same time and where the pre-conditions were identical. Neither the governors nor the other staff members were aware of any discussions or collaboration taking place between these institutions. The probation institutions seem thus to have functioned as *closed systems* in relation to one another.

Changes

According to many of the staff members, much more could have been done for the probationers even with the present administrative, financial and staff resources. When asked what they would like specifically to change, however, a number of them replied that there was nothing they wanted to change. Another group said they would like more staff at the institution. A third group wanted the probationers to remain longer at the institution. The governor and an assistant governor asserted that they wanted the rule system changed, more treatment-oriented staff and the creation of a therapeutic community.

The majority of staff members thought that few changes had been made at the probation institution. Nevertheless, some of them contended that the "attitude had softened" when visiting bans were abolished, the familiar mode of address was allowed when inmates spoke to staff (Swedish has both a formal and a familiar word for "you": it was the use of the latter that came to be permitted) and an inmate council created.

As we have already seen, several changes have taken place. Probably the most significant consequence of these changes was the fact that the probation institution no longer functioned as such. As a result of the re-organization of the prison and probation systems in 1974 it became an open neighborhood prison and probationers were only a minority of its inmates. Many of the probationers had, in accordance with the proximity principle (a dominant feature of the re-organization) been placed in other neighborhood prisons nearer to their homes where they disappeared among the ordinary prisoners. Thus, the most important principle for the establishment of probation institutions, namely to keep probationers and prisoners separate, has been completely eliminated. This decisive change was instigated without any discussion with those concerned at the probation institutions.

As a result of research showing the ineffectiveness of probation with institutional treatment this sanction was abolished and replaced with a possibility to combine probation with ordinary imprisonment for up to three months.

Final Comments

The observation data and interview responses from 1970 and the survey material from offenders sentenced in 1967 lead to a similar picture of institutional treatment and supplement the data obtained from the case records presented in Chapter 5. The results show that the legislature's individual preventive aims, namely that probationers should be treated at probation institutions and be positively influenced psychologically and pedagogically by well-qualified staff and thus prepared for subsequent non-institutional treatment, have not been attained. On the contrary, several findings show that institutional treatment may have made adjustment in society more difficult. The governors interviewed in 1970 and 1976 and the probation institution's annual reports give expression to the idea that the institution can only provide minimal positive assistance and that it runs a clear risk instead of counteracting later readjustment. The probationer seems to a considerable extent to undergo the change of status which Goffman calls *stigmatization* and tries to conceal the fact that he has been at an institution from his friends and particularly from his workmates and employer.

Data obtained from interviews with staff and probationers, as well as data from the records, thus supports a theory of *negative individual prevention.* These results from the study of a probation institution agree both theoretically and empirically with those obtained from other correctional institutions (Bondeson 1974; 1989). There it was demonstrated that, despite the aims and formal structure of the institutions studied, their negative effects were more prominent than their positive effects and that the majority of probationers underwent some form of so-called prisonization.

8

The Law in Books and the Law in Practice

The objectives of the sanctions of conditional sentence and probation and the extent of their realization through sentencing and enforcement are now briefly recapitulated and the factors which hinder the implementation of a treatment program or the achievement of individual preventive aims are examined. The analysis is related to *the different explanatory possibilities*bed in Chapter 1 as to why legislation can lack effects.

The Legislator's Aim of Individual Prevention

The starting point is the legislator's intention to avoid the detrimental effects of imprisoning offenders—*inter alia* high recidivism rates—and to promote their adjustment to the community by using conditional sentence or probation instead. Chapter 3 described how the ideas of the Protective Law Commission and the provisions of the Penal Code are characterized by a treatment ideology which places greater importance on the resocialization of individuals than general obedience to the law.

Realization of the Legislator's Intentions Through Sentencing

On studying the sentencing process, we found results which were both in agreement with, and in opposition to, the legislator's intentions. One intention of the legislator was that those sentenced conditionally should have better prognoses than offenders sentenced to probation. The judges have in fact differentiated between these sanction groups since, in general, the conditionally sentenced offenders had better past records than the offenders sentenced to probation and subsequently recidivated to a significantly less extent.

However, since an *ex post facto* rather than an experimental design was used in this study we cannot say what results would have been obtained if those conditionally sentenced had been placed under one or other of the forms of probation or if the probationers had not received any supervision at all. The judges made correct choices if it can be assumed that the treatment theory which led to the legislation is correct. But that this is not necessarily the case is suggested by the recidivism and prediction studies we have carried out. The possibility cannot be excluded that we are dealing with self-fulfilling prophecies. Post-sentence behavior may be influenced by the decision made.

However, the courts, in addition to the personal or social factors which may be considered significant for the offender's chance of readjustment, have, also imposed more far-reaching measures on the basis of the seriousness of the current offense and previous criminality. This was *not* the legislator's intention since, according to the legislative provisions, both conditional sentence and probation can be imposed in the case of offenses which would normally entail imprisonment.

The multiple regression analysis showed that the judges' choice of sanction is determined more by factors pertaining to criminality than to the offenders' social circumstances and personal characteristics. Thus the legislator's intention that individual prevention should be given primary emphasis in the choice of sanctions is shown by the statistical analysis to take second place.

Realization of the Legislator's Intentions Through the Enforcement of the Sanction

As there are no enforcement measures to be taken with those who have been conditionally sentenced, this sanction will not be analyzed here.

Ordinary Probation

Despite the fact that probation is the most important alternative to imprisonment its goals are not clearly stated, neither in the law itself nor in the preparatory work for the law. One explanation for this may be that probation became a valuable sanction because it does not have the disadvantages of imprisonment. At the same time the Protective Law Commission emphasized that in its report that probation "is intended for offenders who are found to need positive measures in the form of support and help in addition to control in order to promote their adjustment to society" (p.132). According to the Order in Council, non-institutional treatment consists of two elements, control and help. In the instructions on implementation the control function has been stressed and the support function weakened by vagueness.

The Protective Law Commission wanted supervision to be conducted by professionally trained probation officers and assistants. The Minister of Justice contended that it was not possible to meet these requirements. Only a few of the clients in our random sample had professional supervisors.

The Protective Law Commission thought that a private citizen should assist the probation officer with carrying out supervision "as a friend and helper" and his only qualification would be an "ability to win the sentenced person's confidence" (p.158). Neither the Penal Code nor the instructions concerning the implementation of its provisions states with the same clarity the demands which might be made on the lay supervisors.

Given their importance for implementation, their personal and social backgrounds are of interest. We note that 90% of the supervisors were men, 90% were married and their average age was 50. The average age among clients was 27 years. In general the clients wished their supervisors were much younger than they actually were.The majority of supervisors were public servants, social workers and police. Their social backgrounds were markedly different from those of their clients. We also found that the supervisors' attitudes to a number of central issues were related to their age and that the younger and better educated supervisors were more treatment oriented. We also found that while supervisors belonged almost exclusively to the middle classes, their clients mainly belonged to the lower social classes. In addition, we noted a great psychological distance between the two groups. Since supervision consists of interaction between supervisor and client, this interplay was analyzed as well as participants' attitudes within individual pairs of supervisors and clients. In general, it may be assumed that the greater the similarity between supervisor and client with respect to background variables and attitudes, the greater the theoretical possibility of good communication and hence normative influence (see, for example, Segerstedt's theory on symbol environments, 1944).

Supervisors said that their goal was to help their client adjust in the community—a re-statement of the official goal. Although the "Instructions for Supervisors" (1972) recommend that one or more contacts per week be made at the beginning of supervision, the supervisors reported that they met their clients on an average of once every three weeks during the first year. The clients' median answer to this question was that they met together once per month. The meetings usually lasted, according to the supervisors, for about 30 minutes while the clients reported somewhat shorter times.

The supervisors said that it was more common for them to initiate contact, whereas their clients claimed that they themselves took this initiative more often.Tension in the supervision relationship was revealed by the fact that a majority of both groups thought that both parties should initiate contact whilst at the same time only a minority in both groups considered that this happened in reality. The offender was informed at the beginning of supervision that he was obliged to keep in contact with his supervisor but was not informed of his supervisor's obligation to keep in contact with him. Thus, one-fifth of the clients wrongly believed that they alone should initiate contact.

A majority of supervisors met and actually preferred to meet their client at their own place of work or home rather than at the client's home. The clients also, to a great extent, preferred to meet at their supervisor's place of work or home. This suggests that a majority of both supervisors and clients wanted the visit to be as impersonal as possible. The supervisors wanted to establish contact with their client's family, parents and employer to a much greater extent than their clients. This is probably because the supervisors primarily regarded these measures as constituting an offer of assistance whereas the clients to a greater extent perceived them as attempts at control.

A central question concerns the possibility of uniting control and help. Because of his position between the chief probation officer and the client and the double objective of supervision, the supervisor may experience a conflict of loyalty. Double loyalty was illustrated by the fact that three-quarters of the supervisors did not consider it their duty to report the clients' violations to the chief probation officer although in fact they were under an obligation to do so. On the other hand, only a small majority of supervisors thought that the clients should be allowed to read the supervision report although a clear majority of the clients were in favor of this.

The supervisors believed themselves to be on the client's side, and only a minority considered themselves to be on the side of the chief probation officer and supervision board. However, the proportion of supervisors who believed that their clients perceived them as being on the authorities' side was significantly greater; this agreed with the clients' own answers. Agreement within individual supervisor-client dyads is generally low. Thus, their was poor agreement between them on how each party believed the other party perceived him. Other questions concerning trust between supervisor and client showed a similar pattern.

Both parties have clearly divergent views of what supervision involves and what its effects are. Only one of ten supervisors thought that supervision constituted a considerable encroachment on the personal freedom of their client, whereas almost four times as many clients held this view. Two-thirds of the supervisors believed their clients would not manage as well without a supervisor, while only one-fifth of their clients had the same opinion.

These examples illustrate the considerable difficulties involved in combining the double objectives of control and assistance. Other Scandinavian criminologists have come to the same conclusion (e.g. Hauge 1968; Frej 1974; Balvig and Kyvsgaard 1975).

Probation with Institutional Treatment

Like ordinary probation, probation with institutional treatment was principally justified by reference to individual preventive aims. Special institutions were built so that these probationers would not be placed among ordinary prisoners. The institutions were to be staffed with well-qualified personnel who would use the short sentences to influence the probationers psychologically and pedagogically.

The institutions were built, but the Swedish Prison and Probation Administration found it difficult to fill them because the courts did not use probation with institutional treatment as much as had been supposed. In order that the low occupancy rate of the institutions should not be too obvious, special types of prisoners were also placed in these institutions. Since these various categories of inmates lived under different conditions and had different needs, conflicts soon arose between them. When the total re-organization of the prison and probation systems was carried through in 1974, the probation institutions became what the Act on Prison Treatment 1974 defines as neighborhood prisons, i.e. prisons near the homes of those serving imprisonment for up to one year. The original intentions were thereby completely eliminated.

Even the probationers were different from those the legislator had in mind. Institutional treatment was primarily intended for young offenders with a relatively good prognosis who were capable of profiting from the short time they had for treatment. However, not all of them were young or had a good prognosis. In principle, the institutions were to be used for offenders who were convicted for the first time but a majority of those actually placed there had previously been convicted—some had even served long prison sentences. Nor were the institutions supposed to be used for offenders with alcohol or drug problems but such offenders became common. This sanction was not to be imposed with persons of poor mental capacity or who were mentally ill but even such offenders came to make up a fairly large group. The staff at the institution complained about the incorrect way the courts used the sanction, saying that they had to receive a clientele for whom the institution was not intended.

Furthermore, the staff were recruited from traditional prisons. The majority had worked for many years within the prison system. This meant that the staff were clearly in danger of being influenced by the traditions and values of the very prisons from which the probation institutions were intended to be completely different. Nor was staff training different from that of other prison staff groups.

The staff reported that it devoted most of its time to administrative or traditional supervisory tasks whilst asserting at the same time that it was more important to talk with the probationers. There were numerous conflicts between the managerial, more treatment-oriented staff members and the custodial staff members.

Treatment was not essentially different from that found in the traditional prisons. Contrary to the intentions, a plan of treatment was not drawn up at the institution we studied. The treatment board meetings did not work well either. The probationers mostly worked at nailing loading platforms together—an activity did not require any special thought or skill. So far as vocational training and work was concerned the particular institution studied here had rather less to offer in the way of work and vocational training than traditional prisons. Both probationers and staff complained about the monotony of the tasks in the workshop. The annual reports from the institutions called attention to the danger of the work at the institution causing the probationers to develop negative attitudes to work outside the institution.

One psychiatrist, who chiefly prescribed sedatives, was available for consultation once a week. The post of psychologist was vacant at the time of this study. Group discussions were not organized on a regular basis and they tended more to impart information than to be concerned with therapy. The institution's inmate council, which was to provide a forum for the inmates to discuss their views of the treatment at the institution with the staff, did not normally exist. Little in the way of leisure activities was organized by the staff and only rarely were meetings with persons from outside the institution arranged. According to the research observer, the treatment consisted primarily of teaching the probationers to abide by a number of detailed regulations. This was clearly in conflict with the intentions of the Penal Code.

The Protective Law Commission had stressed the importance of appointing counselors who could see to it that institutional treatment was made more effective. Two positions for assistant governors were made available at the probation institution. They were, however, most often held by temporary staff members who found it difficult to feel the security that their jobs required if a treatment program was to be carried through—something which often had to be attempted against the wishes of the custodial staff.

One of the most important tasks of the institution was to prepare the probationers for treatment in the community by arranging work and a place for them to live. However, the majority of the probationers studied here already had work and a place to live before they were committed to the probation institution. On that ground we might question the suitability of removing them from their social environment.

The assistant governors waited about two weeks after offenders were committed before they began the work of preparing for their release as they considered it unprofitable to start sooner. Work furloughs were granted only infrequently and only at the end of a probationer's stay. Aptitude tests were normally not given. The assistant governors claimed that because of the harsh conditions of the labor market, it was very difficult to find work for the probationers.

The findings presented in Chapter 7 (regarding the treatment given at one of these institutions) which were based on interview and observation data, agree quite closely with the data taken from the records presented in Chapter 5 concerning recidivism and conditions of work during the period of non-institutional treatment. Yet these studies dealt with quite different samples—the one being sentenced to probation with institutional treatment in 1970 and the other during 1966–67. It was clear also from the records that probation institutions had difficulties in arranging meaningful work on release for the probationers. As many as one-fifth lacked work when they were released. Less than half secured work through the institution or the probation service. More than one-third of the institutional group were unemployed for at least the first three months after release. As one might expect, there is a clear relationship between unemployment and recidivism.

A similar picture is revealed by survey material based on offenders who were sentenced to probation with institutional treatment in 1967. The institution is reported to have found work for only a small number of probationers and, moreover, almost none of those for whom the institution did obtain work were satisfied with their jobs. About half of the group reported that they wanted to hide from their workmates and employers that they had been in an institution.

It seems indisputable that the probation institutions have, contrary to intentions, become similar to ordinary prisons. The institution could be described more as a *coercive organization*, using Etzioni's terminology, than as a normative institution. During a visit in 1976, the then governor asserted that the probationers who succeed after release do so despite the treatment given at the institution and not because of it.

Although the institution is small and open, signs of a prison subculture were detected among the probationers. Although they as individuals do not perceive the staff entirely as "screws", they often believe the other probationers do. Despite the rapid turnover of probationers and the rather large age differences, group cohesion among probationers is at least as great as it is at traditional prisons. Despite the short time spent at the institution, half the probationers claimed that the experience had been detrimental to them. They had become nervous, dependent, apathetic and idle, they had lost confidence in others and they wanted to take revenge when they were released. Apart from the negative effects of their stay at the institution, the offenders underwent the change of status which Goffman calls *stigmatization.*

The Effect of the Sanctions

There are considerable differences between the recidivism rates of the sanction groups. When using offenses registered in the Central Criminal Register during a 2-year period as a criterion, the recidivism rates were 12% for the offenders with conditional sentences, 30% for the offenders sentenced to ordinary probation without institutional treatment and 61% for those sentenced to probation with institutional treatment. These figures show that the legislator's aim of individual prevention was well realized in the case of conditionally sentenced offenders, but was realized to a lesser extent in the case of ordinary probationers and to a far less extent in the case of probationers sentenced to institutional treatment.

However, a fair assessment of the effects of the sanctions requires that the varying social backgrounds and offender careers of the individuals in these three sanction groups be taken into consideration. Using a predictive instrument based on some forty background factors and having reasonable prognostic power, account can be taken of the offenders' differing prognoses by dividing them into different classes according to their total risk scores. However, even when the risk scores were held constant, considerable differences between the recidivism rates of the sanction groups were found. These differences were statistically significant and it seems that they cannot be explained away by reference to deficiencies in the predictive instrument or other underlying factors. When a large number of possible sources of error were reviewed we were unable to detect any reduction in the differences of recidivism rates. On the contrary, in some cases they showed an increase.

Since there was very little recidivism among the conditionally sentenced offenders regardless of their risk category, we conclude that the legislator's intentions concerning this sanction were fulfilled. There were more recidivists among those sentenced to ordinary probation regardless of risk group. Thus the legislator was less successful in reaching the goal of individual prevention with this sanction. Recidivism was even greater among those sentenced to probation with institutional treatment regardless of risk group.

About half the recidivism occurred during the first six months after the imposition of the sentence or after release. Those sentenced to probation with institutional treatment recidivated especially quickly. One-quarter committed new offenses during the first three months after release.

That the probation institutions partly failed to arrange work for their probationers is indicated by the fact that one-fifth of the probationers were released without jobs. Three-quarters of these offenders recidivated as compared with half of those who had some form of employment. However, about two-thirds of those for whom the institution had found work recidivated as compared with one-third of those who had found work for themselves, a finding which suggests that the employment obtained by the institution was not always the best. This difference remained even when the variable prior work stability was held constant.

There were, on the whole, few significant relationships between the form of supervision, as it was described by both supervisor and client, and the client's likelihood of relapsing into new crime. However, control-oriented supervision does seem generally to have produced poorer results than support-oriented supervision. False treatment optimism also seems to be detrimental. A great deal of interaction between client and supervisor correlated with a high rate of recidivism for offenders in the low risk groups. Confidence in the relationship showed covariance with low recidivism, especially in the high risk groups. Informal supervisor style had favorable effects on offenders in both risk groups.

An attempt was made to explain the recidivism by means of a multiple regression analysis. For all three sanction groups taken together, the sanction variable shows the highest association with recidivism ($r = .42$) and also has the highest explanatory value ($R = .42$ and $R^2 = .18$). Work stability and housing prior to sentence come out as the second and third explanatory variables but they contribute only minimally to increased explanatory value. In a separate analysis of both probation groups together, including factors pertaining to circumstances after sentence was passed, the sanction still turns out to be the first variable, followed by unemployment after sentence and alcohol abuse after sentence. A corresponding analysis of the probation with institutional treatment group, excluding the sanction variable, produces unemployment after release and abuse of alcohol after release as the first and second explanatory variables. However, previous type of sentence and age come just before these two variables for the group of probationers who were not sentenced to institutional treatment.

Criminological Interpretation of the Findings on Treatment

The fact that conditionally sentenced offenders succeeded better than probationers, even when allowing for their better social prognoses, may be explained by the fact that they were deprived of no treatment worth the name since they were not placed under supervision and to a high degree they escaped being stigmatized by the people in their surroundings since there was a general absence of controlling bodies.

Similarly, the reason for those placed on ordinary probation succeeding better than those sentenced to probation with institutional treatment is probably to be found in the fact that they did not miss out on any treatment of value at the institution nor were they taken away from their environment or stigmatized by people in their surroundings to the same extent as those who were sent to a probation institution. We have seen that the institution's capacity to improve the social environment and provide psychological-pedagogical treatment lacked reality.

The intention of the legislator with probation was justified by reference to individual prevention. But if the treatment which is supposed to lead to the intended resocialization of offenders does not involve positive measures, and if the client perceives it as constituting control rather than support, then more "treatment" will be experienced only as more "punishment". That a more intervenient measure produced worse results is thus understandable.

Both the recidivism figures and the description of treatment for probationers indicate that resocialization failed despite the individual preventive aims. As I have pointed out in an earlier research study, a positive individual preventive aim can even have *negative individual preventive effects* (Bondeson 1974).

This distinction is important at a time when the claim that it makes no difference what we do with offenders has become quite common. All treatment is said to accomplish the same results. It is true that my research from 1974 showed that corrective institutions, irrespective of goals and formal structure, created similar subcultures among the probationers and led to criminalization and psychological injury. But it also showed that the longer the inmates were "treated", the worse the outcome. Recidivism data, which were later collected, indicated that prisonization also made subsequent social adjustment more difficult (Bondeson 1989). The present non-institutional study also shows differences between various sanction forms. Providing no treatment, as was the case with the conditional sentence, produced the best result, supervision alone gave an intermediate result and supervision combined with institutional treatment gave the poorest result. It is not merely that institutional treatment failed to reduce recidivism—it appears actually to have increased it. Similarly, supervision also appears to have increased the rate of recidivism rather than preventing or reducing it.

The results obtained in this study seem to show that the less there is of coercive treatment, the better the individual preventive effects.

It is, however, a distinguishing characteristic of a great deal of treatment research that while its methodology is well developed, the status of theory is often low. In general, no explanations have been given for the negative results attained in research conducted on the effectiveness of correctional treatment (see e.g. Lipton, Martinson and Wilks 1975).

Socio-Legal Interpretation of the Legislative Effects

A criminological analysis would normally end by asserting that the treatment does not have the intended effect. But can an analysis using a sociology of law framework contribute further to an *explanation* of the results obtained? Is it possible, for example, that the treatment did not achieve its purpose because the treatment program was not carried through? If this is the case, why was the program not carried out according to intentions?

In what follows I shall make use of the model of the effects of law and the explanations concerning the absence of effects which were presented at the outset of this study. The reader is referred to the Figure 2 and the scheme accompanying it in Chapter 1. The purpose of the explanations given below is to account for the difference between the law in theory and the law in practice.

1. The Individual Prevention Theory May Be a Treatment Ideology Which Has Other, Legitimizing, Aims. Such a theoretical explanation brings the expressed aim of the legislator concerning individual prevention into question. Using sociological language it can be said that the manifest function is not necessarily the actual intended aim. Marxist analyses often assert that legislation serves purposes other than those which are expressed and that its aim is to conserve or justify certain social conditions. Thus, Elwin et al. (1975, 67–69) believe that the individual prevention theory, which emphasizes classification and treatment, must be related to the genesis of the capitalistic industrial society *inter alia* because it was irrational to punish an offender who could serve production, and by the same token, rational to render an offender harmless for a long time if he interfered with production.

Without referring to capitalistic industrial societies—the individual prevention theory has not been unknown in socialist industrialized societies either—one could argue that the treatment notion serves the purpose of legitimizing a given penal system. It is possible to think for example, that the legislator wanted to retain substantial parts of classical penal law founded on retribution and fair or reasonable proportionality but, thinking that this doctrine chimed badly with the rational and enlightened spirit of the time, made an attempt to unite these contradictions by constructing a harmonious treatment ideology. The packaging would in this way appear more acceptable and the legislator would appear to be both rational and humane.

However, I consider a simple conspiracy theory unlikely as it seems to conflict with the historical development of modern criminal policy.

In Chapter 2 we saw that English courts devised different means of avoiding too severe an administration of justice. In the same way, both judges and laymen in Massachusetts tried in a highly pragmatic way to save people from cruel and destructive prison sentences either by getting round the law or sentencing offenders to probation. We also saw that probation was not supported by legislation until the Supreme Court declared that the judges were acting illegally. Thus enabling legislation was forced into being for something that had long been an accepted juridical practice.

Impulses came to Europe and Sweden for what was then called conditional sentence, partly from America and partly from the positive school of penology and the International Association of Criminalists. They emphasized crime prevention through individual prevention in part because of the growth of criminological science which for the first time provided a foundation upon which to base the study of the offender instead of working, as legal science had, with offense abstractions.

The subsequent development of the conditional sentence in Sweden reveals a pragmatic attitude to the new criminal policy. Other reforms which were implemented before the introduction of the Penal Code, also suggest that the legislator had serious intentions of humanizing crime policy and even making it more effective.

Thus, when considering the historical development of conditional sentence and probation, both internationally and nationally, it does not seem especially likely that the legislator's only aim with a doctrine of individual prevention was to legitimate either some conditions in society or the classical theory of penal law. However, this does not prevent the legislation from having such *effects.* The arguments I have put forward here against a pure conspiracy theory are not objections to the latter type of functional reasoning. But here I am more interested in the first type of argument, namely whether the legislator intended to preserve the penal system and justified this by referring to individual prevention because this would make that aim more easily accepted.

Had the legislator not wanted the offender to be helped to adjust in society, the law might still have been called a "protective law" but without being given a content and resources for the realization of a treatment program. The Protective Law Commission emphatically stressed the importance of providing the non-institutional sector with personnel as well as economic and organizational resources in order to make the realization of their intentions possible. However, both the progressive-sounding term "protective law" and some of its concrete content disappeared in the Penal Code. This far, therefore, it can be said that the Penal Code was able to utilize the Commission's theory of individual prevention in order to legitimate the preservation of some classical principles of penal law. But since the greater part of the Commission's proposals concerning conditional sentence and probation were adopted, I would be inclined to argue that the Penal Code was to a relatively great extent inspired by what was perceived as a theory of individual prevention.

2. The Individual Prevention Theory Is Not Sufficiently Clearly and Unambiguously Worded to Ensure Certainty of Implementation. This can *inter alia* depend on contradictions in the law caused by compromises during the preparatory work. We saw in Chapter 3 that certain contradictions concerning individual prevention can be traced in the work of the Protective Law Commission and that these were accentuated in the Penal Code where greater emphasis was placed on general prevention.

The Minister emphasized general preventive aspects still further by including a section giving guidance on the choice of sanction (Penal Code, Chapter 1:7). The majority of judges answering some interview questions in a study of perceptions of justice (Bondeson and Bodin 1977) seem nevertheless to have interpreted this fairly vague paragraph as placing greater emphasis on individual prevention rather than general prevention. To the extent that there are expectations that the goal of individual prevention will be reached by individualized treatment, a contradiction exists between this goal and that of general prevention, since the latter is founded on the notion that punishment should be felt as disagreeable and this should result in greater general obedience to the law.

The Protective Law Commission was influenced by the positive school of penology, the International Association of Criminalists and the International Society of Social Defense, all of which bodies stress the prevention of crime as the most important task of criminal policy. However, the Commission could not completely reject the classical notion of penal law which stipulates that crime must be followed by punishment, that this punishment must be proportional to the crime and that consideration must be given to demands concerning general prevention. The Protective Law Commission's final report, "Protective Law", explained how, in the work of the Commission, various advantages and disadvantages were weighed against each other to obtain what was considered the most satisfactory and presumably the most practicable solutions.

The comments of various bodies on the Commission's recommendations as well as the Minister's proposals in the Government Bill and the examination made by the Law Council, all gave consideration to requirements of general prevention when the individual elements of the sanctions were drawn up. Since the amendments which were made in the Commission's proposals involved less emphasis on the demands of individual prevention, treatment theory came less clearly to expression in the Penal Code whilst at the same time the contradictions increased. This shift towards general prevention has gone even further in the Commentary to the Penal Code III which is used by judges and reflects prevailing legal practice.

The ambiguities and contradictions which exist in the preparatory work and then in the law and its interpretation can be expected to leave their mark on the implementation of the sanctions, both at the sentencing and enforcement levels.

Over and above the conflicts which exist concerning notions of individual and general prevention, the individual prevention theory is vaguely formulated. For example, it is not explicitly stated just when supervision and institutional treatment are required. The content of treatment, which was partly described by the Protective Law Commission, almost completely disappeared in the Penal Code.

3. The Legislator's Theory of Individual Prevention Is Not Implemented by the Responsible Bodies. There can be various reasons for deficient implementation.

3.1 *Vagueness in the law and its preparatory work as well as in subsequent regulations may cause uncertainty among sentencing and implementing authorities.* We have seen how ambiguities in the legislation concerning what should be the necessary conditions for supervision or institutional treatment and in the aims of these treatment forms, make it difficult for the courts to apply individual preventive views with any consistency. The *traditional determination of pun-*

ishment—which has been found partly to guide the choice between the sanctions of conditional sentence, ordinary probation and probation with institutional treatment—conflicts with the legislator's intentions. It is nevertheless defended in the Commentary to the Penal Code III (p.55), which claims that the courts' free assessments are bound to give rise to uncertainty and that even if the traditional determination of punishment has drawbacks, it is preferable, probably because of its long tradition and a well-established practice. This argumentation in the Commentaries can also be a rationalization to defend a classical doctrine of penal law and the *status quo* in judicial practice.

There is a clear tendency among the bodies which directly implement the law, to create a *uniform administrative practice* instead of attempting individualized treatment. Supervision, which should cease as soon as it was no longer needed, continued as a matter of routine for the entire three-year probation period. The Protective Law Commission had warned against just such a development. The reason for such enforcement is probably connected with, among other things, ambiguous stipulations regarding the purpose which supervision should serve and when it no longer should be considered necessary.

The supervision period was shortened when the reorganization of the prison and probation systems took place in 1974. New provisions recommended that supervision be reviewed after one year and made it obligatory to review it after two years. But the new legislation appears scarcely to have succeeded in adapting the supervision period to the individual; it has simply created new intervals.

This routinization can be seen as an effect of *bureaucratization*. It is interesting to compare this with the first amateur use of supervision in Massachusetts, which normally only lasted a few weeks. Similarly, the period of treatment at probation institutions, which was supposed to vary between one and two months depending on the offender's treatment needs, in the majority of cases was actually terminated as soon as the minimum time had elapsed. This routinization probably depends partly on the setting of ambiguous goals for treatment, partly on the probationers' demands for fairness and partly on the need of a bureaucratic organization to simplify decisions. These three explanations are mutually related.

Vagueness in the regulations can also give rise to variations in decision-making which are not based on considerations of treatment. The issuing of special instructions and the imposition of sanctions for misconduct varies among supervision boards and, since it cannot be fully accounted for by differences in offender populations, should rather be interpreted as *differences in perspective and practice among the boards* (SOU 1975:16, 197–198).

Earlier we looked rather closely at the conflict which arises among supervisors because they are required to meet two different demands in their work, that of control and that of support. The Protective Law Commission's proposal to provide the offender with "help and support as well as control" in order to facilitate his adjustment in society, was partially diluted by defining control as adherence to the law and any instructions based on it, whilst support was defined as obeying the law. What was already vaguely formulated in the bill became even more ambiguous in the orders and regulations on implementation and contributed to creating uncertainty among the supervisors about their most important duties. We have also seen how this situation can create a double loyalty—one to the supervisor's superiors and another to his client. In its turn, this can lead to irresolution and an inability to act.

3.2 *A theory of individual prevention or a treatment ideology is not necessarily embraced by the legal actors who have to implement the law. This may lead to open or concealed conflict.* When judges determine punishment concerning the sanctions of probation and conditional sentence, at least in part in traditional ways, it may be because they have been trained in classical penal traditions and have practical experience drawn from other sanctions such as imprisonment or fines. The more vaguely the law is expressed, the greater the risk that judges make use of an earlier acquired way of thinking about punishment and are influenced by their *professional role* and other social roles when they decide on these sanctions.

A judge is chairman of the supervision board and here too there is a risk that he may take certain behavior patterns, learnt in the courtroom, with him to the supervision board meetings. This would make the Protective Law Commission's intention that a dialogue built on trust should be established between members of the board and client, difficult of achievement.

As we saw earlier, the staff of the probation institutions were recruited from within the prison system and they had often worked for a long time in closed prisons. They thus took social roles and attitudes with them from the custodially-oriented prisons—attitudes and roles which hindered the realization of the treatment program at the institution. The more vaguely the original wording of the treatment program, the greater the scope for these earlier behavior patterns to influence events.

We have further observed that there is a paternal type of supervisor who is relatively authoritarian, has little training in social work but long experience as a supervisor. Police officers are prevalent among this type of supervisors. It is not difficult to see that the police may experience a *role conflict* between their professional role and the helping role of a supervisor. They very likely perform the controlling duties of their work very well, something which is indicated by the high rate of recidivism among their clients. However, the control function has not been compensated for by a more developed support function.

3.3 *The organizational structure and functioning of the probation service may hinder the mediation of a treatment theory and lead to an inability to act.* Without making an in-depth study of the probation organization, it seems that certain aspects of its structure make it difficult to achieve treatment goals. As we saw in Chapter 2, the organization was limited and formally each probation officer was responsible for a large number of clients (at one time the caseload was over one hundred, later it came down to about sixty and today the aim is to limit it to about thirty). Moreover, the same organization has always been responsible for both probation and parole clients. This has meant that the greater part of the supervisor's time has been devoted to conditionally released prisoners who often have even greater problems than the probationers. Because these officers of necessity spent a lot of time solving the acute problems of parolees, they may have failed to develop methods for dealing with the real problems of probationers.

Moreover, the probation organization has a number of varying functions. It can be described as an organization for social inquiries, counseling, sanction implementation and treatment functions. It is subordinate locally to the supervision board and nationally to the Swedish Prison and Probation Administration, both of which are decision-making bodies. Although the probation organization is expected to implement the legislation's individual preventive aims and carry out an assisting and supporting function, it has lacked power to make its own decisions. It is the supervision board which makes the final decisions, especially on matters of control. This distribution of the decision-making functions has probably weakened the probation organization. Its organization structure can be understood historically but appears hardly defensible today. When the organization consisted of a small number of officers whose qualifications perhaps little known, it was natural for decisions to be made by a supervision board headed by a jurist. But the organization has since expanded considerably and now employs well-trained social workers. It is therefore difficult to understand why the organization should be called, and function as, a service body for the supervision boards.

The chief probation officer and his staff appear to feel that their work lacks a clear goal and they do are uncertain which functions should be given priority. *Work instructions* are vague and antiquated and date back to 1963, i.e. before the Penal Code came into force. Some probation assistants, who were interviewed during the summer of 1976, stated that they lacked written instructions and up-to-date work regulations. They complained that adequate information was not supplied to new recruits and that there had been no discussions about aims and methods. It was only quite recently that they had started staff group discussions led by a psychologist on ways of dealing with clients and other practical problems. The Swedish Prison and Probation Administration admits that probation and parole staff have been neglected in this respect.

Moreover, the organization is unable to meet the client's material needs because its financial resources are too limited. The organization is, in principle, dependent on the social services for the payment of allowances to clients. In interviews probation staff have stated that a great deal of time is spent negotiating allowances for clients with the often reluctant social service bureaux.

3.4 *The reinforcement of management and administrative authorities may create a bureaucracy in which means are converted into goals.* The reorganization of the prison and probation systems which became operative in July 1974 saw a considerable increase in the number of probation staff. Thus, one of the organization's earlier weaknesses was at least partially remedied. However, this reinforcement of staff (a threefold increase in the 5-year period 1974–78) does not necessarily mean that the supervision of probationers improved. Just over one-third of the extra personnel were assigned to new areas of activity in connection with the compilation of presentence inquiry reports, contacts with offenders remanded in custody, contacts with offenders at the neighbourhood prisons and with parolees.

The Sundsvall Experiment, which also involved a threefold increase in probation staff, demonstrated that little of these additional resources affected the lay supervisors and their clients (Kühlhorn 1975; 1979). Simple administrative tasks, such as the distribution of a resource catalogue to the supervisors, did not present any problems but treatment strategies scarcely changed. Comparisons made before and after the experiment in Sundsvall, with Karlstad functioning without extra resources as a control town, showed that the frequency of contact between supervisor and client did not increase despite recommendations that it should. Moreover, there was a decrease in Sundsvall in the number of supervisors who claimed that their client perceived them as a personal friend, in the number of supervisors who believed they succeeded in helping their client and in the number of supervisors who felt supervision had positive significance for their clients.

The reorganization of the prison and probation systems in 1974 resembled the model on which the Sundsvall Experiment was based, i.e., an increase in staff, investment in professional staff, supervision discontinued after one or two years, responsibility for pre-sentence inquiry reports transferred to the probation service and an increase in activity at the neighbourhood prisons. The following conclusion about effects was drawn after a preliminary evaluation of the experiment: "From our experience from Sundsvall, experiments conducted in other countries and common sense, there are no grounds for optimistic expectations" (p. 93).

From organizational theory we could instead talk about a *bureaucracy*, which, with rapid growth, transforms means to goals (Merton 1957). Indeed, it seems from my interviews that when there was only one probation officer in a district he actually had more time for home visits than was the case when there were over thirty persons in the probation office.

The staff complain about the frenzy for forms saying that it seems as though the filling in of forms has become a goal in itself.

Normally, an organization has certain rational goals which it strives to reach but there may well exist limitations in the organization's members (Simon 1971) or within the organization itself (Homans 1950).

When an organization lacks clear goals, work instructions, decision-making functions and material resources, it risks becoming impotent. In the light of this, we find it easier to understand that so much of the staff's time is spent discussing their own problems.

3.5 *It may be difficult for both professional and lay supervisors to apply treatment theory by themselves alone.* The great majority of probationers are supervised by laymen. Since these supervisors are not public servants (at least not in their role as supervisors) their chances of establishing a personal relationship built on trust with the client are greater than with professional supervisors. On the other hand, their chances of helping clients with practical matters are limited, partly because they do not always have the necessary knowledge of various social measures and partly because they are not always able to conduct this work during office hours. Similarly, the probation officers and assistants are in a better position to help the clients with practical matters and less able to function in close and open contact with them.

Thus, while the professional probation staff have greater resources for assisting clients with practical matters, the lay supervisors have greater resources for offering personal help. Since the client may need both practical assistance and personal support he can have use of both the professional services of the probation staff and the personal support of the laymen. This was exactly what the Protective Law Commission intended but the idea was accepted neither by the bodies of critical assessment nor the Minister of Justice. The reason for this rejection may have been that the Commission did not base its treatment arguments on a clear distinction between control and support. Interviews with probation staff brought out that they felt that the client believes their function to be one of control whereas they should primarily have the function of providing practical assistance. There is a definite risk that the lay supervisors in the present system function as semi-professional supervisors although they lack the resources and time to do so satisfactorily. Despite the fact that the number of professional supervisors has been increased, they nevertheless find it difficult to keep up with all the extra work for which they have been made responsible and to give priority to any particular area since their work lacks a clear goal. In this situation there is a risk of *professionalization* which to a great extent coincides with the tendency to bureaucratize. Employees seek criteria for their professional status which are not necessarily related to the client's real needs. We have already seen examples of the professionalization of probation in America.

It seems to me that there are obvious dangers in the situation where bureaucratization and professionalization of the probation services give rise to an organization with its own needs—ones which are not directly related either to the client or to society. Since the demarcation between the correctional system and the social service system is so obscure, treatment work may even be duplicated, to the detriment of both the client and society.

4. Offenders Do Not Perceive Treatment in Accordance with Its Intentions. The offender may find it difficult to see the sanction as constituting an aid to his adjustment for a number of reasons. He may feel he was unfairly judged, he may not want to adjust to society, he may not think that he needs help or he may think that the assistance he is offered is not real help.

It would scarcely be unreasonable for the offender to mistrust treatment that has been vaguely formulated in legislation and further weakened in its application. Yet, to make use of the help that is offered he must be willing to co-operate. And to co-operate with his supervisor he must trust him. In fact, offenders do not always trust their supervisors nor do they always regard supervision as constituting help.

5. The Fault Lies in the Treatment Theory Itself.

5.1 *It is difficult for a client to make use of treatment which combines control and support.* The offender was introduced to non-institutional treatment by being notified that if he misbehaved during probation, his probationary period could be extended for up to five years, i.e. he would be "punished" by being subjected to more "treatment". This is hardly an effective way to lay the ground for positive attitudes to supervision or supervisors. The offender is informed of his duty to keep in contact with his supervisor. If he does not, he risks being taken into temporary custody by the police. And this is not to regarded as punishment either—it is simply to permit his situation to be looked into. Furthermore, the offender must follow the general rules of good conduct. He might also be given special instructions or conditions to follow. These used to cover such things as alcohol consumption, so-called voluntary treatment, work, housing and personal finance. If he breached any of these special conditions, more would be imposed. Again, none of the conditions were to be regarded as constituting punishment. Misconduct in any form could cause probation to be discontinued and the offender to be sentenced to prison instead. With all these threats hanging over his head for a number of years, it is perhaps understandable if the offender finds it difficult to regard supervision as constituting assistance. How can the offender avoid being suspicious of the assistance which hides behind these so-called measures of support?

Just as there are a great number of regulations governing the control function of supervision, there are very few governing the support function. Systematic treatment programs have not existed. Treatment has been dependent on the circumstances, on whether the client and supervisor were able to establish good contact and whether the offender dared to confide in his supervisor despite formal rules which oblige supervisors to report to their superiors. Theoretically, if the client tells his supervisor of a previous offense which has not been detected, he risks having his probation sanction replaced with a prison sentence. According to the Protective Law Commission, the lay supervisor should be a confidant and friend—but how can the client see him as such when he is obliged to report to the authorities what the client has told him?

In light of the above, it is perhaps not surprising that many offenders feel that supervision has not helped them, that they would have managed just as well without a supervisor and that supervision is a considerable encroachment on their personal freedom.

5.2 *The client does not need treatment.* Apart from the fact that it may be difficult to combine support and control in supervision, it is possible that the client does not need supervision with either support or control as its most important ingredient. The courts decide that in certain cases supervision, possibly including institutional treatment, is necessary, but we are rarely informed on what grounds this decision is based. Since the court is not obliged to account in detail for its reasons they cannot be discussed. However, for the probationers studied here, as many as one-third of the supervisors declared that their clients would manage just as well without supervision.

5.3 *The client needs material and practical assistance rather than treatment.* The probation groups considered here often have different kinds of problems. They have had little schooling and have rarely received vocational training.

They have difficulties in obtaining work and their personal financial situation is usually poor. Their financial situation is often aggravated by the imposition of fines and/or damages. Their debts can easily reach the point where they no longer are motivated to work. They sometimes run into problems in their attempts to secure financial assistance from the social service agencies because they are clients of the correctional services. Many offenders either share accommodation or live in below-standard conditions. In many cases, it would seem that the client is in greater need of material and practical assistance than so-called treatment.

6. Treatment Fails for Reasons Pertaining to the Offender's Personal and Social Circumstances. Since treatment aims at promoting the offender's adjustment, this explanation is simply another way of saying that the treatment has failed. However, the offender may have great problems due to poor social heritage, lack of ability, mental handicap and alcohol problems. For some observers these conditions prove that "the clients are so bad it doesn't matter what you do" whilst for others such difficulties constitute a real challenge to help such clients. Obviously, treatment has not been effective enough in changing the offender's personal and social circumstances. We have noted that unemployment and alcohol abuse are important factors in recidivism.

7. Treatment Fails for Reasons Pertaining to Other Societal Conditions. What can criminal policy do about social heritage? What can it do about extreme poverty? What can criminal policy do about the exclusion from society of the socially handicapped? What can it do about the class society?

By asking these questions we can clearly see the extent to which criminal policy is limited. If the probation services were integrated with the social services, the situation for probation and parole clients would at least not be worse than that of other social service clients. If this were done, the offenders' financial problems might more easily be solved.

Possibilities, based on legislation, ought to exist for providing employment other than work substitution schemes for people who have become marginalized in society. The present social security legislation seems to have placed the socially handicapped outside the normal labor market. Society should try to help these groups to procure employment on the open market.

8. Treatment Fails for Reasons Pertaining to Stigmatization. The *stigmatization* theory is based on the notion that an individual's evaluation of himself is influenced by social control measures (Becker 1963, 1964; Goffman 1968). The sentence which is imposed on the offender may identify him as a criminal. The reactions of the people around him may then reinforce his new identity. This identity can, in turn, affect his choice of member and reference groups. This differential association (Sutherland and Cressey 1978) further strengthens the offender's self-image as criminal and, because of altered behavior patterns, can result in new social control measures being adopted. In this way, the processes of stigmatization and ostracism risk becoming irreversible. When a sentence is imposed on an offender, legal and non-legal factors which strengthen each other begin to interact and the process which is thus activated is subsequently difficult to interrupt.

The Protective Law Commission seemed to be aware that such a labeling process can be caused by time spent in prison and that it can make subsequent social adjustment more difficult for the offender. However, the Commission did not express any concern that supervision might contribute to such labeling of offenders as well. In all probability the labeling process is greater in the case of incarceration but that does not exclude the possibility that even less drastic measures can have similar effects.

The fact that clients who did not have serious criminal records or social histories and who met their supervisors frequently, recidivated to a greater extent, can scarcely be explained by anything other than stigmatization theory. Well-adjusted offenders probably have more to lose from being caught up in the control system. The label need not consist of a factual condemnation. The offender may *feel* that the treatment has rendered him socially incompetent and degraded him. Such a denigrating self-evaluation may in itself be sufficient to make social adjustment more difficult. If the offender who is placed under supervision feels *infantilized* and degraded, he may well believe that people in his environment see him in the same light. He may think that the responsibility for his behavior has been taken from him and, at the same time, that the people around him regard him as incompetent. Mead's theory of the way in which our self-concept is influenced by other people's views of us, could also include "imaginary others". Eysenck's theory (1964) of how the offender is *fixated* with the offense through punishment is also partially related to the labeling theory.

If we include the concepts of infantilization and fixation in the stigmatization theory, we find that a number of the negative results that have been observed in treatment research can be understood. This applies not only to correctional treatment. For example, Holstein and Jersild (1976) found that no treatment at all was more effective than every type of treatment then available for Danish drug addicts. They interpret their results as support for the stigmatization theory.

Research which *evaluates social programs* in various fields (Caro 1971) has also produced a long series of negative results (see Weiss 1972, 126). Thomas and Znaniecki's earlier studies of Polish immigrants (1918) showed that the help they were offered could be directly detrimental to them. Other studies worth mentioning are Powers and Witmer's (1951) project on prevention of juvenile delinquency, and Meyer, Borgatta and Jones' experimental investigations of social assistance (1965).

9. The Combination of Different Explanations. All the explanations given here to account for the fact that the law governing probation did not reach its goal of individual prevention, could be valid. It is also possible that many of the above-mentioned factors reinforce and supplement each other. The legislator's treatment theory is vaguely formulated and thereby gives little guidance to those who implement the law. The legislative text gives fuller expression to the negative sanctions rather than the positive inducements. In its turn this influences a number of instructions on implementation. The client is faced with injunctions and threats rather than being offered real treatment. As the treatment organization is badly built up in terms of personnel, economy and decision-making, it has difficulty in offering services other than control. The client is suspicious of what is called treatment which he perceives as punishment. Thus he cannot easily make use of the help which he is actually in need of. He already has serious personal and social problems which are in danger of being aggravated by the sentence imposed. Instead of being helped, he might then be harmed.

Final Comments on Support and Control

If the aim really is to give the offender help and support in order to facilitate his adjustment to society, his real *needs* should be determined. An investigation of the needs the client himself experiences has probably never been undertaken neither officially nor scientifically (cf. Martin 1965).

According to the Protective Law Commission, the pre-sentence social inquiry reports, which are compiled in order to lay a ground for court decisions on probation and conditional sentences, should also be used as a foundation upon which to base the treatment program. Despite the Commission's extensive discussion of such treatment planning, these reports have not been used in this way. In fact, the social enquiry investigators have sometimes so misunderstood their role that they have argued in terms of general prevention when recommending sanctions (Ferrer and Walhjalt, Kriminalvårdsstyrelsen 1974). Thus, we are once again confronted with the problem around which this whole study has revolved, namely the possibility of combining punishment and treatment, or as it is referred to in the probation system, control and help. We have found interesting shifts in both legal and non-legal norms. There is a shift from support to control at the legislative level—the Protective Law Commission stressed individual prevention to the detriment of general prevention more strongly than the Penal Code does. Regulations which are based on the law also stress control more strongly than support. In the formal instructions given to supervisors we can, by studying successive editions, see a tendency over time for this trend to be reversed and the support aspect of supervision is once again being given greater consideration than the control aspect. Finally, the training literature which is distributed by the Swedish Prison and Probation Administration and the National Association of Lay Supervisors clearly stress the support function. The following passage, taken from a training program administered by the Swedish Prison and Probation Administration is interesting from the point of view of the sociology of law: "Many of the regulations which govern supervision in the correctional system are, in today's perspective, out-of-date. In practice the law is not implemented literally but rather the attempt is made to shape work with what is practical in the particular case."

Thus, the administration which issues the instructions and trains the supervisors in fact advises them to disregard the law's regulations. The different considerations regarding control, which were introduced into the Penal Code, have partially been invalidated by those whose job it is to apply the law. A system similar to the common-law system of Anglo-Saxon countries has developed in Sweden in the form of *informal legal norms* which are apparently sanctioned by the supervising body, i.e., the Swedish Prison and Probation Administration.

The law in practice approximates to the original intentions of the Protective Law Commission, yet those who apply the law are unaware that they in fact comply with the legislator's intentions. From a historical perspective we can see that the circle is almost complete but this is rarely noticed because the usual time perspective is too short. It seems to be time for a new legislator to codify what has become prevailing practice or even to lead the way and guide it.

The analysis made within the framework of the sociology of law of the effects of a particular piece of legislation has thus shown among other things that even though the legislator expressed a treatment ideology through an individual preventive aim for the sanctions, the underlying treatment theory has been seriously undeveloped. This appears to have led to a content of treatment different from that intended by the legislator and to the intended resocialization of offenders being less than effective. The legislator wished to achieve change in the form of lower recidivism rates and reduced criminality through a criminal policy which was treatment-oriented instead of punishment-oriented. But these goals seem, in part, to have been rendered impossible of attainment because of the lack of clarity and consistency in the legislation and its implementation.

9

Lines of Development and Suggestions for Reform

Science and Politics

When a research study leads to disappointing findings—as is the case here—it is not unusual for the scientist to be asked what should be done instead. Unfortunately, on the basis of the present findings the existing system can be criticized but not improved with any certainty. For that more rigorous experimentation would be necessary to test the alleged superiority of a given sanction or treatment method over some other sanction or method.

In the absence, however, of opportunities for this experimentation it may be useful to see if our findings give some indications about what should be changed and in what way. This is perhaps not an unreasonable exercise since the scientist has access to systematically collected data in a way which the practitioner and the politician do not. I shall therefore try to draw conclusions from my findings, identify faults in the system and suggest how these could be improved.

Basing my suggestions on the findings does not mean they are always based on present data or that every detail has been scientifically tested. I have also drawn on the results of other relevant studies.

It is inevitable that the author's own *values* come to expression. Even within the positivist research tradition the researcher's values influence the choice of problem and method. An early example of a scientist who re-examined the social sciences' supposed objectivity and freedom from value judgments can be found in Myrdal (1968; 1972).

Within American criminology, Becker (1967), on the basis of a new approach to value-relevant research, considers that the criminologist should identify himself with *the underdog*. But Gouldner (1968) has criticized this idea on the grounds that it is liberal rather than radical (Gouldner also thinks one should identify with the oppressed but for different reasons) whilst Riley (1971) criticized them both for not taking sufficient account of the fact that no social science analyses can be objective. But Riley has also questioned why the assertions based on a sociology of knowledge should be the only ones to be considered objective. In England, traditional criminology has been subjected to sharp criticism by Taylor et al. (1973) who have also put forward proposals for a so-called radical criminology (1975).

For my part, I tend to adopt what Anttila and Törnudd (1973, 26, 145ff) call a *value-conscious research.* They advocate the avoidance of value judgments in science but say that when the researcher introduces a value premiss, this should be done so as openly as possible. Whilst, therefore, the reform proposals which follow are founded on scientifically assessed data it should be stressed that these may be uncertain or incomplete. Moreover, the gap between the results of research and a readiness to act on them is filled with assumptions based on theoretical and empirical knowledge, the unsystematic experiences of oneself and others, one's own values and those of others, one's own intuition and one's own guesswork (Weiss 1972, 125).

Punishment, Treatment, Least Possible Intervention and a Welfare Ideology

The Theory of Individual and General Prevention

Historically, the classical doctrine of penal law gave way to a positive doctrine in which interest in the criminal partly superseded interest in the crime. We have examined the complex conflict that exists in the current legislation between general and individual preventive considerations, i.e. between punishment and treatment. The functional incompatibility of such objectives as deterrence or retaliation and therapy have constituted a classic theme in penology during the past few decades. Several criminologists have analyzed the various roles assigned to the criminal and the sick (e.g. Aubert and Messinger 1958), and they have shown how very different are the solutions to human problems offered by the courts and the medical profession (e.g. Christie 1971). Apart from these theoretical efforts, empirical studies on the effects of different correctional treatment methods have produced disappointing results (for early reviews see Christie 1961; Bailey 1966).

The systematic review by Lipton, Martinson and Wilks (1975) is generally considered to have given treatment ideology a death blow. My own review of Scandinavian treatment research paints a more differentiated picture, but unfortunately there are few methodologically reliable studies from these countries so the conclusions are more uncertain (Bondeson 1975).

If the ideology of treatment is disappearing, what will replace it? Some punishment theorists believe general prevention should be reintroduced. Andenaes (1971; 1974a) thinks that the death of individual prevention theory leaves the field open for the alternative theory of general prevention (cf. Christie 1971b). However, as I have pointed out elsewhere (Bondeson 1980b), the correlation between punishment/treatment and effect is not zero but *negative,* particularly if account is taken of spontaneous recovery. Even if we assume that there is no relation between punishment/treatment and effect, we still cannot draw any simple conclusions concerning general prevention.

There is no strong scientific support for the theory of general prevention. Even old examples of how the crime rate would rise to an extent never before suspected if the police were paralyzed (e.g. Trolle 1945), no longer hold. For example, in Finland, the police strike in 1975 did not result in an increase in crime. However, the central issue is whether differences in punishment level are of significance for prevention (see Zimring 1971 for the concept of *marginal deterrence.*) It is too early to generalize from the somewhat disparate results of the studies which are available on general prevention (for early reviews see Zimring and Hawkins, 1974; *General Deterrence,* National Swedish Council for Crime Prevention, 1975). Various studies have shown that *public knowledge* of punishment is quite limited. They have also shown that the public does not seem to attach as much importance to differences in the level of punishment as a utilitarian general prevention theory would predict (Bondeson 1979b; cf. Blumstein and Cohen 1980). Lack of space prevents presentation of the available studies but it does not seem rash to say that empirical studies hardly justify the claim that general prevention theory has generally been confirmed. This would also seem to be the conclusion of the U.S. National Academy of Science which produced a comprehensive and critical review in "Deterrence and Incapacitation" (Blumstein et al. 1978) pointing to basic weaknesses of a methodological and statistical nature. For Scandinavian refutations of the doctrines of deterrence and incapacitation see Mathiesen (1988) and v. Hofer (1993).

Alternative Punishment and Treatment Theories

Classical Theories of Penal Law. One alternative theory is the classical theory of penal law based on retribution and proportionality of crime and punishment. In the vacuum concerning criminal policy that many experience today, there is a risk that the pendulum can drastically swing back from the positive to the classical school. The classical theory, however, is founded on what many experts would nowadays regard as simplified conceptions of guilt and responsibility. The past hundred years have taught us something of the sociological, psychological and biological explanations of criminal behavior as well as the selection mechanisms which determine what crimes are detected and prosecuted. As a result, we have a different picture of the criminal today from that which we had one or two centuries ago when the classical theory dominated. Moreover, political values have radically changed so as to make democracy and solidarity among citizens a desired ideal.

During recent years more refined forms of classical penal thinking have taken shape in Finland and Sweden which emphasize the value of punishment in the creation and maintenance of moral norms. Criticism of the treatment ideology has led to the desire to separate punishment from treatment. The proportionality principle, related to the notion of retribution, means that punishment should reflect the reprehensibility of the crime (see Brottsförebyggande rådet 1977:7; SOU 1986:13–15). This neo-classical orientation resembles the penal philosophy usually referred to in the US as "just deserts" (see "Doing Justice" by von Hirsch 1976).

Decision Criteria and Goals. In the criminal policy decisionmaking process different decision criteria are employed more or less explicitly. For example, the extent and distribution of criminality, the maximization of legal predictability, the cost of various measures and the political feasibility of carrying them through may all be considered. After a comprehensive analysis of such decision criteria, Anttila and Törnudd (p. 140) advance the following *main objectives* for criminal policy: 1. to minimize the costs and suffering brought about by crime and by society's control measures; 2. to distribute the costs and the suffering in a just way.

Over and above these effectiveness criteria consideration is also given to such values such as humanity and justice.

The reform proposals which will be presented her, are, to a great extent, guided by two principles—*the theory of least possible intervention* and *a general welfare ideology* which can be deduced from the goals specified above.

The Theory of Least Possible Intervention. From previous research I have demonstrated that all types of deprivation of liberty led to criminalization and other negative prisonization effects. Thus, although the aim of a variety of correctional treatments was predominantly of individual preventive character, the resulting effects were mainly *negative* (Bondeson 1989). In this study we found that the effects of probation with institutional treatment were more harmful than those of probation without institutional treatment and that the effects of probation were more harmful than those of conditional sentences. Once again we see that a positive individual preventive intention seems to result in *negative* individual prevention.

Thus, these studies of correctional treatment in institutions and in the community lend support to Wilkin's conclusion (1969) that the less we do with offenders the better the outcome. Even when the legislator intended to provide the offender with help and support, he failed, at least with the present sanction system.

If applied, the findings on negative individual prevention should lead to a systematic de-escalation of the whole penal system, i.e. a *depenalization.* On the basis of the general prevention ideology we must intervene in some way, but the lower the punishment level the better. In general, the principle of least possible intervention leads to probation being preferred to confinement and conditional sentence being preferred to probat sentences (see Aspelin 1973). In this connection various monetary penalties could be imposed, possibly in connection with *decriminalization* (Skogh, Brottsförebyggande rådet 1975; see also "Report on Decriminalisation" by Council of Europe 1980). Likewise, greater use could be made of diversion from the penal system through, for example, exclusion of sanction, waiver of prosecution and reduction of reporting (SOU 1976:47). Experiments could be undertaken with such measures as community service or the use of damages as a sanction, possibly in combination with supervised work or other forms of treatment (cf. Anttila 1973; Rentzmann 1975a; Straffelovrådet 1977).

The theory of least possible intervention has several advantages. Firstly, in terms of results, it seems to be the most effective. Secondly, in terms of economy it is more advantageous—the less we do, the less it costs. Thirdly, it satisfies the requirement of humaneness, as punishment is associated with suffering. And fourthly, it satisfies the requirement of fairness, since punishment is accumulated in a small number of individuals who, moreover, have often been "punished" from the outset due to their poor social heritage.

In the United States, the related notion of *diversion* was probably first used by the President's Commission on Law Enforcement and Administration of Justice (Task Force Report: Courts, 1967) but has since given rise to a flora of literature (for an early summary see Vorenberg and Vorenberg 1973) and to the specification of different programs and studies primarily within the Department of Justice, Vera Institute of Justice and American Bar Foundation. Diversion is probably also related to what Schur (1973) calls *radical non-intervention.* For the use of the concept of diversion in German criminal policy see Heinz (1992).

Treatment Ideology. So far offenders have rarely been offered treatment instead of punishment; they have usually been punished as a form of treatment or treated as a form of punishment. It may therefore be argued that it is too early to reject an ideology which has not been adequately tested.

Treatment research has in turn had to conform to the reality of criminal policy. It has seldom had the opportunity to compare pure forms of treatment with pure forms of punishment. It has had to evaluate something called treatment which is in reality punishment and which, at most, may contain certain concrete elements of treatment that are more or less forced on the offender. The majority of studies are based on the evaluation of a specific treatment measure undertaken as a part of a sanction which is otherwise unchanged. It is, for example, hardly surprising that Kassebaum, Ward and Wilner (1971) found group therapy in traditional prisons ineffective in reducing recidivism rates. Such therapy is only a drop in the ocean and cannot be expected to counteract all the negative factors influencing people inside and outside the prison (cf. Landerholm-Ek, Kriminalvårdsstyrelsen 1976).

Similarly, it is hardly reasonable to expect the probation officer's varying case-load to affect the client's degree of adjustment to the community as long as the client is forced to contact the probation officer and the latter has little possibility of taking the client's specific needs into consideration. American research into case-loads has produced similar findings, even from studies of probation involving fewer cases per supervisor and more frequent contacts with clients.

The treatment ideology has been compromised through the use of treatment theory to legitimate punishment measures. The traditional prison sentence would probably have lost much meaning during this century if treatment had not been used as an additional justification for its existence (Christie 1966). Other measures involving lengthy deprivation of liberty have been created with the aim of treating offenders but such measures as youth imprisonment and internment seem to have more or less disappeared from Scandinavian criminal policy (Andenaes 1974b).

Even if the treatment ideology has been misused, we cannot rule out the possibility that offenders in need of treatment may exist, notably the large number of offenders who have problems with alcohol or drugs and for whom some form of therapy may be indicated. Yet, it is difficult even for clients of the non-institutional services to make use of such treatment mainly because of the coercive structure of the system.

The Protective Law Commission had little difficulty in combining punishment and treatment probably because it did not at that time fully understand the detrimental effects of coercion on therapy. The Committee on Correctional Reform succeeded in bridging the gap between control and support but this would probably not have been possible if use had been made of social scientists (SOU 1972:64). The Danish report "Criminal Care—Social Care" (Kriminalforsorg-Socialforsorg 1975), produced by a planning group in which several social scientists took part, concluded that it is not possible to combine treatment and coercion. In the Norwegian report "Non-institutional Correction" (Kriminalomsorg i frihet 1975) the only social scientist in the group (Hauge) entered a reservation against the committee's view that it is possible to combine control and support. The Finnish Correctional Committee in their report from 1972 proposed that coercion should not be combined with treatment and service but that each should be kept within the framework of separate systems (see Anttila 1973).

A Welfare Ideology. One way to avoid the conflict between punishment and treatment might be to talk of a welfare ideology instead of a treatment ideology. It seems as though the socially handicapped groups within the correctional system more often need material resources than treatment. Personal finance, employment and housing present the most acute problems according to both clients and supervisors (see also Hansen et al. 1980). Similar problems were revealed in interviews with inmates at different types of correctional institution (Bondeson 1974, 342–354). In a welfare state like Sweden one might also think it obvious that a welfare policy ought also to embrace those less favored by society and that an equal rights policy should not exclude the less favored groups.

Such a welfare ideology may, however, conflict with general feelings of fairness where it is believed that only those who contribute to the prosperity of the society should be rewarded by enjoying its fruits. Only those who work, for example, should have the right to a pension or sick benefits. Such principles are, however, slowly loosening up. An interesting example of this can be seen in the initiative taken to grant offenders, who were considered hopeless recidivists, early retirement pensions with the aim of preventing them from being sentenced to repeated internment. This experiment seems to function humanely for the individual while at the same time being relatively cheap for the society. In addition, it seems to have led to a reduction in recidivism (Kyvsgaard 1981).

However, the real measure of civic solidarity would be if it were found that, in order to cope in the community, offenders were in greater need of social resources than other needy people. If the clients of the correctional services were to be given better opportunities than ordinary citizens the questions "Are they to be rewarded for committing crimes?" "Is the only way to get special privileges to commit crime?" would at once arise. These questions are of course not easily answered. I merely want to stress the fact that an affirmative answer to these seemingly paradoxical questions is not incompatible with an ideology of welfare and equality.

Moreover, it is known from the psychology of learning that *positive sanctions* work better than negative ones (see Rentzmann 1975b for a review of the literature) and that a reinforcing or extinguishing reaction to a particular behavior must come in direct conjunction with that behavior. This *principle of immediacy* has also been taken into account by certain legal philosophers (Bentham spoke of the principle of celerity), but has, in great part, been neglected in practical criminal policy.

Thus, it is important that punishment, when imposed in accordance with the principle of least possible intervention, follows as quickly as possible after the offense has been committed. The principle of immediacy naturally places great demands on both the police and the judicial authorities. Furthermore, punishment should not be so severe that its deleterious effects cannot be counteracted and compensated for by measures taken in accordance with the principle of welfare ideology.

Changing the Sanction System

In what follows I shall only suggest reforms on the basis of the sanctions studied in the present research.

Greater Use of Conditional Sentence

More offenders who are sentenced to probation or imprisonment could be sentenced conditionally. The recidivism study made in the course of this research showed that conditionally sentenced offenders recidivated about four times less than probationers. The prediction study also demonstrated that such offenders recidivated less than probationers—even when account was taken of their social prognoses. Within the different risk groups there were fewer recidivists among offenders who had received conditional sentences. Moreover, we noted that their recidivism rates were very low throughout—even for the conditionally sentenced offenders who belonged to the high risk groups. These findings suggest that it should be possible to increase the number of conditional sentences without increasing recidivism.

Moreover, we note that the conditional sentence sanction has been increasingly used without leading to an increase in recidivism rates. Carlsson and Olsson's analysis of recidivism statistics (Brottsförebyggande rådet 1976, 24–29) showed that the use of conditional sentences increased both in absolute terms and in relative terms (from 18% of all sanctions to 24%), without affecting recidivism rates. The increase in the use of conditional sentence is most evident in the case of offenses against the person (from 21% to 36%) and thereafter for property offenses (from 22% to 30%). For these offense categories there was no real increase in recidivism rates (from 7% to 8% and from 9% to 10% respectively).

The fact that similar trends are found for offenders with previous convictions is of special interest. It is true that there were few such offenders sentenced conditionally but the number increased twofold (absolutely from 332 to 746 and relatively from 3% to 6%) without a corresponding rise in recidivism (from 15% to 16%). These trends are seen even more clearly in the case of the most common offense categories—offenses against the person and property offenses. Although the number of cases increased more than twofold, recidivism remained unchanged or even decreased (from 15% to 16% and 19% to 9% respectively).

Comparisons among different risk groups as well as comparisons over time thus indicate that the conditional sentence could be used to a greater extent without recidivism rates being affected (see also Sarnecki 1993, 65ff). The fact that there are so few recidivists among conditionally sentenced offenders with previous convictions suggests that there is considerable scope for the increased use of this sanction. It is, nevertheless, impossible to predict how far one can go in this direction before recidivism rates are negatively affected.

Conditional sentence has thus increased relatively more among first-time offenders and probation more among previous offenders in the period 1966–1980. However, recidivism rates have note increased neither for first time nor for previous offenders (v. Hofer 1981).

Unfortunately, there is not much other research apart from the present study, which compares conditional sentence with probation whilst holding criminal antecedents constant. Sparks (1970), reviewing and summarizing the research conducted in this field, implied that many probationers would have managed as well with a nominal measure not involving supervision without increasing the risk of recidivism. He adds that "it would be of interest to compare the effectiveness of conditional sentences without supervision—as now used in many European countries—with probation in those countries" (p. 267).

This is what has been done in the present research but it seems that it is one of the few of this type undertaken. Börjeson (1966), another exception, also found in his prediction study that conditional sentence was the best sanction as far as individual prevention is concerned. Another study similar to the present one was conducted for the Home Office of England and Wales by Hammond (1964; 1969). Fines and conditional sentence were more effective than probation and different forms of institutional treatment. This was true of both first offenders and recidivists as well as different age groups. Collins et al. (1984) also found in a study on alternative probation strategies in Maryland that nonserious offenders sentenced to probation could go unsupervised without increasing the likelihood of recidivism.

Greater Use of Probation

It should be possible to sentence more offenders to probation rather than to prison. Even if the present project does not contain findings that directly lead to this conclusion, support is found for it in other data. Simple recidivism studies have shown that relapse rates are no greater for probationers than for prisoners and are often much lower; probation is therefore usually said to be at least as effective as a prison sentence. In summarizing different research results, Sparks (1970) asserted that even in countries where probation is extensively used, it could probably be used for a substantial number of offenders who are presently sentenced to prison without an increase in recidivism.

Wilkins (1958) found in an early study that there were no significant differences in the recidivism rates of offenders sentenced in two courts even though one of the courts sentenced offenders to probation three times as often as the other. He also drew the conclusion that "a large number of offenders who are now placed in prisons or youth prisons could be placed on probation without any ensuing change in recidivism rates".

Great variation in the courts' use of probation has been noted in several studies. Davies (1964) found considerable variation in California where probation was imposed for 14% of the felonies in one district and 68% of the felonies in another. He also confirmed the fact that no relationship exists between the frequency of this practice and corresponding recidivism rates. Mueller (1965) found that 20% of newly imprisoned males could have been recommended for probation instead as, according to the prediction tables, the probability of recidivism for these offenders was the same as for those who were sentenced to probation. Robert and Seckle (1965) estimated that 40% of the young offenders who were committed to an institution could be immediately released to the community without risking great increases in relapse rates.

The few experimental studies conducted in the United States also indicate that probation is either more effective than, or at least as effective as, institutional treatment. Some of these studies are: the Community Treatment Project in Sacramento and Stockton (Warren 1964; 1967); the Provo Experiment in Utah (Empey and Rabow 1961; 1964), the Silverlake Experiment in Los Angeles (Empey et al. 1966) and the Essexfields Project in New Jersey (Stephenson and Scarpitti 1967). In these experiments the recidivism rates seem to be lower for juvenile offenders in the experimental groups who were treated in the community than for offenders in the control groups who were sent to various institutions. These experiments, however, were not constructed specifically to evaluate probation. (In the Community Treatment Project and Silverlake the treatment for the experimental group could not be described as ordinary probation). Criticism has been leveled at the Community Treatment Project, Essexfields and Provo because of alleged methodological inadequacies concerning assignment to the experimental and control groups as well as for the significance supervision had for the way in which recidivism was assessed for the different groups (Lerman 1968; 1975).

Sparks stressed in his review of Anglo-Saxon research on probation, that almost all the studies showed that the majority of offenders who were placed under supervision did not recidivate within the chosen follow-up time: "These figures are, of course, much higher than the overall success rates typically reported for institutional treatment" (1970, 253; see also Radzinowicz 1959).

There are no Swedish studies which directly compare probationers with offenders sentenced to different types of confinement and which control for the degree of prior criminality (cf. Wolf 1960; 1961). However, the official statistics published by the National Central Bureau of Statistics, "Relapse into Crime 1967–70" (Statistiska Centralbyrån R 1973:1), show that 40% of probationers committed serious offenses within a 3-year period (this figure includes both those who received probation only and those who received probation in combination with institutional treatment).

Table 9.1 shows that there is somewhat greater recidivism among probationers than among offenders imprisoned for one to four months (30%) but considerably less than among offenders imprisoned for five months or more (66%). Probationers clearly recidivate less than youth prisoners (81%), internees (79%), to those given treatment under the Child Welfare Act (56%), or to youth training schools (clearly over 70%; see also Bondeson 1989).

If we compare offenders who were sentenced *for the first time* (or given waiver of prosecution) in 1967 with those who had been previously sentenced (or given waivers of prosecution), we find partially opposite tendencies for probationers and prisoners. Thus, offenders sentenced to probation for the first time recidivate more (30%) than offenders sentenced to imprisonment from one to four months or five months or more in prison (13% and 24% respectively)—but clearly less than young offenders sentenced to youth imprisonment (78%) or sent to youth training schools (68%). Among offenders with *previous convictions*, probationers recidivate to the same extent as offenders sentenced to imprisonment for from one to four months (44%) but clearly less than offenders sentenced to five months and more (69%), and much less than young offenders sentenced to youth imprisonment (81%), offenders sentenced to internment (79%), or juveniles sent to youth training schools (80%).

The very low recidivism rate among offenders *sentenced for the first time* to prison for from one to four months leads one to suspect that a special type of offense was involved in these cases. Official statistics show that slightly more than three-quarters of these offenders were found guilty of driving under the influence of alcohol. The recidivism rate of these offenders is as low as 10%. Only 5% of offenders sentenced for the first time to imprisonment for from one to four months had committed property offenses but as many as 38% of them recidivated. This proportion of recidivists is higher than that for first-time probationers who had committed property offenses which remains at 30%.

Property offenses are the dominant offense type among probationers, both among those sentenced for the first time and those with previous convictions (84% and 86% respectively). Property offenses increase significantly among offenders with previous convictions sentenced to imprisonment from for one to four months. Only in the case of offenders with previous convictions who had been sentenced to prison for five months or more did the level of property offenses reach that of probationers. Since property offenses in all sanction categories result in higher recidivism rates than other categories of offenses, probationers should be compared with the former categories.

Forty-eight percent of probationers who had committed property offenses and who had *previously been sentenced recidivated,* but this proportion increases to 69% for offenders sentenced to prison for one to four months and 72% for

TABLE 9.1 Recidivism within a 3-Year Period for Offenders Sentenced for Serious Offenses in 1967 with Previous Convictions Held Constant

Sentenced in 1967 to:	First Time Convicted* Abs.	First Time Convicted* Recid. %	Previously Convicted* Abs.	Previously Convicted* Recid. %	All Convicted* Abs.	All Convicted* Recid. %
Cond. sentence	2 398	10	508	14	2 906	10
Probation	2 974	30	3 659	47	6 633	40
Prison 1-4 months	2 680	13	3 341	44	6 021	30
Prison 5 months or more	176	24	2 239	69	2 415	66
Youth imprisonment	18	78	280	81	298	81
Internment	-	-	578	79	578	79
Child Welfare Act	409	48	270	61	679	56
Other sanctions	141	18	509	38	650	33
All sanctions	8 796	20	11 384	52	20 180	38

*Including waivers of prosecution. Foreign citizens have been excluded.
Source: Statistiska meddelanden no R 1973:1, Table 8 (here simplified).

offenders sentenced to prison for five months or more. Property offenses dominate the other sanctions in the same way and recidivism is here as high as approximately 80% (youth imprisonment 82% and internment 79%).

We have thus seen that, for property offenses, the type of offense most relevant to probation, the rate of recidivism among probationers is *lower* than for all sanctions privative of liberty regardless of whether we consider those with first or previous convictions.

Unfortunately, there is no detailed information available about the weight of the criminal records of those sentenced to probation and imprisonment. We do know however, that individual prevention was taken into consideration when the probationers were sentenced and that the sentenced offenders had poor prognoses. Those who were sentenced to prison for the first time had generally committed special types of offenses such as violent offenses, driving under the influence of alcohol or objecting to military service and were deprived of their liberty for reasons of general prevention. The small number of offenders who had committed property offenses were sentenced for robbery, embezzlement, fraud under aggravating circumstances, or a combination of these and other offenses. For this reason, it can fairly safely be assumed that offenders sentenced to probation belong to higher risk groups than offenders sentenced to prison. If this assumption is correct, we would expect a higher rate of recidivism among offenders sentenced to probation than among those sentenced to prison. But, if the recidivism rate is found to be lower this can mean that the sanction of probation is less likely to lead to recidivism than imprisonment. Without a predictive instrument, however, we cannot be sure about the effects of these sanctions.

Carlsson and Olsson (Brottsförebyggande rådet 1976) analyzed recidivism in connection with different sanctions and in particular, they compared probation with prison sentences. Broadly speaking, they reached the same conclusions as those presented above but in some respects their interpretations differ. In the main, they based their study on offenders sentenced in 1966 and found that probation resulted in *higher* recidivism rates than prison sentences. The sanction groups differ, however, in a number of respects. The men who were sentenced to prison were considerably older than those who were sentenced to probation (51% of the first-time prisoners were 30 or more by comparison with only 16% of the probationers) and recidivism was three times as great among young offenders as among older offenders with first convictions for both sanctions. When the authors held the age factor constant, they found that the number of recidivists was greater among probationers than among prisoners for the men who were sentenced for the first time, while the differences were reversed for those who had previously been convicted. Furthermore, in an analysis dealing only with men who were sentenced for the first time, when they eliminated drunken drivers the differences still remained, except for certain age groups and for prison sentences of five to twelve months. When analyzing the material by main offense, they found that the recidivism pattern differed from that established earlier only in the case of the offense of theft and gross theft. With respect to property offenses, they contended that the trends demonstrated earlier held true for men who were sentenced for the first time (within a 5-year period, 35% of prisoners and 39% of probationers recidivated).

These findings may seem somewhat surprising. If we look at the original recidivism statistics from the National Central Bureau of Statistics and compare property offenders sentenced to probation or prison for from one to four months in 1966 *for the first time,* we find a 1% difference in favor of prisoners during a 5-year follow-up period and a 1% difference in favor of probationers during a 3-year period. If we examine the 3-year periods for which there are published recidivism data (offenders sentenced 1966 through 1970) we find, so far as property offenses are concerned, that probation has a lower recidivism rate than imprisonment for from one to four months during four of the five years reviewed. And the lower age of those sentenced to probation—a factor which is associated with higher recidivism—was not taken into account.

Thus, we see that there are small variations in the recidivism figures for the different years and that there may be small shifts in the statistics depending on whether we base them on all the offenders sentenced or only the men. It is also important to stress that Carlsson and Olsson's concentration on offenders who were sentenced for the first time involved atypical offense categories with lower recidivism rates among those sentenced to imprisonment whilst property offenses dominated among all offenders except those who were sentenced to imprisonment.

If instead we look at *all the offenders sentenced for property crimes* for the period 1966–67 and compare probationers with offenders sentenced to prison for one to four months, we find differences in recidivism of about 25% for offenders sentenced to imprisonment for one to four months and 30% for offenders sentenced to five months or more, both in favor of probation.

We might ask, however, if it had not been more meaningful to compare non-institutional treatment with institutional treatment instead of comparing probationers with prisoners. With the former comparison, those sentenced to probation should be split into two groups, one containing only ordinary probationers and another containing those sentenced to probation with institutional treatment. As we saw earlier, there were twice as many recidivists among offenders who were committed to a probation institution. We could also compare the ordinary probation group with offenders sentenced to other kinds of confinement, in particular youth imprisonment, and perhaps even to training schools and internment. The sanctions of probation and youth imprisonment both require that there exists a treatment need whereas ordinary imprisonment does not. When we compare the ordinary probation supervision group with other sanction groups who were also thought to be in need of treatment but who instead received it through institutional treatment, the considerably lower recidivism rates among the probationers is even more striking.

Abolition of Probation with Institutional Treatment

In this study we have demonstrated that probation with institutional treatment results in much higher rates of recidivism than probation without such treatment (61% and 30% respectively). We also noted significant differences in recidivism rates when the offender's social prognosis was taken into account. Within every risk group there were more recidivists among probationers who had been sentenced to probation with institutional treatment.

Thus, from the viewpoint of individual prevention, it seems to be better to sentence an offender to probation without institutional treatment. However, if we compare probation with institutional treatment for one month with imprisonment for more than four months and with, especially, youth imprisonment (about 10 months), we find that these latter forms of confinement result in even higher rates of recidivism (66% and 81% respectively).

To the extent that an alternative to youth imprisonment is desired (one of the reasons for establishing probation institutions) the shorter periods probationers spend at institutions would seem to be preferable to longer periods of confinement under other sanctions privative of liberty.

Probation with institutional treatment was often imposed on offenders for reasons of general prevention even though the primary aim of probation was supposed to be individual prevention. As we saw in this study, there was also little scope for any real treatment at the probation institution.

However, when considering the mental and social handicaps from which the majority of probationers sentenced to institutional treatment suffered, it appears to me that confinement was not an adequate measure—whether it be called treatment or punishment. It would be better if the probation services paid greater attention to this group. Furthermore, since many of these offenders misuse alcohol and drugs, some of them ought also to receive expert help for these problems.

From the beginning the probation institution, contrary to intentions, mixed probationers and various categories of prisoners. With the re-organization of the prison and probation systems in 1974, probation institutions were transformed into neighbourhood prisons, thus abandoning the last of the original intentions.

Considering the fact that the intentions behind probation with institutional treatment were contradictory, and, in addition, were poorly realized, the abolition of this form of the probation sanction seems logical.

Changes in Probation

Probation can probably be rendered more effective. It is almost certainly easier to improve the non-institutional services than to improve institutional corrections (Bondeson 1974; 1989).

The Order in Council on the non-institutional services (SFS 1964:632) requires that probation provide both *control and assistance.* As this study has shown, there are great difficulties associated with combining these two functions. Several other studies have reached the same conclusion. With the re-organization of the prison and probation systems, which took effect on 1 July 1974, the importance of control was reduced by shortening the supervision period and by removing certain of the conditions which could be imposed on the probationer. Further progress can probably be made in this direction. However, it is hardly realistic to suggest the abolition of the controlling aspect of probation under the present circumstances. Since the non-institutional services may henceforth be expected to receive new kinds of offenders, who have hitherto been handled by the institutional sector, they cannot readily eliminate all possibilities for exercising control.

The control function could, however, in part be given a new form. Firstly, it should be separated as far as possible from the assistance function, and, secondly, it could be made less irksome by combining it with reinforced resources for helping clients.

The double system of supervision with professional and lay personnel certainly involves great advantages, which, however, are not fully utilized. An analysis of these two roles shows how different they actually are. Such an analysis ought to be used to cultivate the roles so that each actor could make the most of his part.

Laymen do not directly represent the authorities in the eyes of clients which is why a client may more easily confide in his lay supervisor. *Personal support should therefore be provided primarily by laymen who should not take on the function of formal control.* Professional supervisors possess special knowledge and must work subject to professional responsibility. *Practical support and formal control should therefore be the primary function of the professional probation officer staff.* The two latter functions ought also to balance each other and provide the probation officer with a badly-needed reward and control system (cf. the proposal of the Protective Law Commission described in Chapter 3 and Frej, Sundsvall Experiment, 1974). By partially redefining the roles of laymen and probation officials and at the same time providing substantially increased assistance, the control function could be perceived less negatively by clients.

Reduced Formal Control

Supervision Should as Far as Possible Be Given a Voluntary Character. The ideal would naturally be to make assistance so attractive that those who really need it would ask for it and thereby render supervision a voluntary measure. Theoretically, this would be the best solution, as research has shown that it is difficult to combine treatment with coercion. The Social Welfare Committee came to the same conclusion (SOU 1974:39) and suggested that supervision be made voluntary within the social services. The Danish report "Criminal Care—Social Care" (Kriminalforsorg-Socialforsorg 1975) came, in principle, to the same conclusion for the non-institutional services.

In the present study we found that almost half the clients thought they themselves ought to decide if supervision should be provided or not. Almost one-fifth of the supervisors shared this view. The majority of clients believed they would manage just as well or even better without a supervisor. One-third of their supervisors also thought their client would get by just as well or better without a supervisor.

The real problem with voluntary supervision is to determine whether those who really need control or help actually receive it. There is a risk that the offenders who are in most need of support are least aware of it or least willing to admit it. We would thus not reach the most needy clients. I believe therefore that for the present we must refrain from making supervision totally voluntary and instead make it voluntary to the greatest extent possible. The degree of client contact should be determined from case to case and decided upon in the first place according to the individual's need of assistance and in the second place in accordance with society's need to control the offender.

Shortened Supervisory and Probationary Periods. The Committee on Correctional Reform proposed that the supervisory period be shortened. Accordingly, the maximum period for supervision has been shortened from three years to two and is subjected to obligatory review after one year. The Committee had suggested that the probationary period, which can exceed the supervision period, should be reduced two years. It is, however, still three years. The probationary period could reasonably be two years as is the case with conditional sentences. The supervisory period should be continually reviewed and the client's needs should, as far as possible, be taken into account.

Fairness requires that supervision should not continue longer than is justified having regard to the seriousness of the offense.

As in a number of other studies, we noted that recidivism often occurs fairly soon after sentence. In this study that there were practically no cases of recidivism after two years and half of the all observed recidivism occurred within six months. Thus, the important thing is to concentrate help efforts on the first period after sentence is passed when problems seem to be greatest (cf. the first amateur supervisors in Massachusetts). Supervision could, in most cases, be terminated after one year.

Ideally, voluntary help efforts should be offered before the trial and as soon as possible after the offense has become known so as to attempt to solve the personal and social problems which may have caused the criminal behavior. The Committee on Correctional Reform suggested that this principle of immediacy be met by appointing a voluntary contact person who would have no control function. To date, very little use has been made of this function.

Special Probation Conditions Should Be Kept to a Minimum. At one time, special conditions were imposed in one-quarter of all cases of probation. The Commission on Correctional Reform proposed the abolition of certain conditions and a more restrictive use of others. The Commission's report points out that probation conditions have not always been well-suited to their purpose and may have contributed to client hostility towards supervision.

In this study, we saw that there was very little agreement between the supervisor and client as to which of the conditions were applicable in particular cases. However, both parties did agree that many breaches of these conditions occurred. It is clear that the special conditions and instructions were not effective as neither party attached any special importance to them.

In the Danish report "Criminal Care—Social Care", it was suggested that special conditions of probation should be completely discarded. We ought to add that such conditions have been used to a greater extent in Denmark than in Sweden. We do not know just how common the practice is today as this information is no longer given in the reports of the National Central Bureau of Statistics. The Swedish Prison and Probation Administration estimates that they were used in only about 10% of cases.

Special conditions should be used only when they are clearly justified, primarily from the point of view of treatment, and only when they can be carried into effect. Unnecessary conditions can actually counteract their objective. Possibly the chief probation officer should decide on the use of certain special conditions to greater extent instead of the supervision board, thus making the procedure more flexible and more informal. Special conditions could be both imposed and withdrawn swiftly where this was really justified.

Deprivation of Liberty Should Not Be Used as a Sanction for Breach of Probation Conditions. According to the provisions obtaining at the time of this research, a client could be temporarily taken into custody or even be made subject to ordinary deprivation of liberty if he violated any general or specific conditions of probation. The 1973 statistics show that there were 853 such cases in that year (SOU 1975:16, 198). There was great variation between probation districts which, in part, reflected the differing practice of the different supervision boards. After reviewing the annual reports from the supervision boards included in the present study, we noted a trend towards the reduced use of taking into custody and other measures for misconduct. This trend was apparent even before the reorganization of the prison and probation systems came into force in 1974.

Even if an offender has not misbehaved he can be taken into custody. A client might be arrested by the police if, for example, he had not kept in contact with his supervisor. I consider it a doubtful practice to deprive clients of their liberty when no new offense has been committed.

In the proposals from the Danish committee there was a desire to do away with the possibility of depriving clients of their liberty for breach of probation conditions. Nevertheless, a minority opinion pointed out that because this measure was rarely used, retaining the possibility to use it could serve as a threat to difficult clients. However, it could be argued that this threat means very little if it is not carried out. If officials make empty threats, they risk losing credibility.

Even if breach of special probation conditions were not dealt with by deprivation of liberty, this would not mean that such conditions are worthless. As I stated earlier, they can be justified from the point of view of treatment. They may also be imposed for control purposes. Their violation could be taken into account—as in the Danish proposal—when an offender is sentenced for having committed new offenses.

The Supervisor's Obligation to Report Should Be Abolished. Greater collaboration between professional probation officials, supervisors and clients (see below) would eliminate the necessity for the supervisor's formal obligation to report. As this study has shown, the obligation to report can disturb the supervisor-client relationship. Letting the client read the report or write it together with the supervisor does not resolve the problem of establishing trust. In any case, the majority of supervisors we asked did not want the client to take part in the writing of the report.

It will be remembered that supervisors were unwilling to report on their clients' offenses. Information on new offenses comes in any case mainly through police channels. If, therefore, supervisors were no longer obliged to report on their clients' offenses, the probation organization would not be deprived of vital information.

Increased Formal and Informal Assistance

The idea of allowing the professional probation staff to take the primary responsibility for providing practical support and allowing the supervisor—or preferably a contact person—to be responsible for providing personal support, requires close collaboration between these parties and the client (see also Hansen et al. 1980).

Better Collaboration Between the Probation Organization, the Contact Person and the Client. Collaboration between the professional probation staff and lay supervisors has been relatively limited and has primarily concerned the quarterly reports. Since it has proved difficult to get these reports sent in to the probation office it seems reasonable to suppose that this form of collaboration is not experienced as adequate and meaningful. It would be desirable to replace these reports by regular meetings of all involved parties. Such meetings should not, as the present reports do, mainly constitute a retrospective, controlling activity, but be primarily used for *looking ahead and planning various measures to be taken*. Some way of checking that the various measures were carried out in accordance with the intentions behind them would need to be built in but this should be in the hands of all parties.

The first meeting should, following the principle of immediacy, take place at the earliest possible moment. The chief or regular probation officer should, together with the contact person and client, analyze the client's needs and formulate a plan for the ensuing work. There has for some time been a requirement for a treatment plan to be prepared—or at least a form has to be filled with this aim in mind—but usually the plan seems not to have evolved from a discussion between the parties involved. Regarding the decline of the treatment ideology, it might be more appropriate to call the treatment plan an "action plan" or simply a "work plan" and the meetings could be called *planning meetings*. New meetings should take place continuously to check if the measures have been carried out and are effective and perhaps to suggest new ones. Periodic consultation should take place between the client and either the supervisor or the probation officer to discuss the details in the implementation of the plan. It seems likely that, even before the end of the first quarter, a new meeting should take place to check on and discuss the effectiveness of the measures.

Meetings should be held as long as earlier problems remain or new ones appear. When the client seems to be relatively free from problems and has shown stability for some time, discussions concerning the termination of supervision should begin. Supervision should be terminated as soon as there is no longer any need for it to continue and should not proceed longer than can be justified from the viewpoint of punishment.

Since 1975 the Swedish Prison and Probation Administration has recommended treatment planning. But for the clients of the non-institutional services nothing is regulated in law about the form treatment should take and, in consequence, there are no provisions on treatment planning. The Administration nevertheless thinks that the client, the supervisor and the person handling the case ought to meet and discuss what form treatment should take. "It is desirable to continue with these meetings between the three parties after the treatment plan has been established but as it may prove difficult to secure the presence of the client and the supervisor, the follow-up cannot always be made in this way." (Kriminalvårdsstyrelsen: PM ang. behandlingsplanering 1975, p. 29)

If meetings are to be held between the professional handling the case, the supervisor and the client, resources must be made available so that the probation office can remain open in the evenings. In Malmö, as in the majority of other districts, there is a period of duty outside office hours for only two hours per week.

The SPPA presupposes that treatment planning will take place because an official form, called a "treatment plan", has been sent out. The professional probation staff in Malmö stated in discussions held with them in the summer of 1976 that they had as yet no practical experience in treatment planning but they certainly experienced irritation over having to fill in the new treatment plan forms. A probation officer commented on them as follows: "Some time before 1 April a whole bunch of new forms came in so that the case records and journals would have to handled in a completely new way. The system has many advantages but also makes use of a great many different forms that all of us think to quite unnecessary and pointless. These forms are to be filled in for every new case, they are to be kept regularly, and are to be made out quite differently from previously. We find all this negative."

It should be an important task for the Swedish Prison and Probation Administration to try to counteract *bureaucratic* tendencies which, *inter alia,* have the effect of transforming means into ends. Proposals for an improved work organization within the non-institutional services, which were sent out for comment in 1976, were criticized by field workers for shifting decision-making responsibility away from the probation officers and up to the chief probation officer. This does not seem to be the right way to reduce the sense of alienation which many probation officers appear to experience in their organization.

Qualified Service from the Probation Organization for Clients. The boundary between the non-institutional and the social services is unclear and in all probability results in a great deal of work being duplicated. Probation staff seem to devote much time to helping their clients with acute financial problems, something which would seem to be more properly a duty for the social services. Some clients "go the rounds" and manage to beg some small "go-somewhere-else" sums from both organizations. However, there are plans to relieve social service workers from paying out social welfare benefits in routine cases by transferring such payments to local social insurance offices.

These changes should provide the personnel of the probation services with more time for qualified assistance to all clients with needs. If clients are to be helped to adjust in society, professional staff working during office hours are required. Given that professional staff take over many of the practical problems which have hitherto been handled by laymen would give the latter group more time to work with the clients' personal problems. The professionals' function becomes one of practical support while that of the lay supervisors becomes one of personal support.

Apart from these duties, the professional staff are responsible for the recruitment, training and supervision of the lay supervisors. They also have an important role to play in informing and influencing public opinion.

Ends and means analyses appear to be neglected by the probation organization. Our knowledge of the way in which staff members actually use their time and resources is deficient. The proposal outlined here implies that the staff should use more time to analyze the clients' needs and, together with other authorities and the lay supervisors, work more actively with long-term programs in an effort to solve the clients' adjustment problems. Some of the most important tasks of a practical, supportive nature for probation staff are to find meaningful employment and satisfactory housing for their clients as well as helping them to improve their financial situation.

*1. **Meaningful Employment.*** This study has shown that unemployment is common among probationers and a direct link can often be found between unemployment and recidivism.

A relatively detailed follow-up has shown that quite a large proportion of probationers who were supposed to be helped by a probation institution to obtain work, were without jobs when they were released and that many of these probationers subsequently recidivated. Not only did the probation institution fail to procure work for those committed to it but in addition some clients who were employed before committal lost their jobs. Information from inmates from different types of correctional institutions showed that only half of them had work when they were released (Bondeson 1974, 353). Gustafsson and Treiberg (Kriminalvårdsstyrelsen 1974) also found that about half of the prisoners who were to be released to the Stockholm district did not have work and that unemployment was greater among these offenders *after* their stay at a prison than before they were committed.

It appears to be difficult for the probation services to break the vicious circle that offenders are caught up in after release—poor general education and little or no vocational training, little work experience, employment gaps, mental and social problems, factual or feared labeling, discrimination—all of which make it difficult for the sentenced person to compete for work on the open market and often result in his being marginalized in society.

In principle, the National Labor Market Board is able to offer *vocational rehabilitation* in the form of retraining, work tests and training for people who are difficult to place, alternatives-to-unemployment schemes, archive work, sheltered employment, semi-sheltered employment and domestic work.

Alternatives-to-unemployment schemes have been the most common form of employment for parolees and the other clients of the probation services who are badly equipped to compete for work on the open market. While originally these schemes were thought of as an aid for the unemployed, *special schemes* for the handicapped have developed into a form of sheltered employment. Job preparation schemes are organized at certain centers for handicapped groups such as those seeking work from the correctional services, the temperance services, youth welfare services and the mental health services. Each handicap group is usually placed in a special work team—a form of categorization which can strengthen the feeling of failure.

Where placement in the open labour market is difficult, there should be possibilities for *semi-sheltered employment* instead of alternatives-to-unemployment schemes. This means that an enterprise would receive compensation from the Labour Market Board for providing employment to people who, because of some kind of handicap, cannot do a full, normal day's work. This sort of arrangement was originally intended for people with medical or mental handicaps but it could be extended to people with social handicaps. If private employers, despite compensation, refuse to engage previously convicted persons, public authorities at least should to create such "semi-sheltered employment" for the clients of the non-institutional services.

Collaboration between the Swedish Prison and Probation Administration and the National Labour Market Board has been formally regulated and carried out since 1962. As part of the Sundsvall project with reinforced resources for the non-institutional services, the Sundsvall probation service had at its disposal a labor exchange officer assigned especially to visit and secure work for their clients. This experiment gave positive results, at least in the short term. In Malmö there has been a similar arrangement since 1955 and this too is thought to have achieved good results. In recent years a special consultation group was formed to deal with the collaboration between the two authorities. At the end of the 1960s *special boards for dealing with labor and trades unions questions* were set up at the majority of prisons.

The Committee on Correctional Reform took the view that clients of the correctional services should have access to the same standards and services as other members of society and that this principle should "apply with even fewer restrictions to the clients who are retained in the community" (SOU 1974:64, 167). Similarly, the Minister of Justice stressed the fact that the social activities of the non-institutional services were primarily intended to supplement the efforts of the National Labour Market Board and the social authorities (Prop 1973:1, App. 4, 129).

Have the clients of the correctional system been integrated into society in accordance with the *normalization principle?* According to the statistics of the National Labor Market Board for 1974 assembled by the National Audit Administration, only a small proportion of clients found work on the open market. A rather large group was instead involved in some kind of training. However, alternatives-to-unemployment schemes were still the most common employment available to these clients. There were extremely few opportunities for semi-sheltered employment, sheltered employment and archive work (Riksrevisionsverket 1976, 9).

It appears therefore as if the normalization principle has not become a reality. Insofar as the clients of the non-institutional services are poorly educated and are disadvantaged on the labor market by comparison with comparable groups in the community, this indicates that it is not enough that they be given the "right to assistance and support to the same extent as other citizens" (Prop 1973:1 App. 4, 129). Theoretically, the principle of equality is valid for correctional clients when it comes to avoiding discrimination but if they are so clearly disadvantaged that the equality principle actually discriminates against them, then *special treatment through affirmative action* is called for. In other words, these socially handicapped groups seem to need extra support and assistance so they do not become the isolated rejects of society.

2. ***Satisfactory Housing.*** It has been shown earlier that a large number of the probationers were living under unsatisfactory conditions both before and after they were sentenced. The majority of them were either compelled to

share rooms or live in below-standard apartments and overcrowding was common. Some clients lost their apartments during their short stay at the probation institution.

Another study demonstrated that the during the stay in prison the accommodation situation of parolees had deteriorated: after release fewer would be able to live in their own apartment, more would live at a single sex hostel and the number living alone increased considerably (Gustafsson and Treiberg, Kriminalvårdsstyrelsen 1974, 22).

The Swedish Prison and Probation Administration made a survey of the housing situation for clients during 1975. Among other things, it was found that large groups of clients, particularly juveniles, had only temporary housing arrangements. A total of 16% had some "short-term accommodation" and 10% of these said they had found "temporary solutions" to their housing problems. The corresponding figures for clients with alcohol or drug problems are as high as 73% and 65% respectively. Thirty percent of those who were due to be released from prison within a two-week period either had no place to live or had only made temporary arrangements.

The results from the Administration's investigation agree well with the information given by the inmates in different types of correctional institutions where one fourth said they had neither housing nor work at the time of most recent release. A similar proportion reported problems with housing and work as an important reason for the most recent recall to prison (Bondeson 1974).

The correctional authorities together with the local municipalities are responsible for the housing situation during the entire time that an offender is subject to any form of correctional sanction. The Prison Treatment Act requires that offenders must be assisted in finding a place to live and that housing should be arranged well before release (KvaL, 1974:203, 16). The Order in Council on non-institutional treatment further stipulates that clients should not live under conditions which would counteract the effects of treatment (22§ Frivårdskungörelsen 1964:632).

The *Committee on Correctional Reform* held that a central task for the non-institutional services was to procure satisfactory housing for their clients and that available resources should be allocated primarily to the purchase or renting of apartments. Collective forms of accommodation should be restricted to groups with special social needs (SOU 1972:64, 168).

The National Audit Administration made an economic analysis of the clients' housing situation. Substantial resources—probably considerably more than half the correctional system's total housing grant—were used to cover less than 1% of the housing needs of non-institutional clients (Riksrevisionsverket 1976b, 16). The Committee on Correctional Reform considered that the use of the housing grants was not guided by any unified planning. Given that a general aim of the Commission was the integration of the clients of the non-institutional services into the community, it would seem reasonable not to use such a large proportion of the grant for *special forms of accommodation* rather than "normal" housing. Moreover, this special accommodation only satisfies elementary housing needs and because of the size and isolation of the accommodation provided runs the risk of giving rise to ghetto conditions.

The correctional system must work together with the local municipalities in procuring accommodation for clients in *ordinary housing facilities.* If resources are freed from the funding of special accommodation they can instead be used to facilitate clients in their efforts to find suitable housing on the open market.

Employees of the non-institutional services assert that it is difficult for clients to find ordinary apartments to rent, even in areas where there is a surplus. The owners of the buildings may be unwilling to place their apartments at the disposal of the non-institutional services not only because they consider it financially risky to hire out apartments to sentenced offenders but also because they fear social problems. The municipal housing companies, which have hitherto supplied the majority of apartments, may be unwilling to make further apartments available because they fear the areas in question could be dominated by tenants with social problems. It is therefore important for the probation services to contact *different housing companies* and try to persuade all of them to make apartments available in proportion to the total number at their disposal. It is essential that *rent guarantees* be made to the housing companies. This would, in principle, be the responsibility of the social services. If the correctional services could supervise and provide service to clients in regular housing facilities, the housing companies would harbor less doubt and the support and control aspects of correction would be met.

The housing conditions of the correctional clients are obviously unsatisfactory. Nevertheless, the correctional system might be able in different ways to help clients secure apartments on the open market. Both professional and lay supervisors ought to be given better *information* on what is available locally, through resource catalogues, for example. Resource catalogues should also be made available to clients. As long as there is no acceptable solution to the housing problem, social adjustment is probably particularly difficult to achieve.

3. Improvement of the Client's Financial Situation. We have earlier shown that the wages of male probation clients are lower than those of other workers in the country. About two-thirds of them had, before being sentenced in 1967, an annual gross income of less than 15,000 Swedish crowns whilst the median annual income for 1970 was about 16,000 Swedish crowns (about 2,000 US dollars). Moreover, a large number of these clients had fines and/or damages to pay off. Both clients and supervisors stated that the clients' greatest problems concern their financial situation.

In the Sundsvall project it was found that about half of the clients in the Halmstad and Eskilstuna districts had net incomes in 1971 of at most 15,000 Swedish crowns. Only one-third of the citizens in the control group (same sex, age, nationality and social group) had such low earnings. In addition, rather more than every third client had fines to pay off, the same proportion owed court procedure costs and every fourth client owed damages. The debts owed for fines and legal expenses were in most cases not more than 1,000 Swedish crowns whilst amounts owing for damages often were more than 5,000 Swedish crowns. In addition to court procedure costs many of the clients were burdened with debts in the form of unpaid rent, maintenance allowances, taxes, hire-purchase contracts, debts to relations, etc (Sundsvallsförsöket: Frej 1974; Kühlhorn 1975).

Even greater debts were reported by inmates from different types of correctional institutions where the median sum owed was as high as 10,400 Swedish crowns (Bondeson 1974, 349). Of special interest in this connection was that a high proportion of these inmates also believed that the full sums owing would be demanded of them. Only those subject to internment, with a median debt of more than 50,000 Swedish crowns, believed that the amount they would in fact be required to pay would be considerably lower.

A person with many debts has a reduced motivation to work because a considerable proportion of the money he earns must go to paying debts. He may frequently change his place of work in an effort to avoid debt collectors or forfeiture of goods. Interviews with those released from prison showed that problems with debts cause anxiety which can drive them "underground" (Rosendahl and Thorsson 1975, 126; and Pockettidningen R 1975:6). The National Audit Administration stated that "the financial situation is so bad for a relatively large group of correctional clients that social assistance and monetary support from the correctional services cannot put their economy on a sound footing" (p. 31).

The National Audit Administration also pointed out that the financial situation of clients had not been the subject of any great interest on the part of correctional authorities. Systematic budget planning has not been undertaken by either the institutional authorities or the non-institutional authorities. However, in conjunction with the payment of market wages to the inmates of certain prisons, some attempts have been made to assist prisoners with *financial planning.*

Probation officers and client evidently do not know what debts the clients have incurred, which of them may be postponed and which debts may be remitted. According to the National Audit Administration, correctional officials are not generally aware of the fact that maintenance allowances may be remitted. Detailed advice should be given in a resource catalogue concerning the regulation of debts. Complicated cases may warrant expert help.

In cases where expert help proves insufficient, certain changes in legislation may be called for. For example, a moratorium delaying the repayment of debts for a year or so, could be permitted. If the offender behaves during this time the state could make an agreement with his creditors whereby they receive part of the money which the client owes and the rest of the debts would be written off. Some experts have demanded that repayment of damages, under certain circumstances, be reduced and some form of insurance allowed to take over (cf. Hellner 1976; Skogh, Brottsförebyggande rådet 1975). Probation fees, as introduced in several American states (see Ring 1989) have not been seriously considered in Scandinavia. Making the offender pay for the supervision seems to put excessive burden on him and would hardly bring substantial benefits to the state.

4. Treatment and Training Arranged by the Probation Organization. If clients need *psychological or medical assistance,* probation officers should be able to arrange specialist services. Given the number of offenders with drug or alcohol problems, this kind of assistance is probably needed in a large number of cases. However, there are great problems associated with providing adequate care for these groups.

It has not been possible, in certain districts, to arrange meaningful collaboration between the probation organization and the local psychiatric clinics. Since the reorganization of the prison and probation services became operative, psychiatric consultants have been assigned to the non-institutional services but, because of a general lack of psychiatrists, progress in this area has been slow.

It has been well documented that there are serious deficiencies in the basic *education* of probation and parole clients. As a result of this lack of fundamental education, two-thirds of these clients have *reading and writing disabilities* and one-third have considerable difficulties in this area. Although, scholastically speaking, they deviate greatly from the normal population, their intellectual capabilities are within the normal range. Clients have considerable difficulty in making use of vocational training because of these handicaps and many do not continue with vocational courses. It seems that there is a great need for introductory or supplementary education to prepare clients for vocational training. Since it has been shown that about half the clients with reading and writing disabilities are interested in this idea and a further quarter do not reject it, there is good reason to initiate such courses. The chief probation officer and his staff could set about seeking out potential students and advertize courses focusing on the correction of reading and writing difficulties as a first step in a vocational training program.

Psychological factors such as lack of self-confidence may lie behind alcohol problems as well as language handicaps. Moreover, social problems are generally associated with previous difficulties in the family, at school, with friends, etc. It is therefore particularly important to try to *build up the probationers' self-confidence.* Thus, an important part of treatment is helping clients to gain insight and awareness of their problems. The probation organization should be given resources to experiment in this area so that the treatment form most suitable for individual clients can be made available. The probation staff could also attempt to interest clients in various leisure activities and distribute information on the various client self-help organizations.

It should be emphasized that different forms of treatment and training can be justified and defended even if they do not lead to a reduction of recidivism rates. Maybe the only thing gained from treatment is a feeling of greater self-realization. This ought to be sufficient. When a treatment form is *voluntarily* chosen, we must accept *other goals and methods of measurement than mere recidivism rates.*

5. Treatment Undertaken by Probation Officers. Opinions differ about what are the most important functions of the probation organization. Some persons believe social work should take precedence while others think therapeutic work should dominate. This conflict can also be traced in the American and

English probation services, where one school claims that officers ought to work with *referrals*, i.e. referring clients to the appropriate authorities for help, while others contend that officers should devote themselves to *case-work*, i.e. psychological treatment (Tappan 1960). As we saw earlier, members of the probation staff complain that work goals are not discussed, and that they are in doubt as to which tasks should be given priority.

When probation officers are overburdened with too many clients they find it almost impossible to devote time to any treatment efforts. Different administrative tasks take up a large part of the time available. So-called client work at the office seems to consist primarily of paying out small amounts of money for acute material needs and home visits to look for clients with incorrect addresses. It is natural, in a relatively stressful situation, to emphasize such things as employment, accommodation and finance. These aspects of probation work are fundamental to social adjustment and therefore even to other kinds of treatment.

There are several reasons why probation personnel should have more time for true treatment work. They would get to know their clients better and thereby be more motivated to work with them in providing social care. In the first place, probation staff would like to have more discussions with clients concerning social or psychological problems. It would be both economical and rewarding to combine individual counselling with *group discussions* in which several clients examine their problems together with a probation officer. Secondly, the probation officers could devote more time and interest to the clients' family situation. *Family treatment* could well be added to other general treatment efforts.

However, we should not lose sight of the special difficulties which arise when the probation organization is itself responsible for treatment. To the extent that the client perceives these authorities as representative of a punitive and controlling system, the psychological prerequisites are lacking for true forms of treatment based upon the *principle of voluntary participation*.

Whole-Hearted Support from Volunteers

1. Lay Supervisors Renamed Contact Persons. Many people have reacted against the title "supervisor" for laymen because of its direct association with control. Formally, there is a certain reality behind the use of the term. A supervisor who fulfils the purely formal requirements for control has, in principle, fulfilled his responsibilities while a supervisor who only meets the informal requirements of support may be open to criticism as neglecting his duties. It is thus sufficient, formally speaking, for a supervisor to meet his client briefly at the office once a month and send in a quarterly supervision report in order to be paid. The title of supervisor should therefore be changed so that it is clear to all that the layman's primary function is to offer *personal support*. A suitable title would be *contact person*.

2. The Majority of Clients Ought to Have at Least One Voluntary Contact Person. It is suggested here that reinforcement of the non-institutional services should lie in offering the client whole-hearted support from at least one contact person. This proposal involves a double investment since the contact person provides a service in addition to the qualified service offered by probation officers. By allocating different functions to different people, the dividends ought, theoretically, to be so much greater.

In principle, the contact person's services ought to constitute a voluntary offer of human contact during a difficult transition period. There is a risk that the clients may fear that they are to be controlled by two supervisors instead of one. The ideal for the correctional services would be to make the roles of the probation officers and contact persons so attractive that the client asks for them voluntarily.

3. ***Selection of Contact Persons.*** As far as possible *the client should suggest* his own contact person. This possibility has long been open to clients but few have taken advantage of it. Even when a client does suggest a supervisor, he generally chooses the traditional type, most likely because he is not aware that other supervisor types are accepted. It is vital that the client is made fully aware of the benefits involved in his choosing a contact person, and that the choice need not be limited to a particular supervisor type. On the contrary, the choice should be broadened and the client can contribute to this by selecting new suitable supervisors. *Criteria* for the selection of contact persons ought to be determined more precisely.

In order to make the contact persons desired and chosen by clients who need them, their composition should reasonably be to some extent different from that which obtained for supervisors. The present study showed that supervisors are representative neither of the general public nor of the clients they supervise. They were usually middle-aged, married, and employed as public servants. They had been entrusted with different responsibilities by their municipality and they normally supervised two clients at a time. This is the same picture as has been found in other studies.

This portrait of the typical supervisor has been challenged by a number of official and semi-official bodies. It has been claimed that over recent years the number of female supervisors has been greatly increased and in certain districts even surpasses the number of male supervisors and that the average age of a supervisor is considerably lower, about 30 years. I therefore undertook an additional study of supervisors from the whole country to check these assertions and found that there had indeed been an increase in the number of female supervisors and a lowering of the average age. However, 67% of supervisors were men and the average age of a supervisor was 43.

With information from the greater part of the whole country (30 of 47 districts) we can say that it still was a generation which usually separates the supervisor from his client. More recent studies have confirmed the observation made here that the majority of supervisors are public servants and that they belong to the middle class. Hence there is quite a social distance between the supervisor and the client. The psychological distance between the parties could be seen in the responses they gave to a number of attitude questions dealing with, among other things, supervision. The distance between supervisor and client was also revealed by their inability to correctly perceive each other's views in different matters.

Social psychology provides us with ample reason to suppose that greater similarity in background variables and attitudes between different parties increases the basis upon which understanding and mutual trust can be founded.

We might, however, ask just how alike supervisor and client should be. The question of similar backgrounds is not necessarily of decisive importance and different background variables may vary in importance. If a supervisor and the client have common backgrounds they are generally in a better position to understand each other than if they do not. For example, a client and a fellow-worker speak the same language and probably share similar social backgrounds, so it is likely that they have more in common than the client and a traditional public servant. Work-mates meet more often, have common interests to discuss and therefore may want to meet in their leisure time as well.

The relationship between supervisor and client often seems quite formal. They generally meet once a month and talk for about half an hour. Most of the time the meetings take place in the supervisor's office. Thus, these relationships may be called *formal* or *institutionalized.*

It is reasonable to assume that clients' contact needs are most strongly felt during their leisure hours and not during office hours when, in fact, the majority of probationers usually meet their supervisors. According to our data only a small group of supervisors met their clients in their leisure time to share some activity. This situation is related to the definition of supervision as well as to the choice of supervisor. The supervisors are for the most part very busy people; in addition to the work they have in supervising a couple of clients, they usually have duties associated with their membership in several organizations and often have been entrusted with responsibilities in their local community.

In the majority of cases, it should be easier to find someone with similar leisure interests among people of the same age and with similar backgrounds. In general, younger people devote themselves more to outgoing activities than older people. The need for activity which is found among the young should be exploited in order to break the type of passivity that can lead to alcohol or drug misuse.

Generally, ex-offenders have not been employed as supervisors but it is time that such persons who have succeeded in adjusting in society were recruited even in Sweden. The ex-offenders represent experience which is valuable for the client under supervision. They can also function as role models since they offer a possibility for *identification* which is one of the best prerequisites for the exertion of influence. Organizations such as Alcoholics Anonymous, Synanon and Red Top were met with surprise and contempt in their early stages but are today seen to be remarkably effective in helping misusers to refrain from alcohol and drugs.

Using sociological terminology, contact persons ought to be included in the client's *primary group* and not only belong to his secondary group. An individual's primary group consists of the people who are close to him, such as his family and friends. A person becomes a member of various secondary groups when he joins organizations and clubs and through his work. Normally, primary groups are more important to an individual than secondary groups. This means that they are in a better position to exert influence on him. Many correctional clients have had poor family relationships and have often lacked primary groups in early life. It becomes therefore especially important to try to create primary group relationships with the aim of compensating to some extent for earlier deficiencies. If the goal is to employ contact persons who actually can exert a developing influence on the client, such a primary group relationship is, in principle, a necessary precondition (Krech et al. 1962).

Finally, it should be said that proposals which resemble those are made here have been recommended by various bodies. Thus, the Danish report "Criminal Care—Social Care" (Kriminalforsorg-Socialforsorg 1975) put forward the idea that, over and above anything provided by probation staff, each client should have a contact person who could well be recruited from among his fellow-workers. The Swedish Confederation of Trade Unions has also suggested that supervisors be recruited from the place of work and that a client may need more than one such contact person.

*4. **An Offer of Training to All Contact Persons.*** In this study we have seen that many supervisors lacked special training for their work. Both the Swedish Prison and Probation Administration and the Swedish Association of Probation Officers arrange courses for supervisors but they obviously do not reach everyone. But a change in the content of supervision should also lead to a change in the content of supervision training.

Since the proposal presented here means that the probation staff would be responsible for professional service, such things as knowledge of the working of the labor and housing services becomes less important for contact persons. Instead, it would be more valuable for them to gain knowledge in sociology and psychology as their work is primarily to lend personal support.

*5. **Higher Fees for Contact Persons.*** The remuneration for supervisors has always been very low. Inflation means that the sums provided fall behind in value but the size of the fees also reflects a philosophy concerning lay supervision which must be considered out of date.

It is argued that a low remuneration will ensure that those seeking the job will not be doing so with the intention of making money. However, supervision would not be lucrative even if the remuneration were substantially increased. Moreover, contact persons should not normally work with more than one client at a time which in itself diminishes the possibilities of mere money-making. And if proper recompense is not paid for expenses and investment of effort the effect in all probability will be the preservation of a distorted recruitment of middle-class idealists. The Commission on Correctional Reform argued against raising the remuneration of lay supervisors by saying that it was better to give priority to new appointments in the non-institutional services. This, however, is to ignore the special contribution that laymen can make. This consideration becomes even more important if functions are divided up between two quite different persons as has been recommended here.

Better Information to the Public

It is particularly important that all the involved parties contribute to increasing the public's knowledge of client problems and of the measures taken to solve them. This is a responsibility of the supervision boards and the chief probation officer, but it is just as important that the lay supervisors and clients assist in the dissemination of correct information.

It is known from a number of studies that the public often harbor false ideas about crime and punishment. Thus, for example, in one study it was found that a representative sample of the public overestimated the extent of violent offenses, the gravity of such offenses and the frequency with which they are committed in public places (Bondeson 1979b, see also Kutchinsky 1972).

The mass media magnify the significance of serious offenses, especially violent offenses (Aspelin, Brottsförebyggande rådet 1976). In this way the public can get a false picture of crime in the community and, for example, tends to overestimate the number of homicides and bank robberies and fails to realize that most criminality concerns traffic and minor property offenses.

The National Swedish Council for Crime Prevention has tried to disseminate factual information through a differentiated campaign focused on both individuals and organizations. But it does not seem likely that the kind of information which desirably should be presented to give the public a more balanced picture of reality will be given much currency by the mass media. Several studies have shown that when information of a controversial nature is presented on television or in newspapers it only has a limited effect. The majority do not see or read such material and among those that do, there is a considerable risk that they misunderstand the message. There may even be a boomerang effect, i.e. the content of an announcement or advertisement may be interpreted in a way which is the opposite of what was intended and earlier prejudices are confirmed (Hedebro, Brottsförebyggande rådet 1977).

It is against this background that it becomes especially important for information to be conveyed via those who are in some way involved (see Trankell 1973 and 1975 for a discussion on the importance of personal contacts). This is therefore another reason for recruiting contact persons from all parts of society, not the least from the lower income social groups where attitudes to offenders are often more negative. Using fellow-workers as contact persons would help spread information on the client's difficulties as well as provide a better understanding of the client. This ought to be an important strategy if we want to change attitudes to offenders at the place of work.

Community service as a new sanction in Scandinavia may have the advantage of giving occupation to the offender and at the same time compensation to the victim or to society and thereby being instrumental in creating better relations to the public (for experiments on community service in Sweden see Appendix II and for Denmark and some other countries, see Storgaard, 1989; Bondeson 1990; Straffelovrådet 1990).

Changes in Society

The proposals for reforms presented here have been put forward as a series of particular points, to some extent isolated from a wider context. It is, however, essential to have a *system perspective* when considering change. Partial criminal policy reforms can affect the whole correctional system. Whether they can be carried through can depend on how they interact on and with other societal circumstances. I believe that general prevention can be satisfied by a sanction system with a lower level of punishment and that, in general, individual prevention is best met by resorting to as few intervenient measures as possible. Further, as a consequence of this view, I believe that sanctions privative of liberty should, as far as possible, be replaced by non-institutional treatment, and greater use made of the sanction of conditional sentence and relatively less use made of probation. In addition, dispensing with a sanction, waivers of prosecution and dispensing with the reporting of offenses should be used to a greater extent than at present. This would lead to a general de-escalation of the penal system.

The implementation of a criminal policy which espouses the principle of least possible intervention will depend on the reactions it stirs in different social groups. However, it seems that there is a growing consensus on the desirability of using measures privative of liberty as little as possible.

In a survey conducted among a representative sample of Malmö citizens it was found that as many people considered a suggested reduction by the Minister of Justice in the average number of prisoners (from about 5,000 to less than 1,000) to be satisfactory or too small as thought the average prison population should be greater (Bondeson 1979b; see also "Public Opinion—on Crime and Criminal Justice" by Council of Europe 1979). However, acceptance by individuals is not enough: politicians and social agencies must also be prepared to accept such changes.

The reorganization of the prison and probation systems decided on by Parliament in 1973 presupposed close collaboration between prison and probation authorities on the one hand, and on the other, probation and other social service authorities, so as to integrate offenders into society. *The relationship between criminal policy and general social policy* was formulated by Mr Lennart Geijer, a former minister of justice, as follows: "One must be careful not to isolate criminal policy. Twenty to thirty years ago, criminal policy was a separate activity for the correctional authorities. The situation is changing. The decisive efforts of society to prevent crime will no longer be initiated from the Ministry of Justice. Instead, the important policy areas will be education, the labor market, housing, social policy and a policy for equality" (Rosendahl and Thorsson 1975, 151).

As we have seen in this report, it is not always easy to convert these insights into practical action. The clients of the probation service are also, for the most part, well known to other social service authorities but because collaboration between the different agencies is underdeveloped, it is difficult to avoid duplication of work. The danger is that instead of receiving the extra support they need, clients fall between different social service agencies. It will be difficult to realize a welfare ideology in the treatment of clients as long as co-operation between the correctional services and the social services remains as poor as it has been.

However, during the past decade, a more comprehensive overall perspective has been adopted within the social services. A logical development in this direction would involve *integrating the social and correctional services.* The work methods of the correctional services will in any case be affected by whatever form social service takes in the future. We must wait and see how the overall goals of democracy, equality, solidarity and security will be translated into a practical policy of reform (SOU 1974:39, 239).

We probably do not have certain knowledge about the way in which the various *social systems* affect criminality in industrial society. Christie (1975), who has analyzed criminality from a general societal perspective, has made an attempt to propose macro-level reforms with the aim of creating a more decentralized society in which informal social control is presumed to be able to replace or supplement formal control. However, this raises the not unimportant question of what price people are prepared to pay to reduce crime.

The majority of crime-prevention measures may be described as unfocused or only partially focused. Walker (1972) formulated the following question: what methods are suitable for achieving the greatest reduction in crime in relation to their costs? He considers that the *unfocused methods* are often relatively cheap but also relatively ineffective. Such methods include general prevention, education and propaganda. A more lengthy compulsory school attendance, which was originally introduced with a view to preventing crime, is said today to have a negative effect on stimulating conformity to the law. These findings do not mean that we should refrain from investing in the spreading of information but they may well imply that we should try other methods.

A number of studies have also shown that such *partially focused efforts* as improving slum areas and various programs involving social workers and youth clubs, have not been particularly successful (Suchman 1967; Caro 1971; Weiss 1972). But even if we have not been able to measure the effects of these projects, we surely do need to invest in families, schools and housing with a view to making the community more suitable for children. Various studies have demonstrated that many offenders showed signs of social maladjustment from an early age.

It is also abundantly clear that a welfare society creates its own criminality because of the rich supply of goods and services available (Wolf and Høgh 1966). Criminologists have, however, not devoted enough effort to studying ways of reducing crime by technical control of the crime opportunity structures. These include such *technical constraints* as the control of firearm licenses, of explosive materials and of poisons, TV-surveillance of department stores, bullet-proof shields for bank employees and different conditions of insurance. One may think that such measures fall outside the area of penology and have more of the character of social engineering or administration. Nevertheless, they are probably some of the most effective and least costly measures that can be used in the control of crime (Persson 1975).

If we are unwilling to submit to such controls as, for example, a strict regulation of alcohol consumption, we ought to be prepared to discuss and *review the distribution of responsibility and the burden of guilt* between different groups in the community. One way of more evenly distributing the damaging effects of criminal acts is to compensate the victims through a state insurance scheme—at least when the perpetrator is not found or is without means (Anttila and Törnudd, 138).

If the unfocused or semi-focused methods prove not to be particularly effective in preventing crime, we would have more reason to return to the *focused* methods. It is inevitable that penologists prefer to concentrate on these. A series of studies of self-reported crime certainly show that we are all to some extent criminals but later studies show that even so there is a marked concentration of crime around a limited number of persons. Carlsson (Brottsförebyggande rådet, 1975) demonstrates this from certain theoretical assumptions and Persson (1976) on the basis of empirical data.

Although the forms of treatment used hitherto have not shown positive results, both straight recidivist and quasi-experimental studies indicate that the more punitive the measures taken, the poorer the result obtained. The time seems therefore ripe for testing methods other than the traditional escalations of the penal system which have so far had little success. It is against this background that I have introduced the theory of least possible intervention and a welfare ideology. We have noted two important facts about the majority of offenders who fill our institutions: punishment has little effect on them, and they are burdened by having a poor social heritage. Probationers are similarly underprivileged.

As Jonsson (1969, 291) pointed out, an offender can be rejected by society in two stages—"first rejected as a normal member of society, then down-graded as a recipient of treatment". Thus, if a sanction is called treatment and an offender does not succeed in adjusting in society despite the goodwill implicit in such "treatment", he runs the risk of being *doubly stigmatized* (see also Ahl 1976; cf. Sarnecki 1985).

The distance between socially rejected groups and the established members of society is also increasing in welfare societies. While the offender usually has nothing—except his debts—the average Swede, to an increasing extent, has a house or summer cottage, car, bank accounts, etc. While the average Swede has a negotiated wage with automatic wage increases and reasonable job security, the punished offender stands completely outside the ordinary labor market. In this situation, it is especially important that we do not add further to the offender's handicaps by imposing unnecessarily severe sanctions which push him even further away from ordinary society. The danger is otherwise that we may create a criminal class of which one of the effects is that criminality further increases (Mead 1917). By including offenders in our welfare ideology we improve our chances of reducing crime and at the same time we demonstrate solidarity with all members of our society.

Appendix I: Sampling and Methodology

In this appendix we present a supplementary description of the sampling procedure, data collection and the methods used in the various separate studies. The research sample is, in principle, the same for the sentencing study, the recidivism study and the supervision study. The sentencing and recidivism studies are based on the same case-records but the supervision study is based on questionnaire responses. The institution study is, on the other hand, chiefly based on another sample and uses observational and interview material. Since the research sample is the same in the first three studies, there are possibilities to link these studies together and compare the different methods in a way which is not common within socio-legal and correctional treatment studies. Some problems concerning the reliability of the data are discussed at the end.

Case-Record Material in the Sentencing and Recidivism Studies

The sampling procedure was the same for the parts of the project that dealt with the analysis of the choice of sanction, the recidivism study and the supervision study. Data were collected in the same way for the sentencing study and the recidivism study and similar measures used.

Sampling Procedure

The sample was randomly drawn according to the following criteria:

1. We proceeded from the sanction groups conditional sentence (CS-group), ordinary probation without institutional treatment (P-group) and probation with institutional treatment (PI-group).
2. The population consisted of men sentenced to the above sanctions in 1967.
3. The sentences were passed in the courts whose jurisdictions cover the probation districts of Helsingborg, Lund and Malmö.
4. An approximate base rate of 150 individuals per sanction group was established.

The first step in the sampling procedure was to determine the number of individuals to be taken from each district to form the base sampling rate for each sanction group. The admission papers for offenders committed to Stångby probation institution in 1967 were reviewed in order to appraise the approximate distribution over districts for one of the three sanction groups. The proportions per district were approximately 50–25–25 for Malmö, Lund and Helsingborg respectively. We decided to accept these proportions for the other sanction groups also.

The base rate of 150 individuals could not be obtained for the PI-group as there were only 74 cases during 1967. For this reason, the material was supplemented with PI-offenders sentenced in 1966.

Lists were obtained from the probation organization of all persons sentenced to probation in 1967. Women and men sentenced in courts outside the districts in question were removed from the base material. A new list, in which offenders were arranged according to the time sentence was passed, was compiled for each district separately. From this list, which comprised the populations from which the samples were to be drawn, every individual was selected in varying ratios for the different sanction groups depending on the size of the population and the predetermined base rate. Every third P-offender was drawn from the Malmö and Lund districts, and every fourth from the Helsingborg district.

Approximately 9,000 judgments made by the different courts of the districts in question were reviewed to obtain data on the offenders who were conditionally sentenced in 1967. All the men so sentenced were put together in a register for each court. These court registers were then linked together by district and they became the basis for the regional sub-populations. In order to achieve the base rate and to take account of the different contributions to the sanction groups from each district, every second individual from the Lund and Helsingborg districts was drawn while three out of every four were included from Malmö.

Table App.I.1 shows the sampling procedure for the three sanction groups. The sample consists of 148 CS-offenders, 138 P-offenders and 127 PI-offenders giving a total of 413 offenders.

Methods, Data Collection and Missing Data

The *methods* which are the same for the sentencing study and the recidivism study, seek to describe the offenders' personal and social conditions *up to the time they were sentenced.* The aim was to classify the background data which is made available to the courts for sentencing purposes as completely and objectively as possible. All the CS-offenders and P-offenders had been the subject of a social enquiry report and in addition there were medical reports or other personal reports available for many of the offenders.

By studying previous criminological investigations and analyzing the social enquiry reports, the instrument for the measurement of background variables was gradually constructed. During the preparatory work a number of tests were carried out to ascertain the precision of the instrument.

The final instrument consists of some 80 variables and covers the following aspects of the offenders' lives:

1. Childhood and home conditions up to the age of 16.
2. Personal attributes and scholastic achievements.
3. Previous antisocial tendencies and contact with the child welfare authorities.
4. Present social adjustment concerning accomodation, occupational status, etc.
5. Previous criminal behavior resulting in court appearance.

Data regarding the CS-offenders were collected from the documentation available to the various courts at the time of trial and subsequently kept at the different courts.

Data collection from official records began at the end of 1969 and the beginning of 1970 and took six months to complete. In this period Hansson and Chylicki worked to-

TABLE App.I.1 Sampling Procedure Scheme

Conditional Sentence

District	Number in Population	Sample Ratio	Number in Sample
Malmö	98	3/4	74
Lund	73	1/2	36
Helsingborg	75	1/2	38

Ordinary Probation (i.e. without institutional treatment)

District	Number in Population	Sample Ratio	Number in Sample
Malmö	206	1/3	68
Lund	108	1/3	37
Helsingborg	133	1/4	33

Probation with Institutional Treatment

District	Population 1966	Population 1967	Number in Sample
Malmö	33	36	69
Lund	13	16	29
Helsingborg	7	22	29

gether so that any questions about the information categories might be discussed as they arose. Five per cent of the probation material was double coded.

Coding reliability was shown to be satisfactory.

Coding difficulties varied depending on the nature of the data. The task was simple for data of a factual nature, such as place of birth, number of siblings, etc. However, the categorization of some of the data was more in the nature of content analysis. This applied to information which was based on subjective judgments such as information regarding adjustment to work and school conditions or the quality of the home. Where there were no explicit assessments or actual data in the files, the statement: "information missing" was coded.

As far as the *quality of the data* is concerned, we can say that, as with all case files, the information contained in them is subject to error. Firstly, we might suspect some under-reporting of "symptoms". This is most probably the case with the CS-offenders and those resident abroad. Secondly, there may be a certain distortion, in particular concerning the data on parents and siblings. Such an effect is conceivable since social enquiry investigators may be steered by their own notions and hypotheses about the significance of various behavioral deviations. Thus, they look for specific information about the different family members such as an alcoholic father, a mother who shows signs of mental illness or siblings involved in criminal activity.

In addition to the information about the offenders prior to their conviction, information was collected about the offenders *after sentence.* First, recidivism data were collected from the Central Criminal Register and from the criminal records kept by the National Board of Excise. Secondly, the contents of the personal case records which are kept at the probation offices for both groups of probationers, were analyzed. A detailed follow-up concerning conditions of employment, accommodation and alcohol and drug habits was undertaken.

We were able to obtain and process all the necessary files, case records and extracts from registers, i.e. there were no *external missing data.* However, there were *internal missing data* due to omitted or uncodifiable information.

Questionnaire Responses from Supervisors and Clients

Methods Used with the Pilot and Main Studies

The pilot studies comprised not only a review of the literature, but also visits to the probation offices and probation institutions as well as discussions with the various officers employed by the correctional services. During the pilot study, the case records of the probationers who were included in the sample were reviewed. They contain the social inquiry report, the court's sentence and reasons for sentence, medical reports, treatment plans, supervision reports, case notes, etc. Such material is often the only source of information used in studies similar to our own. These data were processed using special forms but were subsequently judged to be of too varied a quality to warrant further analysis. It was originally our intention to use the supervision reports both to supplement and check on the data obtained through the questionnaire. However, we were forced to abandon this idea because of the diversity of the reports both as to form and content.

Nevertheless, the review of the case records did help us in the construction of the questionnaire. A great deal of work was put into covering what we considered to be the relevant problem areas and into formulating the questions clearly and unambiguously. Pilot interviews were conducted with both supervisors and clients. It became clear that such things as the supervisor's conflict of loyalty and the support and control aspects of supervision would be difficult to measure. Furthermore, the preliminary interviews conducted with probationers at the Stångby probation institution revealed that they often had little knowledge of the legal terminology used concerning them. This showed that there could be difficulties with questions concerning any special conditions of probation imposed since some probationers did not understand this notion.

The final questionnaire contained 76 questions for the P-clients, 63 questions for the PI-clients and 96 questions for supervisors.

Supervisors and clients were asked in an introductory letter not to discuss the questionnaire together. To the extent that they did confer with one another despite this request, a source of error exists. However, this does not seem likely as there was little agreement in answers between pairs of supervisor and client.

Samples

In principle, the client sample in the questionnaire survey is the same as that which formed the basis of the two studies presented above, i.e. men sentenced in 1967 to probation with or without institutional treatment. The sentences were imposed by the courts in the probation districts of Helsingborg, Lund and Malmö. In an effort to reduce the geographical "spread" and thus facilitate data collection, an additional requirement was that supervision should have been started in the same district. The sampling procedure has been described above. The only difference here is that the supplementary year 1966 was not used for the PI-group in this study. We preferred to work with a smaller PI-group (n = 74) rather than obtain differences in the supervision period among sanction groups.

In this way we obtained a *client sample* comprising 212 offenders sentenced to probation in 1967 (104 sentenced in Malmö, 53 in Lund and 55 in Helsingborg).

The *supervisor sample* was obtained by taking the supervisor of each of the clients in the client sample. If the offender was under supervision when the sample was drawn, his present supervisor was chosen but if supervision had been terminated, his last supervisor was chosen. Some supervisors were supervising more than one client in our sample so that we finally had 176 supervisors for 212 clients.

Data Collection and Missing Data

The questionnaire together with an introductory letter and stamped return envelope was sent to supervisors and clients on 8 March 1970. A reminder was sent on 25 March to those who had not returned the questionnaire. After the first reminder, 107 supervisors had returned their questionnaires and 53 clients had returned theirs. On 13 April another reminder was sent out with a new copy of the questionnaire and a further return envelope. This reminder resulted in a further 26 answers from supervisors and 34 from clients. On 12 May we sent a third and last reminder, which resulted in 12 answers from supervisors and 17 from clients. Judging from the substantial decrease in the number of responses to the third reminder, we assumed that a fourth reminder would not appreciably increase the number of answers. Moreover, for ethical reasons, we thought we should not continue to bother the people to whom we were writing; this is a natural consideration particularly in the case of sentenced persons.

Of the 176 *supervisors,* 52 did not answer so that the average missing data rate was 29%. It was lowest for Malmö (21%), intermediate for Helsingborg (35%) and highest for Lund (40%). The reason for such a high missing data rate in Lund may be that a few small parallel studies had been started there soon after our study started. Some of the supervisors from Lund said that they had received another somewhat similar questionnaire a short time after receiving ours and they chose not to answer either. We add that two of the supervisors taken up in the missing data rate had died. Such cases are usually regarded as "natural missing data" and then not included in the missing data figures. We should also point out that the missing data rate is somewhat high owing to the fact that we are dealing with "supervisor units" who are not necessarily identical with physically different individuals.

Of the 212 *clients* to whom we wrote, 108 did not answer. The total average missing data rate of 51% was once again highest for Lund (62%). The rate for Malmö was 49% and for Helsingborg was 44%. Here too there is included a "natural missing data " of two deceased clients.

A special reason for the considerable missing data rate among clients is the fact that they are very difficult to reach. Many of the letters were returned because the addressee was no longer at that address. New addresses were sought and new questionnaires sent out—not always successfully. In some cases three different addresses were tried without result. Despite our repeated attempts, a rather large proportion of clients was never reached. Thirty-four persons, corresponding to 16% of our sample, never received our letters. If we calculate the missing data rate on the basis of the number of clients who in fact received a questionnaire, we reduce it from 51% to 42%.

Supervisors who returned our questionnaires unanswered (11 altogether) gave the following reasons: they had no time; their knowledge of the client was too limited; they did not wish to subject their client to exposure or they mistrusted research projects of this kind; one wanted payment for taking part.

Few clients gave reasons for not answering the questionnaire. It appeared, however, from those giving reasons that either they did not want to be reminded of their sentence or they did not want to take part in a research project.

Analyses of the Missing Data

We attempted to make closer analyses of the missing data. The only background information available was obtained from the probation offices on the *supervisors'* ages and professions. There were no differences in the distributions of these variables. On the basis of this information we draw the tentative conclusion that the supervisors who did not respond do not differ from those that did. Comparisons made with findings from other studies of supervisors also show considerable similarities on background variables (see Chapters 6 and 9).

For the *clients* a comparison was made on 12 variables taken from the case records, of which eight variables concerned the time before or directly related to the current sentence and four to the follow-up period. No differences were found in age, education, social class or early alcohol abuse between those who answered our questionnaire and those who did not. On the other hand, we did find a larger number of clients with previous convictions in the missing data group (a difference of 11%). There were only small differences between the groups concerning the type of principal offense, the severity of total criminality or total risk points. A somewhat greater number of clients from the missing data group were unemployed during the probationary period (a difference of 6%). There are, however, no differences between the groups with respect to alcohol abuse and change of residence. On the other hand, there was more *recidivism* among the clients in the missing data group (the difference reaches 15% with $p = <.05$ for recidivist offenses recorded in the Central Criminal Register).

We then analyzed a further four variables connected with the offense, the sanction and recidivism in an effort to find out whether the higher rate of recidivism among the missing data group could explain the fact that we could not reach these offenders to the same extent as the others. We found a significantly greater number of *probationers who had had their sanction revoked* in the missing data group (14% difference). The majority of these were imprisoned which could account for their not answering the questionnaire. We also studied the sentence imposed with recidivism upon these offenders irrespective of whether probation was revoked and found that first-time recidivists from the missing data group mostly received *sentences depriving them of their liberty* (15% difference). On the other hand, there were no appreciable differences between the groups concerning the type of offense or the length of prison sentence, neither with first nor any later relapse into crime.

Since there are no essential differences in background variables or even in risk scores between the missing data group and the group who answered the questionnaire, we may assume that there are no decisive differences between those clients who answered and those who did not. The only important variable seems to be recidivism. The fact that many of the offenders in the missing data group had their probation revoked either prevented their participation or diminished their interest in taking part in a study of this kind.

The missing data problem associated with dyadic analysis, i.e. studying a given supervisor and his client together, was discussed in the text.

In summary we can say that the missing data rate is considerable particularly among clients. The missing data analyses which we carried out do not reveal any differences between the clients who answered and those who did not. There are no differences in background variables or the total risk score. Many of the offenders in the missing data group had recidivated and had had their probation sanction revoked. This could explain the low rate of participation. It seems therefore that our sample, despite the missing data, represents the parent population tolerably satisfactorily.

Observation and Interview Study of a Probation Institution

Included in the questionnaire were certain questions that PI-offenders were required to answer about their treatment. This rather incomplete information was later supplemented with observation and interviews conducted at a probation institution.

Sample

There is only one probation institution in the southern region, Stångby. This institution covered the three court jurisdictions in question.

Methods

One of my sociology major students who was placed in the Stångby probation institution was chosen as an observer. I was, of course, aware of the dangers present in having an observer who was involved in the social situation which he was studying. The advantages were judged to outweigh the disadvantages, however.

The way the *problem of objectivity* is looked upon within the social sciences has undergone a change during recent years (see Chapter 9). In this context, however, attention is called to Becker's famous article "Whose Side Are We On?" (1963) in which he appeals to researchers to choose sides—either of those who are being treated as deviants or of those who define the others as deviants. Whichever side we choose, we risk being accused of taking someone's part but, according to Becker, if we choose the deviant's point of view there is less likelihood that we provide a one-sided or distorted picture. Or as he formulated it in "Outsiders": "What we are presenting is not a distorted view of 'reality', but the reality which engages the people we have studied, the reality they create by their interpretation of their experience and in terms of which they act. If we fail to present this reality, we will not have achieved full sociological understanding of the phenomenon we seek to explain." (p. 174)

Similarly, Blumer explained in "Society as Symbolic Interaction" (1962) that people adjust their behavior only after they have interpreted a situation and if a researcher wants to uncover this interpretation process he must play the role of an active participant in the social process: "to try to catch the interpretive process by remaining aloof as a so-called objective observer and refusing to take the role of the acting unit, is to risk the worst kind of subjectivism. ..." (p. 188)

We used *different methods of observation and different observers* in an effort to meet the demands of objectivity. The observer, who was at the probation institution from December 1970 to August 1971, made notes of his discussions with the inmates and staff. His role was that of a *participant observer*.

During the spring of 1971, I also engaged two external sociology students to undertake *standardized interviews* with the probationers and staff. Several of these interviews were taped. These interviews were conducted during the period 7 to 16 May 1971. Two supplementary interviews, one with the governor and the other with an assistant governor, were conducted some weeks later.

Preliminary interviews were conducted with initial versions of the interview questionnaire which were subsequently modified and further pilot interviews were conducted. The probationers and staff at the probation institution were informed about the study, among other things, by placing information sheets on the notice boards in the administration building and the inmate pavilions.

All the *offenders* sentenced to probation with institutional treatment who were present during the week in question, were interviewed. There were thirteen such offenders. Offenders sentenced to imprisonment were not included in the study and thus were not interviewed. None of the probatiners refused to take part in the study.

In all, fourteen interviews were conducted with the *staff*, i.e. with the two governors (the one permanent and the other temporarily appointed), three assistant governors, three foremen, a head cook, a chief custodial officer and four custodial officers.

Two members of the custodial staff refused to be interviewed. They were generally regarded as the most conservative members of the staff; both had worked for a long time within the closed prison system. With so few interviewees the absence of two of the more custody-oriented persons could affect the representative nature of the sample to some extent. However, the missing data probably has no significance for the characteristics of institutional treatment as described in Chapter 7.

Other Methods and Reliability of Data

I later supplemented the empirical data in a number of ways. In part this was done by using more refined analytic methods with the various separate studies and in part by bringing these latter together using a variety of comparison analyses. In this way, it became possible to further check data *reliability* (i.e. how accurately the methods measure what they actually measure) and *validity* (i.e. how well the methods measure what they are supposed to measure). By *comparing the different questions, methods and samples* of the project we have seen that both reliability and validity seem satisfactory (comparisons have been presented at appropriate places in earlier chapters).

The data have also been tested by placing them in the framework of *theoretical models*. This so-called *logical validity*, was studied chiefly with models of the legislators' intentions, the judges' choice of sanction and the supervisors' behavior. In addition, an overall model of the effects of the law has been constructed so as to foresee both real and absent legislative effects. The logical validity seems reasonably good.

Validity was further tested by making *comparisons with other studies*. This *pragmatic validity* also indicates that the data are trustworthy. Similar comparisons also show that the data are relatively *representative* so far as the aspects which allow of comparison are concerned. This is particularly so for supervision and to some extent institutional treatment.

In addition, I have broadened the perspective by making *historical analyses*. Firstly, I have studied the origins of probation internationally and of conditional sentence and probation nationally. This provides a better understanding of the purposes which the Penal Code Commission had in mind when it drafted this legislation.

Secondly, I have studied the reorganization of the prison and probation systems which became operative in 1974 and attempted to evaluate its significance for the contemporary situation. Studies have also been made of this legislation and the preparatory work for it. I have also attempted to secure available and appropriate material for an evaluation of this reorganization. In this context, foreign studies of supervision caseloads, reports of the Sundsvall Project and reports from the National Audit Administration have been particularly valuable.

Finally, I later went back to the field and conducted follow-up interviews with representatives of the various sectors studied. I have *interviewed a number of key persons* including legislators, judges, the chairman of a supervision board, the governor of the former probation institution, chief probation officers, probation officers and the officials of the National Swedish Association of Voluntary Supervisors. These experts were given the relevant parts of this report to read, thus enabling me to obtain their views of the descriptions given of their respective fields. They were asked to comment on the text and to describe any changes that have taken place since the empirical studies were made.

Official statistics and *annual reports* were also included in the methods used to check the reliability and the validity of the data.

In summary, criminological and socio-legal investigations of conditional sentence and probation are rarely built around as many different studies as the present project. The advantage of this approach is that comprehensive account can be given of the application of the sanctions studied. A further advantage is that the use of different samples and different methods provides numerous possibilities for checking the reliability and validity of the data.

Appendix II: Developments in the Use of Non-Custodial Sanctions

Norman Bishop

The purpose of this appendix is to give a brief account of the main legislative and organizational changes which have taken place over recent years and relate them to the proposals for reform contained in Chapter 9. A subsidiary purpose is to give a short description of subsequent research on non-institutional sanctions.

A Modified Approach to the Choice of Sanctions

Recurring themes throughout the book as well as in Chapter 9, are the tension arising from the claims of general and individual prevention and the desirability of reducing reliance on imprisonment.

Prior to January 1989 the criteria in the Penal Code for the choice of sanctions required the courts to give consideration to general prevention and especially the desirability of fostering the offender's reformation. Since then, however, the Penal Code provisions on the choice of sanctions have been modified with the intention of increasing the predictability and uniformity of sentencing. The new wording requires the courts to choose sanctions with due regard to the need for uniform sentencing, the penal value of the offense and the scale of punishment provided for in the Penal Code. Specific aggravating or mitigating circumstances affecting the penal value of the offense are exemplified in the new law and the courts must take particular account of circumstances that argue for a less severe sanction than imprisonment. As special reasons for imposing probation the court may consider whether an improvement likely to result in cessation of his criminality has occurred in the offender's situation or whether he is under, or willing to enter into, treatment for substance abuse or some other condition that can be presumed to be lead to cessation of his criminality.

Thus, although the new legislation sets up new principal criteria for the choice of sanctions to replace general and individual preventive considerations, it emphasizes that imprisonment should be used restrictively and retains individual prevention as the main reason for the use of probation (see Lundqvist 1990).

Norman Bishop is former head of the Research Group, Swedish Prison and Probation Administration.

Modified Criteria for the Use of Probation and Conditional Sentence

Major proposals in Chapter 9 referred to the desirability of minimum penal intervention and extended opportunities for the use of non-institutional sanctions. Certain subsequent legislative changes are intended to have these effects.

Up to 1983 a conditional sentence could be imposed if there were firm reasons for assuming that supervision or some other more far-reaching measure was not necessary to restrain the offender from further crime. An amending law which entered into force in that year made this requirement less stringent and simply stated " ... if there are no firm reasons to suppose that the offender will commit further offenses". The intention to widen the scope of the sanction has resulted in a proportionate increase in the use of conditional sentence over recent years. Thus, in 1974 the courts sentenced 27,791 persons to various forms of deprivation of liberty, probation, conditional sentence, handing over for special care or decided that an existing sanction covered a new offense. Conditional sentences made up 19% of this number. In 1991 the number of similar sentences had risen to just over 39,680. Conditional sentences made up 35% of this number.

Prior to 1983 probation could be imposed if were deemed necessary and no more far-reaching sanction was needed. This provision has since been altered and probation can now be ordered "if, having regard to the offender's personal circumstances, there is reason to suppose that it could contribute to restraining him/her from further crime". The change was intended to ensure that probation would not be used for those offenders who could be dealt with by a less severe community sanction. The absolute number of sentences to probation has been fairly constant over the last ten years at about 6,500 per year. But, since the the number of sentences to sanctions mentioned in the previous paragraph have increased, the proportion of sentences to probation has gone down from 23% in 1975 to 16% in 1991.

Both of the above changes can be seen as extensions of the principle of minimum penal intervention.

A New Form of Probation

Improvement of treatment response to the treatment needs of a sizeable group of offenders who are dependent on alcohol or drugs was also urged in Chapter 9. Moreover, it was suggested, the content of supervision should be made as attractive as possible so that coercion could be reduced and the element of choice on the part of the offender heightened. In that connection it should be noted that a new form of probation was introduced in 1988, so-called contract treatment, through the following legislative provision : "Where it can be presumed that the misuse of a dependency-producing substance, or some other special circumstance which calls for care and treatment, has substantially contributed to the commission of the offense, the court shall, when assessing whether probation is a sufficiently intervenient sanction, take special account of the expressed willingness of the offender to engage in some suitable treatment in accordance with an individual treatment plan which can be followed in connection with the implementation of a sentence to probation (SFS 1987:761)."

Unlike ordinary probation, the new provision requires consent ("expressed willingness"). Another difference is that the court must state the length of the imprisonment that would have been imposed had it not decided to sentence to probation with a condition of contract treatment. The purpose is to ensure that contract treatment is used solely as an alternative to imprisonment and not as an alternative to some other non-custodial sanction. It also makes possible a severe reaction if the conditions of contract treatment are not observed satisfactorily. However, if a decision has to be made about enforcing the prison sentence, the court must take account of all the circumstances and not automatically impose the earlier pronounced prison sentence.

Community Service as a Form of Probation

Another change, intended to widen the field of application of probation, has been the initiation of a three-year trial of probation with a condition of community service as from January 1990. Special legislation (SFS 1989:28) enables the courts of five districts to sentence offenders to probation with a condition of performing unpaid work in their spare time for the good of the community for from 40 to 200 hours. Offenders aged 18–25 who otherwise would have been sentenced to a short prison sentence are intended be the main target group. The offender's consent to community service is necessary, i.e. the element of choice also enters into this form of probation. The probation service decides on a suitable workplace, times for performing the work, etc. The courts are required to state the length of the imprisonment that would have been imposed had community service not been ordered. The aim of this last provision, as with contract treatment, is to restrict the use of community service to those offenders who would otherwise have been sentenced to imprisonment. The trial is to be evaluated by the National Council for Crime Prevention. The main findings of a preliminary report are described later in this Appendix. Parliament approved further legislation in 1992 extending the experiment with community service nationwide until December 1995.

Planning the Content of Supervision

A series of proposals in Chapter 9 dealt with improving the content and methods of supervision. To that end it was urged *inter alia* that regular meetings should be held between the professional probation officer, the lay supervisor and the client to plan the content of supervision and assess progress. The importance of dealing with financial problems, work and housing was emphasized. The proposed meetings would make written reporting by the lay supervisors unnecessary.

A provision in a government ordinance (SFS 1977:329) made an initial planning meeting obligatory. A further law (SFS 1979:680) empowered the supervision boards to impose conditions about how probation supervision should be implemented, in particular, the nature and frequency of contact.

A later law (SFS 1983:24) transferred managerial responsibility for probation work from the supervision boards to the chief probation officers. The latter were made accountable to the regional directors of the Swedish Prison and Probation Administration. These changes left the supervision boards acting more like courts in deciding only matters that restricted the personal rights and freedoms of the offender, e.g. temporary arrest if out of contact.

The Swedish Prison and Probation Administration has issued instructions on planning meetings. Apart from contact frequency, special attention is to be given to alcohol and drug dependence. The offender's financial position is also to be examined with special reference to debts of various kinds and the possibility of making a budget and payment plan. In the major urban areas a special post as legal adviser has been created to help with clients' financial problems. Plans for various kinds of assistance are frequently drawn up as "agreements" so as to try to secure a sense of participatory responsibility from the offender. Since the initial planning meeting is followed by further meetings to review progress, written reports from lay supervisors are no longer required.

The importance of planning meetings is reinforced by a new law on pre-sentence inquiries (SFS 1991:2041) which entered into force in July 1992. The changes in sentencing criteria and the introduction of new forms of sanction mean that more flexible forms of pre-sentence social inquiry are required which are better suited to the needs of the courts for deciding on the sanction. The probation service is given full responsibility for conducting the inquiry and decides what shall be its scope. The intention is that the initial planning meeting should use the social inquiry report as a starting point for planning treatment.

Length of Supervision Period

A provision in Law SFS 1983:24 requires supervision to be ordinarily for one year only. With misconduct the supervision period can be prolonged. On the other hand prolongation cannot be ordered for reasons of need or treatment. Conversely, directives to undertake some course or treatment are to be related to need and not to be used as sanctions for misconduct. The reduction of the supervision period was meant to enable a better deployment of probation workers so that they could work more intensively and effectively during the early phase of supervision when the probability of recidivism had been shown to be greatest. The above provisions are in line with recommendations made in Chapter 9. The probationary period, however, has remained unchanged at three years. An exception to these provisions is made with contract treatment. With this sanction the supervision period can be longer than one year, particularly where some form of institutional treatment is undertaken. The extended supervision period is intended to provide for continuing support and control after completion of treatment. The court decides the length of the supervision period in the individual case. Generally speaking, a period six months after the completion of institutional treatment is considered adequate. No prolongation of supervision is possible where the treatment is of ambulant nature or where the institutional treatment is of short duration.

Organizational Developments

It was argued in Chapter 9 that professional probation officers should give more qualified practical service to clients and be responsible for the control aspects of supervision. The lay supervisors should have more the role of contact person and friend. This presupposes adequate staffing and re-definition of role.

Since 1983 caseloads have been reduced to about 30 cases per probation officer. The probation officers are assisted by a small number of psychologists and nurses. In some 30 districts the services of a consultant physician are hired for 3–10 hours per week.

Over the years the number of lay supervisors has steadily diminished. For the budgetary year 1990/91 there were just over 4,800 lay supervisors. The diminution is partly due to an increasing awareness of the demands made by a probation and parole clientele with serious personal and social handicaps and partly to recruitment difficulties. In addition, it is considered that the clearer demands for supervision and control arising from legislative changes have led to increased contact with the professional probation officer and reduced the need for the lay supervisor. Special programs for drunken drivers and drug misusers are also considered to reduce the importance of the lay supervisor. The lay supervisor is no longer expected to exert formal control. The reduced caseloads of the professional probation officers make it easier for them to assume this function instead.

Nevertheless, the importance of lay supervisors was emphasised in Chapter 9 and it was there suggested that they should receive a higher fee and adequate training. In fact, the fee has been increased to 200 Swedish crowns (about 30 US$) per case and month. If they undertake special leisure activities with a client they can receive an extra

35 crowns (about 5 US$) per hour. Although the sums involved are not large they perhaps indicate that the contact role of the lay supervisor is considered important. The Swedish Prison & Probation Administration has also developed training modules which emphasize the lay supervisor's supportive role and the development of creative relationships.

A shift to decentralization and delegation of decision-making from the central administration to regional and local units was another proposal in Chapter 9. Major changes of this kind have now been implemented in both the prison and probation services. Probation offices are now given considerable freedom to use their budgetary allocations according to local plans on the content and methods of supervision. Staff recruitment and the training of senior managers are further examples of delegated questions. One effect of the new managerial emphases is said to be a higher status for local probation administrations both within the correctional service as a whole and in relation to agencies in the organizational environment. Even if the full-scale integration of the probation service with the social services which was proposed in Chapter 9 has not come to pass, decentralization is claimed to have led to fuller and better collaboration.

Ideological Aspects

Both in connection with the abolition of probation with institutional treatment as well as more generally it was urged in Chapter 9 that punishment, control and treatment should be given clearer profiles in the probation sanction. The new legislative emphases on probation as a reaction to an offense with concomitant conditions mean that these elements have been given a clearer profile both in ordinary probation as well as with probation with a condition of contract treatment or community service.

The probation officer's task when preparing a social inquiry report is seen by the Swedish Prison and Probation Administration to be to explain to the client the nature of the possibilities concerning the sanction which are open. For example, there a possibility for the offender to avoid a sentence to imprisonment if he agrees to enter into contract treatment. This can involve living in a therapeutic community for up to a year with abstention from drugs checked by frequent urine testing. Non-compliance with these conditions can mean expulsion from the therapeutic community in which case the court must be informed and will decide what action to take.

The probation officer is expected to try to motivate the offender to accept any help offered. If the help is accepted, the offender must either take the responsibility of abiding by the ground rules or the consequences of non-compliance. In short, the probation officer's job is frequently to ensure that the situation, with its relative gains and losses, is clearly understood by the offender. Within this situation some room for manoeuvre on the part of the offender exists—but with conditions and consequences attached to the courses of action open. The offender must decide what he or she wants to achieve and act accordingly. The Swedish Prison and Probation Administration claims that these policies are carried out and that probation work has improved as a consequence.

Another ideological issue taken up in Chapter 9 dealt with the nature of the help to be offered to the offender and how it is to be provided. The "normality principle", by which is meant using the existing community health and welfare services to the greatest possible extent, was strongly recommended as part of a welfare ideology. Criticism was expressed about the unclear boundaries between the probation and social welfare systems especially concerning assistance to clients with financial and housing needs. Progress in this direction is claimed by the Swedish Prison and Probation Administration so far as financial help to clients is concerned. Today, a client in financial difficulties ordinarily obtains help through the regular social welfare channels and does not receive sums of money from the probation officer.

Although the provision of housing is also the responsibility of the municipality in which the offender resides, the Swedish Prison and Probation Administration considers that this provision does not work well in a time of acute housing shortages and severe municipal budgetary restrictions. Probation and parole clients are frequently seen as less than desirable tenants partly because of such personal problems as alcohol and drug misuse and partly because of their inability to pay their rent regularly. Efforts to put pressure on municipal authorities to be more accepting meet with varying degrees of success.

Similar difficulties have arisen in connection with employment, In order to improve the occupational status of probationers and parolees, concerted efforts by different administrations are often necessary. Two projects, which, in collaboration with the probation service, link the efforts of the employment office with educational and social welfare agencies, have been running for some years in the towns of Malö and Örebro. An agreement on similar forms of collaboration has been drawn up with the Labour Market Administration. Similarly an agreement has been drawn up with the administration which is responsible for collecting monies due to the State (e.g. fines, court expenses, taxes, etc) for the local office to work in collaboration with the probation service to deal with offenders' debts.

The present policy is that the probation service should document the nature and extent of the need to be addressed and try to get the regular community agencies to provide the necessary service. So far as drug misusers are concerned there has been close co-operation between the municipal services (which have sizeable funds available for the prevention of AIDS and drug treatment services) and the probation service to identify misusers under supervision and motivate them to enter treatment. A number of probation districts also run programs for drunken drivers.

Intentions and Reality

The whole purpose of the research conducted by Professor Bondeson was to investigate the extent to which legislative and organizational intentions became working and effective realities. The findings were essentially negative. In this appendix a number of subsequent changes in legislation and organization have been described which, broadly speaking, are in accord with recommendations made on the basis of the research. These changes are, as before, intended to lead to certain improvements and, indeed, the Swedish Prison and Probation Administration claims that a number of improvements in probation practice have occurred. It must, however, be pointed out that no independent scientific research comparable to that described in the preceding chapters has been undertaken to study these legislative and organisational changes and ascertain to what extent intentions and reality are in accord.

Although national criminal policy, legislation and practice has emphasized the importance of community sanctions, it is disappointing to have to report that relatively little rigorous research on conditional sentences and the various forms of probation has taken place since the completion of the research described by Professor Bondeson. A brief account of the few studies undertaken now follows.

Research

Community Service as an Alternative to Imprisonment

Andersson and Andersson (Brottsförebyggande rådet 1991) have presented an interim report covering the first fifteen months of the trial in five experimental districts. A total of 204 offenders were recommended for community service following a pre-sentence social inquiry. Of this number 52% were in fact sentenced to community service. No difficulty was experienced in finding suitable forms of work.

In 25% of the community service sentences the court ordered 40 hours of community service (the minimum period) and in a further 60% to less than 100 hours. The maximum period of 200 hours was used in 14% of all cases. The equivalence of the pronounced lengths of imprisonment to the number of hours of community service varied greatly. Thus, for example, six months imprisonment corresponded to both 100 hours community service as well as 200 hours.

The offenders were mainly, but by no means entirely, within the age range recommended by the legislator. Some 60% had previously been sentenced to a conditional sentence, probation, imprisonment, closed or open psychiatric care, care under the Act on the Care of Drug Misusers or some combination of these sanctions and measures. The principal offenses for which they were sentenced to community service were assault (24%), theft (20%) and drunken driving (17%).

Since the report was of interim character and dealt with only small numbers, no recidivism study was undertaken at this stage. An account of the use of community service in Denmark, which has had longer experience with the sanction than Sweden, is given by Bondeson (1990).

Recidivism Following Probation

Engman and Gustavsson (Kriminalvårdsstyrelsen 1991) have studied recidivism on the basis of a 10% random selection of persons sentenced to probation (including probation combined with imprisonment) between July and December 1983 each of whom was followed up for six years (N = 278). Recidivism was defined as the commission of further offense leading to a fresh sentence to probation or to imprisonment. By the end of the follow-up period 60% of the sample had recidivated. Nearly half of the recidivists had committed their recidivist offense within six months and nearly three-quarters had done so within one year, i.e. while under probation supervision. The recidivism rates were especially serious for those aged up to 25. Sixty-five percent of those in this age group without a previous sentence recidivated. The corresponding figure for those with a previous sentence was as high as 76%.

Comparisons between different recidivism studies are subject to the limitations imposed by varying definitions, follow-up periods, etc. With this reservation it is nevertheless interesting to compare the results of the above study with Professor Bondeson's finding that 12% of the conditionally sentenced, 30% of probationers and 61% of probationers who had undergone institutional treatment had recidivated at least once during a two-year period. The recidivism rate for the two categories of probation combined was 45%. Even allowing for differences in the analyses made in these two studies there would appear to be no grounds for supposing that probation recidivism rates have improved since Professor Bondeson's study and it is possible that they have deteriorated.

The Grut Project

This is a small-scale evaluation to determine whether there were any positive outcome effects resulting from intensive basic education (Ahlberg, Brottsförebyggande rådet 1991). A small group of young drug misusing offenders with educational weaknesses and a median age of 23 entered an intensive basic education course. By improving their education level it was hoped to interest them in continuing with further education or vocational training and that this should lead to lives without crime or drug misuse. A comparison group—not selected randomly—was set up. There was reasonable comparability between the two groups on criteria concerning age distribution, criminality and drug misuse. A before-and-after design was used to control for spontaneous remission effects.

Findings were that the treated group had less drug misuse than the comparison group during the treatment period (p = .10). Criminality was the same in both groups during this period. During the follow-up period there was a considerable and similar reduction in criminality and drug misuse in both the treated and the comparison groups. It was concluded that spontaneous remission was the main cause of the post-treatment improvements noted.

Women, Crime and Supervision

This doctoral dissertation (Ungmark 1992) consists of a study of registered data concerning 157 women under probation or parole supervision of whom 27 were randomly selected for lengthy interviews. With three exceptions all those interviewed were drug misusers.In addition 17 probation officers involved with these clients were also interviewed. The main emphasis is on a qualitative and descriptive account of the coping strategies employed by these drug misusing women offenders.

The study shows *inter alia* that supervisors make less demands on women offenders under supervision than on men offenders largely on account of the feelings evoked in supervisors by their life situation and problems. At the same time these problems, chiefly drug misuse, social marginalization and unhappy relationships, make for a perception of women offenders as difficult, "hard work" cases. The women offenders on their side make use of a variety of defensive techniques to maintain a degree of control over the supervision situation. To some extent the suspicion, denial of feelings and maintenance of distance in relationships in the supervision situation was considered to be a result of their early unhappy life experience reinforced by similar experiences in their relationships with criminal men. But the defensiveness was also partly be attributed to the possibility of getting help and support but, on the other hand, being subject to the supervisor's coercive and sanctioning powers. What the women wanted from supervision was concrete and practical forms of assistance whilst the supervisors wanted to deal with what they saw as the underlying problems. Why some of the women perceived supervision positively and others did not is not explored in the study.

To Cease with Crime

The purpose of this doctoral dissertation (Chylicki 1992) was to investigate the factors that lead to a cessation of criminal careers (desistance). A total of 226 persons born in 1960 who had terminated their criminal careers by the age of 24 is compared with 214 persons, born in the same year, who had not so terminated their criminal careers. Comparisons between the desisters and recidivists were made in respect of factors related to childhood and adolescence, to various forms of social intervention during childhood and adolescence and to the nature of their prison or probation careers. The social situation of the two groups at the age of 24 was also compared. In addition, 24 unstructured deep interviews were conducted with the two groups to throw light on the conclusions drawn from the statistical analyses.

The two groups differed strongly. The early life conditions of the recidivists were worse than those of the desisters. Many more of the recidivist group had been subject to a variety of social interventions. Disturbed relationships with parents, early institutional experience and frequent changes of residence all showed a statistically significant association with continuing criminality. Drug misuse was also significantly more frequent among the recidivists and, at a mature age, significantly more of them could be considered socially marginalized.

A quantitative and qualitative analysis of the impact of correctional measures led to the conclusion that only those which contained opportunities for the development of close and trusting relationships had the potential to be of importance in promoting desistance. This appeared to be more especially true of the contact with a supervisor during the periods of parole or probation supervision. (This finding is in accord with the numerous practical proposals in Chapter 9 for improving the quality of the supervisor-client relationship). The notion that offenders tend to mature out of criminality received support in the study but Chylicki emphasises that the process of maturing is not necessarily related to biological age. Social and mental maturity supervened at different ages for different individuals.

Bibliography

Abrahamson, Bengt. *Organisationsteori.* (Organization Theory). Stockholm: Almqvist & Wiksell, 1975.

Adorno, Frenkel-Brunswik, Levinson and Sandford. *The Authoritarian Personality.* New York: Harper, 1950.

Agge, Ivar. *Studier över det straffrättsliga reaktionssystemet.* (Studies of the Sanction System). Stockholm: Nordiska Bokhandeln, 1939.

Ahl, Kennet. *Grundbulten.* (The Bottom Bolt). Stockholm: Prisma, 1976 (3rd ed.).

______. *Lyftet.*(The Kick). Stockholm: Prisma, 1976.

Ancel, Marc. *La Défense Sociale nouvelle.* (The New Social Defense Movement). Paris: Editions Cujas, 1954.

______. *L'individualisation des mesures prises à l'égard du délinquant.* (The Individualization of Measures Used with Offenders). Paris: Editions Cujas, 1954.

Andenæs, Johs. "Om virkningen av forskjellige reaksjoner mot lovovertredere". (On the Effects of Different Sanctions.) *NTfK*, 3, 117–135, 1966.

______. "Forskning om individualprevensjon og almenprevensjon". (Research on Individual and General Prevention) *NJT, Lov og Rett*, 2, 61–69, 1971.

______. *Straff og lovlydighet.* ("Punishment and Law Obedience"). Oslo: Universitetsforlaget, 1974a.

______. "Signaler i kriminalpolitikken—spesielt om strafferettslige særreaksjoner." (Criminal Policy Signals—Notably Special Penal Law Sanctions). *NTfK* 2, 97–117, 1974b.

______. "Kriminalomsorg i frihet." (Criminal Care in Liberty). *Lov og Rett.* 33–44, 1978.

Anners, Erik. *Humanitet och rationalism.* (Humanity and Rationalism). Stockholm: Rättshistoriskt bibliotek, Nordiska Bokhandeln, 1965.

Anttila, Inkeri. "Kriminalvård i frihet—social service eller kontroll?" (Non-Institutional Corrections—Social Service or Control?). *NTfK*, 1, 24–36, 1973.

Anttila, I. and Törnudd, P. *Kriminologi i kriminalpolitiskt perspektiv.* (Criminology in a Criminal Policy Perspective). Stockholm: Norstedts, 1973.

Aspelin, Erland. "Böter i stället för frihetsstraff." (Fines instead of Deprivaton of Liberty). *NTfK*, 1, 53–72, 1973.

______. "Utvecklingslinjer i svensk kriminalpolitik efter brottsbalkens införande." (Developmental Trends in Swedish Criminal Policy Following the Introduction of the New Penal Code), *NTfK*, 2, 97–122, 1975.

Aubert, Vilhelm, Eckhoff, T. and Sveri, K. *En lov i søkelyset.* (Spotlight on a Law). Oslo: Institut for samfunnsforskning, 1952.

______. *Likhet og rett.* Essays om forbrytelse og straff. (Equality and Law. Essays on Crime and Punishment). Oslo: Pax, 1964.

______ and Messinger, S. "The Criminal and the Sick." *Inquiry.* 137–160.

______. *Rättssociologi.* (The Sociology of Law). Stockholm: Aldus, 1972a.

______. *Lag, samhälle och individ.* (Law, Society and Individual). Stockholm: Rabén & Sjögren, 1972b.

______. *Rettens sosiale funksjon.* (The Social Function of Law). Oslo: Universitetsforlaget. 1976.

Bailey, Walter. "Correctional Outcome: an Evaluation of 100 Reports." *Crim. Law, Criminol. and Pol. Scie.*, 153–160, 1966.

Balvig, F. and Kyvsgaard, B. "Kriminalforsorg i (u)frihed." (Non-Institutional Correction in (non)freedom). App. 5 in *Kriminalforsorg-Socialforsorg.* København: Betænkning 752, 1975.

Barnes, H. and Teeters, N. *New Horizons in Criminology.* Englewood Cliffs: Prentice Hall, 1959.

Becker, Howard. *Outsiders.* Studies in the Sociology of Deviance. Glencoe: Free Press, 1963.

______, ed. *The Other Side.* Perspectives on Deviance. Glencoe: Free Press, 1964.

______. "Whose Side Are We On?" *Social Problems*, 3, 239–247, 1967.

Beckman, Hult and Strahl. *Kommentar till brottsbalken III.* (Commentary on the Penal Code III). Stockholm: Norstedts, 1967 (2nd ed. 1971).

______, Holmberg, Hult and Strahl. *Kommentar till brottsbalken I.* (Commentary on the Penal Code I). Stockholm: Norstedts, 1965 (4th ed. 1974).

Bengtsson, A-G., Fälth, B-M. and Lindberg, M. *Ett nytt sätt att rapportera övervakning vid skyddskonsulentexpeditionen i Bohus distrikt.* (A New Way with Supervision Reports at the Bohus District Probation Office). Göteborg, Socialhögskolan, 1975.

Bentham, Jeremy. *The Principles of Morals and Legislation.* New York: Hafner, 1948.

Bentzon, Agnete Weis. "Artikler om Retsplejens vilkår og virke i de grønlandske samfund." (Articles on the Conditions and Effects of Judicial Procedure on Greenland). *Nyt fra Samfundsvidenskaberne*, 15, 1967.

Berglind, Hans, ed. *Ideal och verkligheter i svensk socialvård.* (Ideals and Realities in Swedish Social Welfare). Stockholm: Wahlström & Widstrand, 1976.

Bishop, Norman. Non-Custodial Alternatives in Europe. *HEUNI.* Publ. No. 14, Helsinki 1988.

Blau, Peter. *The Dynamics of Bureaucracy.* Chicago: University of Chicago Press, 1955.

______, and Scott, R. *Formal Organizations.* A Comparative Approach. London: Routledge & Kegan, 1963.

Blegvad-Persson, Britt-Mari. "The Systematic Position of Sociology of Law in Current Scandinavian Research." *Acta Sociologica*, 10, 22–19, 1966.

______, Bolding, P-O., Lando, O. and Gamst-Nielsen, K. *Arbitration as a Means of Solving Conflicts.* Copenhagen: New Social Science Monographs E6, 1973.

Blomberg, Dick. "Det svenska kriminalvårdsklientelet." (The Swedish Correctional Clientèle). App. to *SOU*, 55, 100–116, 1956.

______. *Den svenska ungdomsbrottsligheten.* (Swedish Youth Criminality). Stockholm: Natur och Kultur, 1971 (3rd rev. ed.).

Blumberg, Abraham. *Criminal Justice.* Chicago: Quadrangle Books, 1967.

Blumer, Herbert. "Society as Symbolic Interaction." *Human Behaviour and Social Processes*: An Interactionist Approach. Boston: Houghton Mifflin, 1962.

Blumstein, Alfred et al. *Deterrence and Incapacitation.* Estimating the Effects of Criminal Sanctions on Crime Rates. Washington, D.C.: National Academy of Sciences, 1978.

______ and Cohen, J. "Sentencing of Convicted Offenders: An Analysis of the Public's View." *Law and Society Review* 14:2, 223–261, 1980.

Bodin, Greger. *En explorativ undersökning om språk, normer, attityder och beteende i kriminologiskt perspektiv.* (An Explorative Study of Language, Norms, Attitudes and Behavior in a Criminological Perspective). Lund: Sociologiska institutionen (stencil), 1971.

Bolding, Per-Olof. *Juridik och samhällsdebatt.* (Law and the Debate on Society). Uppsala: Almqvist & Wiksell, 1968.

Bondeson, Ulla V. "Argot Knowledge as an Indicator of Criminal Socialization—A Study of a Training School for Girls." *Scandinavian Studies in Criminology*, 2, 73–107, 1968.

———. *Fången i fångsamhället.* Socialisationsprocesser vid ungdomsvårdsskola, ungdomsfängelse, fängelse och internering. (Prisoner in Prison Society. Socialization Processes in Training Schools, Youth Prisons, Prisons and Internment). Stockholm: Norstedts, 1974.

———. "A Critical Survey of Correctional Treatment Studies in Scandinavia 1945–1974" in van den Haag and Martinson, eds., *Crime Deterrence and Offender Career.* Pp. 251–334. New York: 1975.

———. *Kriminalvård i frihet—Intention och verklighet.* (Non-Institutional Treatment—Intention and Reality). Stockholm: Liber, 1977.

———. NADSOR. (Non-Custodial Sanctions). Moskow: Juriditeskaja Literatura, 1979a.

———. "Det allmänna rättsmedvetandet" (The General Sense of Justice) in U. Bondeson, ed., *Rationalitet i rättssystemet.* Pp. 123–143. Stockholm: Liber 1979b.

———. "Conditional Sentence and Probation" in N. Bishop, ed., *Scandinavian Criminal Policy 1975–80.* Pp. 59–69. Scandinavian Research Council for Criminology, 1980a.

———. "Nyklassisk straffilosofi och reformpolitik" (Neo-Classical Penal Philosophy and Reform Policies) in S. Heckscher et al., eds., *Straff och rättfärdighet.* Pp. 97–115. Stockholm: Norstedt, 1980b.

———. "Die Effizienz unterschiedlicher Formen der Strafaussetzung zur Bewährung" in P. Dünkel and G. Spiess, eds., *Alternativen zur Freiheitsstrafe.* Pp. 148–164. Freiburg: Max-Planck-Institut, 1983.

———. *Prisoners in Prison Societies.* New Brunswick, N.J.: Transaction, 1989.

———. "Innovative Non-Custodial Sanctions" in N. Bishop, ed. *Scandinavian Criminal Policy and Criminology.* Pp. 59–69 Scandinavian Research Council for Criminology. Stockholm 1990.

———. "Surveys of Victimization in the Scandinavian Countries" in G. Kaiser et al., eds., *Victims and Criminal Justice,* Kriminologische Forschungsberichte. Pp. 333–346. Freiburg: Max-Planck-Institut, 1991.

———- and Bodin, G. *Domarens rättsmedvetande.* (The Judge's Sense of Justice). Lund: Sociologiska institutionen (stencil), 1977.

Brottsförebyggande rådet (The National Swedish Council for Crime Prevention) *Kriminalitetsnivå och belastningsfördelningar* by Carlsson, Gösta. (Crime Levels and the Distribution of Previous Criminal Records). PM 1975:1.

———. *General Deterrence.* Report 1975:2, Liber.

———. *Om skadestånd och straff ur samhällsekonomisk synpunkt* by Skogh, Göran, (On Damages and Punishment in a Socio-Economic Perspective). Kriminalpolitiska gruppen, (stencil) 1975.

———. *Återfall vid olika reaktioner på brott* by Carlsson, G. and Olsson, O. (Recidivism Following Diverse Reactions to Crime). 1976: 2.

———. *Pressens brottsinformation* by Aspelin, Erland. (The Crime Information of the Press). PM 1976: 4.

———. *Försöksverksamhet med intensifierat samarbete mellan kriminalvården och andra samhällsorgan.* (Experiment with Intensified Collaboration between Corrections and other Social Agencies). PM 1976: 6, Report I.

———. *Frigiven—utvärdering av en informationskampanj* by Hedebro, Göran. (Conditionally Released—Evaluation of an Information Campaign). KANSLI-PM 1976: 11.

______. *Åtgärdseffekter—Ett statistiskt exempel* by Carlsson, Gösta. (Effects of Penal Measures—a Statistical Example). KANSLI-PM 1977: 2.

______. *Stämplingsteori—en kritisk granskning* by Knutsson, Johannes. (Labeling Theory—a Critical Survey). Report 1977: 1.

______. *Att informera om avvikande grupper* by Hedebro, Göran, (On Providing Information about Deviant Groups). Report 1977: 2.

______. Kühlhorn, Eckhart et al. *Frivård och rehabilitering.* 1979:3. (Non-Institutional Treatment and Rehabilitation, English Summary, 1979:7).

______. *Nytt straffsystem:* Idéer och förslag, 1977:7. (English Summary: A New Penal System: Ideas and Proposals, 1978:5).

______. Ahlberg, J. *GRUT-projektet i Visby—en utvärdering* The GRUT Project in Visby—an Evaluation). 1991.

______. Andersson, T. and Andersson, L. Samhällstjänst som alternativ till fängelse. (Community Service as an Alternative to Imprisonment). 1991.

Brunander, Lennart. *Om relationen övervakare—klient.* (On the Supervisor—Client Relationship). Stockholm: Pedagogiska institutionen (stencil), 1963.

Buckley, William. *Sociology and Modern Systems Theory.* New York: Prentice Hall, 1967.

Börjeson, Bengt. *Om påföljders verkningar.* (On the Effects of Sanctions). Uppsala: Almqvist & Wiksell, 1966.

______. "Om påföljders verkningar—en kommentar till mina kritiker." (On the Effects of Sanctions—a Commentary for My Critics). *Statistisk tidsskrift,* 5, 384–392, 1967.

Caro, Francis, ed. *Readings in Evaluation Research.* New York: Russell Sage Foundation, 1971.

Carter, R. and Wilkins, L. *Probation and Parole.* New York: Wiley, 1970.

Chambliss, W. and Seidman, R. *Law, Order and Power.* Massachusetts: Addison & Wesley, 1971.

Christiansen, Karl O. "Factors Influencing Recidivism in Criminological Diagnosis. An International Perspective," eds. Ferracuti and Wolfgang. Lexington, pp. 129–178. 1983.

Christie, Nils. "Reaksjonenes virkninger." (The Effects of Sanctions). *NTfK,* 2, 129–144, 1961.

______. "De fratagbare goder. En inntak till beskrivelse av verdiendringer over tid." (Removable Goodness. an Introduction to a Description of Changing Values Over Time). *Tidsskrift for samfunnsforskning,* 119–130, 1966.

______. "Law and Medicine. The Case Against Role Blurring." *Law and Society Review,* 5, 357–366, 1971a.

______. "Forskning om individualprevensjon kontra almenprevensjon." (Research on Individual versus General Prevention). *NJT, Lov og Rett,* 2, 49–60, 1971b.

______. *Hvor tett et samfunn.* (How Close Shall Society Be?). København—Oslo: Ejlers-Universitetsforlaget, 1975.

______. *Conflicts as Property.* Oslo: Institutt for Kriminologi og Strafferett (stencilserie 23), 1976.

______, Andenaes, J. and Skirbekk, S. "A Study of Self-Reported Crime." *Scandinavian Studies in Criminology,* 1, 86–116, 1965.

Council of Europe. *Public Opinion on Crime and Criminal Justice.* Strasbourg, 1979.

______. Council of Europe. *Report on Decriminalisation.* Strasbourg, 1980.

Chylicki, Pawel. *Skyddstillsyn och vilkorlig dom.* (Probation and Conditional Sentence). Lund: Sociologiska institutionen (stencil), 1971.

______. *Att upphöra med brott* (To Cease with Crime). Doctoral Dissertation, Lund: Lund University Press, 1992.

Clarke, R. and Sinclair, I. "Towards more Effective Treatment Evaluation." *Council of Europe*, Strasbourg, 5, 1–34, 1973.

Clemmer, Donald. *The Prison Community*. New York: Holt, Rinehart & Winston.(1940), 1958.

Collins, J.J. et al. "Research on Alternative Probation Strategies in Maryland." *US Department of Justice*, Washington 1984.

Cressey, D. *"Limitations on Organization of Treatment in the Modern Prison" in Theoretical Studies in the Social Organization of the Prison. Social Science Research Council*, New York, 78–111, 1960.

______. *The Prison*. Studies in Institutional Organization and Change. New York: Holt, Rinehart & Winston, 1961.

______. *Delinquency, Crime and Differential Association*. The Hague: Martinus, Nijhoff, 1964.

Dalberg-Larsen, J. *Lovene og livet*. (The Laws and Life). København: Akademisk Forlag (2nd ed.), 1991.

Daun, Å., Börjeson, B. and Åhs, S. *Samhällsförändringar och brottslighet*. (Social Change and Criminality). Stockholm: Tiden, 1974.

Davis, George. "A Study of Adult Probation Violation Rates by Means of the Cohort Approach." *Jnl. of Crim. Law, Criminol. and Pol. Scie.* 55, 70, 1964.

Diana, Lewis. "Is Casework in Probation Necessary?" *Focus*, 34, 1–8, 1955.

Eckhoff, Torstein. *Rettskildelære*. (Theory of Sources of Law). Oslo: Tanum-Norli, 1975.

Edling, S. and Elwin, G. *Obduktion av en död utredning*. (Post Mortem on a Dead Committee). Stockholm: Wahlström & Widstrand, 1972.

Ek, I. and Hultén, M. *Genomgång av institutet skyddstillsyn*. (Analysis of Probation as an Institution). Lund: Sociologiska institutionen (stencil), 1971.

Ekelöf, Per Olof. "En essay om tolkning och mening." (An Essay on Interpretation and Meaning). *Kungl. Vetenskapssamhället i Uppsala årsbok*, 20, 5–53, 1976.

Elmhorn, Kerstin. "Prognosteknik i behandlingsforskningens tjänst." (Prognostic Techniques for Treatment Research). *NTfK*, 3, 136–147, 1966.

Elwin, G., Heckscher, S. and Nelson, A. *Den första stenen*. Studiebok i kriminalpolitik. (The First Stone. Study Material in Criminal Policy). Stockholm: Tiden, 1975 (4th rev. ed.).

Empey, L. et al. *The Silverlake Experiment*: A Community Study in Delinquency Rehabilitation. Youth Studies Center: University of Southern California, 3, 1966.

Empey, L. and Rabow, J. "The Provo Experiment in Delinquency Rehabilitation." *ASR*, 26, 679–696, 1961.

England Jr., Ralph. "What is Responsible for Satisfactory Probation and Postprobation Outcome." *Jnl. of Crim. Law, Criminol. and. Pol. Scie.*, 6, 667–677, 1957.

Eriksson, T., Jansson, C-G. and Larsson, U. "Återfall i brott bland unga lagöverträdare." (Relapse into Crime among Young Offenders). App. to *SOU*, 55, 35–82, 1956.

Etzioni, Amitai. *Comparative Analysis of Complex Organizations*. New York: Free Press, 1961.

______. *Moderna organisationer*. (Modern Organizations). Stockholm: Bonniers, 1966.

Eyben, W. von. *Strafudmåling*. (The Meeting out of Punishment) København: Gads Forlag, 1950.

Eysenck, Hans. *Crime and Personality*. London: Routledge & Kegan, 1964.

Feeley, Malcolm M. *Court Reform on Trial*. While Simple Solutions Fail. New York: Basic Books 1983.

Folkard, S. et al. Probation Research. A Preliminary Report. *Home Office*. London, 1967.

______ et al. IMPACT—Intensive Matched Probation and After-Care Treatment. *Home Office*. London, 1, 1974.

______ et al. IMPACT—The Results of the Experiment. Vol. II. *Home Office*. London: 1976.

Friedman, Lawrence. *The Legal System*. A Social Science Perspective. New York: Russell Sage Foundation, 1976.

______ and Macaulay, S. *Law and the Behavioral Sciences*. New York: Bobbs-Merrill, 1969.

Fuller, Lon. *Anatomy of the Law*. Harmondsworth: Pelican, 1971 (1968).

Gahrton, Per. "Fångars försvar." (The Prisoners' Defense). *Sociologisk forskning*, 1, 109–130, 1968.

Galtung, Johan. "Prison—The Organization of Dilemma" in D. Cressey, ed. *The Prison*. New York: Holt, Rinehart & Winston, 107–145, 1961.

Garfinkel, Harold. "Conditions of Successful Degradation Ceremonies." *ASR*. 420–424, 1956.

Gaudet, Frederick. "The Sentencing Behaviour of the Judge" in Branham and Cutash, eds. *Encyclopaedia of Criminology*. New York: Philosophical Library, 1949.

Geijer, L. and Schmidt, F. *Arbetsgivare och fackföreningsledare i domarsäte*. (The Employer and the Union Leader in the Judge's Chair). Lund: Carl Blom, 1958.

Gerth, H. and Mills, C. *From Max Weber*—Essays in Sociology. New York: Oxford University Press, 1958.

Gilbert, D. and Levinson, D. "Custodialism and Humanism in Staff Ideology" in Greenblatt et al., eds. *The Patient and the Mental Hospital*. Glencoe: Free Press, 1957.

Glaser, Daniel. "Differential Association and Criminological Prediction." *Social Problems*, 8, 6–14, 1960.

______. *The Effectiveness of a Prison and Parole System*. New York: Bobbs-Merrill, 1964.

______. *Evaluation Research and Decision Guidance*. New Brunswick, N.J.: Transaction, 1988.

Glueck, Sheldon and Glueck, Eleanor. *Five Hundred Criminal Careers*. New York, 1930.

______ and Glueck, Eleanor. *Predicting Delinquency and Crime*. Cambridge: Harvard University Press, 1959.

Goffman, Erving. *Asylums*—Essays on the Social Situation of Mental Patients and Other Inmates. New York: Doubleday, 1961.

______. *Stigma*. Harmondsworth: Penguin, 1968 (1963).

Goldschmidt, Verner. *Retlig adfærd*. (Legal Behavior). København, 1957.

Gordan, Kurt. *Att vara övervakare*. (On Being a Supervisor). Stockholm: Bonniers, 1967.

Gottfredson, Don. "Assessments of Prediction Methods" in Johnston et al., eds., *The Sociology of Punishment and Correction*. New York: Wiley, 745–771, 1970.

Gouldner, Alvin. "Organizational Analysis" in Merton, ed., *Sociology Today*. New York: Basic Books, 400–428, 1959.

______. Biologist as Partisan: Sociology and the Welfare State. *The American Sociologist*, 2, 103–116, 1968.

______. *The Coming Crisis of Western Sociology*. New York: Basic Books, 1970.

Green, Edward. *Judicial Attitudes in Sentencing*. London: Macmillan, 1961.

Greve, Vagn. *Kriminalitet som normalitet*. (Criminality as Normality). København: Juristforbundets forlag, 1972.

Grygier, Tadeusz. "Treatment Variables in Non-Linear Prediction" in Johnston et al., eds., *The Sociology of Punishment and Correction*. New York: Wiley, 828–838, 1970.

Grünhut, Max. *Juvenile Offenders before the Courts*. Oxford: Clarendon, 1956.

Hagström, Nilsson and Sillfors. *Frivårdstjänstemännens attityder—en explorativ studie*. (Probation Officer Attitudes—an Explorative Study). Stockholm: Pedagogiska institutionen (stencil), 1971.

Hansen, M.V. et al. *Dømt til hjelp.* (Sentenced to Help). Oslo: Universitetsforlaget, 1980.
Hansson, Kjell. *Övervakarna och övervakningen.* En enkätundersökning bland nykterhetsnämndens övervakare i Lund. (The Supervisors and the Supervised. A Questionnaire Inquiry among Temperance Board Supervisors in Lund). Lund: Sociologiska institutionen (stencil), 1966.
Hansson, Thomas. *Skyddstillsyn och villkorlig dom*—en återfalls- och prognosundersökning. (Probation and Conditional Sentence—a Prognostic and Recidivism Study). Lund: Sociologiska institutionen (stencil), 1971.
Hammond, W. The Sentence of the Court. *Home Office.* London, 1969 (1964).
Hampstead, Lord Lloyd of. *Introduction to Jurisprudence.* London: Stevens, 1972 (3rd ed.).
Hart, H L A. *The Concept of Law.* Oxford: Oxford University Press, 1961.
Hauge, Ragnar. *Tillsynsførerens syn på sin virksomhet.* (Supervisor's Views on Supervision). Part I and II. Oslo: Oslo universitet, 1967.
———. "Institutional Dilemmas in Probation and Parole." *Scandinavian Studies in Criminology,* 2, 41–52, 1968.
———. *Kriminalomsorg i frihet.* (Non-Institutional Correction). Oslo: Norges Vernesamband, 1970 (Universitetsforlaget, 1974).
Heinz, Wolfgang "Diversion in German Juvenile Justice." *Studies on Crime and Crime Prevention,* 146–166. 1992.
Hellner, Jan. *Skadeståndsrätt.* (The Law on Damages) Stockholm: Almqvist & Wiksell, 1976 (3rd ed.).
Hirsch, Andrew v. *Doing Justice.* New York: Report of the Committee for the Study of Incarceration, 1976.
Hirschi, Travis. "Procedural Rules and the Study of Deviant Behaviour." *Social Problems,* 21, 159–173, 1973.
von Hofer, Hans. "Dutch Prison Population." 17:e nordiska forskarseminariet i kriminologi 1975. *Nordiska Samarbetsrådet för Kriminologi,* 104–150, 1976.
———. "Skyddstillsyn och fängelse." (Probation and Prison). *Tidskrift för Kriminalvård* pp. 31–33, 1981.
———. Nordic Criminal Statistics 1950–1980 (81). Promemoria 1983:8. *SCB,* Stockholm, 1983.
———. *Fängelset: Uppkomst—avskräckning—inkapacitering.* (The Prison: Origins—Deterrence—Incapacitation). Stockholm: Kriminologiska institutionen, 1993.
Holstein, B and Jersild, T. "932 kriminelle stofmisbrugere—fem år senere." (Nine Hundred and Thirtytwo Drug Misusers—Five Years Later. *Justitsministeriet, Kriminalpolitisk forskningsgruppe,* København 1976:2.
Homans, George. *The Human Group.* New York: Harcourt, Brace, 1950.
Hood, R and Sparks, R. *Kriminologi.* (Criminology). Stockholm: Wahlström & Widstrand, 1973.
Hughes, Everett. *Men and Their Work.* Glencoe: Free Press, 1958.
Illich, Ivan. *Den farliga sjukvården.* (The Nemesis of Illness). Stockholm: Aldus, 1975.
Inghe, G and Lindberg, T. "Recidivrisken vid olika brottstyper med särskild hänsyn till inflytandet av alkoholmissbruk." (Recidivism Risks with Different Crime Categories with Special Reference to the Influence of Alcohol Misuse). App. to *SOU,* 55, 83–99, 1956.
Ingstrup, Ole. "Frivillighed eller tvang i forsorgen for kriminelle—kriminalforsorg eller social bistand." (Voluntariness or Coercion in Correctional Work—Correctional Care or Social Help). *NTfK.* 1–2, 48–61, 1976.
Israel, Joachim. "Mentalsjukhusens personalorganisation." (Staff Organization in Mental Hospitals). Part I. *SOU,* 24, 22–128, 1963.
——— and Johansson, S. "Kustodialism och alienation bland vårdavdel-

ningspersonalen på ett mentalsjukhus." (Custodialism and Alienation among Ward Staff at a Mental Hospital). *Sociologisk forskning,* 2, 63–77, 1965.

______. "Om konsten att lyfta sig själv i håret och behålla barnet i badvattnet." (On Lifting Oneself up by One's Bootstrings and Not Throwing the Baby out with the Bath Water). Stockholm: Raben & Sjögren, 1972.

Jander, Lind, Näslund and Vogelhut. *En studie av övervakningen i Lund.* (A Study of Supervison in Lund). Lund: Pedagogiska institutionen (stencil), 1971.

Johansson, Sten. *Mentalsjukhuset som organisation.* (The Mental Hospital as an Organization). Uppsala: Sociologiska institutionen (stencil), 1966.

Jonsson, Gustav. *Delinquent Boys, their Parents and Grandparents.* København: Munksgaard, 1967.

______. *Det sociala arvet.* (The Social Heritage). Stockholm: Tiden, 1969.

______. *Att bryta det sociala arvet.* (Counteracting the Social Heritage). Stockholm: Tiden, 1973.

Justitiedepartementet (Ministry of Justice) *Betänkande angående de enskilda övervakarna inom kriminalvården.* (Report on Lay Supervisors in Non-Institutional Corrections). Ju 1967:8.

______. *PM angående övervakning vid kriminalvård i frihet.* (Memorandum on Supervision in Non-Instituional Corrections). Ds Ju 1973:3.

______. *PM angående ny lagstiftning om kriminalvård i anstalt mm.* (Memorandum on New Legislation on Prison Treatment). Ds Ju 1973:9.

______. *PM angående ändrade bestämmelser om ersättning till de enskilda övervakarna inom kriminalvården.* (Memorandum on Changed Provisions on Payments to Lay Supervisors). Ds Ju 1976:3.

______. *Frivård i storstad.* (Non-Institutional Corrections in Cities). Ds Ju 1976:9.

Jørgensen, Stig. *Ret og samfund.* (Law and Society). København: Berlingske, 1970.

Kalmthout, A. and Tak, P. *Sanctions-Systems in the Member-States of the Council of Europe.* Deventer: Kluwer. Part I 1988; II 1992.

Kaplan, Abraham. *The Conduct of Inquiry.* San Francisco: Chandler, 1964.

Kassebaum, G, Ward, D and Wilner, D. *Prison Treatment and Parole Survival.* An Empirical Assessment. New York: Wiley, 1971.

Katz, D and Kahn, R. *The Psychology of Organizations.* New York: Wiley, 1966.

Katz, E and Lazarsfeld, P. *Personal Influence.* New York: Free Press, 1955.

Krech, D, Crutchfield, R and Ballachey, E. *Individual in Society.* New York: McGraw-Hill, 1962.

Kriminalforsorg i frihed. Rapport fra et nordisk kontaktseminar mellem forskere og praktikere. (Non-Institutional Corrections. Report from a Scandinavian Contact Seminar for Researchers and Practiticioners). *Nordisk Samarbejdsråd for Kriminologi,* 1966.

Kriminalforsorg—Socialforsorg. (Criminal Care—Social Care). *Justitsministeriet,* København. 1975:752 (vol 1–3).

Kriminalomsorg i frihet. (Non-Institutional Corrections). *NOU* 1975:61.

Kriminalvetenskapliga institutet. *Fångarnas situation vid frigivningen.* (The Situation of Released Prisoners on Discharge) by Grahm, Sundström and Thorfelt, Stockholm 1968 (stencil).

Kriminalvårdskommitténs betänkande. (Report of the Committee on Corrections), Helsingfors 1972.

Kriminalvårdsstyrelsen. (National Prison and Probation Administration) *Anvisningar för övervakare* (Guidance for Supervisors) 1964, 1972, 1974.

______. *FRÖ.* (Seeds—a Plan for Supervisor Training) 1973.

______, utvecklingsenheten. *Läs- och skrivsvårigheter hos frivårdsklienter* (Functional Illiteracy among Probationers) by Nybäck, Y and Lindström, M, 1973.

———. *Viljesvag och förmodligen lättledd* (Weak-Willed and Presumably Easily Led) by Ferrer, S and Walhjalt, A-M, 1974.

———. *Nyligen frigivna och skyddsvärnet* (Newly Released Prisoners and the Stockholm Discharged Prisoners' Aid Society) by Gustafsson, N and Treiberg, Y, 1974, 6.

———. *PM angående behandlingsplanering.* (Memorandum on Treatment Planning), 1975.

———. *Tidsanvändning på två skyddskonsulent expeditioner.* (The Use of Time in Two Probation Offices) by Bagge, L and Bishop, N, 1975, 11.

———. *Rapport om IMPACT*—ett engelskt frivårdsproject (Report on the English Probation Project, IMPACT) by Leche et al. 1975.

———. *Läs- och skrivsvårigheter bland klienter inom Västerås skyddskonsulentdistrikt* (Funtional Illiteracy among Probationers in the Västerås Probation District) by Stenberg, A, 1976.

———. *Om förändring i fängelse* (On Change in Prison) by Landerholm-Ek, 1976, 15.

———. *Villkorligt frigivna 1973.* (Conditionally Released) 1976, 18.

———. *Skyddstillsynsdömda 1971.* (Sentenced to Probation 1971). 1976, 19.

———. *Kriminalvården* (Annual Reports of the Swedish Prison and Probation Administration) 1967–1992.

———. Engman, K. and Gustavsson, *I. Post-Prison and Post-Probation Recidivism.* Research Paper No. 2, 1991.

Kungl Maj:ts prop 1962 med förslag till brottsbalk, (The 1962 Bill on Proposals for the Penal Code, Part A-C).

Kungl Maj:ts prop 1973:1. App. 4.

Kutchinsky, Berl. "Sociological Aspects of Deviance and Criminality" in Nine Collected Studies in Criminological Research *Council of Europe.* Pp. 9–99, 1992.

Kühlhorn, Eckart. "Frivårdsklienter i Halmstad och Eskilstuna." (Probationers in Halmstad and Eskilstuna) *SOU,* 64, 264–286, 1972.

Kyvsgaard, Brita. *Invalidepension och recidiv.* (Early Pensions and Recidivism). København: Justitsministeriets Forskningsrapport no. 16, 1981.

Lauridsen, Preben Stuer. "En empirisk undersøgelse af juridisk metode." (An Empirical Study of Juridical Method). *Fuldmægtigen,* 47–53, 1972.

Lazarsfeld, P and Rosenberg, M. *The Language of Social Research.* New York: Free Press, 1962.

Lemert, Edwin. *Social Pathology.* New York: McGraw-Hill, 1951.

Lenéer-Axelson, B and Thylefors, I. "En individualterapeutisk effektstudie" (Effects of Individual Therapy—a Study). *APA* 1969:7 (stencil).

Lerman, Paul. "Evaluative Studies of Institutions for Delinquents: Implications for Research and Social Policy." *Social Work.* 13, 55–64, 1968.

———. *Community Treatment and Social Control.* Chicago: University of Chicago Press, 1975.

Levinson, D and Gallagher, E, *Patienthood in the Mental Hospital.* Boston: Houghton-Mifflin, 1964.

Lewis, Diana. "Is Casework in Probation Necessary?" *Focus,* I, 1–8, 1955.

Lindgren, L, Magnusson, D and Stjernquist, P, *Sociala styringsformer.* (Social Steering Mechanisms). Stockholm: Almqvist & Wiksell, 1971.

Lipton, D, Martinson, R and Wilks, J. *The Effectiveness of Correctional Treatment.* New York: Praeger, 1975.

Lundén, A and Näsman, E, eds. *Beskrivningar av de utstöttas livssituation och självbild.* (Descriptions of the Life Situation and Self-Image of Marginalized Persons). Stockholm: Prisma, 1973.

Lundquist, A. "Some Developments in Swedish Criminal Policy during the 1980s" in

Scandinavian Criminal Policy and Criminology, ed. N. Bishop, Scandinavian Research Council for Criminology, Stockholm, 1990.

Macaulay, Stewart. *Law and the Balance of Power*. New York: Russell Sage Fundation, 1966.

Mac Naughton-Smith, P. "The Classification of Individuals by the Possession of Attributes Associated with a Criterion." *Biometrics*. 1963.

Mankoff, M. "Societal Reaction and Career Deviance: A Critical Analysis." *The Sociological Quarterly*, 12, 204–218, 1971.

Mannheim, H and Wilkins, L. *Prediction Methods in Relation to Borstal Training*. London: Her Majesty's Stationary Office, 1955.

Martin, John. "After Care in Transition," in Grygier et al., eds., *Criminology in Transition*. London: Tavistock, 1965.

Martin, J P and Webster, D. *Social Consequences of Conviction*. London: Heinemann, 1971.

Mathiesen, Thomas. *The Defences of the Weak*. London: Tavistock, 1965.

______. *Kan fængsel forsvares?* København: Soc-Pol, 1988.

______. *Rett og samfunn*. (Law and Society). Oslo: Pax, 1975.

Mathieson, David. "The Probation Service" in E. Stockdale and S. Casale, eds. *Criminal Justice under Stress*. Pp. 143–159. London: Blackstone 1992.

Mattson, I and Österberg, C. *Studier av samband mellan behandling och effekt i multivariata icke-experimentella material* (Studies of the Association between Treatment and Effect with Multivariate Non-Experimental Data). Stockholm: Statistiska institutionen (stencil), 1971.

Mead, George. "The Psychology of Punitive Justice." *AJS* 23, 577–602. 1917–18,

______. *Mind, Self and Society*. Chicago: The University Press, 1947 (1934).

Merton, Robert. *Social Theory and Social Structure*. Glencoe: Free Press, 1957.

Meyer, H, Borgatta, E and Jones, W. *Girls at Vocational High*. An Experiment in Social Work Intervention. New York: Russell Sage Foundation. 1965.

Mueller, Paul. "Advanced Release to Parole." *California Department of Corrections*. Research Report No 20, 1965.

Myrdal, Gunnar. *Objektivitetsproblemet i samhällsforskningen*. (The Problem of Objectivity in Social Research). Stockholm: Rabén & Sjögren, 1968.

______. *Vetenskap och politik i nationalekonomin*. (Science and Politics in National Economy). Stockholm: Norstedts, 1972.

Mäkelä, Klaus. "Public Sense of Justice and Judicial Practice." *Scandinavian Studies in Criminology*, 2, 42–67, 1966.

Nasenius, Jan. "Socialvården—värderingar och mål" in Berglind, etc. *Ideal och verkligheter i svensk socialvård*. (Social Welfare—Values and Goals). Stockholm: Wahlström & Widstrand, 31–60, 1976.

Nelson, Alvar. *Brott och påföljd*. (Crime and Punishment). Uppsala: Elander, 1967.

______. "Ingripanden mot brott." (Interventions with Crime). *Svensk Juristtidning*, 54, 207–227, 1969.

______. *Ingripanden vid brott*. (Interventions with Crime) Uppsala: Prisma, 1970.

Newman, Charles. *Sourcebook on Probation, Parole and Pardons*. Springfield: Thomas, 1964.

Nonet, Philip. *Administrative Justice*. New York: Russell Sage Foundation, 1969.

Nordisk Tidsskrift for Kriminalvidenskab Symposienummer ang upprepad brottslighet (Symposium on Repetitive Crime, Special Number) ed. by A. Nelson, 1976:III–IV.

NU A 1980:13 Nordisk Strafferetskomité: *Alternativer til frihedsstraf* (Alternatives to Sanctions involving Deprivation of Liberty) København: Nordisk Ministerråd.

Ohlin, Lloyd. "Predicting Parole Behavior" in Johnston et al., eds., *The Sociology of Punishment and Correction.* New York: Wiley, 282–291, 1962.

______ et al. "Major Dilemmas of the Social Worker in Probation and Parole." *National Probation and Parole Association Journal*, vol 2, 211–226, 1956.

Olofsson, Birgitta. *Vad var det vi sa!* Om kriminellt och konformt beteende bland skolpojkar. (What Did We Say! On Criminal and Conforming Behavior among Schoolboys). Stockholm: Utbildningsförlaget, 1971.

Olsson, Agneta. *Övervakning inom kommunal socialvård.* (Supervision within Municipal Social Welfare). Örebro: Socialhögskolan (stencil), 1975.

Olsson, Anders. *Tillsynspersonal vid två fångvårdsanstalter.* (Basic Grade Staff at Two Prisons) Lund: Sociologiska institutionen (stencil), 1971.

Parsons, Talcott. *Essays in Sociological Theory.* New York: Free Press (rev ed.), 1954.

Persson, Leif. *Den dolda brottsligheten.* (Hidden Criminality). Stockholm: Kriminalvetenskapliga institutet (stencil), 1972.

______. "Tillfället gör tjuven? Ett etiologiskt dilemma inom kriminologin." (Does the Occasion Make the Thief? An Etiological Dilemma in Criminology). *NTfK* 1, 35–59, 1975.

______. *Inbrottstjuvar i Stockholm*—en studie av individuell brottsbelastning, samhällelig brottsnivå och brottsutveckling. (Burglars in Stockholm—a Study of Individual Criminal Backgrounds, Community Crime Levels and Crime Trends). Stockholm: Sociologiska institutionen (stencil), 1976.

Petersilia, J. et al. "Costs and Effects of Intensive Supervision of Drug Offenders." *Federal Probation*, 12–17, 1992.

Pinatel, Jean. *La Criminologie.* (Criminology). Paris: Spes, 1960.

Pockettidningen. "Eftervård efter vad?" (After Care after What?). R 1971:4.

______. "Utbildning-Inbillning." (Education—Imagination) R 1971:5.

______. "Det handlar om stålar." (A Question of Money). R 1976:6.

Pound, Roscoe. *Jurisprudence.* Saint Paul, 1959.

Powers, E and Witmer, H. *An Experiment in the Prevention of Delinquency.* New York: The Cambridge-Somerville Youth Study, 1951.

President's Commission on Law Enforcement and Administration of Justice. Task Force Report: *Courts.* Washington DC: Government Printing Office, 1967.

Prins, Adolphe. *La Défense et les transformations du droit pénal.* (The Defence and Changes in Penal Law). Paris: Misch et Thron, 1910.

Quensel, Carl-Erik. "Om påföljders verkningar." (On the Effect of Sanctions). *Statistisk tidsskrift* 4, 446–464, 1966.

Radzinowicz, Leon. *The Results of Probation.* English Studies in Criminal Science. London: Macmillan, 1959.

Rentzmann, William. "Om alternativer til frihedsstraf." (On Alternatives to Prisonment). *NTfK*, 2, 163–183, 1975 a.

______. "Notat om tvang og motivation" (Notes on Coercion and Motivation) in *Kriminalforsorg-Socialforsorg*, København: App. 6, Betænkning 752, 1975 b.

Richmond, Mary. *Social Diagnosis.* New York: Free Press, 1965 (1917).

Riksrevisionsverket. *Kriminalvård i frihet—klienternas ekonomi.* (Non-Institutional Corrections and the Clients' Financial Circumstances). 1975:26.

______. *Kriminalvård i frihet—klienternas arbetsförhållanden.* (Corrections and Work Circumstances) 1976:238.

______. *Kriminalvård i frihet—klienternas bostadsförhållanden.* (Non-Institutional Corrections and the Clients' Accomodation Circumstances). 1976:994.

Riley, Gresham. "Partisanship and Objectivity in the Social Sciences." *The American Sociologist*, 1, 6–12, 1971.

Ring, C.R. "Probation Supervision Fees: Shifting Costs to the Offender." *Federal Probation*, 2, 43–48, 1989.
Robert and Seckle. "The Board of Corrections Probation Study." *California Board of Corrections*. California, 1965.
Robinson, W. S. "Ecological Correlations and the Behavior of Individuals" in Voss and Petersen, eds., *Sociology, Crime and Delinquency*. New York: Meredith, 147–158, 1971.
Roethlisberger, F. and Dickson, W. *Management and the Worker*. Cambridge: Harvard University Press, 1939.
Romander, H and Bergström, G. "Övervakningsnämnderna." (The Supervision Boards) Stockholm: *Justitiedepartementet*. 1968.
Rosendahl, L. and Thorsson, H. ... *dom andra kallas tjuvar*. Introduktion i kriminalpolitik. (It's the Others Who Are Called Thieves. Introduction to Criminal Policy). Stockholm: Tiden, 1975.
Ross, Alf. *Skyld, ansvar og straf*. (Guilt, Responsibility and Punishment). København: Berlingske, 1970.
Ross, Laurence. *Settled out of Court*: A Sociological Study of Insurance Claims Adjustment. Chicago: Aldine, 1970.
Rubington, E and Weinberg, M. *Deviance*. The Interactionist Perspective. New York: Macmillan, 1973 (2:nd ed.).
Rusche, G. and Kirchheimer, O. *Punishment and Social Structure*. New York: Columbia University Press, 1939.
Rylander, Staffan. *Perspektiv i rättsforskningen*. (Perspectives on Legal Research). Stockholm: Socialhögskolan (stencil), 1974.
Sarnecki, Jerzy. Predicting Social Maladjustment. *The National Council for Crime Prevention*. Stockholm, 1985.
______. "Ungdomsbrottsligheten—En kunskapsöversikt" (Youth Criminality—a Review of Knowledge) in *SOU* 1933:35, Part B, 7–92.
Scheff, Thomas. *Being Mentally Ill*. A Sociological Theory. London: Weidenfeld & Nicholson, 1966.
Schillander-Lundgren, Barbro. "Kriminalvård i frihet. Service-kontroll." (Non-Institutional Treatment. Service or Control?). *NTfK* 2, 113–119, 1973.
______ et al., eds. 50 *år med frivården*. (First Years of Probation and Parole Work). Norrköping: 1991.
Schur, Edwin. *Law and Society*. New York: Random House, 1968.
______. *Labeling Deviant Behavior*—its Sociological Implications. New York: Random House, 1971.
______. *Radical Non-Intervention*. New York: Prentice Hall, 1973.
Schwartz, R. and Skolnick J., eds. *Society and the Legal Order*. London: Basic Books, 1970.
Segerstedt, Torgny. *Ordens makt*. (The Power of Words). Uppsala: Argos, 1968 (1944).
Selznick, Philip. *TVA and the Grass Roots*. New York: Torchbooks, 1966 (1949).
______. *Law, Society and Industrial Justice*. New York: Sage Foundation, 1969.
Siegel, Sidney. *Nonparametric Statistics for the Behavioral Sciences*. New York: McGraw-Hill, 1956.
Simon, Frances. "Prediction Methods in Criminology." London: HMSO, *Home Office*, 1971,7.
Simon, Herbert. *Administrativt beteende*. (Administrative Behavior). Stockholm: Prisma, 1971.
Sjöberg, Lennart. "Är frihet det bästa straffet?" (Is Freedom the Best Punishment) *Nordisk psykologi*, 3, 212–217, 1969.
Skogh, Gunilla. *Arbetsuppgifter och attityder hos frivilliga övervakare inom kriminalvården*. (Tasks and Attitudes among Voluntary Correctional Supervisors) Uppsala: Psykologiska institutionen (stencil), 1972.

Skolnick, Jerome. *Justice without Trial.* New York: Wiley, 1966.

SOU 1951:41. *Ungdomen möter samhället.* (Youth Meets Society). Ungdomsvårdskommitténs slutbetänkande.

———. 1953:14. *Förslag till brottsbalk.* (Proposals for the Penal Code). Straffr ättskommittén.

———. 1956:55. *Skyddslag.* (Protective Law. Final Report of the Protective Law Commission). Strafflagberedningens slutbetänkande.

———. 1961:16. *Kriminalvård i frihet.* Betänkande av 1956 års eftervårdsutredning. (Non-Institutional Corrections. Report of the 1956 After Care Committee).

———. 1965:55. *Barn på anstalt.* Barnanstaltsutredningens betänkande. (Children in Prison. Report of the Committee on Children in Prison).

———. 1972:64. *Kriminalvård.* Betänkande avgivet av kriminalvårdsberedningen. (Prison and Probation Treatment. Report of the Committee on Correctional Reform).

———. 1972:72. *Rätten till ratten.* "Social kontroll av grövre trafikbrottslighet" (The Right to Drive. Social Control of Gross Criminality on the Road) by Hans Klette, 9–123.

———. 1972:76. *Unga lagöverträdare II.* 1956 års klientelundersökning rörande ungdomsbrottslingar. (Young Offenders II. The 1956 Investigation into Youth Crime). Report by Gösta Carlsson.

———. 1973:25. *Unga lagöverträdare III.* 1956 års klientelundersökning rörande ungdomsbrottlingar. (Young Offenders III. The 1956 Investigation into Youth Crime). Report by Birgitta Olofsson.

———. 1973:26. *Lag och rätt i grundskolan.* Betänkande angivet av en arbetsgrupp inom samarbetsorganet för åtgärder mot ungdomsbrottsligheten. (Legislation and Law for Primary Schools. Report of a Working Group on Counter-Measures to Youth Crime).

———. 1973:35. *Kriminologisk forskning.* Betänkande avgivet av kommittén för kriminologisk behandlingsforskning. (Criminological Research. Report of the Committee on Criminological Treatment Research).

———. 1974:39. *Socialvården.* Mål och medel. Principbetänkande av socialutredningen.(Social Welfare. Ends and Means. Report of the Social Committee). (Summary: SOU 1974:40).

———. 1975:16. *Kriminalvårdens nämnder.* Betänkande av övervakningsnämndsutredningen. (Supervision Boards, Report of the Committee on Supervision Boards).

———. 1976:47. *Färre brottmål.* Betänkande av åtalsrättskommittén med förslag till ökade möjligheter till åtalsunderlåtelse och förundersökningsbegränsning. (Fewer Criminal Cases. Report of the Committee on Prosecutions with Proposals on Increased Opportunities to Waive Prosecution and Limitations on Initial Investigations).

———. 1976:50. *Statligt personskadeskydd.* Yrkesskadeförsäkringskommitténs betänkande. (Protection for State Employers. Report of the Committee on Insurance and Professionally Incurred Harm).

———. 1977:83 *Tillsynsdom.* (Supervision Sentence). Betänkande av ungdomsfängelseutredningen.

———. 1981:90 *Frivårdspåföljder.* (Non-Custodial Sanctions). Delbetänkande av frivårdskommittén.

———. 1986:13–15. *Påföljd för brott.* (Sanctions for Crime). Huvudbetänkande av fängelsestraffkommittén.

———. 1993:35 *Reaktion mot ungdomsbrott.* (Reactions to Youth Crime). Betänkande av Ungdomsbrottskommittén, Del A-B. Justitiedepartementet.

Sparks, Richard. "Research on the Use and Effectiveness of Probation, Parole and Measures of After-Care" in Practical Organisation of Measures for the Supervision and After-Care of Conditionally Sentenced or Conditionally Released Offenders. Pp. 249–273. *Council of Europe.* Strasbourg, 1970.

Stangeland, P and Hauge, R. *Nyanser i grått.* (Nuances in Grey). Oslo: Universitetsförlaget, 1974.

Statistiska Centralbyrån, *Kriminalstatistik.* (Criminal Statistics 1972– 1973.

______, Statistiska meddelanden: *Återfall i brott 1967–70,* R 197:1 (Statistical Information: Relapse into Crime 1967–70, R 1971. (Also for the Periods 1966–69, 68–71, 69–72 and 70–73).

______, Statistiska meddelanden. 1967. *Den grövre brottsligheten 1967* (Statistical Information: Gross Criminality 1967. (Also for 1968–70).

______, *Rättsstatistisk årsbok 1992.* (Yearbook of Judicial Statistics 1992). Stockholm 1992.

Stephenson, R and Scarpitti, F. *The Rehabilitation of Delinquent Boys.* Final Report to the Ford Foundation. N J: Rutgers, 1967.

Stjernquist, Per. *Laws in the Forests.* A Study of Public Direction of Swedish Private Forestry. Lund: Gleerup, 1973.

Storgaard, Anette. *Alternativer til frihedsstraf.* (Alternatives to Imprisonment). Aarhus: Universitetsforlaget, 1989.

Strahl, Ivar. "Rörelsen för socialskydd (défense sociale)—den senaste idériktningen inom straffrätten." (The Social Defense Movement—the Latest Notion in Penal Law) *Nordisk Kriminalistisk Årbok,* 19–58, 1955.

______. *Den svenska kriminalpolitiken.* (Swedish Criminal Policy). Stockholm: Aldus, 1967.

Straffelovrådet. *Alternativer til frihedsstraf* (Alternatives to Deprivation of Liberty). København: Bet. no 806, 1977.

______. *Betænkning om samfundstjeneste.* (Report on Community Service by the Danish Penal Council). København: Bet. no 1211, 1990.

Street, D, Vinter, R and Perrow, Ch. *Organization for Treatment.* New York: Free Press, 1966.

Strömholm, Stig. "Lagtolkningens funktioner" (The Function of Legal Interpretations) in Edling and Elwin, eds., *Rättssociologi.* Stockholm: Wahlström & Widstrand, 111–143, 1973.

Suchman, Edward, ed. *Evaluation Research.* New York: Russell Sage Foundation, 1967.

Sundin, Bertil. *Individ, institution, ideologi.* (Individuals, Institutions and Ideologies). Stockholm: Aldus, 1975 (1970).

Sundsvallsförsöket (Projektet frivårdsförstärkning). (The Sundsvall Experiment.) *Undersökningsrapport från en dagboks- och en observationsundersökning av skyddskonsulenternas och assistenternas arbetsuppgifter vid skyddskonsulentexpeditionerna i Sundsvall och Karlstad.* (Report of a Daily Record and Observational Study of the Tasks of Chief Probation Officers and Probations Officers in Sundsvall and Karlstad) by Frej, Gunborg, 10 (stencil), 1973.

______. *Att skaffa jobb åt straffade* (On Getting Offenders Jobs) by Kühlhorn, Eckart, 11, 1973.

______. *Övervakning inom kriminalvården* (Supervison in Corrections) by Frej, Gunborg, 16, 1974.

______. *Kriminalvård i frihet—en preliminär utvärdering av ett försök i Sundsvall* (Non-Institutional Treatment—a Preliminary Evaluation of the Sundsvall Experiment) by Kühlhorn, Eckart. BRÅ, 1975:1.

Sutherland, E and Cressey, D. *Principles of Criminology.* Lippincott, Philadelphia 1978 (10th rev ed.).

Sveri, Knut. *Kriminalitet og alder,* (Age and Criminality). Uppsala: Almqvist & Wiksell, 1960.

______. "Om användningen av straffrättsliga påföljder i Norden, Vättyskland och England" (On the Use of Penal Reactions in the Nordic Countries, West Germany and England). *SOU* 1986:15, 55–77.

Sverne, T and Hinderson, B. "Frivårdens ansvar." (The Responsibility of the Probation Service). *NTfK,* 3–4, 201–210, 1975.

Swedner, Harald, *Socialvård och samhällsförändring.* (Social Welfare and Social Change). Stockholm: Almqvist & Wiksell, 1970.

Sykes, Gresham. *The Society of Captives.* A Study of a Maximum Security Prison. New Jersey: Princeton University Press, 1958.

Tajthy, Zsolt. *Den sociala strukturen på en skyddstillsynsanstalt.* (The Social Structure of a Probation Institution). Lund: Sociologiska institutionen (stencil), 1972.

Tappan, Paul. *Crime, Justice and Correction.* New York: McGraw-Hill, 1960.

Taylor I, Walton, P and Young, J. *The New Criminology.* For a Social Theory of Deviance. London: Routledge & Kegan, 1973.

______, Walton, P and Young, J. *Critical Criminology.* London: Routledge & Kegan, 1975.

Thomas, W and Znaniecki, F. *The Polish Peasant in Europe and America.* Boston: Badger, 1918.

Thornstedt, Hans. "Förarbeten." *Juridikens källmaterial* (The Preparatory Work. Legal Source Material) by Eek et al. Stockholm: Norstedts (8 ed.), 1975.

Toby, Jackson. "An Evaluation of Early Identification and Intensive Treatment-Programs for Pre-Delinquents." *Social Problems,* 13,2, 1965.

Trankell, Arne. *Kvarteret Flisan.* (The Flisan Town Quarter). Stockholm: Norstedts, 1973.

______. "Svenskars fördomar mot invandrare" (Swedish Prejudices against Immigrants) in *Invandrarproblem.* Stockholm: Norstedts, 1975.

Trolle, Jørgen. *Syv maaneder uden politi.* (Seven Months with No Police). København: Nordisk Forlag, 1945.

Unger, Roberto. *Law in Modern Society.* New York: Free Press, 1976.

Ungmark, I., *Kvinnor, brott och övervakning* (Women, Crime and Supervision). Doctoral Dissertation, Department of Education and Psychology, University of Linköping, Linköping 1992.

United Nations. *Probation and Related Measures.* 1951.

______. *Practical Results and Financial Aspects of Adult Probation in Selected Countries.* 1954.

van Dijk, J.J.M., Mayhew, P. and Killias, M. Experiences of Crime across the World: Key Findings of the 1989 International Crime Survey. Deventer: Kluwer, 1990.

Varga, Csaba. "The Foundation of a New Socialist Type of Codification." *Acta Juridica Academiae Scientiarum Hungaricae* 1–2, 111–138. 1975.

______. "Modernization of Law and its Codificational Trends in the Afro-Asiatic Legal Development." *Institute for World Economics of the Hungarian Academy of Sciences.* Budapest, 1976.

Vestergaard, Jørn. "Kriminalforsorgens dobbeltvirksomhed." (The Double Activity of Corrections) *Social Rådgiveren,* 5, 165–173, 1976.

Vorenberg, E and Vorenberg, J. "Early Diversion from the Criminal Justice System: Practice in Search of Theory," in Ohlin, ed., *Prisoners in America.* New York: Prentice Hall, 151–183, 1973.

Waaben, Knud. *Strafferettens almindelige del.* (The General Part of Penal Law). København: GAD 1989 (2nd ed.).

Walker, Nigel. *Sentencing in a Rational Society*. Harmondsworth. Penguin Books, 1972.
Warren, Marguerite. "Recent Findings in the Community Treatment Project." *California Board of Corrections, 4*. California, 1964.
______. et al. "Community Treatment Project." *California Youth Authority*. California, 7, 1966.
Weber, Max. *Wirtschaft und Gesellschaft*. (Economy and Society). Tübingen: Mohr, 1956.
Weiss, Carol. *Evaluation Research*. Methods of Social Science Series. New York: Prentice Hall, 1972.
Wilensky, Harold. *Intellectuals in Labor Unions*. Glencoe: Free Press, 1956.
______ and Lebeaux, C. *Industrial Society and Social Welfare*. New York: Russell Sage Foundation, 1958.
Wilkins, Leslie. "A Small Comparative Study of the Results of Probation." *BJD*, 8, 201, 1958.
______. "An Essay in the General Theory of Prediction Methods" in Johnston et al., eds., *The Sociology of Punishment and Correction*. New York: Wiley, 249–256, 1962.
______. *Evaluation of Penal Measures*. New York: Random House, 1969.
Wolf, Preben. "Om recidiv efter betinget dom." (On Recidivism Following a Conditional Sentence). *NTfK*, 4, 314–329 (1969) and 1, 49–72 (1961), 1960 and 1961.
______. and Høgh, E. *Kriminalitet i velfærdssamfundet*. (Criminality in the Welfare State) København: Paludan, 1966.
Wunderman, H. *Klientelet vid skyddstillsynsanstalten Aspuna 1967*. (The Clintèle of the Asptuna Probation Institution). Stockholm: Kriminalvetenskapliga institutet (stencil), 1968.
Yearbook of Nordic Statistics 1993. Copenhagen: Nordic Statistical Secretariat, 1993.
Young Adult Offenders. *Home Office*. London: HMSO, 1974.
Zimring, Franklin. "Perspectives on Deterrence." Crime and Delinquency Issues. *National Institute of Mental Health*. Washington, 1971.
______ and Hawkins, G. *Deterrence*. Chicago: University of Chicago Press, 1974.
Övervakarnas Riksförbund. *Övervakare—en lekman i samhällsarbetet*. (The Supervisor—a Layman in Social Work). Brevskolan (2nd ed.), 1974.
Øyen, Else. *Socialomsorgen og dens forvaltere*. (Social Welfare and Its Practitioners). Bergen: Universitetsforlaget, 1974.
Other sources mentioned in the text but not included in the bibliography consist chiefly of laws, decrees, annual reports and mass media reportage.

Abbreviations:
ASR =American Sociological Review
BJC =the British Journal of Criminology (former BJD)
BJD =the British Journal of Delinquency
Nou =Norges offentlige utredninger (Norwegian State Commission Reports)
NTfk =Nordisk Tidsskrift for Kriminalvidenskab (Nordic Journal of Criminal Science)
SOU =Statens offentliga utredningar (Swedish State Commission Reports)

About the Book and Author

Despite current interest in alternatives to imprisonment, little is known about their effectiveness. In this book, Professor Bondeson undertakes a unique socio-legal and criminological study of the impact of three alternative sanctions—conditional sentence, ordinary probation and probation with institutional treatment.

Beginning with the goal of resocializing offenders, Bondeson uses sophisticated methods to determine whether current legislation is having positive results. She examines in a recidivism study the effects of different treatments in order to assess the outcome of various sentences. She also analyzes the factors that lie behind a judge's choice between sentencing possibilities.

The findings show considerable and surprising differences among the rates of recidivism even when selection bias is held under control. Conditional sentences had the lowest rate of criminal relapse; probation had higher rates, and probation with institutional treatment had markedly higher rates. An in-depth study of probation consistently shows that probation was perceived by supervisors as providing help whereas most offenders perceived it as a stigmatizing means of control. The author shows that despite the legislators' intent to improve the possibilities for resocialization, the opposite result was achieved. Bondeson concludes by describing two general principles for effective reform: a theory of least possible intervention and a general welfare ideology.

Ulla V. Bondeson is professor of criminology at the University of Copenhagen and former professor of sociology of law at Lund University. She has been president of the Scandinavian Research Council for Criminology and is currently vice president of the International Society of Criminology.